The Listener's Companion
Gregg Akkerman, Series Editor

Titles in **The Listener's Companion: A Scarecrow Press Music Series** provide readers with a deeper understanding of key musical genres and the work of major artists and composers. Aimed at non-specialists, each volume explains in clear and accessible language how to *listen* to works from particular artists, composers, and genres. Looking at both the context in which the music first appeared and has since been heard, authors explore with readers the environments in which key musical works were written and performed.

Experiencing Stravinsky: A Listener's Companion, by Robin Maconie, 2013
Experiencing Mozart: A Listener's Companion, by David Schroeder, 2013
Experiencing Jazz: A Listener's Companion, by Michael Stephans, 2013

EXPERIENCING JAZZ

JAZZ

A Listener's Companion

Michael Stephans

THE SCARECROW PRESS, INC.
Lanham • Toronto • Plymouth, UK
2013

Published by Scarecrow Press, Inc.
A wholly owned subsidary of
The Rowman & Littlefield Publishing Group, Inc.
4501 Forbes Boulevard, Suite 200, Lanham, Maryland 20706
www.rowman.com

10 Thornbury Road, Plymouth PL6 7PP, United Kingdom

British Library Cataloguing in Publication Information Available

Library of Congress Cataloging-in-Publication Data

Stephans, Michael.
    Experiencing jazz : a listener's companion / Michael Stephans.
            pages cm. — (Listener's companion)
    Includes bibliographical references and index.
    ISBN 978-0-8108-8289-8 (cloth : alk. paper) — ISBN 978-0-8108-8290-4
(ebook)
    1. Jazz—Analysis, appreciation. I. Title.
    ML3506.S77 2013
    781.65—dc23   2013019838

Printed in the United States of America.

Each thing you hear
determines the direction
that you go. You just follow the music
and if you follow the music, you
can go anywhere.

—Steve Lacy

My first relationship to any kind of music is as a listener.

—Pat Metheny

CONTENTS

Foreword by Doug Ramsey   ix

Preface by Dave Liebman   xi

Acknowledgments   xiii

1   Ears, Mind, Heart: A Path to Open Listening   1

2   Groundwork: Developing Listening Skills   10

3   Jazz as a Mirror of Our Times: From Birth through the 1940s   32

4   Jazz as a Mirror of Our Times: From the 1950s to the Present   53

5   Functions and Forms: Jazz on and off the Bandstand   77

6   Points of Departure: Small Groups and Big Bands   90

7   Horn of Gabriel: The Trumpet
       (*Getting Personal with Dave Douglas*)   112

8   Raspy, Gaspy, Smooth, and Silky: The Trombone
       (*Getting Personal with Roswell Rudd*)   139

9   Reeds and Deeds I: The Tenor Saxophone
       (*Getting Personal with Joe Lovano*)   160

10 Reeds and Deeds II: The Alto Saxophone
(*Getting Personal with Rudresh Mahanthappa*)   186

11 Reeds and Deeds III: Highs and Lows—The Soprano and
Baritone Saxophones (*Getting Personal with Dave Liebman*)   208

12 Reeds and Deeds IV: Top and Bottom Woodwinds—The Clarinet,
Flute, and Bass Clarinet (*Getting Personal with Bennie Maupin*)   224

13 I Got Rhythm I: The Piano (*Getting Personal with Alan Broadbent*)   243

14 I Got Rhythm II: The Acoustic and Electric Basses
(*Getting Personal with John Patitucci*)   281

15 I Got Rhythm III: Give the Drummer Some!
(*Getting Personal with Jim Black*)   308

16 I Got Rhythm IV: A Little Discussion about Percussion
(*Getting Personal with Joe Locke*)   344

17 I Got Rhythm V: The Guitar (*Getting Personal with John Scofield*)   363

18 The Singer and the Song (*Getting Personal with Dwight Trible
and Roseanna Vitro*)   385

19 Is Jazz Entertainment or Is It Art?   419

20 The Shape of Things to Come: Jazz in the 21st Century   430

Afterword   447

Glossary   449

Appendix A: Surfing the Jazz Net   451

Appendix B: CDs and DVDs   457

Works Cited   463

Other Sources   465

Name Index   469

Title Index   479

Recording Index   483

About the Authors   487

FOREWORD

Doug Ramsey

With few exceptions, the latest popular hits that wallpaper the airwaves and the Internet offer little to challenge listeners. Appreciation of their transitory value requires little musical knowledge or experience. Nor do we expect current pop music to be more than it sets out to be—entertainment. In contrast, other types of music present greater demands and offer greater rewards. The deep satisfaction of a Charlie Parker solo, a Bob Brookmeyer orchestration, the three-way dialogue of the Bill Evans Trio, and the complexity of a Wadada Leo Smith ensemble do not yield themselves easily to those new to jazz listening. Indeed, many listeners won't make the effort to discover those treasures. If you picked up this book, you must be an exception.

There was a time when popular music and jazz were not mutually exclusive. At dances and by way of radios and jukeboxes, listeners to big bands got bonuses: the work of brilliantly creative soloists, composers, and arrangers. Jazz values may not have been the goal of all those young fans, but those principles were built into much of the popular music package. That time is long gone. The stepped-up pace of a culture founded on short attention spans, quick cuts, and easy gratification leaves fewer people inclined to devote time to listening, which over the years would enrich their lives in ways that only music can.

The more we listen, the more we hear. There is no substitute for time spent listening. It develops the nexus of emotion, intellect, and physical response and helps make hearing superior jazz a profound experience. Still, the help of a knowledgeable guide can be invaluable. With this welcome volume, Michael Stephans is that guide. A prominent teacher of creative and technical writing at the university level, he is supremely effective at illuminating what he has learned playing drums with a diversity of leading jazz figures. He has worked with Bob Brookmeyer, Bennie Maupin, Alan Broadbent, David Liebman, Pharoah Sanders, and Bob Florence, among others. Michael's passages on melody, harmony, and rhythm bring insights even to those of us who think we already understand the basic elements of music. His explication of the nature and effects of harmony is enormously helpful. He beguiles his readers into practicing syncopation, helping us understand why, as Dizzy Gillespie frequently said, rhythm is the true heart of jazz.

Early in the book, Michael urges us as listeners to surrender to jazz with the same open acceptance as the improvisers who make it. In return, I urge you to open yourself to the flow of the melody, harmony, and rhythm of this book as you would to a Louis Armstrong or John Coltrane solo. If you do, you will be pleased to find your hearing improved and your enjoyment increased.

PREFACE

Dave Liebman

What is it that makes jazz so special? Surely there is a lot of music that has commonalities with jazz: solo excursions coexisting with group participation; spontaneous improvisation; a "groove" of some sort; virtuosic expertise on an instrument; passion and sophistication all mixed together, and more. So *why jazz*?

Simply because it represents *the* music of our time coalescing in American cities created by people from all cultures mixed together, most notably in its birthplace, early 20th-century New Orleans. Jazz, being a folk music of sorts, reflected the life of the people of this epoch, their joy, sorrow, aspirations, and celebrations. Certainly African Americans are well represented, yet as I write in 2012 it is a fact that jazz increasingly includes people from all over the world. Musically speaking, the technical aspects of jazz are heard far afield from its home environment, in pop music and contemporary classical settings, and of course, more and more in "world" music. Jazz is the lingua franca of the past 100 years—and as an educator, I can attest to the abundance of jazz learning going on worldwide on the university level. Jazz, despite the impression that it may be of importance to only a few listeners, is here to stay in one form or another.

Art can communicate on any or all three of the levels that Michael refers to in this book as ears, mind, and heart. One may be attracted to a work of art because the technique is so dazzling, or because the mood that the piece conjures up strikes a responsive note. Sooner or later it is the spirit and passion of the artist that truly affects the receiver of the art. For jazz, the listener may at first enter the door of appreciation on any one of these levels. Other arts have a more shall I say "dramatic" atmosphere when they are presented . . . ballet, theater, poetry, painting and sculpture, and so on. One can physically see the artistic creation. But music is much more elusive, especially when it appears to move fast, as improvised music often does as a result of several improvisers offering their experience, knowledge, heart, and soul in the moment, creating a special synergy. The way Michael presents the material in this book offers a perfectly balanced approach to entering the world of jazz as a listener at first on the "mind" level, but with the understanding that one will sooner or later hear the music from the heart.

I have known Mike for the past six years since he moved to the area of northeast Pennsylvania where I live (a fertile area for jazz musicians, by the way). Michael is first and foremost a great jazz drummer with an encyclopedic knowledge of the music. We have shared some great moments recording and performing together. Besides other musical abilities (trombone and singing, for example), Mike is a published poet and excellent prose writer, as you will see. What makes him the perfect person for a book of this sort is that he truly wants to communicate with people about this special music that we hold so dear. People who dedicate themselves to jazz are well aware of the necessity of honesty and sincerity when entering this universe.

Experiencing Jazz: A Listener's Companion is a "perfect storm" of sorts, written by a master musician, poet, and writer describing the special world of jazz past, present, and future in a lively, nonacademic tone, which for anyone who has an inkling of interest in jazz will further their appreciation of the music.

ACKNOWLEDGMENTS

A book like this one would not have seen the light of day without the generosity of the musicians who contributed their thoughts and feelings about the music as well as their advice to new listeners. I humbly thank Joe Lovano, Bennie Maupin, John Scofield, Dave Liebman, Rudresh Mahanthappa, John Patitucci, Roswell Rudd, Dave Douglas, Jim Black, Joe Locke, Roseanna Vitro, Dwight Trible, and Alan Broadbent for each one's kindness, perceptiveness, and candor.

I am also grateful to my lifelong friend and co-conspirator Steven Sanders, for his support and encouragement, and for sharing his breadth of authoring experiences with me. Others who were of help through the birthing process include Scarecrow Press senior acquisitions editor Bennett Graff, educator-supreme Patrick Dorian and his better half copyeditor-supreme Mary Dorian, the eminent author and jazz journalist Doug Ramsey, the eternally young singer/songwriter Bob Dorough, woodwind wizards and friends Bennie Maupin and Dave Liebman, writer/bassist Bill Crow, Coltrane scholar Lewis Porter, and my big brother and mentor the late Bob Brookmeyer, who was encouraging from the very beginning of this trek.

Most of all there is Kathleen—my cheerleader, informal editor, and critic. Her love, patience, and honesty continue to be a beacon of lunazurean light. . . . *Namasté*.

I

EARS, MIND, HEART

A Path to Open Listening

WHY LISTEN TO JAZZ?

Imagine this scenario: A friend is in town visiting and wants to go out and hear some live jazz. You have never been to a jazz club and have maybe heard only a few jazz recordings. Other than that, you think that you might have heard jazz as part of a movie soundtrack or while in the grocery store or shopping mall. Even though you know as much about jazz music as you know about Einstein's theory of relativity, you're curious and think you might like to learn more about it.

So imagine this scenario a bit further: You ask your friend to tell you a little about the music. "Jazz music is cool. A bunch of guys on the stage, usually with their eyes closed, making funny faces and playing some pretty far-out stuff on their instruments. It's really entertaining." Or maybe your friend says something like, "Jazz is not for everybody. You have to be ready to experience something deeply complex and mysterious." A little confused or intimidated by either of these descriptions, you suggest the sports bar down the street. At least there, you can watch the Dodgers play the Braves, and that—unlike listening to jazz—doesn't seem so much like work.

My guess is that a scenario like this one plays itself out frequently in cities and towns across America. A great many people are hesitant to leave their homes and their big-screen TVs after work to go to a club,

Figure 1.1. At the Deer Head Inn in Pennsylvania. Courtesy of Laurie Samet.

plunk their money down, and listen to some music that is completely foreign. So why bother? What makes experiencing jazz so special? What is it about jazz that defines its uniqueness among the many musical genres out there today? And if it is so unique and—as suggested in many music texts—is America's original contribution to the arts, then why isn't it played all that much on either AM or FM radio stations? And why have jazz CD sales decreased noticeably over the years? Finally, why is it so difficult to gain public support for jazz?

This book will attempt to bring you, the potential listener, a little closer to this very special music. As a professional jazz musician and teacher, and one who has been "on the frontlines" working for decades to keep jazz alive for present and future generations, I feel especially well qualified to share what I know with you about this music. I have been lucky enough to have performed with many jazz greats—in some cases, legends—and have spent much of my life playing, practicing, and listening to jazz. My mentors have been jazz giants, well known throughout the world as absolute masters of interpretation and improvisation. And I have had other teachers who are brilliant but relatively unknown musicians plying their craft in places like Sacramento, California, and Austin, Texas.

I continue to be a student of the music, through exposure to the innovative work of many of the younger jazz artists on today's scene. In turn, I have tried to share their music and wisdom with my own students and here with you, in this book—whether you are a musician or a listener. The idea is that if I am able to present jazz as a living, breathing, and vital art form—one that can be accessible to all—then perhaps you may begin to discover what is so special about the deeply honest and emotional qualities of jazz and those who sacrifice so much of themselves to bring it to us.

In this age of high technology, jazz may well be one of your connections to a most organic fundamental human spirit—one that gets to the core of who each of us really is, as well as who we might be capable of becoming, if we open our ears, our minds, and most importantly, our hearts to it. Jazz is a story of humanity; it is *our* story, musician and listener alike.

WHAT IS THIS THING CALLED JAZZ?

So what then is jazz? We have about as much chance of coming up with a universal definition of jazz as we have of flying merely by flapping our arms on a windy day. Many scholars, critics, and jazz musicians themselves have tried, often to no avail, to breathe life into the term, often with mixed results. Here are some of the more colorful and interesting attempts at definition:

> Hot can be cool and cool can be hot, and each can be both. But hot or cool, man, jazz is jazz.
>
> —Jazz trumpeter Louis Armstrong (1901–1971)

> Jazz is a language. It is people living in sound. Jazz is people talking, laughing, crying, building, painting, mathematicizing, abstracting, extracting, giving to, taking from, making of. In other words, living.
>
> —Critic and jazz broadcaster Willis Conover, 1976

> Of all the sophisticated forms of music, jazz is the most self-revealing, the music where there is the least room for the person to hide who he or she is.
>
> —Critic and novelist Nat Hentoff, 1976

> Jazz is playin' from the heart, you don't lie.
>
> —Cornetist Bunk Johnson (1879–1949)

And some of the more ridiculous:

> Jazz is music invented by devils for the torture of imbeciles.
>
> —Henry Van Dyke (1852–1933)

> The "jazz mania" has taken on the character of a lingering illness and must be cured by means of forceful public intervention.
>
> —Russian composer Boris Gibalin, 1958

> Jazz originally was the accompaniment of the voodoo dancer, stimulating the half-crazed barbarian to the vilest deeds.
>
> —Anne Shaw Faulkner, 1921

And finally, two profound thoughts about jazz by master saxophonist John Coltrane, as noted in the New York Jazz Museum pamphlet *About John Coltrane* (1976):

> If you are playing jazz, you have to play what comes out at any moment—something you have never said before!

> I think the main thing a musician would like to do is to give a picture to the listener of the many wonderful things he knows of and senses in the universe.

So where do these various perceptions of jazz leave us? We know that jazz is a form of music that has been around since the early 20th century. We know that, unlike many other more commercial types of music being played today, jazz places unique emphasis upon improvisation—that is, making up music on the spot, based upon certain guidelines established by the musicians on the bandstand or concert stage.

IMPROVISATION: THE HEART OF THE JAZZ EXPERIENCE

Suppose you've just emerged from the subway on 42nd Street in New York City. Suppose also that you have no particular destination in mind, so you decide to head east on 42nd and see where it takes you. You cross

Broadway, then 6th Avenue, enjoying the sights and sounds as you walk. The only guidelines you have are to have some lunch and head back to your hotel by dinnertime.

As you come to Madison Avenue, you make a split-second decision to turn right and head south. You have never been on this street before, and everything you see and hear is new to you. At this point you decide to find a restaurant for lunch. Your only guideline is your budget; as a result, you discover a tiny Indian restaurant on 38th Street. The prices are reasonable, so you make the decision to have a meal there.

And so goes your afternoon. Street after street, you move spontaneously and without an agenda. The only thing you come to expect is the unexpected itself.

Now, move the scenario from the streets of New York City into your kitchen. You're tired of the same old recipes, and you haven't made your weekly trek to the grocery store. So you decide to just throw something together. But what? You decide to make up a recipe on the spot, using whatever ingredients you have at hand. So into the skillet go the sliced onion, the ground beef, a little chili powder, some sliced tomatoes, and a few black olives. You have no idea what you are preparing, but you do know that you will serve these prepared ingredients over a bed of white rice. If this experiment tastes good, you might try to prepare it again sometime. If not—well—you'll try to invent something else another time.

These two scenarios represent an important part of life and they are certainly at the very core of jazz music for both the performer and the listener. When the jazz musician is through playing the melody of a song, he or she then embarks upon an improvisational journey, not unlike an afternoon in New York City or an adventure in your kitchen. There are some guidelines, however; just as you know how to put one foot in front of the other when you walk down the street, the jazz musician knows how to play a musical instrument and understands the structure of a song, before he or she moves into unfamiliar territory, choosing this note or that, this musical phrase or that, just as you might instantaneously choose one city street over another in your travels, or one spice rather than another in your instant recipe.

This sense of spontaneity that provides the basis of improvisation is what is often known as being in the moment. As Buddhism and other spiritual philosophies often suggest, there is no past and no future; there is only the present moment in which we find ourselves—either as musicians or listeners. Buddhists call this state of attentiveness *samadhi*. When we musicians improvise, we are often seated squarely in the present moment of spontaneous creation. That is not to say that we don't use the lessons of the past to create our improvisations. We bring certain fundamental tools to a performance—things like the knowledge of theory, harmony, and rhythm, as well as the full range of human emotions we feel at that time—in order to craft our improvisations in some way that brings deep personal meaning to us and hopefully brings the listener into our world, if only for a little while. As my friend and colleague New York pianist Jim Ridl pointed out in a personal interview on June 9, 2011, "Jazz is a complex medium of expression. It calls for both musical intelligence and passion. The musician draws on multiple sources: music of all kinds, personal life experience, current events, history, and culture, and something intangible within the self, whether it be called soul, inspiration, the Muse, or the Spirit." Creating jazz, to paraphrase the legendary trombonist and composer Bob Brookmeyer, is the act of telling your story and mirroring the world at large—with all of its emotional ups and downs. In this sense, the jazz improviser says things through his or her instrument that all human beings are capable of feeling as a part of life. That is where the connection between musician and listener has the potential for creating a moving and memorable experience.

GETTING STARTED: A FEW WORDS ABOUT FOCUSING

When we go to the movies or the theater, we watch the production and listen to it simultaneously. This is a given; however, when a film or play has depth and is totally engrossing and engaging (think of your favorite movie, for example), something happens to us. We often move beyond the mere act of observation and into the realm of participation; that is, we empathize with one or more of the characters and laugh at his or her bumbling mishaps (in a comedy) or cry when he or she encounters tragedy (in a drama). We also revel when justice is served and evildoers get their comeuppance. In other words, we are able to experience a film or play, rather than passively watch and listen to the production.

The above analogy holds true for jazz as well, although the act of experiencing jazz can often be more subtle than experiencing comedy or tragedy. In other words, the whole range of human emotions is not as readily visible as it would be in a film or a play. As you experience a jazz performance, you must be open to whatever feelings you might be having at the very moment you are hearing the music. Since art often mirrors life, you may well experience a wide range of emotions, from pleasure and excitement to sadness and contemplation, and all that falls in between.

Even as jazz musicians strive for a state of *samadhi*—that is, total immersion in the creative act—so, too, can listeners move into a state of absolute concentration. As a listener, you have only to be completely open to the music unfolding on the bandstand or on your iPod or CD player. As multimedia composer and violinist Stephen Nachmanovitch suggests in his book *Free Play*, "For art to appear, we have to disappear" (51). In other words, we essentially have to abandon conscious thought while listening to (or playing) music. We have to train ourselves to be present; to allow ourselves to focus upon what is going on at that very moment—much as a child focuses upon something as simple as the act of building a sandcastle. That means, in a sense, to become what we're doing. So when we hear jazz, we have to give ourselves over to the experience, without preconception, judgment, or distraction. In this sense, we are truly experiencing jazz, not merely listening to it.

Sounds easy, right? But if my own students are any indication, experiencing jazz can be a real challenge. With our attention spans becoming shorter and shorter, due to the dynamic advancements in computer technology as entertainment, the idea of sitting through a jazz concert or listening to an entire John Coltrane recording in a college music library or at home may seem too much like work.

So how do we create a sense of focus if we want to be able to give our total concentration to a jazz performance? My jazz appreciation students, who over the years have been mostly nonmusic majors, have discovered that such listening is a challenge, especially when they are exposed to music that is often under three minutes in duration, and when they are overexposed to a hit song by a well-known popular musician. For example, you might hear a new song by a good singer, and as a result, you download that artist's song or purchase the CD. After several months of listening to the hit song on your iPod and on the radio and hearing it as background music in boutiques, grocery stores, and elevators, you become understandably bored with it.

Jazz, on the other hand, is not a commodity that can be canned and packaged into a three-minute recording. It is not an entertainment and has little "commercial potential." Musicians don't become jazz musicians because the music provides a lucrative means of making a living. As such, the first thing a new listener can do is to cast aside all previous notions of what jazz is and to accept it on its own terms. Before you decide whether you like a particular jazz performance, you must give your attention fully to it. This means openly embracing whatever you hear and avoiding comparisons with any other musical genre. It also means taking the time to learn about and from the men and women who create the music—for they and the music they play are inseparable. This is one of the keys to the *samadhi* of listening. A fellow musician once said to me that we [jazz musicians] are vessels through which the music of the universe passes—and this is what flows through us and into you, the listener, if you are open to what we have to say: our stories, our lives.

THE GOAL OF THIS BOOK

Consider this book to be an open invitation and a welcome to the world of jazz and to those men and women who have dedicated their lives to creating and sustaining it. *Experiencing Jazz* will serve as an introduction for listeners to some of the fundamentals and practitioners of this unique American art form, and to those characteristics of the music that make it so personal and rewarding to those who play and those who listen. We will also learn about jazz by discussing the social contexts that have always been an important part of its growth and development as an art form.

This book may be unique among jazz appreciation texts for two distinct reasons.

Unlike many other survey and historically based books, *Experiencing Jazz* approaches the music from the standpoint of musical instruments and their masters, rather than chronologically based eras and the leading musical innovators of each era. In other words, a more traditional text would discuss tenor saxophone innovator Coleman Hawkins in a chapter dealing with the swing era; so we would view Hawkins in a historical context, a shining light among other similar icons, active from the late 1920s through the '40s. This text, however, will allow you to learn about "the Hawk" in the context of the tenor saxophone, its evolution and major players. For example, as we have a look at the instrument itself, we'll also discuss Hawkins's style, especially as it differs from the other major approach to the horn favored by one of the Hawk's contemporaries, Lester Young. And as we move forward in time, we'll discover the music of other great tenor saxophonists who were influenced by either Hawkins or Young, men like Sonny Rollins, Stan Getz, and John Coltrane—all of whom had their own disciples, including Wayne Shorter, Michael Brecker, and David Liebman.

And finally, we'll be introduced to some of the exciting young saxophonists currently on the scene, such as Donny McCaslin, Chris Potter, Joshua Redman, Chris Speed, and others.

Another example of this unique approach would be to examine the alto saxophone, not in a historical context, as much as in a stylistic one. We'll discuss the major differences that exist among a wide variety of alto saxophonists, beginning with Duke Ellington soloist Johnny Hodges (1920s through the '50s) and bebop innovator Charlie Parker (1940s through the '50s), and moving through later masters like Jackie McLean, Lee Konitz, Paul Desmond, Eric Dolphy, and Ornette Coleman. Then we'll move into the present and offer profiles of newer alto players such as Kenny Garrett, Tim Berne, and Rudresh Mahanthappa.

The second reason that *Experiencing Jazz* may be unique among jazz appreciation texts is that it has been written by a jazz musician who continues to be active on both the East and West coasts, as well as on the European jazz scene. While there have been many fine volumes written that provide historical and critical analysis of the music, there have to date been only a small number of books written by jazz musicians themselves specifically with the listener in mind. Hence, *Experiencing Jazz: A Listener's Companion* is just that: a guided tour of the jazz world by a practitioner who is eager to bring you closer to the heart of the music and those who create it. So rather than the historical or meticulously critical context so prevalent in many other texts, this book will look at the artists themselves in the context of the instruments they play (or played), and will bring you squarely into their worlds via profiles, stories, and interviews. In many cases, we will hear from a number of musicians—directly in their own words—about music making, earning a living, and what they would like listeners to know about how best to experience their music.

At the end of the day, an important element of learning how to listen to jazz is simply to listen. The web links that are listed in this book will provide a lot of opportunities to hear and see some truly amazing and inspiring performances, by both older and newer artists.

David Liebman, the world-renowned saxophonist and teacher, has suggested frequently that an artist's work mirrors his or her thoughts and feelings, and that he or she lays them bare for everyone to see and, in the case of music, to hear. It is my contention that as we listen to jazz, we not only see and consider the very intimate workings of the musician's mind and heart, but of our own being as well. And in the best possible sense, we will be all the richer for it.

2

GROUNDWORK

Developing Listening Skills

WHAT TO LISTEN FOR IN A JAZZ PERFORMANCE

Developing the ability to listen to music happens on three distinct levels: in the early stages of our exposure to jazz, we first must hear it; then we learn to go beyond the mechanical act of hearing and begin to learn how to really listen to the music that is being created. Once we become used to listening to a jazz performance, we have the potential to cast aside all extraneous thoughts and opinions and really experience what we're hearing. In this sense, we become a vital part of the jazz experience—the beneficiaries of the musical gifts being offered to us from the concert stage and the bandstand.

Let's imagine you and a friend sitting ringside in the Blue Note, a world-famous jazz club in Greenwich Village, New York. The James Moody Quartet takes the stage and prepares to play the first of two hour-long "sets" of music. The announcer informs us that for this engagement, the venerable saxophonist Moody will be joined by the brilliant young pianist Renee Rosnes and two of the city's best rhythm players, bassist Todd Coolman and drummer Adam Nussbaum. This particular group has played with the saxophonist many times before and is sure to provide some musical fireworks for the attentive crowd. Moody turns to the rhythm section (as pianists, bassists, and drummers are collectively known) and counts off

Charlie Parker's famous bebop composition "Anthropology." Your friend turns to you and says, "Wait till you hear this." You may feel intimidated because you're not sure what you'll be hearing over the course of the next couple of hours. Imagine then, how much more valuable this evening's journey into the jazz experience would be if you had an idea what was taking place up there on the bandstand.

THREE COMPONENTS OF MUSIC

In order to begin this journey, we must have a brief look at three of the building blocks of jazz. It's accurate to break a lot of music down into these basic components: melody, harmony, and rhythm. The Native American Ojibwe people call the intersection of interrelated things *miziweyaa*, or a place where things come together for us. So when we receive music created as a result of the blending of these three components, we would do well to understand the unique quality of each and how they work together to create sounds and feelings. Let's have a look at these briefly and see what relationship they have to one another and to jazz. All three are building blocks for musicians, yet may be completely foreign to listeners, except in a very general sense. Let's make them a little more accessible for the nonmusician by speaking of melody, harmony, and rhythm as each one relates to our daily lives.

> Melody is the golden thread running through the maze of tones by which the ear is guided and the heart reached.
>
> —Anonymous

When we hear a melody, we don't really think of it as much more than a memorable (or should we say "memorizable") assemblage of musical notes, which when taken together, constitute what is known as a "song." And if we hear that melody enough times, then it becomes recognizable—so much so, that we may even be able to hum or sing it ourselves. However, contemporary media such as AM and FM radio and "canned music" or Muzak often pummels us over the head with a song, to the point that even though we can sing both the words and the melody, we may likely grow weary of hearing them over and over again. Maybe the old saying "Familiarity breeds contempt" is true. In other words, while overexposure to a song helps us learn the words and the music, hearing the melody countless times on the radio, in restaurants, in grocery stores, boutiques, doctors' office waiting rooms, and many other similar locales lessens the emotional impact of the melody to the point that it trivializes the song into becoming merely background music. We hear it, but we don't really listen to it. One example would be the pop song made famous by James Taylor called "You've Got a Friend." Originally written by Carole King and recorded in 1971 by both artists on separate albums, it was Taylor's version that was one of the hits that catapulted him to fame. While the melody and the words to the song were very appealing to listeners, it became much more than just a nice song about love and friendship. "You've Got a Friend" could be heard on mainstream radio station playlists as many as six or seven times a day, if not more. And as if that weren't enough, it ultimately showed up as canned music in many other venues where "listening" was not the first priority. In that sense, this lovely little tune became something we might hear, but not something we would actively listen to. In other words, "You've Got a Friend" became background music.

Jazz at its best, on the other hand, is foreground music. Each jazz musician states a melody in his or her own personal way. You could place a dozen saxophonists side by side and ask each one to play the melody of any given song, and the odds are that you will hear 12 different versions of the same sequence of the notes comprising the melody. Each saxophonist would stamp his or her own personal touch on the song, and each one's interpretation would be different than the others.

One of the challenges—and delights—of a jazz performance is that when the musicians have finished stating the melody of a song and begin their improvisations, they are creating new melodies on the spot—things you've never heard before and are unlikely to hear the same way again. Experiencing the music of saxophone legend Lester Young is a vivid example. Young (or "Prez," as he was known) played solos that sounded as though they had been formally composed first, then performed—even though his solos were completely improvised every time. A similar experience occurred for me personally when I toured with the iconic trombonist Bob Brookmeyer's quartet in the mid-'80s. We played recognizable songs like "My Funny Valentine" every night—and every night, Brookmeyer's solos were little gems, yet sounded like they, too, were written, rather than improvised. We must have played "My Funny Valentine" a dozen times on that tour, and each time Brookmeyer reinvented the melody and reshaped it as though he were a sculptor and the original melody a block of clay.

In the process of experiencing jazz, you might go to a jazz club several nights in a row to hear a particular group, and while it's altogether possible that you'll hear them play the same songs each night, the soloists will create their own personal variations—instant reworkings of the original melody—that will be different each night. That's one of the beauties of this music: as a listener, you can always expect the unexpected . . . if you are prepared to really listen to the music. So listening for the composed melody of a song and then to the soloists "composing" their own variations on the spot is a good first step toward the development of solid listening skills.

HARMONY IN LIFE AND IN MUSIC

If only the whole world could feel the power of harmony.

—Wolfgang Amadeus Mozart

You use a glass mirror to see your face; you use works of art to see your soul.

—George Bernard Shaw

"Harmony" is often as elusive to define as a concept like "liberty." On the one hand, we might say that harmony can be described as a pleasant arrangement of parts, such as the color combinations found in paintings, combinations of words and lines in poetry, or combinations of notes in music. Going by this perception, it's possible to think of harmony as elements working together to create a whole in which all parts are compatible with (and even complementary to) one another.

On the other hand, perhaps there is a way to look beyond definitions of this sort to get to the essence of what harmony really is. Have you ever seen a flock of migratory birds flying in a "V" formation during the twilight hours in a late October sky? If you have, and if you were completely focused upon the beauty and symmetry of that scene without any other thoughts or distractions, then perhaps you were experiencing harmony—that is, connectedness—with life in the here and now. So then if we experience a kind of connectedness to whatever exists in a particular moment, then it may be said that we are in harmony with the universe.

In sum, we see that harmony is a concept that can exist on a number of levels. Jazz musicians often create harmony (or more accurately, harmonies) when they use their instruments to combine notes to create "layers of sound." Take, for example, any seven notes on the piano. Now play them all at the same time. The sound you are hearing is a component of harmony called a "chord." If you were the famous American composer and jazz master Duke Ellington, you might take each of those seven notes and assign them to a particular instrument—seven different instruments, each playing a different note. Seven musicians creating musical harmony.

Imagine melody then as a horizontal line, moving in time from left (beginning of a tune) to right (its conclusion). Now imagine that as it moves from start to finish, it takes on more weight by adding layers of other notes above and below the single notes moving the song along. As a result, the song gains more depth. The top layer of a chocolate cake is fine, but the addition of six more layers beneath can make it irresistible. Perhaps we might say that harmony works to thicken and enrich a simple melody, giving it depth and character in the process.

If you look at the overall concept of universal harmony as one of connectedness in any kind of music, you will see that it can be the glue that binds and blends elements. Two brief examples: Johann Sebastian Bach has shown us that if you take a simple melody and layer a second melody on top of it, each one complements the other. And the two taken together comprise what's known as "counterpoint." Bach was the master of this form and another, which is called a "fugue," and he composed many of these, much to the delight of listeners throughout the centuries.

The second example of how the global concept of harmony works in music is of a more personal nature. As a result of being part of a State Department tour of South America, I had the chance to hear and play with many fine musicians. One event stands out as particularly memorable. We were in Cartagena, Colombia, filming a concert sequence on one of the city's beautiful beaches. On one of our breaks in shooting, I had the pleasure of meeting and improvising with a group of native drummers and singers. The impromptu get-together was intense and joyous, and even though we didn't speak each other's verbal language, we were on a completely level playing field, thanks to the music we made. You might say that we were in complete harmony with one another. We had created a momentary miziweyaa there on the beach, much to our delight and the delight of those who came over to listen.

Jazz musicians create this kind of communal harmony in performance, by establishing connectedness with themselves and, as a consequence, with their listeners. We put the music out there into the air as a sonic gift to you, our listeners. Jazz is the sum total of all of our life experiences; our ups, our downs, our wins and our losses. We tell you our stories, just as though we were sitting across a table from you in a small café, sharing secrets and some quality time. And if you are an open, attentive listener, and free of preconceptions and judgment, we will be in harmony together, a pleasurable experience that is capable of giving both fulfillment and quiet understanding. Indeed, it will be miziweyaa, a place where things come together for us as musicians and listeners.

FASCINATIN' RHYTHM: A LITTLE PREVIEW

Johann Wolfgang von Goethe, one of history's most versatile and creative minds, had this to say about rhythm: "There is something magical about rhythm; it even makes us believe that the sublime is something of our own" (*Individual Points*, 1824).

And over 100 years later, the eminent jazz writer Leonard Feather had this to say: "Jazz without the beat, most musicians know, is a telephone yanked from a wall; it just can't communicate" (*Show*, January 1962).

Indeed, rhythm is one of the primary elements that have the power to bring melody and harmony to life. But even so, we embrace rhythm from a much deeper place. For example, our hearts beat in a regular rhythmic pattern; there is rhythm in our breathing in exercise or at rest; when we walk down the street, we walk in a tempo that is completely our own.

While rhythm is a vital part of our existence, and while most music maintains a rhythmic foundation, the rhythmic art occupies a special place in jazz. Syncopation, or the deliberate displacement of conventional rhythms, has been a part of jazz since its infancy and is another of the true characteristics of the music.

Using walking once again as an example, let's consider what "deliberate displacement" might mean for us as we engage our feet and stroll down the street. If you remember the art of skipping, then you're on your way to understanding the heart of syncopation. Here's a refresher:

R = right foot / L = left foot
Begin walking at a comfortable medium speed: R / L / R / L / etc.

Once you have established a consistent walking rhythm, try this:
R / L / R-R / L (repeat this in succession a number of times)

Notice that the double Rs are almost twice as fast as your normal foot-falls.

Now say the pattern as you walk, using numbers: "1—2—3-ah—4"

You can also begin this experiment with your left foot rather than your right and you can also skip continuously, rather than alternating the double-step patterns with the single steps, creating a pattern that would look like this:

R-R / L-L / R-R / L-L / etc.

and making a sound like this:

1-ah / 2-ah / 3-ah / 4-ah / etc.

Congratulations! You've just become a syncopator!

As you might guess, syncopation moves away from the rigidity of metric pulse. Walking becomes even more fun when we are able to skip, slide, hop, glide—in short, dance. In the late 1890s, a style of music known as ragtime became the rage, primarily because of the rhythmic looseness of movement in songs like "Maple Leaf Rag" by Scott Joplin, and because that very looseness translated very well into body movements on the dance floor. Needless to say, ballroom dancers were appalled by the new syncopated style of movement, since it broke away so drastically from the stiffness of more traditional dances like the Viennese waltz. Yet there were others who were inextricably drawn to the rhythms and movement of ragtime and early jazz. Young people, in particular, loved the rhythmic free-for-all aspect of this new way of moving to the music, just as their parents found it to be suggestive, paganistic, and downright vulgar—all the more reason for teenagers to be attracted to it.

> Suddenly, I discovered that my legs were in a condition of great excitement. They twitched as though charged with electricity, and betrayed a considerable and dangerous desire to jerk me from my seat.
>
> —Gustav Kohl, "The Musical Possibilities of Rag-Time"
> (*The Metronome*, 1903)

Syncopation, then, is the component of rhythm that changes walking into skipping, and with the birth of ragtime, into syncopated dancing. Without these seemingly erratic herky-jerky rhythmic movements, dances like the One-Step, the Black Bottom, the Charleston, the Lindy, the Shim-Sham, or the Varsity Drag would not have come into existence. The relationship between syncopation, jazz, and dance is one that was cemented early on and lasted for over half a century, well into the 1950s. And syncopation was and is the foundation for all rhythm in jazz from every era.

> I got rhythm. . . . Who could ask for anything more?
>
> —George and Ira Gershwin (1930)

WHAT IS A "SOLO"?

We've already talked about improvisation in a very general sense. So now let's move into the heart of the music even further and focus upon the art of soloing.

When you are experiencing a jazz performance, either live or on video, you are witnessing the music of not only the entire group—for instance, when it plays the arranged melody of a song—but most likely, you are also hearing and seeing one or more of the musicians play solos during the performance. So what then is a "solo"? Let's ask an imaginary jazz musician ("JM") some questions about soloing in a jazz band:

MS: How do you know what to play during your solo?

JM: Well now, that's a good but complex question. Let me see if I can break it down for you: If the group is playing a song like "Watermelon Man," then my solo would be based upon the chords that the composer wrote to support his melody. There are a number of notes that make up each chord and, as a soloist, I'm free to choose which of those notes I want to play in my solo. For instance, if the chord contains five notes, then I'm free to construct my own melody, using those chordal notes as a basis for my improvisation. That's a simplified explanation of the technical element of the solo.

MS: Why do many jazz musicians close their eyes when playing solos? Is it just for dramatic effect?

JM: You know, there's another dimension to playing a solo besides the technical one. For many of us, soloing is a deeply personal act, one that goes beyond just running the notes in a chord and finding new ways to organize them. If you think of playing jazz as sort of a conversation among musicians, then you're off to a good start—except that you as a listener are part of that conversation! Without you, we'd just be playing for ourselves. When you hear a solo, you're hearing more than a series of notes and tones; you're listening to someone share his or her feelings with you. A soloist doesn't offer these things to you for drama's sake. It's like when the great saxophonist Charlie Parker suggested that a jazz solo is made up of a musician's personal experiences, thoughts, and wisdom. In other words, the jazz musician is offering his or her story to you, using sounds rather than words to tell it.

MS: Sort of like an actor "lives" the words in a play or a movie?

JM: In a way, yes. However, whereas the actor becomes the character he or she is portraying, the jazz musician doesn't "become someone else." He, too, loses himself in the creative moment, but he digs deep into his entire being to be able to do it. And the absence of self becomes essential during the creative process at work in a solo. The brilliant saxophonist John Coltrane called this phenomenon "selflessness." Up to a certain point, the instrument is a vehicle to help me say what I've got to say musically; however, there comes a moment where I give myself so fully to my solo, that I cease to exist. I become the music that is pouring out of the horn.

I know that this is pretty mystical sounding, but that's the way playing music can be. It's such a powerful feeling. Unlike actors, we are not assuming the role of another person. But just like when the actor becomes the role he's playing, we, too, immerse ourselves in the music to the point where we don't play the music; it plays us.

MS: Are you saying, then, that there's something spiritual about a solo?

JM: I think so, though maybe not for every jazz soloist. I can't make that kind of comfortable generalization. But I can say that when everything is just right between me and the rhythm section and between us and our listeners, I do think that something indefinably magic happens. Call it spirituality; call it whatever you want. When everything feels right, the music plays itself. We are just the vessels through which it passes, in order to reach you—in order to touch you in some way that maybe even you can't define.

MS: Any parting words of advice for listeners?

JM: Just these: Keep your eyes, ears, and hearts open to our music. We're all in this together!

WHAT TO WATCH FOR IN A JAZZ PERFORMANCE

Whatever size city or town you live in, there is a distinct possibility that a jazz group might be playing somewhere in the vicinity. Many venues that feature the music, either on a full-time basis or as part of a diverse weekly music series, have persisted even in difficult economic times. From nightclubs to coffeehouses, colleges, concert halls, and other performance spaces, "live" jazz is often accessible within a feasible distance. While seeing and hearing jazz performances on a DVD on your computer or via You-Tube are certainly worth it, there really is no substitute for experiencing the immediacy and intensity of the music being created on the spot, a short distance away from your seat. This is not to negate the value of seeing jazz on film, especially historic performances and memorable concert footage; however, experiencing a live jazz concert is being able to have a front-row seat during its creation. Unlike downloading music onto your computer for repeated listening, once the last notes in the "live" set have evaporated, the performance becomes consigned to memory. As the late woodwind artist and jazz icon Eric Dolphy said about live performances: "After you hear music, it's gone in the air. You can never recapture it again" (*Last Date*, Limelight Records, 1964).

In the following sections, we'll look at three different kinds of groups and three distinct types of settings for live jazz performance: one by an established group in a concert setting; another by an "impromptu" group in a Los Angeles jazz club; and finally, we'll look in on a jam session held in an unusual venue in Pennsylvania.

SIGHTS AND SOUNDS I:
AN ESTABLISHED GROUP PERFORMANCE

Formed in the mid-1990s, the Bennie Maupin Ensemble may well be one of the most intriguing and original-sounding groups on the jazz scene today. The brainchild of woodwind artist and multi-instrumentalist Bennie Maupin, the ensemble is a quartet that features mostly original music composed and arranged by Maupin. The unique instrumentation features musical instruments that provide many different tonal "colors" to each composition. Maupin plays a variety of saxophones, flute, occasional piano, and the bass clarinet (see figure 2.1)—the instrument that brought him

Figure 2.1.   The Bennie Maupin Ensemble: Concert in London. Courtesy of Garry Corbett.

into the limelight with trumpeter Miles Davis and keyboardist Herbie Hancock in the late '60s and the early '70s, respectively. Darek "Oles" Oleszkiewicz, one of Poland's most famous musical exports, is also one of jazz's most original voices on the acoustic bass. Percussionist Darryl Munyungo Jackson is an entire orchestra unto himself, creating wild and exotic sounds on each of Maupin's compositions, and utilizing dozens of percussion instruments to do so. I play drums in the ensemble, and I am also the resident spoken-word artist when the occasion calls for it.

The ensemble has played in many different settings both in the United States and in Europe, including clubs, colleges, museums, cultural centers, and concert halls. This performance took place on the concert stage in Cheltenham, England, as part of the annual Cheltenham Jazz Festival.

You take your seat in this beautiful old-world theater and wait for the musicians to enter the stage. While you're waiting, you notice the way the group is set up. The drums are at stage right, facing diagonally toward the center. A bit farther back in the center is the acoustic bass and its electronic amplifier. The vast array of percussion—including conga drums, bongos, a wooden sound box called a cajon, African slit drums, and various cymbals—is located at stage left. The three physical positions form a kind of semicircle that surrounds the saxophones, flute, and bass clarinet, which are positioned right in the center.

The house lights dim and finally go dark, leaving the stage bathed in a variety of colored lights. After the ensemble is announced, they enter the stage from the left side and take their places. For several moments, the hall is completely quiet, so much so that you can almost hear your own breathing. The group is completely motionless, heads bowed, eyes closed.

After what seems like an eternity of silence, Maupin begins clacking the keys of his bass clarinet. The rhythmic click-clack sounds are soon complemented by Jackson's cajon and a variety of woodblocks struck with a yarn mallet. After several moments, Oles joins in, lightly slapping his bass in a similar rhythm with the flat of his hand. I am the last to enter, punctuating the others' rhythms with sticks on metal drum rims, and on the wooden shells of his drums. There is no written music for what listeners are hearing—we ensemble members are having a "musical conversation" with one another, using the edges and surfaces of our respective instruments to create a sonic tapestry that weaves together an exciting blend of rhythms.

While the three of us continue to improvise underneath him, Maupin begins playing a continuous 12-note theme on the bass clarinet until, magically, the entire group stops playing at once. Keep in mind that there is no one conducting us, waving a baton, cueing stops and starts. We all just seem to know when to stop playing and when to begin the tempo again. It seems almost telepathic. As a listener, you wonder how we could possibly know how to do this.

No sooner does the group stop in unison, when we start again in complete sync with one another—only this time, the acoustic bass doubles Maupin's bass clarinet melody, as Jackson moves to conga drums, and I add the drum set into the mix. The music begins to expand into a thicker and fuller sound, leading into a bass solo by Oles, with Maupin using his bass clarinet to punctuate the bassist's improvisations. It sounds almost as though the two are having a discussion, undergirded by the dancing drum grooves of Jackson and me.

Maupin takes the next solo and shows why he is considered to be without peer on his instrument. At times, he reaches into the bottom of the horn and produces notes so low that you can almost feel your seat rumble. Other times, he soars beyond the upper reaches of the instrument and produces a scorching series of bleats and cries that sound almost human.

Darek, Munyungo, and I follow him, and together we explore the feeling of the piece, as we are hearing it then and there.

Once Maupin returns to the 12-note melody, the music ends as it began, with each member of the ensemble returning to the tapping, clicking, and clacking sounds, until it all fades away, as if slowly evaporating into the air.

The audience (including you) responds enthusiastically. Whether it's because of the infectious, pulsating rhythms of the music, or the fact that this music is unlike anything you've ever heard before, you find that you and your fellow listeners are enjoying the direction set by the ensemble, and you wonder what they're going to do next.

No sooner does the piece called "Tapping Things" end, when Maupin turns to the percussionist, and merely nods. Jackson begins playing the osi drum (or "slit drum," as it is more commonly known). His solo begins softly as he plays this instrument with his fingers, palms, and the flat of his hands. Each part of the resonant wood between the slits produces a warm, melodic tone, and Munyungo creates a simple melody that he keeps returning to throughout his improvisation. As the solo continues, Maupin switches from bass clarinet to an alto flute, a deeper-pitched member of the flute family. Oles picks up on Jackson's slit drum melody and plays it in unison with the percussionist. I use soft yarn mallets to create a floating, ethereal sound, and thin metal beaters to scrape the cymbals for a *zzzzzzing!* effect. Maupin enters and plays the melody of "Penumbra," the title track from the ensemble's CD. A brief flute solo follows, and the song ends with a mysterious whisper as Jackson uses his voice to move air very softly into the microphone.

If we were fortunate enough to meet Mr. Maupin after a concert, we might have had the opportunity to ask him questions about the music we just experienced. Here are some questions we might've asked, followed by Mr. Maupin's actual answers (in a 2010 personal interview):

MS: How do you decide what compositions to play before each set?

BM: We use our spare moments in taxis, airports, hotel rooms, and restaurants to discuss the compositions that we may perform. The music actually begins with those dialogues and continues onto the bandstand. It's very rare that I create a set list, as things change so much from moment to moment. Over a 10-year period of creating together, we've developed a deep connection that allows us the freedom to manifest our direction through musical signals and nonverbal communication. I hope I'm not confusing you.

MS: How does each member of the ensemble know when one solo is ending and when the next one begins, and how does each musician know when it's his turn to solo?

BM: We listen very deeply to one another. The flow of our ideas reveals in themselves, our starts and stops, and seldom do I know who will solo next. In order to maintain the freshness in our presentations, we've given ourselves the freedom to do what's natural. The goal is to keep the music feeling organic, and not to struggle with making it a mechanical effort.

MS: I notice that the members of the group seem to get softer and louder together at the same time. Is that planned, and if not, how do they know when to do that?

BM: There are certain times that I'll simply motion to someone to solo. It all depends on where we are in the program and the overall mood that we've created. It's all about being in the moment.

SIGHTS AND SOUNDS 2: AN IMPROMPTU PERFORMANCE

One of Los Angeles's most venerable jazz clubs, Charlie O's Bar & Grill, was truly what is called a jazz "hang." The expression comes from the time-honored pastime of frequenting a venue, "hanging out" with other listeners. Charlie O's was a destination of choice not only for new and seasoned listeners, but also for many of L.A.'s greatest jazz musicians, who when they weren't playing there, often spent the evening at the bar listening to their colleagues on the bandstand and swapping stories that may or may not be true, depending upon who you ask.

Tonight on our make-believe hang, we're going to witness an impromptu performance. Unlike the Bennie Maupin Ensemble, the group we'll be seeing and hearing this time is not one that appears regularly in many different settings. This group plays together occasionally and may or may not perform any "original" compositions by its members (as opposed to "standards" from the *Great American Songbook*); however, the members of this group all know many compositions in the jazz repertoire and, because of their experience and intuition, they are able to sound like a totally polished and organized ensemble.

Like the Bennie Maupin Ensemble, the impromptu group led by saxophonist Don Menza is a quartet; however, this group uses piano in lieu of a percussionist, making this quartet's instrumentation a more traditional grouping: tenor saxophone, piano, bass, and drums. Saxophonist Menza has been a fixture on the West Coast jazz scene for over 40 years and is an internationally known powerhouse player whose big, muscular sound is reminiscent of several of the legendary masters of the instrument like Sonny Rollins and Dexter Gordon.

The rhythm section includes bassist John Heard, drummer Roy Mc-Curdy, and pianist Tom Ranier. All three are among the crème de la crème of L.A. jazz artists, and while not an official "band," they have played together as a rhythm section many times before, usually under Heard's leadership. Together with Menza, these gentlemen will offer a variety of songs for two complete sets.

Since there are no bad seats in this intimate setting, we take a high table against the wall, putting us about 10 feet away from the bandstand. We are surrounded by photographs and paintings of a veritable Who's Who of the L.A. jazz community, as well as many legendary artists such as Count Basie, Dizzy Gillespie, and Billie Holiday.

John Heard gets up on the bandstand, picks up his bass, and asks Ranier for a tuning note, to make sure that he and the pianist are in tune with each other. Menza enters and also adjusts his tenor saxophone's pitch to the piano note—all because it is extremely important that the quartet play in tune. The slightest deviation from the central pitch might make some of the quartet's notes sound sour and dissonant, rather like biting into an overripe lemon.

After a brief discussion with the rhythm section, Menza snaps his fingers on two and four, setting the tempo for a brisk version of "Night and Day," a song written in 1932 by American composer Cole Porter, and a frequent favorite among many jazz musicians.

Pianist Tom Ranier plays a brief introduction, accompanied by Heard and McCurdy, and then Menza plays the melody of the song, just as Porter wrote it, over three-quarters of a century earlier. After stating the complete melody one time through, Menza stands off to the side as the pianist begins his improvisation. Ranier plays an extended solo, starting simply with a few notes. He plays a short musical phrase that Heard echoes on his bass, and he answers on the piano moments later. Ranier then builds his solo slowly over the chords of the melody, into a swirling cascade of notes, his fingers blurring over the keyboard. The entire effect is exhilarating, like being on a roller coaster, climbing slowly to the top of a grade and then teetering, tottering, and plummeting to the bottom of the track.

Saxophonist Menza moves up to the microphone, and when he senses that Ranier's solo is winding down, he jumps into the mix and begins powerfully. Unlike the pianist, he starts his solo with a furious swarm of notes, played at lightning speed. It's hard to see how Menza can move his fingers so quickly over the saxophone keys, creating long runs of notes that move from the bottom sounds of the horn to the very top of its range. He arches his horn upward and swings it down in an arc, then back up again, crafting a solo that also builds to an intense finish.

John Heard plays the next solo and seems deeply involved in the process. He hunches over the bass and actually sings the notes at the same time that he plays them. Ranier and McCurdy play very lightly behind him, since the bass is not as loud an instrument as the others in this quartet. Heard plucks and slaps the bass strings, and his hands scuttle like crabs up and down the expanse of the instrument, from the lowest rumbles to the highest pitches—almost guitar-like in tone quality. It almost seems hard to separate the bassist from the solo he's playing. Eyes tightly closed, he is animated and smiling throughout. It appears that the crowd of listeners is really into this particular solo, and many actually applaud before Heard has finished.

In the background up to this point, drummer Roy McCurdy steps into the limelight after the bass solo and develops a solo of his own that is, unlike the others, completely unaccompanied. You watch and listen as he begins only on the cymbals. He creates a glistening wash of sounds and glasslike pitches on the three cymbals and on the two smaller ones mounted on a stand that he plays with his left foot. McCurdy begins adding the drums themselves into the mix, introducing tom-toms, bass, and snare drums here and there in a very rhythmic way. His hands and feet seem completely independent of one another, yet the total sound of the drum set thickens into a dancing, driving series of beats that are models of jazz syncopation.

Menza then reenters and plays alone with the drummer for a while in a very "conversational" way; their exciting dialogue wins the immediate approval of the audience. Then Ranier and Heard join in simultaneously as Menza restates Cole Porter's melody and the group ends the performance in a way that makes it seem like a written arrangement, even though they created the ending right there on the bandstand. There are shouts of "Yeah!" and whistles of approval, accompanying the tumultuous applause, and everyone on both sides of the bandstand is smiling.

After the set is over, we approach Don Menza and tell him how much we enjoyed his group. We admit to him that we are new listeners and that there is so much we don't understand about what we've just experienced. We ask him the questions listed below, which are followed by his actual answers (in a 2010 personal interview):

> MS: Since this is not a regularly performing group, how is it that everyone knows all of the same songs?

> DM: Not everyone knows all the same songs—especially nowadays and in my case with such a generation gap—I get to play with a lot of different players and very often much younger musicians. Knowing this, I usually prepare for this and make sure I have some sort of (clearly written) lead sheet, and if one or two or maybe all of the rhythm section doesn't know the song I call up, at least they will have a reference to the harmonic structure and the form of the song I want to play. This does happen quite frequently, as I travel a lot to different countries and I've learned over the past several years that it's better to be prepared. I like to play many different songs from the 1930s / '40s / '50s as well as many different jazz standards, and it's virtually impossible for everyone to know all the tunes all the time wherever I go.

> MS: How do you decide who plays solos on each song in your set?

> DM: Once I have started a tune, I will feel out the rhythm section—sometimes letting the piano player play after I have played the main theme. This gives me a chance to hear how comfortable they are with what we're playing. I can make eye contact with the bass player and a simple nod or no from him tells me he wants to or doesn't want to play a solo on this particular song. The same goes for the drummer.

> I don't always start every tune the same way. Sometimes a piano intro—sometimes drums or bass alone—sometimes me—sometimes no intro—this can be discussed briefly on the bandstand. Not everyone plays on every tune—this can make things more interesting for the listener. And I must say that every night is different when it comes to solo order. Again, it makes things more interesting for us as well as the listener. WELCOME TO THE WORLD OF JAZZ!

SIGHTS AND SOUNDS 3: A JAM SESSION

Let's set the stage for a real live jam session. To experience it, we must understand how a jam session works, who is involved, and why it can be a positive, unpredictable, and often exciting experience for our eyes and ears.

Figure 2.2. A jam session. Courtesy of Laurie Samet.

So let's start with the session organizer:

Bill Goodwin is a world-class jazz drummer who has played and recorded with many stellar musicians from award-winning alto saxophonist Phil Woods to iconic singer-songwriter Tom Waits. Goodwin is also a gifted teacher and has taught jazz drumming in a variety of settings, to students of all ages, from teens to professionals.

He lives in the Pocono Mountains west of New York City, a community well known as an enclave for artists, and most particularly for its mentoring of aspiring young jazz musicians. Goodwin is one of the primary forces behind the annual Celebration of the Arts (COTA) festival, which for more than 30 years has provided many opportunities for musicians of all ages to play for appreciative fans and listeners in an outdoor festival setting. He has also been on the faculty of the COTA camp, which offers a chance each summer for students to spend a week-long intensive retreat, studying and playing jazz with well-known musicians and teachers.

Goodwin has also been a frequent performer at the Deer Head Inn, one of the oldest and most respected jazz clubs in the country. In addition to playing at the club, he presides over its weekly Thursday night jam sessions.

Bill has invited us to come down and experience one of the Deer Head's jam sessions. We are not sure how a jam session differs from the other kinds of performances already described. Bill explains that his core band, which consists of saxophone, guitar, bass, and drums, will play a set of music for the first hour. After that, Bill will invite players who are in attendance to come up and join the quartet for a song or two, depending upon how many musicians have come out to the club to play that night. Guests are invited to "sit in" with the group, once Goodwin has had the chance to ascertain whether they are prepared for the experience. What this means is that players must be familiar with the songs that are going to be performed before getting up on stage and jamming with the band. Preparation involves knowing the chords that accompany the song's melody, as well as how to improvise on the notes in each of those chords. Many musicians have the misconception that to play jazz, you can just get up on stage, close your eyes, and "play what you feel." Goodwin is emphatic that there is a lot more to playing jazz than that; consequently, he often gently discourages those who he believes are not ready to sit in with his group, and yet encourages them to study the fundamentals necessary to come back another time and give it a try.

Tonight's jam session is graced with some very good guests, since it's Bill's birthday and many friends and well-wishers are here for the celebratory get-together. Here's what we will experience:

The quartet, which features saxophonist Adam Niewood, guitarist Bill Washer, and bassist Tony Marino, has asked Billy Test, an accomplished and imaginative young pianist, to join them this evening. Goodwin suggests that the rhythm section begin as a trio alone, with an old song called "I Remember You" as the first piece. The pianist, who looks like he is still in high school, negotiates the melody and chord structure of the song as though he were a much older, more experienced musician. It's obvious that the trio is swinging and having a good time—smiles all the way around. The piano solo is followed by a leaping, loping bass solo in which Marino explores the full range of his instrument, from guitar-like runs in the upper register to deep rumbles that you can feel more than hear! The torch is then passed to Goodwin, who builds an exciting drum solo out of the song's melody. As the song ends, the audience shows its enthusiasm and approval, by lots of applause and cheers. The trio adds the saxophonist and guitarist for one more song, after which the session begins.

Since this is a jam session, Goodwin sees a man in the audience who has become a living legend among jazz vocalists and fans. Bob Dorough, all 80-plus years of him, is invited up to the bandstand to sing a tune. He chooses a song by the late Charlie "Bird" Parker (himself a bebop legend and a brilliant, innovative saxophonist) called "Yardbird Suite." Originally, the song had no lyrics; however, Dorough—a master songwriter and totally unique interpreter of any song you put in front of him—supplies words to the music. Everyone in the group knows Bird's tune, so all Goodwin has to do is count off the tempo—"One . . . two . . . one-two-three-four"—and off they go. Dorough sings with great gusto, and his voice, gravelly and playful, is right in sync with the band. After his vocal, he dances off to stage right, smiling and clapping his hands on two and four, as Adam Niewood takes the first solo. His tenor saxophone sound encompasses the entire tradition of the horn, from bebop master Sonny Rollins through the sheets-of-sound approach of John Coltrane. Guitarist Washer is next, and his solo is fleet fingered and melodic. Unintimidated by his elders, Billy Test plays an exciting two-fisted piano solo. Dorough in the meantime is beaming at the young man and nodding his head in approval, before recapping the lyric and ending the tune.

Alto saxophonist "Sweet" Sue Terry is invited up to the stage to jam with the group. When asked what she would like to play, Terry suggests "Alone Together," a song that is popular among jazz musicians for its lovely harmonies and chord changes. I have also been asked to sit in, and so I replace Goodwin in the drum chair. So now the band has two saxophonists along with guitar and the rhythm section, with a guest drummer.

There are a couple of virtues present that can make a jam session memorable. First of all, everyone on stage is congenial, relaxed, and respectful. Second, the communal aspect of the performance is very much in evidence. All members of the ad hoc ensemble work together—as members of an instant musical community—to offer a spirited and flowing performance, as though the group were an actual working band.

"Sweet Sue," being the invitee, takes the first solo. She quickly dispels any notion one might have that suggests jazz is a man's art. Her solo bristles with electric energy and a searing, yet pure sound. As she reaches for notes in the upper register of her alto, Terry stands on her tiptoes, as though she were a prima ballerina doing a plié onstage at Carnegie Hall. Niewood follows her on soprano saxophone and matches her intensity with his own, as she looks on, smiling and nodding approval.

As if it were planned (which it wasn't), bassist Marino and I drop out as Billy begins his piano solo. Since he is playing without accompaniment, Billy disregards the tempo and plays a style called "rubato," which means literally to move away from a regular pulse and just let the musical passage flow, much as a river flows—seamlessly and infinitely. When he looks up at us, it is our signal to move back into tempo with him as he moves to conclude his solo. The saxes reenter with the melody and we all "take the tune home," which means that we strive to end it in an extemporaneous, yet organized fashion.

Sue sits the next one out as vocalist Nancy Reed is invited up to the bandstand. When asked what she would like to sing, Nancy offers a song from the swing era called "I Didn't Know What Time It Was," which she begins with Bill Washer alone; a lovely blend of guitar and Nancy's warm and honeyed alto voice. She and the guitarist perform the song once through by themselves, and the rest of the group enters the second time through at a medium slow tempo. Nancy "scats" a chorus—which means that she uses her voice as though it were a horn and improvises over the chord changes, using the same kind of phrasing that, say, a saxophonist or trumpeter might use when soloing. Adam and Sue both follow with solo statements of their own, at which time Nancy returns with the lyric and we end the song.

Goodwin returns to the drums and the group finishes up with an exciting jazz-funk version of pianist Herbie Hancock's song "Chameleon." The amazing thing throughout is how cohesive all of this sounds. Not all jam sessions are like that; indeed, many are rather sloppy, disorganized affairs. However, Bill Goodwin knows how to preside over these kinds of get-togethers.

I take the liberty of asking Bill Goodwin to sit down for a few minutes after the jam session has come to an end and answer some questions for us. The questions, along with his actual answers, follow:

MS: What is the first thing you do when organizing one of your Thursday night jam sessions at the Deer Head Inn?

BG: I have a steady band for my jam session night, except for the bass player. My first priority is to be sure I have a good bass player. He or she must know a lot of standard and jazz tunes and must not mind playing all night, since not too many bass players come to jam regularly. Fortunately, the bass players I get to come out and jam are well equipped to handle an entire evening of music with session attendees.

My quartet usually plays the first set—which turns out to be sort of a master class for aspiring players who come out to sit in with the group. Our set usually lasts for about an hour, and we try to set the tone for the evening. Once we take a break, I circulate among the players and create either a mental or an actual list of those who've shown up to participate in the jam session.

MS: I notice that quite a number of people show up and want to play. How do you know which of them to invite up to the stage to play with you? How do you screen them?

BG: Anyone who shows up and makes themselves known will be sounded to play. Not everyone wants to, but I must ask! If you are dropping by to play with us, then first arrivals get priority on the list, unless a really great player shows—generally someone well known by me and others in the jazz community—in which case I may grant a rare line jumping.

In terms of screening the musicians who want to sit in with us, I generally ask them what specific tune they'd like to play; fortunately, I have a knack and the experience to sort of feel out those I don't know, to see whether or not they're up to the task of joining us for a number. Most often, they are . . .

MS: What if someone makes it past your screening process and gets up there and quite obviously doesn't know the song that you're playing?

BG: Well, there's no way to be sure if a player who we don't know can hack it, until they're actually up there on the bandstand with us. Everybody gets at least a tune, then—if they play well—I decide if they get more, and invite them to remain on the bandstand with us for another tune.

MS: What, to your way of thinking, is the true value of the jam session these days?

BG: These weekly jams of mine provide a venue for musical and social exchange for professional and aspiring musicians in our community. And for me, the sessions provide focus and validation that after all these years as a professional touring and recording musician, it's still fun and often magical to play this music. And it's great to be able to support and encourage our younger musicians as they grow into the music.

Jam sessions are all about community; all about sharing common experiences, about conversing, about the give-and-take of everyday life; a true musical meeting of the minds and hearts of the community members—including the audience. They are often at the core of the jazz experience and, at their best, they are prime examples of democracy in action.

3

JAZZ AS A MIRROR OF OUR TIMES

From Birth through the 1940s

Culture [is] . . . a product of man. He projects himself into it, he recognizes himself in it; that critical mirror alone offers him his image.

—Jean-Paul Sartre, *Les mots* (1964)

What do you think an artist is? An imbecile who only has eyes if he is a painter, or ears if he's a musician, or a lyre at every level of his heart if he's a poet, or even, if he's a boxer, just his muscle? On the contrary, he is at the same time a political being, constantly alive to heart-rending, fiery or happy events to which he responds in every way. . . . Painting is not done to decorate apartments. It is an instrument of war.

—Pablo Picasso, *Les lettres françaises* (1943)

Art doesn't exist in a vacuum. All artists—whether musicians, visual artists, actors, dancers, poets, or writers—are products of the societies and cultures in which they live. The relationship of the artist to his or her environment is crucial to the development and realization of the art that he or she creates. Artists are, more often than not, tuned in to their physical, psycho-social, and cultural surroundings and respond to them accordingly, using whatever tools are available to do so.

It's no secret that artists are often thought of as a highly sensitive lot; but in what way? To answer this question, we must first look inward. Look around you, not only at your profession, your family, or your circle of friends; but look also at the culture and society that surround and permeate your life. How does what's going on in the world around you affect how you look at life and how you perceive your place in the grand scheme of things? More specifically, in what ways does the culture of which you are a part affect your life? Many of us find ourselves bombarded by media culture, whether it's via television, radio, the Internet, or print media. Just how much do these media hold sway over our philosophical outlooks, our cultural choices, or even our spiritual beliefs?

> I heard the news today, oh boy . . .
>
> —John Lennon and Paul McCartney, "A Day in the Life" (1966)

In our busy lives, we don't often stop and ask ourselves philosophical questions like the examples above. However, it is exactly these kinds of inquiries that have been of great interest to artists from all eras and, cultures. Many artists are hypersensitive to their surroundings and, as a result, they deliberately respond to them in a variety of ways. For example, Pablo Picasso graphically depicted the horrors of war in his painting *Guernica* (1937), in which oppression, chaos, and violence are major themes that concerned him as he created the painting. The composer Aaron Copland wrote an orchestral piece called *Music for a Great City* (1964), which captures the intense sounds and feelings of urban life in New York City in the mid-20th century. The beloved Frank Capra film *It's a Wonderful Life* (1946) reflected not only the downturn in the postwar American economy in the 1940s but is also relevant to the economic crises facing many people across the country at this writing in the new millennium. And John Lennon's much-revered song "Imagine" has become an anthem for nonviolence and a call for peace among peoples of the world. These are but a few examples of ways in which artists attempt to illustrate how they perceive and react to the culture and society in which they live. So in sum and as an example, while we may maintain an antiwar philosophy, our beliefs in peaceful coexistence are something we espouse in casual conversation or communication with another person or group of people. Artists, on the other hand, use the tools at their disposal to offer the same kind of message that we might offer, through showing us either the horrors of war (Picasso's painting) or the possibility of lasting peace (Lennon's song).

Jazz musicians have never shied away from reacting to the culture of the time in which they lived, through their music and, on occasion, through their words. The history of jazz is intertwined fully with the history of America itself. So then, in order to really experience the music, you have to understand the context from which it evolved. Since this is a listener's companion and not really a jazz history book, in this chapter and the next, we will touch upon only some of those historic milestones that may have had significant influence upon the music from the time of its inception through the present day.

CULTURAL HISTORY AND THE MUSIC: SOME BRIEF GLIMPSES

Jazz has a long and notable history as a mirror of the culture that has surrounded it since its inception in the early part of the last century and, in some ways, even earlier. Jazz has always been and will always be a musical force that has mirrored the cultural and social environment in which it is created. Let's have a brief look at some examples as we move through history, beginning in the late 1800s.

UP FROM SLAVERY: MUSIC FROM THE FIELDS

It is generally acknowledged that work songs and field hollers were transmitted orally from person to person in Southern slave communities in order to help field hands communicate and get through the long, arduous days picking cotton and doing other forms of manual labor for white slave owners. It was here and in black churches that the call-and-response mode of singing was created, where one person would sing a phrase and others would respond to it by singing either the exact same phrase or a completely different (but unified) response, as you can see in this work song:

> Shuck That Corn before You Eat
>
> Caller: All dem purty gals will be dar,
> Chorus: Shuck dat corn before you eat.
> Caller: They will fix it for us rare,
> Chorus: Shuck dat corn before you eat.
> Caller: I know dat supper will be big,
> Chorus: Shuck dat corn before you eat.

Caller: I think I smell a fine roast pig,
Chorus: Shuck dat corn before you eat.
Caller: I hope dey'll have some whisky dar,
Chorus: Shuck dat corn before you eat.
Caller: I think I'll fill my pockets full,
Chorus: Shuck dat corn before you eat.

—William Wells Brown, *My Southern Home* (1880)

Hymns sung in the black churches had a similar quality to them, as evidenced in this famous gospel song:

Swing Low, Sweet Chariot

Congregation sings this chorus (in response to each verse):
Swing low, sweet chariot,
Comin' for to carry me home!
Swing low, sweet chariot,
Comin' for to carry me home!

Verse (sung by the minister or a designate):
I looked over Jordan and what did I see,
Comin' for to carry me home,
A band of angels comin' after me,
Comin' for to carry me home!

Congregation repeats the chorus (first four lines)

Verse:
If you get there before I do,
Comin' for to carry me home,
Jess tell my friends that I'm acomin' too,
Comin' for to carry me home!

Congregation repeats the chorus (first four lines)

Verse:
I'm sometimes up and sometimes down,
Comin' for to carry me home,
But still my soul feels heavenly bound,
Comin' for to carry me home!

Congregation repeats the chorus (one last time)

—Wallace and Minerva Willis (1840)

One way that these communal songs reflected the tenor of the times was in their codified meanings. In other words, many of these verses were actually secret codes that would convey messages within the slave community. In this instance, for example, the chariot in the title was code for a wagon or other form of transportation used to help slaves escape from bondage. The hymn delivered the message that a wagon would arrive soon to carry slaves to freedom and that they should be on high alert.

The work song, the gospel hymn, and the rhythms and fervor that carried them both along have played a vital role in the development of jazz since its birth. However—from a cultural perspective—had there been no slavery and racial oppression in America during the 19th and 20th centuries, it seems doubtful that early jazz would have evolved as it did, assuming that it evolved at all. So then, out of the deplorable concept of subservience of one human being to another has come a music that reflects a cultural dimension of the very racism from which it came. Most important, the collective musical spirit of the slave communities in both the fields and churches across America during those times has been historically instrumental in creating one of the most endearing qualities of jazz music of any era: its communal spirit.

THE EARLY DAYS IN NEW ORLEANS

America has often been referred to as a melting pot, a veritable gumbo of people from every corner of the globe. The diversity of ethnicities in the United States is overwhelming in its breadth. For example, my college classes at Pasadena City College in California were composed of Americans of African, Asian, Hispanic, Eastern and Western European, Middle Eastern, Native American, and Caucasian descent. At first, each ethnicity in a class would form its own support group; however, as time passed, new friendships were made and cultures fused in very interesting and productive ways, creating a rich and memorable environment each semester.

Much the same way as the diversity in my classes ultimately yielded a truly wild and invigorating mix of experiences, the music of 19th- and early 20th-century New Orleans was the product of a dazzling array of peoples and their respective cultures. In the early 1800s, the city was rife with all manner of European musical influences, including orchestral, brass, and string band music, as well as Christian hymns and chorales. At first, each of these various immigrant groups sought to preserve the cultural heritage of its homeland by attempting to keep its music alive and intact—that is, free of outside influences. However, as time passed, the influence of African American music—with its field hollers, voodoo rites, and work songs—exerted itself mightily throughout the Crescent City. Other cultures couldn't help but be affected by the infectious rhythms and melodies of the slaves. In fact, on any given Sunday, you might wander into Congo Square and experience the songs, dances, and celebrations of the city's slave populace. The abandon with which the music was performed had a profound effect upon European music, notably in terms of its syncopated rhythmic conceptions.

The most memorable effect that African and African American music had upon European music in the late 1800s was the birth of ragtime. The term itself referred to a merging of African syncopated rhythms with European musical traditions, creating a sort of a quirky, nonrigid "ragged time." While there were brass bands, string bands, and solo string instruments like the banjo that played ragtime music, its primary source was the piano—more specifically, a man named Scott Joplin. Ironically, Joplin was not from New Orleans but Missouri, and he was the best known of all ragtime composers. His most famous compositions, like "Maple Leaf Rag" and "The Entertainer" (known to us as the theme from the movie *The Sting*), live on today and remain popular in piano repertoire.

Was ragtime actually jazz? The answer to that question depends upon whether or not you see improvisation as the core and essence of the jazz art. If you believe as many jazz critics and listeners do, then ragtime would not be considered jazz but a precursor to it, primarily because the ragtime of Joplin's day was completely composed. The truth is that there were no improvisations whatsoever. The thing that linked ragtime to jazz was its syncopated melodies and variations, which were very exciting, rhythmic, and danceable in their day. Accepting the definition above, we might suggest that the rag became jazz in the hands of Jelly Roll Morton, who not only played ragtime but composed similar music that allowed space for his improvisations. To summarize, then, ragtime itself laid a foundation for jazz, but it had little else to do with jazz because of its lack of room for solo interpretations.

Not only did African American music exert a significant and lasting influence upon European music at that time and vice versa (as evidenced by the birth of ragtime), but European music—notably classical forms and structures—played a distinct and somewhat unusual role in the black community, apart from the ragtime phenomenon. "Creoles of color" were the result of liaisons between French and Spanish slave owners and their female slaves. As time passed, these unique African Americans were afforded opportunities previously available only to whites. Musically, they were highly trained and sophisticated interpreters of the European musical tradition—and ironically, they looked down their noses at the music of the slave culture.

Even though the Emancipation Proclamation was signed in 1863 and the 13th Amendment to the U.S. Constitution was enacted in 1865, free African Americans continued to work backbreaking jobs for long hours, in the employ of white men. Consequently, the field hollers and work songs previously alluded to continued to proliferate among the ex-slave population. Black Christian churches, the result of a significant shift away from Caribbean and African forms of voodoo, continued to increase in number, and with them, the further growth and development of gospel music and eventually the blues. African American brass bands also became common in New Orleans and played for all manner of community celebrations, including weddings, funerals, and a variety of religious holidays.

All in all, musical styles began to coalesce as a result of the integration of cultures, and no ethnicity was left unchanged. It was here that the early seeds of jazz took root and began to grow.

THE ROARING TWENTIES

"Roaring," among its various definitions, means "moving at a high rate of speed." It's a word that can describe something that is always moving, always dynamic. There is a kind of excitement attached to these words that would fit neatly into our description of America in the 1920s: ever moving, ever changing, ever dynamic—take your pick. Any of these terms would apply nicely to the feeling of that decade.

The year before the new decade introduced the notorious Volstead Act, which was the foundation for Prohibition—a largely unsuccessful attempt to curb the production and consumption of alcohol. This was an era of organized crime, speakeasy saloons, and the formal advocacy of women's voting rights via the 19th Amendment to the Constitution. Continued racial tensions focused upon not only African Americans but also a number of ethnic immigrant groups as well, including Asians, Jews, Irishmen/women, and Italians. Racist groups such as the Ku Klux Klan were active in the Southern and Midwestern states, and "quotas" were imposed in the North upon immigrants attempting to disembark in the country. Once a quota of immigrants had been reached, all others were turned away and forced to settle in other countries.

The 1920s were also an era of significant technological growth, with automobiles becoming more accessible to the general public through mass production. There were the diversions of radio and the movies, both in their infancy, yet each amassing an enormous following.

The arts also thrived in the '20s, notably in urban centers like New York City, which witnessed the birth of the Algonquin Round Table—a literal roundtable gathering of many of the city's (and the country's) finest artists and writers, at the Algonquin Hotel in Manhattan. Weekdays would find literary stars and personalities as diverse as George S. Kaufman, Dorothy Parker, Harpo Marx, and Alexander Woolcott sharing lunch and a lot of verbal jousting and jamming on a variety of topics, many of which became the stuff of literary legend.

New York also saw the birth of the Harlem Renaissance, the first important gathering of African American artists, writers, and musicians. While it was not confined to Harlem, this movement brought many black authors, artists, and musicians to national and international prominence. Writers such as W. E. B. Du Bois, Langston Hughes, and Zora Neale Hurston; artists such as Aaron Douglas, Palmer C. Hayden, and Laura Wheeler; and musicians including Eubie Blake, James P. Johnson, and composer William Grant Still—all flourished at that time.

Music was a key ingredient of the Roaring Twenties. While songs such as "I'm Just Wild about Harry" and "Puttin' on the Ritz" were popular on the radio and early phonographs, it was jazz that defined the music of the decade—hence the alternate name of the '20s was the "Jazz Age." It can be said with some degree of certainty that Harlem, along with New Orleans and Chicago, played an enormous role in the development of jazz in the 1920s. While Buddy Bolden, King Oliver, Louis Armstrong, Sidney Bechet, and others were among the shining stars of the Crescent City jazz scene, the Harlem Renaissance produced talent of the magnitude of band leaders/composers Duke Ellington and Fletcher Henderson, and some really formidable pianists like James P. Johnson, Thomas "Fats" Waller, Willie "The Lion" Smith, and Ellington himself. The music was played in Harlem nightclubs like the Cotton Club (home of Ellington's "jungle music"—racially tinged compositions written for stereotypical African-styled exotic revues and for the largely white audiences who attended them) and Small's Paradise. It was also performed as part of Broadway shows such as *Shuffle Along* (1921) and *Runnin' Wild* (1923). Ironically, some of the best jazz to be heard in New York at that time was the product of "rent parties," informal get-togethers held by tenants in apartments across the city, in order to help families raise money for rent, groceries, and other necessities. Jazz musicians—notably pianists from the "Harlem Stride" school of two-fisted piano playing—would provide the music for these parties and would often compete with one another in "cutting contests" in order to see who could come out on top.

While New York was an active center for jazz in the Twenties, Chicago was considered by many to be the true hub of the music, at least for a number of years in the decade. That the Windy City became a major focal point for jazz should come as no surprise. Due to a number of significant factors, including America's entry into World War I and the designation of New Orleans as a port to be utilized by the U.S. Navy, the infamous Storyville district of New Orleans was shut down in 1917. The district had been the center of much of the city's jazz activity before that time and was the source of income for many a musician. Small bands played in saloons and dance halls, while solo pianists played in the parlors of the district's many bordellos. Storyville was also the home of sporting houses, gambling, saloons, and dance halls. The demise of Storyville, as well as the potential for musical employment and trade and factory work in Chicago, led to what historians have called the Great Migration, which brought many Southern blacks into the Midwest and other areas that seemed removed from the limited work opportunities and the overt racism of the South.

Among the New Orleans musicians who migrated to Chicago were cornetists King Oliver and Louis Armstrong, pianist Jelly Roll Morton, and clarinetist Johnny Dodds—all of whom formed small bands that achieved significant success both locally and nationally. In fact, the Great Migration to Chicago by New Orleans musicians diminished the latter city's importance as a vital nerve center for the music.

In Chicago, there were plenty of cabarets and speakeasies, as well as many venues to play jazz. The South Side—a predominantly black area of the city—was home to many night spots, ranging from dance halls like Lincoln Gardens to nightclubs like the Sunset Café and the Plantation Café, and theaters such as the Vendome Theater, which hired Armstrong and his group to play for silent films. Some of these jazz venues were called "black and tans," where blacks and whites socialized and enjoyed the music together.

The same culture that brought the two races together also gave rise to a population of young white musicians who were inspired by the New Orleans transplants. Most of these Chicagoans lived on the West Side of the city in more affluent white neighborhoods and attended area high schools. One would suspect that playing jazz was a supreme act of rebellion for many of these kids, since there was still much resistance to this music on the part of earlier generations, who would have preferred that their kids study and listen to classical music. Sound familiar? It should, when you consider how parents showed displeasure with rock and roll back in the 1950s and psychedelic music in the '60s. It's not a coincidence that the same disconnect between generations is evident today, manifest in a similar parental resistance to the acceptance of hip-hop and other similar genres of "youth music." History has a way of repeating itself.

In 1922, one such rebellious group of young Chicago musicians—arguably the most famous—came into existence. The teenagers called themselves the Austin High Gang, so named because many of them attended that high school in the West Side suburb of Oak Park. It is reputed that when these young aspiring jazz musicians heard the New Orleans Rhythm Kings on the nickelodeon at the local soda shop, they were so inspired by the music that they decided to get a band together and try to emulate what they were hearing. The gang's roster of members grew and included what would be some of the finest white jazz musicians to come out of Chicago during the next two decades. Famous alumni of the Austin High Gang included cornetist Jimmy McPartland, tenor saxophonist Bud Freeman, clarinetist Frank Teschmacher, drummer Dave Tough, and eventually, clarinetists Benny Goodman and Pee Wee Russell, guitarist Eddie Condon, and drummer Gene Krupa. These musicians collectively and individually created a "sound" that was lighter and more "airy" than the New Orleans bands they emulated. They favored more formal ensemble passages, as well as the individual soloist approach created by Louis Armstrong, rather than everyone soloing at once, as was the custom with the New Orleans bands. And another big difference was the use of the saxophone—in this case, the tenor horn—in both solos and ensembles.

Jazz musicians, as we shall see in other places in this guide, sometimes fall victim to their lifestyles. Alcohol, drug addiction, and unhealthful living habits are just a few of the perils encountered in the jazz life. An early example of such a tragic downfall is that of Bix Beiderbecke, one of the greatest musicians to come out of Chicago in the 1920s. Beiderbecke was actually born and raised in Iowa, and was an immensely gifted musician and composer and, like Louis Armstrong, a virtuoso on the cornet. He was a fine pianist as well, and he composed a number of exquisite solo pieces that are still performed today. In a very short time, Bix rose to the upper echelon of the white jazz scene in Chicago, and soon after in New York. Although his personal irresponsibility and self-destructive tendencies with alcohol shortened his life considerably, Beiderbecke influenced countless trumpet players from all eras of jazz.

THE THIRTIES: THE GREAT DEPRESSION
AND THE BIRTH OF THE SWING ERA

Due to the near-catastrophic economic events that took place here in America and Europe toward the end of the first decade of our new millennium, there has been a renewed interest in the Great Depression—the events that led up to it, how Americans were affected by it, and how the country survived it.

Following a period of economic hyperactivity and financial carelessness, the Great Depression began with the stock market crash of 1929 and continued until 1939, although some historians believe that it ended only in 1941 when America entered World War II. It was a life-altering experience at almost every level of American society. Stock market investors' portfolios were ruined, and almost half of the country's banks failed. America's manufacturing output was cut roughly in half, and unemployment plagued over 25 percent of the work force. People who had never known poverty were faced with a new and stark reality. Bread and soup lines were not uncommon, and entire families were forced to live in makeshift camps called "Hoovervilles." Men and women lost the ability to put food on the table and as a consequence were demoralized, frustrated, and angry. Many Americans began questioning the concepts of democracy, capitalism, and the American dream. It was a bleak time in American history.

It was also a hard time for musicians, who relied upon recordings, radio performances, and dance jobs to make a living. While certain venues like Harlem's Cotton Club retained its clientele (often well-to-do white listeners), these were exceptions rather than the rule. Many clubs had to close their doors due to the poor economy and subsequent lack of disposable income available to the listening public at that time. Radio became the medium of choice for music lovers and folks seeking to escape from the realities of the Depression. It provided all manner of broadcasts, from comedies and mysteries to westerns and dramas; however, it took a sizable bite out of the dwindling recording industry. Instead of spending money (assuming you had any) on phonograph recordings, all you needed to do was create a makeshift space in your living room, kick off your shoes, turn on your Philco radio, and dance to the music being broadcast live from big city dance halls or from radio's *Make-Believe Ballroom.*

Some bands were able to survive the dismal economic situation. Duke Ellington and his orchestra held forth as one of the handful of groups who played on a regular basis at the Cotton Club. Ellington's aggregation, along with a number of other jazz bands, also received the support of the criminal underworld and such notorious figures as Al Capone, which allowed them to remain active and intact as a steadily working unit. Louis Armstrong was another of the decreasing number of working musicians who seemed to be able to maintain financial stability through touring with his bands, crisscrossing the country, playing one-night stands and theaters, and—when possible—recording.

Other musicians and bands didn't have quite the good fortune that Ellington and Louis Armstrong enjoyed. As can be seen, if you were a jazz musician during the '30s, you did anything you could in order to support your family. The situation brightened a little when Prohibition was repealed in 1933, whereupon more clubs reopened their doors and new venues came into being as well.

With the inception of the previously mentioned *Make-Believe Ballroom* in 1935, America had its first radio program to feature phonograph records, rather than live, on-location, or in-studio performers. While the downside of this was loss of radio work for organized bands, the positive side was that if you recorded a phonograph record and it received repeated airplay on radio stations across the country, your stock went up considerably and so did opportunities for more musical engagements. This may be specifically what Louis Armstrong and others were thinking when they recorded their music: if radio shows, due to a lack of funding, were unable to host live bands for on-air performances, and if playing phonograph records by jazz groups repeatedly proved to be more economical, then the band that made records stood more of a chance for wider exposure and, perhaps, more employment. It was (and still is) only natural that legions of listeners wanted to actually have the experience of seeing the groups perform their hits in person.

While it's open to debate, many jazz historians believe that the swing era began in the autumn of 1934, when Benny Goodman and his big band won the residency on the *Let's Dance* radio program. Beginning in December, the band performed regularly on the show for half a year, and brought Goodman squarely into the public eye (or more appropriately, the public ear) and onto the national scene, thanks to the miracle of radio.

The movement away from New Orleans and Chicago-style jazz to tightly knit larger ensembles like Goodman's and Artie Shaw's big bands was of particular interest to young people, who seemed to welcome the change. While *Let's Dance* was aired quite late on the East Coast, it reached a wider (and a more wide-awake) audience at 10 p.m. on the West Coast. As a result, the Goodman band, for example, had a much broader fan base there than in the East or even the Midwest—a fact which seemed to be a big surprise to them.

As mentioned later on, the effects of the Depression were not felt as acutely in Kansas City, Missouri, due largely to the fact that it had been rife with gambling, prostitution, alcohol, and drugs, well before Prohibition. And even when Prohibition was taking hold throughout the country, Kansas City ignored it almost completely, as though it didn't exist. Between Tom Pendergast's totally corrupt local administration and the emergence of bootlegging and organized crime, attempts to prohibit any vices, let alone alcohol, were doomed to failure in Kansas City. Pendergast's goal was to make the city a lucrative festival of illegal entertainment, and he would stop at nothing to realize that goal.

As a result of the Pendergast "machine," there were at least 50 clubs in the nightclub district of Kansas City in the 1930s that offered live jazz as part of their evening's festivities. Clubs like the Sunset Club, the Cherry Blossom, and the Reno Club featured jazz from solo pianists (often playing boogie-woogie) to big bands like those led by Count Basie, Bennie Moten, and Jay McShann.

Just as the prevailing mood in Kansas City was one of energetic proportions, so, too, was the music that permeated the scene at that time. Even though many of the clubs hired only pianists to play in the earlier hours of the evening, it was later that the fireworks began, when bass players and drummers joined in and formed supporting rhythm sections for saxo-phonists, trumpeters, trombonists, and other instrumentalists who would drop by and exhibit their musical wares. These jam sessions were highly competitive affairs, and if you were, say, a trumpeter joining the group to "sit in" on a song, you had best be prepared to give it your best effort—because there might well be another trumpet player in the house waiting to come up on stage and show you up musically. These sessions were also sometimes known as "cutting contests," in that on any given tune, there might be a string of horn players waiting to play—one after the other—to see who would come out on top as the best soloist. Sometimes these sessions went on for hours and tested the staying power of the rhythm section that had to support—and sometimes endure—a seemingly endless string of soloists. The audiences loved the energy; the club owners loved the fact that the jam session musicians were playing for free; and the musicians themselves enjoyed the esprit de corps as they jousted with one another.

Looking back on those days during the Depression, there were so many out-of-work musicians hoping to make a name for themselves, or perhaps to just blow off a little bit of steam in order to momentarily escape the frustrations of unemployment, that the all-night jam session provided the perfect outlet for many.

Today's jam sessions, like the one we experienced in chapter 2, came out of the jazz culture of those early days; however, modern-day sessions are much less overtly competitive than their predecessors, since the culture we live in is not born out of the desperation that existed during the Great Depression. However, 21st-century jam sessions still often exhibit the friendliness and the feeling of community that was very much in evidence in Kansas City and other urban jazz centers in the 1930s.

THE FORTIES: WORLD WAR II AND THE BEGINNINGS OF A COUNTERCULTURE

The Depression finally ended in 1941 when the United States entered World War II. The country's commitment was clear, and its mobilization astonishingly rapid. America threw its weight behind arms production, delivering literally thousands of planes, tanks, guns, and munitions. Every industry went to work for the war effort, and as men went off to battle, over six million women replaced them in factories and other workplaces.

Needless to say, the transition of women from the home into the work force wreaked havoc on many families. Often, grandparents would assume parenting roles, thereby creating role confusion and conflict for many children, who suffered the additional burden of being uprooted from their homes and moved into strange and often unstable new environments. Further instability came from the fact that due to the stresses placed upon husbands and wives as they struggled to maintain their sanity at home and abroad, the number of divorces during the war years increased dramatically.

Adding to the chaos, millions of rural Americans, realizing that the war effort would bring much-needed employment, moved from agricultural areas of the South and the Midwest to major urban areas on both coasts and on the Gulf Coast. There they found work at military bases, factories, and in a wide variety of service industries. As a result of this migration, cities became overcrowded, civil services and schools were overburdened, and food was in short supply. Even though the Great Depression had ended, Americans found themselves in the midst of tremendous change in all walks of life.

The jazz world was also affected by these far-reaching changes. For example, big bands, which only a few years earlier had been at the height of their popularity, found that their audiences were shrinking. There are a lot of opinions as to what factors caused this decline; however, many jazz historians agree that with the inception of the GI Bill and the financial and educational opportunities it afforded war vets and their families, more and more people moved out of urban centers and into affordably financed tract houses in planned "sub-urban" neighborhoods, situated outside of metropolitan areas. As a result, people lost physical proximity to music venues, ballrooms, art galleries, museums, and other similar cultural centers traditionally located in the urban landscape. Add the lure of the new medium of television to the mix, and armchair entertainment took precedence over a night on the town. With fewer people in the audience or on the dance floor, venue owners could ill afford to pay musicians a decent wage in light of decreased revenues.

There were some other factors that helped make the 1940s challenging and frustrating, as well as a time of transitions, both cultural and musical. As the United States entered the war, many jazz musicians enlisted or were drafted into the armed forces. Some, like band leaders Artie Shaw and Glenn Miller, parlayed their fame in civilian life into leading big bands composed of talented servicemen. Others, such as saxophonist Lester "Prez" Young, were drafted into service and thrust into irrelevant nonmusical scenarios that, in Young's case, were degrading and potentially violent.

Unique in both appearance and in style, and one of the two major innovators on the tenor saxophone in the 1930s and '40s, Prez was a true original, both musically and personally. Unfortunately, uniqueness and originality clashed with the regimentation and conformity so indigenous to the army, and as a result, Prez suffered mightily at the hands of his superior officers as well as his fellow soldiers. Ultimately, he was caught injecting heroin and was soon after court-martialed and given a dishonorable discharge.

Lester Young's negative experiences in the army were not unique. Jazz musicians as a whole frequently suffered indignities and even violence in the armed forces, largely because of their status as "artistic types" and because of their more relaxed attitudes toward African Americans. Specifically, there was an enormous culture clash between musicians and nonmusicians, the latter group maintaining a kind of "not-one-of-us" mentality. Jazz musicians, on the other hand, came from a much more open background, where musical interaction was often integrated, with whites sharing the stage with black musicians. This was also at a time when more and more band leaders like Benny Goodman and Artie Shaw were hiring black musicians to be part of their ensembles. This kind of liberal orientation did not sit well with enlisted men who were not jazz fans and had little or no exposure to either the music or the people who created it—either black or white. Add to that the tensions of soldiering and the anxieties associated with going to war, and you have trouble waiting to happen on any given day.

Other cultural events helped shape the music at that time. Just as the war effort resulted in more centralized control of industry, so, too, did the broadcast and recording industries find that large entertainment companies like the William Morris Agency were earning significant profits, while radio and recording companies were earning markedly less. Complicating the situation was the government's limitation on the use of two important physical components of records: vinyl and shellac. And as if that wasn't bad enough, in 1942 the American Federation of Musicians went on strike against the recording industry, which resulted in a recording ban that lasted over a year and a half. During that period of time, musicians were prohibited from recording any music whatsoever for release to the listening public. If recording did take place during the ban, a voice-over was required on the recording, announcing that the performance was not to be sold or distributed.

TO BE OR NOT TO BOP

The war ended in 1945, shortly after the United States dropped atomic bombs on the Japanese cities of Hiroshima and Nagasaki, killing at least 150,000 people. The level of anxiety implicit in trying to achieve postwar equilibrium—socially, psychologically, and professionally—was great among many people, and it appears likely that one major reason for this postwar unease was the development and ultimate destructive capabilities of the bomb itself. It was the first time Americans—and in a larger sense, the world—had ever seen destruction on such a massive scale. Perhaps unexpectedly, the seeds of fear had been planted in Americans and others, who worried that such a deadly and devastating weapon would ultimately spell the destruction of humanity.

Musicians in general and jazz musicians in particular felt the postwar blues quite acutely. With the decline of the swing era as well as the diminishing possibilities of making a living playing music, many musicians sought other forms of income, while others abandoned music completely. It was at this time that the jam sessions that were prevalent in the late 1930s in places like Kansas City and New York City became even more common. Most notably, Minton's Playhouse in New York was the scene of some of the most intense, fertile jam sessions in jazz history. While Minton's opened its doors in 1938, it was not until the early '40s that it gained serious notoriety as a hotbed of innovation and a proving ground for new talent—and a new form of jazz called bebop. Young musicians had free reign to experiment and to find new forms and structures in which to create jazz. And thus began the movement away from jazz as entertainment, toward the cultivation of jazz as a uniquely American art form—one to be listened to and absorbed on a number of different levels, rather than danced to or enjoyed as a pleasant diversion.

As a result of this shift in concept away from jazz as entertainment or dance music, the jam session became an even more important arena for musical development in a highly competitive setting. If, say, you were a trumpet player, then you would have to prove your musical worth and hopefully enhance your reputation by "sparring" on the bandstand with the likes of Dizzy Gillespie or Miles Davis, on any given night at Minton's. In a cultural sense, the jam session was a community event—sort of a meeting place where musicians and listeners could enjoy one another's company, both on and off the bandstand. However, when a new musician entered this communal setting, if he unpacked his horn, he had to prove his musical worth by locking horns with session regulars. This was often an exhilarating event for listeners, who often cheered for their favorites and either ignored others or booed them off the stage.

Even though jam sessions could be entertaining, it was clear that entertainment was not the goal of these events. The new generation of jazz musicians no longer wanted to please their audiences by providing deliberate entertainment or playing dance music. The goal for them was the creation and exploration of new ways to improvise and to expand their musical "vocabulary." If you think of playing jazz—or any music for that matter—as a way of speaking a language, then you might better understand what young innovators like trumpeters Dizzy Gillespie and Miles Davis, alto saxophonist Charlie Parker, pianists Thelonious Monk and Bud Powell, bassists Charles Mingus and Oscar Pettiford, and drummers Kenny Clarke and Max Roach were trying to do. They had no desire to re-create earlier styles of jazz, nor did they wish to remain stuck in what they saw as the mire of swing music. So then, the worth of the jam session for a musician was that it provided a venue to be able to shape his musical skills and personality, without the pressures of audience expectations.

Parker and Gillespie were the enfants terribles of bebop. They aroused a great deal of excitement, controversy, and even animosity among listeners and musicians alike. Their frontline combination of trumpet and alto saxophone produced a searing, sharp-edged sound that was at once attractive to some (notably those musicians and listeners who were ready for something new) and repulsive to others (those who favored earlier, sweeter-sounding, less challenging forms of jazz). Lines of verbal battle were drawn and lively, colorful responses from both old and new camps were in plentiful supply; for example, here are some words by protestors:

> Bebop has set music back twenty years.
>
> —Tommy Dorsey

Playing "bop" is like playing Scrabble with all the vowels missing.

—Duke Ellington

Bebop sounds to me like a hardware store in an earthquake.

—Jimmy Cannon

The jazz critic and producer Leonard Feather responded to these and other negative comments and defended bebop by calling the dissenters "moldy figs" and likening them to fascists who believed that bop wasn't "pure" jazz. Arguments, published retorts, and even fistfights broke out between the defenders of this new music and the fans of swing and earlier forms of jazz.

Charlie "Bird" Parker, on the other hand, countered all such comments by largely ignoring them; but he spoke about bebop (a name that he and many others, by the way, detested) on a broad philosophical level by suggesting: "Music is your own experience, your thoughts, your wisdom. If you don't live it, it won't come out of your horn."

And Coleman Hawkins, the patriarch of the tenor saxophone and one of jazz's most respected icons, offered this perceptive observation: "There's no such thing as bop music, but there's such a thing as progress"—and "progress" is what the innovators of bebop had in mind. What began as a way of intimidating amateurs at jam sessions into packing up their horns and heading off into the night, became a lively and dynamic, yet challenging form of jazz. It challenged musicians and listeners alike with its complex melodies, quicksilver tempos, and general disdain for anything you could sing along with or dance to.

So how is it, then, that this new form of jazz came about? What in our cultural life helped give birth to these new musical expressions? In a sense, bebop was a rebellion against the cultural conventions of the late 1930s and early '40s. It was born in the ghettos of big cities like New York City, Los Angeles, and Chicago, among others, where jam sessions and cutting contests were the norm. Younger African American musicians were bored by what they felt were the plodding rhythms and predictable melodies and harmonies of swing music. As a result, drummers like Kenny Clarke and Max Roach began developing a more syncopated style, one that emphasized speed as well as rhythmic complexity and dexterity. Pianists like Bud Powell and Thelonious Monk created a kind of accompaniment called "comping," which consisted of syncopated "jabs" of chords behind the horn solos. Remarkably, they comped for their own solos as well, where the right hand would play the single notes in the solo and the left hand would play the accompanying chords. And the horn players—usually tenor and alto saxes, trumpets, and trombones—developed more complex melody lines over standard chord progressions from popular swing-era songs like "Cherokee," and they often performed these new melodies at breakneck tempos. Charlie Parker and John Birks "Dizzy" Gillespie were at the core of these new and audacious developments; they were true masters of both the music and their respective instruments.

The beboppers were also disenchanted with mainstream culture and, as a result, created an outward visual style that probably infuriated earlier generations of musicians and listeners as much as their musical innovations did. Zoot suits, beards and goatees, berets, dark glasses—these were uniforms worn by this new generation of jazz musicians. Ironically enough, one of the inspirations of the bebop generation was himself a swing-era saxophonist named Lester "Prez" Young, who along with Coleman Hawkins was one of the two fathers of the tenor saxophone. Young typified individualism. He was an original, yet impeccable dresser, from his trademark pork pie hat to his suede shoes, and he spoke and lived in a manner that was uniquely his own. Many expressions still in use today can be attributed to Prez; for example, the word "cool" and the expressions "You dig?" ("Do you understand?") and "I've paid my dues" ("I've been through a lot") are uniquely his, as well as dozens of others that became popular among beboppers and hipsters in the 1940s and '50s.

Naturally, the rebellious nature of the music and those who created and developed it were, as mentioned earlier, cause for alarm and disapproval among older generations. If you think ahead in time to how strongly parents have disapproved of their kids' musical tastes—from ragtime to Elvis; from the Rolling Stones, James Brown, and Bootsy Collins to rap and alternative rock styles—you have a fairly clear picture of the disconnect that has always seemed to exist between generations when it comes to taste in any of the popular performing arts.

Up to the point that Charlie Parker came on the scene in the early '40s, hard drugs (as opposed to alcohol and marijuana) were not all that prominent or even visible on the jazz scene. Bird was a heroin addict, and the fact that he was also a frighteningly brilliant alto saxophonist may have given many other young musicians the impression that in order to play at that level, one also needed to be high on the drug. Even though Bird occasionally tried to discourage others from using heroin, many of his followers fell victim to the drug—a habit that eventually cost many gifted young musicians, artists, and writers their careers and sometimes their lives. Ironically, many of the younger jazz musicians from this period who may have prided themselves on leading unconventional lifestyles bought into the myth of heroin and engaged in a dangerous, life-altering kind of conformity.

Possibly as a result of Bird's well-publicized addiction, as well as the counterculture aspect of the bebop musicians' lifestyles and overt mannerisms, the general public's perception of jazz musicians in the '40s and into the '50s was not very favorable. These musicians were often perceived of as weird looking, drug addled, and irresponsible types who were part of society's underbelly. While this stereotype had only a small degree of truth attached to it, the negative seeds had been planted in the public's mind. However, jazz, being the dynamic art that it is, would weather the storm of public disdain and misconception and continue its evolution in some very exciting and interesting ways in the decades to come.

4

JAZZ AS A MIRROR OF OUR TIMES

From the 1950s to the Present

THE FIFTIES: TV, FROZEN FOOD, HARD BOP, AND THE BIRTH OF THE COOL

There seems to be a popular notion that the 1950s were sort of a placid and forgettable Pleasantville—a postwar era that was marked by weekly television shows accompanied by bland TV dinners served on folding tables, as families gathered 'round the tube to eat processed meat loaf dinners and watch *The Honeymooners*, *The Texaco Star Theater*, or *Father Knows Best*.

In reality, the '50s was a decade (give or take a couple of years on either end) of growth and a great deal of transition in all walks of life.

Even though there were migrations into the outlying areas of many urban centers a decade or so earlier, suburban living really came into its own in the '50s. There was a significant expansion in industry and, concomitantly, in corporate development. As a result, jobs were more plentiful and opportunities for a good education became more prevalent. Perhaps as a result of these two developments, America was becoming more of a consumer society than ever before. Shopping centers had begun springing up, and all manner of new and "improved" personal and household products became the focus of the advertising industry.

But the nostalgic "Happy Days" image of the '50s that was romanticized and portrayed several decades later on the popular television show of the same name was in truth only a small part of what life was like back then.

Several important historical elements shaped the thinking of the American people. One was the rise and fall of Senator Joe McCarthy, who fueled the country's paranoia by claiming that American society was in imminent danger from the infiltration of anti-American communists. Such infiltration, he claimed, was happening all over the country in large and small cities and in America's heartland as well. McCarthy was very good at mining the unease and anxieties of Americans who were already worrying about nuclear attack from the Soviet Union. He also accused many people from all walks of life of being communists, without the slightest proof of any kind. Eventually, McCarthy was excoriated at the national level and lost almost all his credibility, even though he had already done considerable damage with his unfounded rants and accusations.

On a more positive note, earlier "separate but equal" legislation was overturned by the U.S. Supreme Court, with the *Brown v. Board of Education* decision, which ruled that racial segregation was unconstitutional. African Americans such as Rosa Parks, Medgar Evers, and others made history by standing up to racism, thus heralding the beginning of the end of decades of widespread mistreatment and cruelty to black Americans across the country.

The '50s also saw the birth of a group of poets and writers who embraced bebop and an alternative lifestyle to what they felt was the bland and shallow existence of mainstream culture. "The Beat Generation" included such important wordsmiths as Jack Kerouac, Allen Ginsberg, Lawrence Ferlinghetti, Bob Kaufman, Diane di Prima, John Clellon Holmes, and many others. The Beats identified readily with what they perceived as the militant, rebellious nature of bop, and even incorporated jazz into their own public readings. Many of the Beats had a real and abiding affinity for the music, as evidenced by these lines from a Bob Kaufman poem about Charlie Parker called "Walking Parker Home":

> In that Jazz corner of life,
> Wrapped in a mist of sound
> His legacy, our Jazz-tinted dawn
> Wailing his triumphs of oddly begotten dreams
> Inviting the nerveless to feel once more
> That fierce dying of humans consumed
> In raging fires of Love. (111)

In terms of the fine and performing arts, the '50s gave birth to rock and roll, which began its steady climb as the nation's most popular music. Drawing from black rhythm and blues (R & B) as well as rockabilly music (a hybrid of western swing, country blues, and traditional country music), rock became immensely popular with African American, Hispanic, and Caucasian teenagers and drew from all three ethnicities to create its first "stars." Chuck Berry, Little Richard, Fats Domino, and Jackie Wilson were among the best-known black artists to emerge onto the early rock and roll scene, while crossover artists like Buddy Holly, Carl Perkins, Jerry Lee Lewis, and Patsy Cline straddled the fence between rockabilly and pure country. Mexican American Ritchie Valens was an early trend-setting voice for Hispanic contributions to the new pop music. And at the center of the rock and roll explosion was Elvis Presley, whose status as a rock and pop icon has been indelibly etched into the annals of American music and culture.

In the ace of such enormous attraction of American youth to rock music, jazz continued to lose ground in terms of acceptance and popularity. Even so, it was still a time of tremendous growth and development of the music. Specifically, approaches to composing and playing jazz split into two distinct camps: "cool" jazz and "hard" bop. If you think of jazz as a river, these two jazz styles were its two new tributaries, each flowing in a similar but separate direction.

Many jazz historians agree that cool jazz came into being when trumpeter Miles Davis and composer/arranger/pianist Gil Evans came together to create the landmark recording *Birth of the Cool* in the waning years of the '40s. Davis, who had been refining and reshaping his trumpet style, and Evans, a musical visionary who embraced nuance and pastel-like musical colorations, formed a nine-piece ensemble that consisted of a unique combination of instruments, including French horn, tuba, trombone, several saxophones, and a rhythm section. Using this ensemble sound as a soft cushion for Davis's trumpet, Evans, along with session participants baritone saxophonist Gerry Mulligan and pianist John Lewis, arranged most of the music, which was penned by a variety of composers, including Mulligan, pianist Bud Powell, and Davis. The end result was a sonic reconstruction of bebop, one that removed the hard edges of the trumpet–alto sax frontline sound of Dizzy Gillespie and Charlie Parker, and replaced it with a much more orchestrated and tonally varied approach to the music. In the middle of all this was Davis's relaxed and lyrical trumpet playing, as well as solos by other members of the nonet.

Figure 4.1.   Miles Davis in the jazz-rock period. Photofest.

Evans and Miles took the *Birth of the Cool* aggregation into a Broadway club called the Royal Roost for several weeks in the autumn of 1948. Early in 1949, they went into the studio and began recording the compositions for Capitol Records. The final recordings for the session were made a year or so later, and the original album with all 12 tracks was ultimately released in 1957. Miles Davis and Gil Evans would go on to create some of the most memorable orchestral-based jazz later in the '50s and early '60s, and it's not an exaggeration to say that their collaborations have influenced large jazz ensemble music to this day.

This recording—and to a larger extent, the persona of Miles Davis—helped the concept of coolness enter the American consciousness. The music, even at its most complex, had no swagger, no rough edges, and was both smooth and subtle in its approach to melody, harmony, and improvisation. It sounded like Miles Davis looked—well-dressed, relaxed, and confident in its authenticity. Miles's cool sensibilities and the subtle, understated way that he played the trumpet influenced entire generations of musicians, writers, poets, and visual artists.

Birth of the Cool also signaled a serious shift in the approach to jazz composition and improvisation. Many musicians—notably those on the West Coast—embraced the new sound and approach, and the "Cool School" included many musicians such as saxophonists Stan Getz, Lee Konitz, and Warne Marsh; trumpeters Chet Baker and Jack Sheldon; trombonist Bob Brookmeyer; and pianist Russ Freeman—some of whom will be discussed in more detail in later chapters of this book. However, to label these and other musicians as "cool" players would be to place an unfair label on each of them. Many of the so-called cool players could turn up the heat when called upon to "burn," or play with ferocious intensity.

Even so, there was a backlash to both the harmonic complexities of traditional bebop and the cool approach to jazz on the part of many musicians, notably African Americans from the East Coast who also came from the bebop tradition; however, these musicians chose to retain the visceral, extroverted nature of the music, utilizing simpler harmonies and grooves—almost as a rebellious response to what they saw as an overly arranged and homogenized form of jazz. Their approach embraced the hard-edged sound of the sax-trumpet (and sometimes trombone) frontline, as well as aggressive rhythm section playing. The critics at that time dubbed the music "hard bop," and it became quite popular among jazz fans who found themselves turned off by the cool approach.

One of the major contributors to the hard bop movement was Art Blakey, whose thunderous drumming and exemplary leadership of the Jazz Messengers fostered the growth and development of many great players from the '50s until his death in 1990. Another was pianist Horace Silver, whose music and quintet were all about the "grooves" that would get people's feet tapping and hands clapping. Other hard boppers included saxophonists Jackie McLean, Hank Mobley, and Sonny Rollins;

trumpeters Lee Morgan, Blue Mitchell, and Donald Byrd; pianists Bobby Timmons, Kenny Drew, and Sonny Clark; organist Jimmy Smith—and many others. The three major record labels that supported hard bop and preserved it for future generations to enjoy on both vinyl and CD were Blue Note, Prestige, and Riverside. Blue Note, in particular, produced many consistently excellent recordings by all of the musicians mentioned above, plus many more.

One interesting sidelight was the unmistakable influence of the black experience on hard bop. From the rhythms and harmonies of church hymns and call-and-response songs like "Swing Low, Sweet Chariot" to the ever-present undercurrent of the blues and the realities of urban and rural black life—all found their way into the music and yielded some of the most powerful jazz ever created. The extroverted quality of the compositions and the energy and intensity of the performances were immediately attractive to many jazz fans, regardless of their ethnicity. Blakey and Silver were masters of this style—which was often called, among other things, "soul jazz"—and they gained many fans throughout their long and illustrious careers.

We can nicely sum up hard bop and soul jazz with these recorded words to the audience by trumpeter Lee Morgan at New York's "Jazz Corner of the World" (Blue Note Records) one night back in 1959:

> If you feel like pattin' your feet, pat your feet;
> and if you feel like clappin' your hands, clap your hands;
> and if you feel like takin' off your shoes, take off your shoes.
> We are here to have a ball.
> So we want you to leave your worldly troubles outside
> and come in here and swing!

THE SIXTIES: REVOLUTION AND THE WINDS OF CHANGE

There is no easy way to put the 1960s into a nice, neat little box and explain what exactly happened in that decade and how it affected jazz. To be sure, the '60s were a time of great change in all corners of American life, from day-to-day living to politics, the arts, education, and other forms of culture. The cozy conservatism of most of the 1950s gave way to new and revolutionary perspectives and the desire for genuine ideological changes in how to live one's life.

It is agreed upon by many cultural historians that as baby boomers became young adults, they were no longer satisfied with what they saw as the comfortable complacency of the previous generation. In other words, the baby boomers of the '60s didn't wish to become their parents, and thereby a schism between past and present was created. Thus, the term "generation gap" came into being and has been with us ever since.

Colleges and universities became the stormy center of protests, centering mainly upon the military-industrial complex and America's presence in Southeast Asia. Antiestablishment rebellion filled the air and ranged from intense discussions to outright confrontations, complete with riots and tear gas. Militancy was the order of the day. Young people "dropped out" of mainstream society in ways that the previous generation found baffling and quite disturbing.

This was the time of the "hippie," a word that may have come into being in the early part of the decade. Derived from the word "hip," which meant "in the know" or "cool," the hippie or "freak" (which was the preferable term) was—at least in the beginning—someone who created and opted for a radically different lifestyle. The name really took hold when the beatniks in San Francisco migrated to the city's Haight-Ashbury District from North Beach. Their supposed free-and-easy lifestyle was immensely appealing to many of the area's young and impressionable college students who, in effect, emulated what they saw as a true counterculture.

In reality, much of the hippie culture was devoted to hallucinogenic herbal drugs like marijuana and hashish, and to psychedelics like LSD and peyote, and to what was often called the "free love" movement. Many hippies joined communes and attempted to lead what they felt were simpler lives in rural areas, with varying degrees of success. On a deeper level, some turned to Eastern religious practices and mysticism and authors such as Dr. Timothy Leary ("Tune in, turn on, drop out") and Alan Watts, who was one of the leading interpreters of Buddhism in the Western world. Still others formed radical and sometimes violent protest groups such as the Students for a Democratic Society (SDS), the Weathermen, and the Black Panthers. However, for those on the outside looking in, the hippie movement was often considered to be nothing more than an excuse to take drugs, have sex, and in general, to evade responsibility. Much of the main-stream population was baffled and wary of a generation of long-haired, col-orful youths in bell-bottoms and tie-dyed shirts, who seemed to want to do little more than get high and float through life. Hence, the generation gap.

Unlike the Beats, jazz was not the anthem of the '60s counterculture. Folk and rock had become firmly entrenched as the music of choice, with folksingers/composers like Bob Dylan and Joan Baez writing protest songs, and the Grateful Dead, Jefferson Airplane, and the Byrds often singing the praises of the psychedelic experience. And Jimi Hendrix—who was truly in a class by himself—brought elements of the blues and psychedelic or "acid" rock together in a totally unique and innovative way. But as far as jazz goes, it was not on the hippie radar.

The black counterculture, however, was unique in its militancy in that writers, poets, and musicians figured prominently at its core and the desire for racial equality and justice burned brightly at its center, fueled often by the anger and frustration of being the objects of racial discrimination and violence. To be sure, dissatisfaction with previous generations and the sta-tus quo made the rebelliousness of young African Americans seem similar to that of their white counterparts; however, the issue of racial equality was the linchpin of the black power movement and the many artists and writ-ers who were inspired by it. Singer-songwriters like Richie Havens and Gil Scott-Heron were especially prominent at the time, and the Last Poets—who combined the spoken word with percussion—were the grandfathers of the hip-hop music that is so popular today.

While there were many black writers and poets like Maya Angelou and Gwendolyn Brooks who figured prominently in the quest for racial equality in the '60s, one wordsmith in particular became a major voice for his gen-eration. Amiri Baraka had already established a significant presence in the literary world as LeRoi Jones, who among his 40 books of essays, fiction, poetry, and music criticism authored one of the definitive books about the blues. *Blues People* became required reading in college classrooms and has long been considered a classic portrait of this uniquely American music. Likewise, *Black Music*, one of his books about jazz, offers an insightful and memorable look at the music and the musicians who gave so much of themselves to create it. Baraka was—and still is—deeply involved in the recognition and preservation of black culture in America.

As Baraka indicated in much of his writing, the jazz world of the '60s was in a tumultuous, ever-changing state, buoyed at the very least by the

tremendous unrest and rebellion taking place in American culture. Actually, as if to presage the cultural and musical changes to come, jazz began
its radical transformative journey in the late 1950s, principally with the
innovative music of alto saxophonist Ornette Coleman. With aptly named
albums like *Tomorrow Is the Question* and *The Shape of Jazz to Come*,
Ornette, like Charlie Parker over a decade earlier, turned the jazz world
on its ear, and both excited and infuriated jazz fans everywhere. His
quartet, which featured the pianoless combination of alto sax, trumpet,
bass, and drums, featured Coleman's angular, jumpy compositions, most
of which had abandoned harmony and chord changes altogether. This
approach allowed the group to improvise freely without the restrictions
of chords usually played by the piano. While more traditional musicians
and listeners often found Coleman's music to be dissonant and grating,
many others found themselves exhilarated by both the music and, in the
case of young musicians, the possibilities to break free of what they often
called the tyranny of harmony. Listeners—again, particularly younger
jazz fans—found Coleman's music a welcome change from the past, and
they embraced it wholeheartedly. On the whole, though, while Ornette
was an innovator and certainly created music that challenged the jazz
tradition and popular culture, his music was not directly a reflection of
the social and psychological tension that was building into the next tumultuous decade.

Coleman in his quest for musical freedom did, however, influence many
musicians both younger and older, who took the foundation he had built
and personalized it both artistically and politically. Jazz musicians became
more involved in the culture of the '60s, insisting through both words and
music that social and political systems needed to be overhauled. Among
the more established players who created some beautifully meditative,
powerfully stunning, and politically relevant music, two stalwarts from the
bebop era come to mind: Charles Mingus, the volcanic and volatile bassist and composer, who wrote and recorded songs like "Fables of Faubus"
(aimed at the racist governor of Arkansas, Orval Faubus) and "Meditations
on Intergration"; and virtuoso drummer Max Roach, who together with his
wife, vocalist/actress Abbey Lincoln, produced music that decried racism
and poverty and celebrated important and revolutionary African Americans like Marcus Garvey and Malcolm X. One of the drummer's greatest
achievements was *The Freedom Now Suite*, a multipart work he recorded
in 1960 for Candid Records, which deals with the many faces of prejudice

against black people. The recording has achieved legendary status as one of the greatest concept recordings ever created in the jazz world.

Even though John Coltrane will be discussed in a later chapter, it is wholly appropriate to mention him here, when speaking about jazz as a sort of barometer of the times. The late '50s found Coltrane in one of his major transformative periods, experimenting with complex harmonies and chord changes, often played at breakneck tempos, while at the same time exploring simple song forms and traditional and popular melodies. However, with the advent of the new decade, Trane formed a quartet that, after a few personnel changes, became one of the greatest small groups in all of jazz. This group, often called the "Classic Quartet," provided Trane with the opportunity for tremendous growth as both an instrumentalist and a composer. The music, often fiery and sometimes overpowering, could be on the quiet and more meditative side as well.

While not as overtly topical as some of his contemporaries, Coltrane was all too aware of the many injustices and cruelties perpetrated upon black Americans at that time, as well as much earlier. He had an intense interest in African music and culture, as well as in Eastern religious practices. Unlike others, Coltrane did not react to racism and violence with anger, but with profound sadness. When four young black girls died in a church bombing on Sunday, September 15, 1963, in Montgomery, Alabama, and when the individual who was charged with the crime was found not guilty of murder (and given a six-month sentence for possession of dynamite), many people—black and white—were shocked and angered by both the act and the acquittal. John Coltrane instead expressed his sadness for this tragedy by recording and performing a composition written shortly after the multiple murders. Called simply "Alabama," the song may well be one of the most moving pieces of music in all of jazz.

Interlude I: "Alabama"

You've just downloaded Coltrane's *Live at Birdland*, a recording made in 1963 of Trane's classic quartet holding forth at a club that was sometimes called the "Jazz Corner of the World." The group, which featured pianist McCoy Tyner, bassist Jimmy Garrison, and Elvin Jones, has just finished playing a very intense version of a Mongo Santamaría song called "Afro

Blue." With very little pause and even before the applause dies down from the last song, McCoy Tyner and Jimmy Garrison create a low-pitched continuous rumble not unlike distant thunder. Coltrane stands off to one side motionless, head bowed. After a few moments, he begins to play softly over the meditative drone of the piano and the bowed bass. There is no tempo whatsoever—only a hypnotic, floating cloud of sound, on top of which Coltrane's somber tenor saxophone makes the musical statement that is the melody of the piece. After creating this mood, the quartet pauses and lets the silence take over. It's so quiet in the club that you could hear a pin drop. Trane reenters, and playing four distinct notes, he sets a medium slow tempo, which Garrison and Jones pick up on. Jones is so rhythmically advanced that if you close your eyes, he sounds like two or three drummers playing at once. Garrison plays what's often called "walking bass," which is really playing the note on each beat in any given tempo (in this case, a little slower than the speed at which we might actually walk leisurely down the street).

After another pause, the group reenters, with Coltrane playing the hymn-like melody once more. His saxophone voice sounds as though it were singing a spiritual like "Go Down Moses" or a Jewish prayer like "Shalom Alechim." You could almost put words to his musical statement. The effect is one of a voice in the wilderness, and Coltrane's sound is deep and dark. In the end, you may agree that this song is a lament for the four innocent little girls who lost their lives at the hands of a bigoted murderer, as well as for all of us who hear beyond the notes and into a deeper, unspoken meaning. Such is the power of music.

An interesting factor in the creation and development of the new music in the '60s was that many young musicians found this radical approach to jazz to be very appealing, particularly in light of the cultural and political upheaval that was beginning to happen in cities and towns across America at that time. In short, jazz became a more openly political music, one that often mirrored the rebellion and dissatisfaction of the status quo, in both black and white communities, from smaller cities to larger urban centers. Among the younger players, saxophonist Archie Shepp was among the most important of the African American post-bebop players—certainly one of the most intellectually engaging and outspoken members of his generation of black musicians. In the '60s, Shepp was known primarily as an avant-garde jazz musician, that is, one who, like Ornette Coleman, abandoned traditional jazz form in order to explore more adventurous and freer realms of improvisation. But he was unlike many other "free" jazz musicians in two distinct ways: First, his approach to the sound of the tenor saxophone was steeped in the deep and throaty tradition of the swing saxophonists Coleman Hawkins, Chu Berry, and Ben Webster. Plus, his affiliation and eventual performances and recordings with John Coltrane gave him a stature among the newer players, which lent a well-deserved "legitimacy" to his reputation among fellow musicians and fans alike.

The second factor that made Archie Shepp unique among the new generation was that he was deeply committed to portraying the plight of black Americans in his music. You don't have to look very far to find anyone whose music mirrored the culture of his times more than Archie Shepp. His most memorable compositions included portraits of Malcolm X, the Attica prison riots, lynchings, hypocrisy, and of course the never-ending quest for racial equality.

In addition to his musical contributions, Shepp also became well known as a dramatist and wrote a number of memorable works for the theater. And in the early 1970s, he established a three-decade residency as a professor at the University of Amherst, where he taught a variety of African American courses centered on black history and culture.

While there is no doubt that in the 1960s America was filled with unrest and turmoil, the '60s will always have the distinction of being a time that jazz moved further away from mainstream culture as a form of entertainment and moved headlong into the realm of art as social and political statement, through either words or music or both. Most important, it was a time of heightened creativity and exploration—both in concert and on recordings. So in summary, jazz in the '60s became more of a beacon of truth for artists and listeners than at any other time in its history.

THE SEVENTIES: AN EVER-CHANGING MAINSTREAM

While the dynamic cultural and political climate of the 1960s continued into the next decade, many of the radical ideologies of that era became more "mainstream" in the '70s. The rebellion and disillusionment with the establishment, which was previously embraced largely only by radical groups like the Weathermen, the Black Panthers, and Students for a Democratic Society, became more widely accepted, particularly in the first half of the new decade. However, while many people truly believed that political and social change was necessary for the betterment of America and the world, there were others who merely took on the trappings of "radical chic," looking and acting like supporters of hippie culture without having any idea what the essence of that culture really was. "Power to the people," along with similar slogans, became big business, showing up frequently on T-shirts, baseball caps, bumper stickers, and other such commodities. Perhaps as a result of the commodification of radical culture, many of these fringe groups dissolved into memory.

Taking hallucinogenic and other drugs, espousing the virtues of the free love movement, and wearing long hair, tie-dyed shirts, and low-rise bell-bottom jeans appealed to young people who "dropped out," not so much out of disillusionment with American society, as out of the quest for good times, and of course to drive their parents to the brink of madness, which seemed (and seems) to be one of the raisons d'être of each younger generation.

Many cultural historians and critics seem to view the '70s as a highly forgettable and shallow decade. Howard Junker, the founder of *Zyzzyva*, one of our most well-respected literary magazines, has been frequently quoted as saying: "The perfect Seventies symbol was the pet rock, which just sat there, doing nothing."

Indeed, when many of us look in retrospect at that decade, we may tend to remember it as the shallow era that gave us the disco dance craze, mood rings, sea monkeys, Nehru suits, *The Brady Bunch*, secret agent movies, easy-listening music, and an onslaught of highly forgettable rock bands. However, while these things were surely prevalent throughout the cultural ethos of the times, they were only part of a much larger picture of what was actually happening back then. Cultural historian Bruce J. Schulman sums this up accurately in his book *The Seventies: The Great Shift in American Culture, Society, and Politics*:

> In race relations, religion, family life, politics, and popular culture, the 1970s marked the most significant watershed in U.S. history, the beginning of our time. One year alone, 1973, witnessed the end of American intervention in Vietnam, the U.S. Supreme Court decision on *Roe vs. Wade*, the exposure

of the Watergate conspiracies, the Indian occupation of Wounded Knee, and the first Arab oil shock. Billie Jean King won the battle of the sexes [on the tennis court, against Bobby Riggs] . . . and a young evangelical preacher named Jim Bakker hit the airwaves, intent on creating "God's television."(xii)

Add three tragic assassinations (John and Robert Kennedy, Martin Luther King), two executive office resignations in the face of impeachment (Richard Nixon, Spiro Agnew), technological marvels (the videocassette recorder, the first computer microprocessor, the first test-tube baby, to name only a few), and most pointedly, the growing recognition of the talents and abilities—in short, the equality—of women in the work force, politics, and education. As you can see, the '70s were much more than the banal decade they were made out to be.

Musically, the early to mid-'70s was a fruitful and productive time across many genres, including folk and rock music and rhythm and blues (R & B). In the folk arena, there were many fine acoustic singer-songwriters who followed the Baez-Dylan generation, creating and performing intensely personal work that resonated with large audiences. It was at this time that folk-based artists such as Joni Mitchell, James Taylor, Jackson Browne, Jonathan Edwards, and the harmonious Crosby, Stills, Nash, and Young began receiving national attention. Likewise, rock and roll bands like the Byrds, the Grateful Dead, Cream, the Jimi Hendrix Experience, and the Allman Brothers came to the forefront of that music and topped the charts with many fine recordings. Interestingly enough, these groups were influenced by jazz, in that their live performances included "jams" on a variety of songs; like jazz musicians, they would play and sing the "head" (the melody) of a song and follow it with a series of extended improvisations that were often blistering, groove-oriented affairs.

Grooves were also the foundation for both beat-heavy disco dance music and, more importantly, the R & B groups of the '70s. It was at this point in time that "funk" captured the national ear of both black and white listeners. Unlike rock and roll, whose grooves tended to be rhythmically predictable and rather flat, the R & B rhythms tended to be more funky and syncopated—and very danceable as well. Early funksters included George Clinton, Bootsy Collins, and of course "the Godfather of Soul" James Brown, who had been on the R & B scene already for two decades, and who helped create funky music early on. Brown was also among the first to add a horn section to his band—a phenomenon that, along with electronic keyboards and back-up vocalists, would become the norm in much of '70s funk.

Jazz itself was, as usual, undergoing a series of significant developments as well. The avant-garde so prevalent and well suited to the cultural and social turbulence of the '60s seemed to become less relevant to the culture of the decade and fell somewhat out of favor with all but a modest number of listeners. As a result, many of the creative improvising musicians who embraced the postmodern idiom went on to establish "loft" communities and other small performance spaces where they could present their music. Additionally, many of them (such as Archie Shepp, trumpeter/composer Bill Dixon, and pianist Cecil Taylor) began teaching at major universities such as the University of Massachusetts Amherst, Bennington College, and University of Wisconsin, respectively.

But the real seeds for jazz in the '70s were actually planted in the '60s. For instance, in 1963 the hard bop trumpeter Lee Morgan wrote and recorded a song called "The Sidewinder" that had a "boogaloo" beat, one that was similar in feel to much of the R & B music of that era. Originally written as a throwaway "filler" for the rest of the record, "The Sidewinder" helped propel the entire album into the public eye, and it even appeared for a time on the pop charts. As a result, the trumpeter recorded subsequent tunes with that pre-funky feel but did not achieve the commercial success of "The Sidewinder."

In the late 1960s, a number of small groups, such as those led by vibraphonist Gary Burton and guitarist Larry Coryell, began experimenting with rock rhythms as foundations for their compositions and solos. Coryell, in particular, was an early influence, especially since he employed more of a rock guitar approach that didn't typically favor the more traditional mellow jazz guitar sound. Burton and Coryell recorded several records at that time, which contained elements of both folk music and rock. One such notable disc was called *Duster*, and it laid some of the groundwork for similar efforts to come.

However, it was really trumpeter and jazz icon Miles Davis who brought jazz-rock into the public eye. His explorations with rock rhythms as well as electronics began with his later quintet recordings like *Filles de Kilimanjaro* and *Miles in the Sky*, both recorded for Columbia Records in 1968. His pianist, Herbie Hancock, played electric piano on these discs and provided a dense and swirling atmosphere, which was propelled along by the imaginative and complex jazz-funk rhythms of drummer

Tony Williams. Miles also added various electric guitarists after *Filles de Kilimanjaro* and moved even further away from the standard saxophone, trumpet, and rhythm section concept that was so much a part of his musical history in the '50s and '60s.

With the advent of *In a Silent Way* (1969), Miles's move away from the post-bop quintet setting was complete. This was an amazing recording, one which not only utilized rock rhythms and instruments (this time including the organ) but also crossed over into a very mystical realm, notably on the title track which, to many listeners, still remains a dark, magical beauty of a composition. The successful breadth of this music may have largely been due to the presence of Josef Zawinul, a brilliant keyboardist, composer, and arranger. Born and raised in Austria, Zawinul brought a certain type of intercontinental musical sensibility to the recording, the result being an interesting mix of jazz, rock, and European classical music forms.

That same year, Miles returned to the studio and recorded what has often been called the first real fusion of jazz and rock genres. A series of grooves, riffs, and improvisations based upon sketchy themes, *Bitches Brew* is considered to be a landmark recording—one that would influence scores of musicians for decades to come and would also create a foundation for "fusion" music, which would predominate much of the new jazz of the '70s (read a firsthand account of these recording sessions by saxophonist Bennie Maupin in chapter 5).

As a result of Miles's commitment to bringing what he felt was new life to jazz, a significant number of Miles's alumni would go on to form their own forward-thinking groups and would each, in their own way, develop different styles and approaches to the foundation that Miles created. Pianists Herbie Hancock (Head Hunters), Chick Corea (Return to Forever), and Joe Zawinul (Weather Report); saxophonist Wayne Shorter (Weather Report), drummer Tony Williams (Lifetime), and guitarist John McLaughlin (the Mahavishnu Orchestra)—all formed groups that would achieve worldwide fame, largely as a result of each musician's association with Miles Davis during the late '60s and '70s.

Always on the cutting edge of fashion as well as music, Miles Davis also embraced the 1970s style of dress, wearing clothes that reflected the looser, more organic lifestyle espoused by the hippie movement. His performances became even more hypnotic and spontaneous, similar to the extended jam-like approach taken by rock bands like the Grateful Dead, the difference being that a Miles Davis performance was all music—no announcements, often no real pauses between compositions—very stream-of-consciousness stuff. In fact, in 1970 Miles played opposite The Dead for four nights at the Fillmore West in San Francisco.

In addition to other appearances that year at the club, opposite rocker Leon Russell and bluesman Elvin Bishop, Miles also played at the Fillmore East in New York City, sharing the bill on one occasion with the Neil Young and Steve Miller bands, and on another with singer-songwriter Laura Nyro. All of these appearances at non-jazz venues served to expand Miles's fan base, particularly among young people who seemed to be open to the Davis group's atmospheric explorations. Remember, this was the psychedelic era, when the idea of experimentation—both personally and artistically—was very much a part of popular culture.

Not everyone was accepting of the "new" Miles Davis. People who loved Davis's earlier bands were very vocal in opposition to his new musical directions. Many critics, listeners, and even musicians felt that he was "selling out" and merely attempting to win over the rock and roll audience, in order to make more money with recordings and live appearances. Saxophonist Dave Liebman, who began recording with Miles in 1972 and toured and recorded again with him during the next two years, recalled in a personal interview why Davis embraced rock music and youth culture as he did during that time:

> One thing you can say about Miles is that he knew the score, meaning in the case of the "switchover" from jazz to rock, a move that earned never-ending enmity from some of his peers, one must factor in nonmusical aspects as well as the music itself. Facts show that record sales of the quintet recordings were comparatively low and small in numbers, resulting in what may have been implicit or explicit pressure from Columbia Records, his home label for years by the late '60s. Paradoxically, it happens to be that these recordings contain some of the most influential compositions and improvising of all time. One must note that with the explosion of pop music in the late '60s, the record business was about to enter its golden period for the next 25 or so years, financially speaking. But more so and especially in the case of Miles Davis historically, there was in his MO what seemed to be a natural instinct to always, above all, be the leader of the pack. He just couldn't stand anyone getting ahead of him, including his own sidemen, who were, it seemed at the time, clearly poised for a move in the so-called "fusion" direction. Miles was if anything one of the most perceptive people around concerning timing, not only musically as we know, but in all ways. In retrospect, it appears that the fusion period he embarked upon in the late '60s was inevitable.

So, was Miles's music in the 1970s jazz with a rock flavor, or merely jazzed-up rock? Or was it both—or neither? Whatever it was, Miles's musical approach at that time confounded both critics and listeners, who either liked or hated it, depending upon whether or not their perceptions of the man and his music allowed him to forge yet another path that would deviate radically from the musical style he had embraced before. Davis was no stranger to these stylistic shifts and the furor that they often caused among critics and listeners. Listeners who thought that his late '50s masterpiece *Kind of Blue* was the be-all and end-all were ultimately infuriated and perplexed by the avant-garde leanings of his second great quintet with Wayne Shorter, Herbie Hancock, Ron Carter, and Tony Williams. Likewise, those who saw that quintet as being one of the finest small bands in the history of jazz were often angered by Miles's explorations into rock and funk music. "Why can't he just stick with the ballads?" or "Why did he abandon the quintet to play rock music?" became the hue and cry of listeners from the '50s and the '60s, respectively, who wanted to compartmentalize Davis's music into a consistent and comfortably predictable niche. However, to paraphrase Bob Dylan, the times they were a-changin', and Davis was changing along with them. In sum, Miles Davis—more than any other jazz artist—paid attention to the culture and the music of the '70s and found a way to reflect those changes in his own approaches to jazz. And, as mentioned earlier, Miles Davis opened the door for stylistic explorations and further fusions of jazz and rock that would last well into the next three decades.

THE EIGHTIES: NIGHT AND DAY

The shift in consciousness from the late 1960s through the '80s was really significant, and for many members of the Woodstock generation, disturbing. Hippie and alternative lifestyles and perceptions had given way to an enormous cultural swing of the pendulum, to what has often been called "The Me Decade." The organic, "back-to-the-land" enthusiasm of the hippie movement had all but evaporated, to be replaced by a more materialistic credo, one that placed an emphasis upon upscale living. The BMW replaced the Volkswagen bus, and gourmet cuisine, rather than mung beans and alfalfa sprouts, became all the rage. Instead of retreating from mainstream society, the '80s generation embraced it all the way.

The children of hippies often entered the white-collar workforce, becoming stockbrokers, attorneys, and mortgage bankers, and the acquisition of luxury replaced Flower Power as a way of life.

On the political front, 1980 saw the election of Ronald Reagan to the presidency, an event that many say marked the return of conservatism both in government and in many walks of life. Many supporters of Reagan's economic policies suggested that his tax cuts and expansion of free trade, among other things, helped create an era of unbridled prosperity, which resulted in increased income in each economic segment of society. Critics of Reaganomics, however, believed to the contrary that the '80s were an era of false prosperity evidenced by a continuous growth in the federal deficit, accompanied by a significant increase in the national debt—both of which precipitated an enormous rise in personal debt and homelessness. Whatever the case, many Americans were spending more money in the marketplace and living at a higher standard than in previous decades.

In terms of music, some rock stars moved from the role of counterculture heroes into the glittering realm of celebrity, where the music took a back seat to corporate creations in both appearance and lifestyle. MTV was born in 1981, and Madonna was the decade's "Material Girl." However, the decade also saw the birth of more rebellious music in the form of punk rock, alternative rock, and especially rap or hip-hop, which would exert a noticeable influence upon jazz in the decades to follow.

Jazz itself in the '80s was alive and well and ever-changing. Since Miles Davis's early experiments with the forms of both rock and R & B, jazz musicians searched for new ways to fuse the harmonic and melodic sensibilities of the music with the attractive, often intricate rhythms of funk, Latin American, and Indian music. The bands of Chick Corea, Herbie Hancock, Stanley Clarke, Weather Report, the Mahavishnu Orchestra, and many others continued to thrive, and they even broadened their fan bases in this decade. Fusion jazz emphasized the importance of formidable instrumental technique and often blistering odd-meter tempos, while all the while laying down funky grooves. The music became highly orchestrated and was exciting to watch as well as hear. Unfortunately many fusion groups (excluding those mentioned above) deemphasized improvisation and harmonic sophistication in favor of bravura performances, and much of the music began to sound homogenized and repetitive.

The '80s also saw the birth of what is now often called "smooth jazz," or more accurately, "adult contemporary pop." Many jazz musicians perceived smooth jazz not as jazz at all, but more as background music, such as the Muzak often heard in banks, elevators, department stores, and doctors' offices. An offshoot of fusion music, smooth jazz stylings were marked by simple and watered-down rock and funk rhythms and one-dimensional melodies, with little in the way of intricate improvisations.

Interlude II: Smooth Jazz Appreciation?

After playing excerpts of six or seven tracks from various smooth jazz CDs by Kenny G, George Benson, Boney James, Earl Klugh, and others, I asked my class of college students to react to the music, to express their opinions about what they just heard. I told them that I would not offer my opinion at that time, since what I thought about the music was not relevant to the discussion. Mostly, I did not want to color their opinions with my own, being a bona-fide veteran jazz musician.

There was an interesting variety of responses from the group. Some blasted the music and accused it of not being real jazz, while others said that although the music was pleasant, it couldn't really be thought of as jazz, based upon the music we'd heard thus far in the semester. Still others claimed that the music was, in fact, jazz since it had soloists who were clearly (at least to them) improvising. All agreed that the music was "pretty." However, the one response to smooth jazz that I found most telling was one from an older student who rarely said anything in class. Unsolicited, she raised her hand and said that the music she'd just heard was perfectly suited to cooking, serving, and eating a nice meal, and afterward, especially good as an accompaniment to doing the dishes. Another student promptly raised his hand and asked, "Professor, is this what jazz has become?"

How should I have answered that question? How would you have answered it?

Although jazz-rock fusion had become quite popular in the '80s, there was another interesting development in the music, one that revisited jazz's recent history. The "jazz renaissance," as it was sometimes known, was not really a trip down memory lane (as early jazz had always been). It was centered on the bop and post-bop traditions, to be sure; however, what the musicians were attempting to do was to emulate the approach to the music, rather than its content. In other words, members of this new "retro-jazz" movement concerned themselves less with the compositions and arrangements of their predecessors, and more with maintaining the essence of the music itself—straight-ahead swing. Young musicians like trumpeter Wynton Marsalis and saxophonist-brother Branford Marsalis, pianists Mulgrew Miller and Marcus Roberts, bassists Christian McBride and Robert Hurst, and drummers Jeff "Tain" Watts and Marvin "Smitty" Smith carried the straight-ahead jazz torch by creating acoustic jazz that was both modern and reminiscent of the hard bop of drummer Art Blakey and his Jazz Messengers, pianist Horace Silver's quintet, alto saxophonist Cannonball Adderley's quintet, and of course both of Miles Davis's famous quintets from the '50s and '60s. Without a doubt, the younger neo-traditionalists put their own generational spin on bebop, endowing it with new energies and approaches—all without blatantly imitating the earlier genre.

Ironically, the practitioners of the 1980s jazz renaissance seemed to mirror the conservatism of the political and social culture mentioned earlier. Wynton Marsalis's small groups, among others, wore suits (or coats) and ties and appeared to model themselves after bands like Blakey's and the Miles Davis groups of the '50s and early '60s. Indeed, a lot of musicians wore coats and ties to gigs and recording sessions in New York City and other urban centers in those days—so at least in that sense, imitation became the sincerest form of flattery, beginning in the '80s.

But conservatism existed in the music as well. Wynton Marsalis openly expressed his dislike of fusion music and had even fewer kind words to say about avant-garde jazz. His credo seemed at the time to be to preserve "the real jazz" by bringing it squarely into the '80s—in effect, pouring new wine into old bottles. His and others' attempts were met with a variety of critical responses, from enthusiastic to downright damning.

Even though the contributions of the jazz renaissance and jazz-rock fusion movements were significant and are still in evidence in today's music, many critics and jazz fans believe that the 1980s didn't really produce any one figure who could be called an innovator—someone whose musical vision was so unique that he or she could be called a jazz icon; someone whose contributions to the music would be the stuff of legend, of musical immortality. In other words, the decade failed to produce any legendary figures like a Duke Ellington, a Miles Davis, or a John Coltrane.

THE NINETIES AND BEYOND: LIVING WITH UNCERTAINTY

America rode a veritable roller coaster in terms of both national and international politics, in the last decade of the century and the first decade of the new millennium. While a significant surplus and a growing economy existed when President Bill Clinton left office, a monumental deficit—as a result of the Gulf War and other foreign and domestic factors—burdened the country after successor George W. Bush departed eight years later. Unemployment rose from record lows to significant highs. And as if that wasn't enough, our complacency as a nation was shaken by the growth of international terrorism, the tragedy of 9/11, the South Central Los Angeles riots, and other acts of violence here in America in places as dissimilar as schools, government offices, and shopping centers. Many of us have been shocked, dismayed, and frightened by these and other horrific events—and yet, curiously enough, our condemnations of such tragedies seems to ebb and flow with each new occurrence. Many social scientists and psychologists suggest that the apathy that often sets in after a tragic event may well be a by-product of distractions created by escapist media such as television, movies, and of course, the computer. Yet of the three, it has been the computer that has revolutionized the way we perceive life and live it.

With the birth of the Internet in the early 1990s, life as many of us knew it would change forever, both in terms of culture and society and in the music world. Replaced largely by e-mail (and ultimately, texting and tweeting), the art of writing and mailing letters and postcards became almost an anachronism. Online commerce, thanks to mega-bazaars such as Amazon and eBay and thousands of chain and individual store websites, often minimized the number of trips to the shopping mall we might make to search for all manner of goods. Following suit, many service-oriented businesses created their own websites to further enhance their customer base. Cellular technology put everyone in conversation with everyone else at any hour of the day or night, diminished landline use significantly, and rendered pay phones almost obsolete. Electronic media began to supplant print technology in terms of getting news updates instantaneously, rather than having to wait for tomorrow's edition of your local newspaper to read about some event of international, national, or local importance. And finally, the inception of social networking websites such as Facebook and Myspace allowed us to renew old friendships and forge new ones, all in the comfort and privacy of our own homes.

Just as cyber-technology created new ways of living, so, too, did the computer age impact the music world, in terms of sustainability of both performance and the life of an ensemble. File sharing of CDs became common and highly disputable, especially among musicians and record companies who were losing revenue as a result of this type of cyber-piracy. And the idea of sending one's "demo" CD to a major record company for consideration to release it was disappearing rapidly. Whereas in the past there were significant numbers of established jazz record labels such as Riverside, Prestige, Blue Note, Impulse, Verve, and Columbia, the last two decades have been a struggle to survive for many record companies. Downloading music to personal MP3 players like the iPod effectively eliminated the middleman; that is, you no longer had to visit the nearest record store to buy a CD. In fact, you didn't have to buy a CD at all. Downloading the music onto a computer became the order of the day. As a result, jazz musicians began to take greater control of their music, including production, distribution, and marketing of their recordings. We shall explore this phenomenon in greater detail in a later chapter.

Here is a short list of some other ways that jazz in the late 20th and early 21st centuries has harnessed computer technology as a means of preserving the past, illuminating the present, and supporting jazz's potential for a healthy future:

1. Individual and group websites have become the "business cards" of musicians and bands. Many feature biographies, photographs, sound samples, video clips, links to other sites, and even "stores" where visitors can buy CDs and related merchandise.
2. Music commerce websites such as CD Baby, CD Universe, and of course Amazon replaced physical record stores like Tower Records and Virgin Records, both of which filed for bankruptcy as music downloads continued to increase in popularity.
3. Music-hosting websites were developed to help musicians promote themselves and their bands. Reverb Nation, Host Baby, and others

have provided the means to develop electronic press kits and improved cyber-traffic to websites for musicians across genres.

4. Record label websites, in addition to advertising and music reviews in major jazz magazines such as *Downbeat* and *Jazz Times*, have helped smaller record companies stay alive.

5. Special interest/genre blogs such as National Public Radio's *A Blog Supreme*, Devra Hall Levy's *Lush Life*, and Scott Yanow's *Jazz World* have helped bring fans closer to the music and musicians.

JAZZ IS DEAD . . . LONG LIVE JAZZ!

It seems safe to say, then, that the notion on the part of media critics and others that jazz music is becoming extinct is inaccurate. Jazz continues, as it always has, to be in a state of transition, both in terms of the music itself and the ways in which it reaches the listener. The music is fluid and dynamic, and while it may seem to appeal to only a small segment of the public, it is by no means "dead."

So then, to "reflect" one's culture via the musical art or, for that matter, any art form at all, really means to react to the nature and characteristics of that culture, in order to create a work of art. Since its beginnings, jazz has truly mirrored each era of American culture. It continues to do so today, even though it has not been considered a commercially viable music for many years. At the end of the day, there is more to making music than fame or celebrity and the wealth that often accompanies them. Jazz musicians and devoted listeners know that there is more to this music than entertainment value and monetary gain. How can we hang a price tag on the pure expression of human emotion? Jazz has been one of the ties that bind people and cultures together, across America and around the globe, and it will be with us for a long time to come, if we realize the importance of placing value upon human feeling in any society. Nurturing the willingness to communicate the truth and beauty of living fully in our culture and in the world itself continues to be what jazz is all about.

5

FUNCTIONS AND FORMS

Jazz on and off the Bandstand

In our day-to-day lives, we communicate with others on an individual basis—that is, as one person conversing with another. Also, we often communicate as part of a larger group; for instance, a group of friends at lunchtime, or perhaps something more formal—such as a committee or a team or a jury—in order to perform a task or pursue a mutual interest. People interacting with other people do so in a variety of ways, from medium-sized groups, such as those mentioned, to many types of large aggregations, such as religious congregations, university divisions, and a variety of clubs and special-interest groups. However, it's safe to suggest that all groups, no matter what their size, rely upon healthy group dynamics or energy in order to reach a level of maximum productivity and effectiveness.

The scope and nature of effective group dynamics extend well beyond the confines of everyday and professional life into the realm of many of the fine and performing arts such as music, dance, and theater. In the world of music, ensembles ranging from the Juilliard String Quartet and the New York Philharmonic to Bruce Springsteen and the E-Street Band, the Lincoln Center Jazz Orchestra, and the Keith Jarrett Trio all work to create aesthetic experiences to be shared by audiences in concert halls, stadiums, art galleries, nightclubs, and other places where people gather to experience music. The same can be said about dance and theater repertory companies, each of which rely upon a high level of group dynamics and interaction in order to create a successful performance, as well as a strong connection to their audiences.

In much the same way that we interact with another person or persons for the good of the order, jazz musicians likewise interact with their peers in order to create high-quality music in a variety of settings, from duos to large ensembles. Whatever the size of the group might be, it's safe to say that the goal of the jazz musician remains the same: to create sounds and feelings with other musicians, which will offer an engaging listening experience for those who are receptive to it. The bandstand and the concert stage provide fertile ground for developing and refining this goal. Jazz artists create and follow certain performance guidelines that foster the twin concepts of "community" and "democracy." At its best, a jazz performance can be a communal affair in that the musicians are mutually supportive of one another and are of like mind when it comes to creating music with both earnestness and integrity. The community is further expanded to include the audience who, in a sense, become "community members" and participants, by virtue of bearing witness to the creation of the music and by reacting to it, both consciously and subconsciously.

The concept of democracy as we know it is nowhere better exemplified than on the concert stage or the bandstand. Everyone has an equal share of the responsibility for a performance, and each member's contribution is valued as part of the whole. In the best ensembles, both large and small, there are few power struggles or conflicts of interest. The goal is to create the greatest music possible, to the best of one's ability. A masterful jazz performance is the result of men and women working together in harmony and with single-mindedness of purpose, in order to realize this goal. In these ways, jazz—and all music, for that matter—has been considered a significant example of democracy in action.

WYNTON MARSALIS ON JAZZ AS A
MODEL FOR DEMOCRACY IN BUSINESS

Upon being named one of America's best leaders by Harvard's Kennedy School of Government and *U.S. News & World Report* in 2006, the Pulitzer Prize–winning trumpeter and composer Wynton Marsalis was interviewed by *USA Today* in 2007, where he drew some interesting parallels between organizing a jazz band and building and managing a business enterprise. The article was called "Hot Corporations Know How to Swing," and Marsalis draws some interesting parallels between equanimity on the bandstand or concert stage and in a corporate environment.

In the interview Marsalis suggests that there are two elements among others that must be present for a jazz ensemble—a type of "corporation" in and of itself—to be able to reach a desirable and even memorable performance level: integrity and mutual respect. The most memorable jazz groups—as well as other types of musical ensembles—place great value on these two attributes. The respect a musician has for his bandmates' skills and abilities, and for the music that they are creating as a group, is key to how successful that group will be in reaching a high level of musicality and inspiration.

Actually, thinking of a musical ensemble as a corporation is not so far-fetched, when you consider that one of the definitions of the word "corporation," according to the *Pocket Oxford Dictionary*, is "a group of people authorized to act as an individual" (188). So let's think about this for a minute. When you attend a concert or go to a club to listen to the music, what you are hearing and experiencing is, in fact, "a group of people [the musicians] authorized [by the nature of the performance] to act as an individual [the total ensemble]."

In other words, when you hear a small group, a big band, an orchestra, a chorale, or any other musical ensemble, you are often hearing and experiencing the whole as the sum of its parts, rather than each part itself. So when you listen to Duke Ellington and his orchestra play "Satin Doll," you're not listening to each member of his band individually; you are hearing them collectively, as a unit. Likewise, when you listen to the Miles Davis quintet, you are really hearing a group sound, due to the efforts of its individual members to present a unified musical experience. These musicians don't work individually in their own little vacuums when they play together; as true partners, they support and inspire one another, feed each other new ideas, and attempt to create a total group sound and feel.

Marsalis also suggests that effective results are achieved in both musical groups and corporations only when individual egos are deemphasized and participants work together to reach a common goal. He is emphatic when he points out that if a corporation can develop and sustain a democratic environment, much as the best jazz groups do, then it will surely become a successful and "swinging" group of people.

Interlude I: Jazzocracy = Jazz + Democracy

Eminent bassist and author Bill Crow offered this great example of democracy in action in saxophonist Gerry Mulligan's ensembles:

> One example I can give you is the Gerry Mulligan Concert Jazz Band, which was one of the best bands I have played with. Gerry was the leader, and the band primarily reflected his musical point of view. But he respected [trombonist/arranger] Bob Brookmeyer's musical taste and gave him a lot of room both to play . . . and to influence the way the band phrased and blended together. And he gave everyone else in the band some solo space. Gerry liked to invent backgrounds for the different soloists, and we all joined in, making . . . the solo backgrounds into new structures from night to night. Even in Gerry's quartets, he gave everyone a lot of their own space. And on the Columbia album he did when [trumpeter] Art Farmer was in the group, he asked us to write tunes for the album. That was generous of Gerry, since he was a prolific composer himself. (Crow)

Interlude II: "Do As I Say, Not As I Do!"

I had spent a number of months working with a famous tenor saxophonist out in Los Angeles in the '80s. The man was a fine musician whose ship had come in when he recorded one of the first "smooth jazz" records. It received quite a bit of national attention and he worked a lot as a result of the exposure he got from the record.

When this saxophonist called me to join his quintet, he asked his new bassist and me to try to sound like the bass player and drummer from the recording. While I liked the way those guys played on the date, there was really no way I would be able to imitate the drummer's style, without sounding artificial and, to my way of thinking, "clunky." In any event, the new bassist and I gave it our best shot, and we wound up playing at the Troubadour and Concerts-by-the-Sea in L.A., and other venues in San Francisco, Seattle, and Portland.

The problem for the bassist and me in that band was that Mr. Sax was very explicit about what he wanted us to play, while he and the pianist, a brilliant and explosive player, got to play whatever they wanted without inhibition. For me, it was like always being the best man at a wedding and never getting to be the groom. While these two guys had complete free rein in their solos, the bassist and I were relegated to playing unobtrusive, boring rhythm patterns. There was no interplay, and back in the rhythm section, we just plodded along. Not much democracy happened in that band.

Without democracy, there is always the possibility of a revolution—either on or off the bandstand. So one night somewhere in the middle of a week-long gig in L.A., the bassist and I decided to participate in a more integral fashion. We responded to the sax and piano solos as humans would in actual conversation; we bobbed and weaved, floated like butterflies, stung like bees. We were all over the music, supporting the soloists in imaginative, energetic fashion. The audiences loved it; however, at the end of the run, Mr. Sax paid both of us and then promptly fired us. So much for equality on the bandstand.

I was told months later by my successor in the drum chair that the saxophonist played tapes of us for the new guys and asked them to try to play like us! And so it goes . . .

TEAMWORK ON AND OFF THE BANDSTAND

As Marsalis has suggested, a jazz band, no matter its size, is successful and engaging if it can operate with unity of purpose, in terms of both the music it produces and its internal philosophy of how a group functions, creates, and thrives. He and others across disciplines have emphasized the importance of integrity in the life of any established aggregation of people, whether they exist as musical groups or businesses. Marsalis's analogy could be expanded to include many different kinds of groups, including those mentioned previously. In any of these groups, the idea of working together to achieve a common goal is important, yet the creation of a successful, focused team is not without its challenges. There are often major conflicts between self and other, where one's ego can become an obstacle to the realization of a group's goal. For example, if one player on a football

team has his own idea of the way to execute a play and acts on it in opposition to the team's consensus, the play may not be successful and points may
be lost. Likewise, if the violist in a string quartet decides that she is going to
put a whole new spin on the viola part, while performing a chamber piece
by Haydn, the results may well be disastrous. The point is that the same
negative outcome may be true in any group situation: to emphasize self
over others often undermines collective efforts to achieve a desired objec-
tive. Marsalis's point is well taken when he asserts that "Groups who work
together 'swing.' They believe 'we' is more important than 'me,' and by
doing so, absorb mistakes." In other words, a true group effort—working
together harmoniously to achieve a common goal—is almost as important
as the actual outcome.

The importance of the "we" to teamwork is further supported in the
academic world. For instance, the Administrative and Business Services
Division of the University of California at Irvine released a paper in 1998
that dealt with, among other things, the identification of some basic principles of teamwork. The report states among other things that "at its best,
teamwork requires a willingness on the part of individuals to enter into
interdependence, involving risk" (Brase). One of the foundations of interdependence is an all-pervading trust among members of a group of people,
as well as a belief that "self" is less important than collaboration.

Selflessness is considered by many jazz musicians as the foundation for
musical teamwork. For many great musicians such as saxophonist John
Coltrane and pianist McCoy Tyner, bassist Jimmy Garrison and drummer
Elvin Jones—all members of his classic quartet—making transcendent
music as a group meant "giving yourself up to the music"; entering into
a state of interdependence with one another and, in doing so, creating a
musical experience founded upon risk, trust, and mutual respect; in other
words, submerging your ego to create a collective consciousness that would
act as an entity unto itself—the very essence of jazz!

A SMALL GROUP IN ACTION

On the bandstand, here's how this principle works. Imagine five musicians
on the stage at the Village Vanguard, the legendary jazz club in New York
City. The group instrumentation is trumpet, tenor saxophone, piano, bass,
and drums. The trumpeter counts off the tempo and the group launches

Figure 5.1. Dexter Gordon and Benny Bailey at the Village Vanguard in New York. Courtesy of Tom Marcello.

into "Isotope," a blues composition by the late tenor saxophonist Joe Henderson.

The trumpeter and the saxophonist play the song's melody in unison one or two times, with the rhythm section accompanying them by creating a rhythmic groove and supporting the statement of the melody with certain punctuations that give it more weight. For instance, the drummer might play some of the notes of the song in unison with the horns in order to add a percussive quality and heft to their statement of the melody. As an example of how this works, try singing any song that you like, and while singing, tap out the song with your hand. In effect, you are giving the song more dramatic emphasis by adding the rhythm of the song's melody with your hand. This is often what members of a rhythm section might do to add depth to the melody being stated by the horns.

Once the melody has been stated, the saxophonist takes the first solo. Using the chords created for the melody by the composer, he creates instantaneous countermelodies that, while using the predetermined chords, may sound nothing at all like the original song itself. Johann Sebastian Bach perfected such embellishments in classical music centuries ago, by creating melodies and then turning them inside out, creating a swirling, complex tapestry of sound. One need only listen to "The Well-

Tempered Clavier" to bear witness to Bach's greatness as a composer and improviser. Even though the jazz soloist uses Bach's approach in an entirely different milieu, the results are the same: a set of variations based on an established theme, created on the spot. This is what jazz musicians often call being "in the moment."

There is, however, much more to the concept of soloing than the spontaneous creation of a variety of countermelodies. The level and depth of emotion that a soloist feels may be one of the reasons why so many jazz musicians close their eyes while soloing. The celebrated trombonist and composer Bob Brookmeyer once suggested that jazz musicians bring a great deal of their personal humanity into the act of improvisation. Playing a solo, according to Brookmeyer, was akin to telling one's life story, replete with all of its joys and sorrows, its humor, and even its anger. Brookmeyer and many other jazz musicians believed that, at its best and most memorable, a jazz solo is a deeply personal statement about one's life.

Meanwhile, back on the stage, the saxophonist in our example improvises and works in collaboration with the rhythm section which, individually and as a unit, supports the solo, simultaneously interacting with the soloist, almost as though they were all having a conversation. The saxophonist creates a musical phrase, and that phrase might be picked up and echoed by one or more members of the rhythm section. This "call-and-response" style evident in so many jazz performances had its origins notably in the field hollers and church music of the Southern slaves before, during, and after the Civil War period of America's history. Here's how it works: If, for example, we were having a discussion, you might make a comment or offer an opinion, whereupon another group member might say, "Yes! That's correct," or "Are you sure you mean that?" He or she would be reacting to your thought, punctuating it with his or her own commentary. This is precisely what jazz artists do during a performance. While there may be a solo statement made by one player, it is being supported and "commented upon" by one or more of the other group members. Each member of the group depends upon the others in order to make this happen, and they do so by listening to and concentrating upon every note and phrase the soloist plays.

The saxophonist explores every nook and cranny of the chords and melody of the song and takes whatever time is necessary to build a solo. Once the solo runs its natural course (only the soloist knows when that is), he stops playing and the next soloist begins the journey. In this case, the trumpeter may be next. The process begins all over again with each new solo. It is altogether possible that every member of the quintet will solo, or it may be that the horns and the piano will be the only soloists. Such decisions—though they may be preplanned on occasion—are often made extemporaneously on the bandstand, using eye contact or hand signals, not unlike those used by members of a basketball or football team in play.

After all solos, the melody may be restated one or two times (depending upon its length) before the band ends the performance. This may happen a number of different ways: First, there may be a written musical arrangement—called a "roadmap" by many jazz musicians—that dictates in what way the song will end. In other words, the musicians will adhere for the most part to the notes on the page to guide them to the song's conclusion. A second form of ending may be completely unplanned and is left up to the province of the group members. The group simply constructs an ending on the spot that will, at best, seem prearranged, even if it is merely the result of some close listening on the part of all five musicians.

SOUND ON SOUND: A CLOSER LOOK AT A BIG BAND

The creative process and the teamwork described earlier in this chapter happen not only in small ensembles, but also on a more grand scale in any significantly larger aggregation. One of the most exciting things about a performance by a big jazz band is the sheer wall of sound created by the trumpets, trombones, saxophones, and rhythm section. Unlike the deafening qualities of, say, heavy metal rock—where the music reaches a mind-numbing decibel level and is often obscured by an electronic tidal wave of distortion—big band jazz can and usually does cover an entire range of dynamics, from very soft to quite loud, all without obscuring or compromising its musicality.

Big bands were—and still are—often composed of three "sections" or subgroups. The first is called a brass section, which usually consists of four or five trumpets and three or four trombones. All are brass instruments that are capable of a variety of sounds via the use of devices called "mutes," which are inserted into the bell of an instrument to change the sound of the instrument. For example, when a metal Harmon mute is placed in a trumpet bell, the sound of the instrument goes from very open and pure to a rather tight, pinched timbre. Miles Davis was one of the major proponents of this sound and truly made it his own for almost four decades.

Figure 5.2. Anat Cohen at the Jazz Standard in New York. Courtesy of Michael Skliar.

The second major section in a big band is the saxophone or reed section. In conventional big bands, the sax section usually consisted of two altos, two tenors, and one baritone saxophone, all of which are reed instruments. It was not unusual, even in the early days of the big band, to find members of the sax section "doubling" on other instruments—that is, playing other woodwind instruments besides their appointed horns. The innovative band leader Fletcher Henderson and the legendary pianist–band leader–composer Duke Ellington wrote music that required their woodwind players to double on a variety of other instruments such as the clarinet, the flute, and the bass clarinet, in order to expand the tonal colors of their orchestras. Doubling on a variety of reed instruments became the norm as big bands evolved through the next 70 years.

The rhythm section is the third major component of a big band and has undergone significant changes since its inception in the early part of the last century. The first big bands utilized the tuba and banjo—holdovers from the Dixieland era—along with piano and drums. Henderson's band and Ellington's early ensembles employed both of these instruments early on; however, within a few short years, the tuba was replaced by the string bass (also called the bass violin or, later, the acoustic bass), and the banjo was consigned to history in favor of the guitar. Today's rhythm sections consist largely of piano, bass, and drums, with the frequent additions of guitar and percussion.

While teamwork and the nurturing of mutual respect are integral to the effectiveness and power of small jazz ensembles, nowhere are these ideals more prominently on display than in a big band. In the best of these larger jazz groups, a listener can often tune in to a real sense of community among the musicians. When you watch and listen to an accomplished big band perform, you become acutely aware that the 16 men and women up there on the stage are playing as though they were of a single mind interpreting a piece of music, playing and being in tune with one another. In a sense, a big band is a community unto itself.

A BIG BAND IN ACTION

We've looked at how teamwork, attentiveness, and mutual respect work in jazz combos on the bandstand or concert stage. Let's examine how these characteristics might reveal themselves in a big band setting:

It's December of 1960 in New York City. You are once again at the Village Vanguard, this time to hear the baritone saxophonist Gerry Mulligan and his Concert Jazz Band play a grouping of five or six compositions—commonly called a "set" of performances, usually lasting 45 minutes to an hour. The piece you will be hearing next is called "Let My People Be," a composition by Mulligan, arranged (orchestrated for big band) by bandmate Bob Brookmeyer.

The song begins with Mulligan sitting down at the piano and playing some blues in a medium tempo. After a few moments, he is joined by the bassist and the drummer and they set a light, swinging groove. From the trombone section, Brookmeyer stands up and brings the band in at the first written section of the piece. Trumpets, trombones, and saxophones play the simple blues melody one time through, and Mulligan "answers" the horns with his piano solo. The horns respond with another prearranged melody of their own, and Mulligan, with continued support from the bassist and drummer, responds to them again with musical commentary from the piano. This call-and-response pattern continues for several blues "choruses"—each being 12 "bars" (at four equal beats apiece); the band "calls" and Mulligan "responds." This section leads into a valve trombone solo by Brookmeyer with rhythm section accompaniment. After about two minutes, the brass and saxes play written figures that Brookmeyer responds to in his improvisations. His "response," as in Mulligan's solo, answers the written figures played by the horns. This is a structure similar to the proceedings on any Sunday morning in an African American church, where the pastor sings or shouts a phrase from the litany and the congregation offers a spirited response. The level of communication is exacting and intense.

The tenor saxophonist Jim Reider is next, and he offers an improvised solo that calms things down a bit. His improvisations are relaxed and lyrical (songlike), and the brass and sax sections play written passages underneath him, rather than answer his solo phrases as in the two preceding solos. Once Reider has concluded his improvisations, the rhythm section takes over and provides a soft pillow of sound to introduce the final and most exciting solo of the composition. The trumpeter Clark Terry moves from his place in the trumpet section to center stage and begins his solo softly. He uses a toilet plunger cup occasionally throughout his improvisations, to create vocal effects that make the horn sound almost like a human voice. Terry takes his time and builds his solo slowly, creating a mounting intensity that is truly breathtaking. Along the way during the trumpeter's solo, something amazing happens: Bob Brookmeyer begins playing a figure called a "riff," and the other trombonists pick it up and play it as well. Then one of the saxophonists adds his own musical phrase in counterpoint to the trombones, and his sectionmates join in the fun and play his riff as well. Finally, as Terry builds and builds his solo and climbs into his horn's upper register, the trumpet section adds their own totally unplanned musical phrase, so that at this point the band becomes a sanctified church and is responding to Preacher Terry's shouting with commentary of its own. Eventually Terry's solo reaches a climax, and he rejoins the trumpet section's riff. The musical arrangement resumes on Brookmeyer's cue and the band winds down, playing one long note out of tempo and holding that note as Mulligan brings the song to its conclusion by slowing his piano chords until Brookmeyer waves the band out entirely. Fortunately, that evening at the Village Vanguard was recorded for posterity. You can hear this actual performance on the CD titled *The Gerry Mulligan Concert Jazz Band, Live at the Village Vanguard*.

To witness the creative process on the bandstand with either a small group or a big band is to be privy to and part of a community that values art as something deeply personal and valuable for all who are present and open to the experience. As we move forward and closer to the music and the musicians who create it, this book may well become a true companion for us, and help us to understand the importance and value of mutual respect, teamwork, and the creative imagination in all of our lives, on both sides of the bandstand.

6

POINTS OF DEPARTURE

Small Groups and Big Bands

Of all the different genres and styles of music, it is primarily jazz and classical music that maintain the greatest variety in terms of the size and character of the ensembles that perform it. For instance, the vast repertoire of Western classical music was created by composers for solo players on all instruments, all the way up to mega-sized groups; so at one end of the spectrum, you have a solo piano sonata by Mozart, and at the other, a piece for four orchestras by Karlheinz Stockhausen. Similarly, jazz music—either composed or completely improvised—has been written and/ or performed by unaccompanied soloists (such as pianists Fats Waller and Keith Jarrett, or saxophonists Sonny Rollins and Anthony Braxton) and by increasing numbers of participants, up to big bands that are augmented by strings and extra brass, woodwind, and percussion instruments. Neither country and western music, nor rhythm and blues, nor rock and roll can make this claim, even though artists in each of these genres, such as Lyle Lovett, James Brown, and Frank Zappa, respectively, have performed their music using large ensembles. It remains that classical music and all forms of jazz are rich with variety in both ensemble size and instrumental combinations. In this chapter we will have a look at the evolution of some of the most notable small ensembles and big bands and will offer some suggestions for listening and experiencing this multidimensional music.

SHAPES AND VISIONS: SMALL GROUPS IN JAZZ

The small jazz ensemble, such as the one described in the last chapter, is quite common in size to all eras and styles of jazz. Early versions of these bands included the Original Dixieland Jazz Band, King Oliver's Creole Jazz Band, Louis Armstrong's Hot Five and Hot Seven, and Jelly Roll Morton and His Red Hot Peppers. These and other small bands from the 1920s and '30s have been profiled in many jazz history texts (see "Other Sources" in the back of this book), and were hotbeds of talent on every instrument. Many of jazz's early innovators honed their art and craft in these groups, and fortunately, their recordings are still available today. When you listen to their music, the collective energy level of the musicians is one of the first things you notice. They improvised together as a unit and created an exciting group sound that was unique to that early period. Armstrong in particular was a formidable musician who echoed the power of his predecessors, trumpeters Buddy Bolden, Freddie Keppard, and Armstrong's mentor Joe "King" Oliver; and Armstrong distinguished himself as the first great soloist in jazz, with his 1928 recording of "West End Blues."

Interlude I: A Little Look at "West End Blues"

Sometimes in the creation of jazz, as in many other endeavors, everything just gels, and "good" becomes "extraordinary." Chalk it up to good chemistry, all the planets being in alignment, luck; whatever it is, there is a kind of magic that happens and, as a result, a masterpiece is created. This is exactly what happened in late June 1928, when Louis Armstrong and his Hot Five went into a studio in Chicago and recorded a number of songs, including "West End Blues." Many jazz historians, critics, and seasoned listeners believe that his performance on this song continues to be one of the greatest in jazz.

"West End Blues" begins with Louis playing a 15-second unaccompanied solo (often called a "cadenza"). One thing you'll notice here when you listen closely to the track is how effortless Louis makes his playing seem. That is often the mark of a true master on any instrument. The notes in his improvisation just seem to tumble out of his horn and cascade

Figure 6.1. Louis Armstrong. Courtesy of the William P. Gottlieb Collection.

into the air like fireworks. After his introductory solo turn, Louis steps into the background and passes the baton to trombonist Fred Robinson, and then to clarinetist Jimmy Strong. Behind Strong's solo, Louis "scat" sings; that is, he creates a wordless vocal, using his voice as though it were a horn, complementing and "answering" the clarinet solo. The masterful pianist Earl "Fatha" Hines plays the next solo, followed by an absolutely astonishing solo by Louis, which begins with him holding a breathtaking high note over the rhythm before letting loose with a fierce and beautiful outing—one that is considered by many to be one of the greatest solos in jazz's 100-year history. Louis had definitely come into his own as a soloist, and "West End Blues" put him squarely on the map and certainly on the path to musical immortality.

One of the things Louis Armstrong's famous solo proved was that jazz could be a soloist's music, rather than only that of an ensemble where the horns all solo at the same time. Louis set the standard that day in June of '28, and jazz musicians from every succeeding generation have been trying to reach it ever since.

In looking at the place of the small group in jazz, it is crucial to understand its importance to the music's development as an art form. Much of the innovation in the music at that time took place in these small ensembles, and without them, there wouldn't have been a foundation upon which to build later styles and approaches to both ensemble playing and solos.

While big swing bands began to hold sway in the 1930s and '40s, small groups persevered nonetheless, although in far fewer numbers. Eddie Condon and his various ensembles kept the home fires burning for Dixieland; clarinetists Benny Goodman and Artie Shaw and pianist William "Count" Basie led exemplary swing combos, which consisted largely of members of their respective big bands; and in Europe, the legendary Belgian Gypsy guitarist Django Reinhardt, along with violinist Stephane Grappelli, created a unique and exciting quintet called the Hot Club of France. Even so, audiences wanted to not only hear the music but to be able to dance to it as well—and the most popular vehicle for doing so turned out to be the big band. A grand night out in 1938 might have been to go to the Roseland Ballroom in Manhattan or the Schrader Hotel in Milwaukee to dance to the vibrant, exciting big-band music of Count Basie or Benny Goodman. In a sense, this was high-quality party music on a grand scale. And if you weren't able to attend in person, you could always rearrange your living room furniture, turn on the radio, tune in to *Let's Dance*, and "cut a rug" with your favorite partner.

With the birth of bebop in the early 1940s, there was a significant resurgence of the small group. The music began to move away from the confines of big-band swing, even though it grew out of that popular movement, and jazz began to lose a significant portion of its audience—notably because the new bebop style was not created as a vehicle for dancers, but for listeners. And for the most part, bebop was a small-band music. Again, as with the early jazz groups, the small "combo" of the 1940s was a breeding ground for the musical ideas and personalities of that era: alto saxophonist Charlie Parker; tenor saxophonists Sonny Rollins and Dexter Gordon; trumpeters Dizzy Gillespie, Clifford Brown, and Miles Davis; trombonists J. J. Johnson and Kai Winding; pianists Thelonious Monk and Bud Powell; bassists Charles Mingus and Oscar Pettiford; and drummers Max Roach and Kenny Clarke—to name only a few—were all instrumental in bringing bebop to life and exerting a tremendous influence on generations of musicians yet to come. And all of these men accomplished much of their finest work at that time in the small-group setting.

Interlude II: Food for Thought

You need to ask yourself at this point what you think the purpose or goal of the jazz experience might be for a listener. Is it music to entertain us? Is it best presented as music for us to dance to? Or might it be merely good background music when we're dining in restaurants, relaxing in a Jacuzzi, doing dishes after dinner, or watching a movie?

Or might jazz be something much more personal? If a jazz musician is expressing his or her emotions through an instrument, what should your response to that act be?

This was the dilemma faced by confused listeners in the 1940s, who equated jazz with dancing and having a good time. With the advent of bebop, this situation created a real schism between those who sought to experience the music in a whole new way and those who wanted jazz to remain a music that existed to provide fun and pleasure for dancers and partygoers.

Small-ensemble jazz continued to flourish in the 1950s and '60s, perpetuating bebop while going far beyond its stylistic confines. It was in this intimate setting that Miles Davis and John Coltrane recorded two of the greatest jazz records of all time: *Kind of Blue* (1959) and *A Love Supreme* (1964), respectively. Pianist Bill Evans (who played a significant role on *Kind of Blue*) led one of the most innovative piano trios in the history of jazz; and another pianist, Dave Brubeck, experimented with rhythms and time signatures not ordinarily employed in jazz and, as a result, recorded *Time Out* (1959), which became a best-selling album among both jazz and nonjazz listeners at that time. New and revolutionary music was also being played and recorded by Davis and his groundbreaking 1960s quintet and Coltrane's classic quartet, and by the small ensembles of the volcanic and mercurial bassist Charles Mingus, the radically innovative saxophonist Ornette Coleman, the quirkily brilliant pianist and composer Thelonious Monk, and by many others. Small groups could be found performing in jazz venues everywhere, from large metropolitan cities like New York and Los Angeles, to smaller cities and towns throughout America. At that time, one could travel to places as diverse as Miami, Indianapolis, Seattle, or Baltimore and find a nightclub that featured jazz trios, quartets, quintets, and often larger groups holding forth sometimes as many as six nights a week. It was truly a dream situation for many musicians back then, as well as those devotees who came out to listen to and support the music.

The next several decades saw the ever-increasing popularity of rock and roll, particularly with the inception of British groups like the Beatles and the Rolling Stones, as well as American bands like Jefferson Airplane, the Jimi Hendrix Experience, the Byrds, and countless others. The popularity of rhythm and blues was also growing among the general public, and seminal figures such as James Brown, Otis Redding, Aretha Franklin, and Stevie Wonder were gaining prominence not only in America, but in Europe as well. With the explosion of rock and R & B, jazz became a rarer commodity, and clubs where one could hear the music were struggling to survive. Even so, the decline in popularity of jazz did not affect the levels of innovation taking place, notably once again in small-group settings. In the mid- to late '60s, jazz musicians began experimenting with ways to fuse elements of rock and rhythm and blues with improvisation. The most notable of these experiments took place in small- to medium-size group settings by Miles Davis who, after several years of flirtations with rock rhythms, turned the jazz world upside-down with his historic 1969 recording of *Bitches Brew*, the first really significant melding of jazz and rock to catch the attention of fans of both music genres.

Interlude III: In the Studio with Miles Davis

My friend and musical associate Bennie Maupin, who played bass clarinet in the original *Bitches Brew* sessions, remembered them—and his times in the recording studio with Miles Davis. Here is an excerpt of his recollections from a personal interview:

> The music was wide open for exploration and Miles was very gracious to me, especially when you listen to the recording—I just play all over it. It was like being in a "sound candy" shop; it was like, "Have fun." . . . We were exploring the sounds; and Miles gave me the opportunity to do that—which really changed my life. We took the emphasis away from the notes and put the

emphasis on the sound and the rhythm, so a lot of what you hear are basically "shapes." [Miles] had a direction in mind, and I think that he was the only one who knew what that direction was.

It was like walking into a room where you don't know where anything is and it's dark, and you keep bumping into things. Pretty soon, your eyes get adjusted to where you are and it's fine. That's sort of how I felt being there. I was just bumping into everything; but every time I would have these collisions, [Miles] would look over at me and it would be a sign of approval. He loved it!

The amazing thing about this recording is that there were no rehearsals. . . . Everything was very sketchy. He really challenged everybody's imagination to create something out of what just was basically the air.

This enormous stylistic shift by Davis opened the door to the birth of jazz-rock or "fusion music," which evolved into a highly technical and precise form of jazz, buoyed by fantastically complex rhythmic patterns played by masterful drummers and (usually) electric bassists. Many of the stylistic innovations of this form of jazz were made in small ensembles, not coincidentally led by alumni of various Miles Davis groups from the mid-1960s and later. Tony Williams, Wayne Shorter, John McLaughlin, Joe Zawinul, Chick Corea, Dave Liebman, and John Scofield were among the most notable Miles alumni to explore and expand Miles's vision. Jazz-rock music still exists today, although it's not nearly as popular as it was in earlier decades.

The two decades leading up to the new millennium and the first decade of the new century have produced a wildly diverse panoply of jazz styles, from mainstream bebop, post-bop, and the avant-garde to fusions of jazz and world music, jazz and folk music, and jazz and classical music. And once again, many of these stylistic developments have taken place in small groups, consisting of adventurous players of all ages whose skills and dedication to exploring new modes of expression, as well as revisiting and reconstructing older forms, have stretched the boundaries of jazz in a stimulating variety of ways. Among the younger generation of musicians, the small groups of pianists Jason Moran, Vijay Iyer, and Helen Sung; guitarists Kurt Rosenwinkel and Marc Ribot; bassists Drew Gress and Scott

Colley; drummers Jim Black and Brian Blade; trumpeters Dave Douglas and Ralph Alessi; trombonists Josh Roseman and Isaac Smith; saxophonists Chris Speed and Rudresh Mahanthappa; and vocalists Patricia Barber and Jay Clayton are standouts for the freshness and originality of their visions.

The previous generations are also well represented, with groups led by the likes of pianists Geri Allen and Bobo Stenson; guitarists Bill Frisell and Pat Metheny; bassists Charlie Haden and Dave Holland; drummers Jack Dejohnette and Billy Hart; trumpeters Wadada Leo Smith and Roy Hargrove; trombonists Roswell Rudd and Ray Anderson; saxophonists Joe Lovano, Dave Liebman, and John Surman; and vocalist Norma Winstone—all continuing to expand and redefine their musical voices and concepts, using mostly small ensembles as the vehicles for their continued growth as instrumentalists and composers.

And finally, living masters such as saxophonists Sonny Rollins, Wayne Shorter, and Lee Konitz; guitarist Jim Hall; bassist Ron Carter; drummers Roy Haynes and Jimmy Cobb; pianists Cedar Walton, Steve Kuhn, and Kenny Barron; and vocalist Sheila Jordan—all continue their lifelong explorations, often in the intimate settings provided by small groups.

Keep in mind that these short lists of innovative and original musical voices are in no way complete. Small groups were and continue to be an important vehicle of creative expression for many more fine musicians throughout the music's 100-plus-year history. One of the aims of this book is to bring as many of these fine artists to light as space will allow.

SUCH SWEET THUNDER: A BIT OF BIG BAND HISTORY

The concept of community in big bands may have been born out of necessity. In the 1920s, '30s, and part of the '40s, many big bands traversed the country's highways and back roads in cars and buses, playing in large and small towns on makeshift wooden stages in hotels, dance halls, American Legion halls, warehouses, school auditoriums, and other such places. Night after night and week after week, the members of these bands traveled together, stayed together in hotels or people's homes, and ate meals together. In short, they became microcosmic communities whose missions were to bring their music to people everywhere in America.

It may well be that the traveling big band got its start in the mid-1920s, when big bands began journeying to the smaller cities and towns in a state or region to play for people who, due to their geographic location, didn't have the opportunity or the funds to travel to larger cities to hear and dance to the music. These early road bands were called "territory bands," in that they often crisscrossed geographic territories in many regions of the country for weeks and months at a time, making music for large crowds as well as small audiences. Many of our finest jazz musicians cut their musical (and perhaps social) teeth in these road bands. Count Basie, Duke Ellington, Fletcher Henderson, Cab Calloway, and many other legendary musicians spent significant amounts of time on the road, beginning in those early days.

Among the more famous of the early aggregations were those led by Fletcher Henderson and Duke Ellington. Henderson's band was lively and energetic, while Ellington's early ensembles were uniquely his own, due largely to his composing and arranging skills. Both bands featured gifted soloists. Henderson was blessed with the talents of Louis Armstrong and saxophonist Coleman Hawkins, while Ellington featured trumpeter Bubber Miley, clarinetist Barney Bigard, and alto saxophonist Johnny Hodges, who was a major presence in the Ellington band for 38 years. Henderson was an accomplished composer and arranger and was active as a band leader primarily in the 1920s, and later was an arranger for clarinetist Benny Goodman's big band. He was one of the first arrangers and band leaders to pit the brass section against the saxophone section, using the call-and-response approach to ensemble writing, as mentioned earlier in the Gerry Mulligan Concert Jazz Band performance.

Edward Kennedy "Duke" Ellington was completely in a class by himself. His creative output was nothing short of phenomenal, with at least two thousand compositions to his credit. Ellington's music—and his orchestra—defied easy categorization. Sometimes, the music was dreamy and impressionistic; other times, it was exotic; still other times, it was relentless in its swinging feeling. Ellington was an exemplary musician and gifted visionary whose orchestra was his "instrument." Whether alone or in collaboration with the brilliant arranger and composer Billy Strayhorn, Ellington created beautiful tapestries of sound and feeling. The band's soloists were men of legendary proportion: trumpeters Cootie Williams, Rex Stewart, and Clark Terry; saxophonists Johnny Hodges and Paul Gonsalves; clarinetist Barney Bigard; trombonist "Tricky Sam" Nanton; bassist Jimmy Blanton; drummers Sonny Greer and Sam Woodyard—all totally individualistic musicians, each with the gift of a recognizable style. Ellington even went so far as to write concerti for a number of these fine musicians, including Bigard, Williams, Stewart, and Gonsalves. The Ellington band, in its several incarnations, endured for close to a half century and stands as a testament to one of jazz's great geniuses.

Interlude IV: Duke Ellington—Painter of Soundscapes

The Duke was often thought of as a master painter, in that he drew so many different tonal "colors" out of his orchestra. Whereas many big bands both before and after the swing era were fairly consistent in terms of the sounds of each of the sections (trumpets, trombones, saxophones, rhythm section), Ellington chose to utilize a much more diverse sound "palette" than any of his contemporaries. To achieve this, his saxophonists also played flutes, clarinets, and bass clarinets, in addition to their regular instruments. Trumpeters and trombonists utilized a variety of "mutes" (inserted into the bells of their horns) in order to change the tones of their instruments. Duke's drummers often added other percussion instruments such as the chimes and the timpani to extend the colors even more than those produced by drums and cymbals.

Figure 6.2. The Duke Ellington Orchestra, early 1940s. Courtesy of the William P. Gottlieb Collection.

Yet, the most amazing thing of all was the way Duke would combine these unique timbres in order to offer truly original-sounding compositions and arrangements. Let's look at one of these pieces. "Mood Indigo" is one of Duke Ellington's most famous and beloved compositions. There are many versions of this piece recorded by the Ellington Orchestra listed on Amazon, and literally hundreds more versions that have been recorded by other artists. An embarrassment of riches!

Our version of "Mood Indigo" begins with a brief, classical-sounding piano introduction by the Duke, followed by a soft, slow, and silky-smooth statement of the melody, which is stated by the unusual combination of a clarinet, a muted trumpet, and a muted trombone. Since this is one of the earlier versions of this piece, we will also hear banjo and tuba plunking and puffing away unobtrusively beneath the melody.

Once the melody has been stated, the clarinetist takes the spotlight with a spry and playful improvisation based upon the chords found in the original melody. The trumpeter (still muted) follows with his own reinvention, which leads into a light and airy Ellington piano interlude; then it's back to the original statement of the melody by the horns, and the end of the performance. The solos on this recording are short—probably due to the fact that most 78 rpm records could hold only about three minutes of music. All in all, this version of the Ellington classic is a little gem—one that has been reissued on many different collections over at least the last 70 years.

While Ellington's band was, at various times, a concert ensemble, a show band, and a jazz band for listeners, it was never really known as a "dance band." There were other bands that offered more opportunities for listeners to dance to the music—either in the hotel ballrooms of the day, or even in the makeshift dance floors next to radios in living rooms across the country. Benny Goodman, Artie Shaw, and Count Basie were three of the best and most memorable. Goodman's rise to fame came after much work and frustration. Keeping a band together—much less a big band—in the 1930s was no easy proposition; yet Goodman was tenacious in his belief that people wanted something more than stock or standard arrangements to dance to. He formed his first big band in the spring of 1934 and later that year became the "house band" for the *Let's Dance* radio show.

Interlude V: Dancing in Apartment 206

It's their dancing you remember most; more than the polished hard-wood floors . . . more than the mahogany cocktail table your father lifted aside or the Moroccan rug your mother rolled back against the couch. . . . You can still hear echoes of muted trombones and the hollow reediness of a clarinet played by Artie Shaw, his orchestra rising above a comfortable crackle in the big old radio; the sounds their four feet made, drawing small jeweled boxes on the living room floor . . . your father's voice in unison with the clarinet: "It had to be you. . . ."

—adapted from Michael Stephans, "Home: 1949,"
The Color of Stones (1997)

After the show ended, the Goodman band hit the road and played in cities and made its way to Los Angeles. After that particularly disastrous tour across country, where response to the band was often either ambiva-lent or negative, they were ultimately greeted by legions of fans outside the Palomar Ballroom in Los Angeles, waiting to hear and dance to the swing music they had been hearing on the radio. Many of these fans were college students who found the new swing music to be intoxicating and fun. Admittedly, Goodman wanted to play it close to the hip by starting the evening out with his more commercial arrangements—which fell flat with the audience; however, when he launched the band into Fletcher Henderson's arrangement of "King Porter Stomp," the fans went wild. It was then that jazz reached a new pinnacle—one that would briefly and lovingly catapult jazz, particularly big-band music, into nationwide ac-ceptance and popularity. The swing era was born, and Benny Goodman was crowned its official "king."

The Palomar performance, which quite fortunately was broadcast coast to coast, was a tremendous success, and the Goodman band was revered by teenagers everywhere. All along, he believed that jazz and big band music could be fused in a way that would make both listeners and dancers happy. And he was right. The culmination of his efforts to present the music the way he felt it should be presented took place on a wintery night in 1938 in New York City at Carnegie Hall, a venue that had not ever presented jazz. Understandably, the band was quite nervous and played rather stiffly, until—on a song called "Don't Be That Way"—drummer Gene Krupa unleashed a machine-gun barrage of notes and drove the band into a spirited, uninhibited finale and an intensity level that remained on the stage for the rest of that historic evening. The Carnegie Hall audience quite uncharacteristically clapped, shouted, and took to the aisles to dance to the music. Fortunately for all, the evening was recorded by Columbia Records and remains a part of their catalog even today. Benny Goodman and his band made history that January night, and their memorable performance helped seal the clarinetist's place in jazz history for all time.

Another big band that earned an iconic place in the jazz world belonged to William "Count" Basie. Even though he is often associated with Kansas City and the tremendous jazz scene that proliferated and thrived there in the 1930s and '40s, Basie was born in Red Bank, New Jersey, in 1904. He worked as a theater organist in Harlem for a time, then wound up playing in other theaters in various parts of the country. One such venue was the Eblon Theater in Kansas City, where Basie eventually settled. Basie made an important connection with Oklahoma bassist Walter Page and, in the late 1920s, was a member of various territory bands including Page's band, the Blue Devils. At the time of the Depression, notably when Wall Street crashed, Basie returned to Kansas City and spent time as the pianist with Bennie Moten's Orchestra before striking out on his own. Basie formed his first big band in 1937 and kept its various incarnations alive through the next 47 years. Many great jazz stylists were members of the various editions of the band. There was, first and foremost, tenor saxophonist Lester Young—The "Prez"—whose light and buoyant tone and formidable technique became world renowned as a major alternative to the heavier, darker sound favored by tenor giant Coleman Hawkins. There were trumpeters Buck Clayton and Harry "Sweets" Edison, both powerful yet lyrical players who were immensely popular among fans. There was the legendary Basie rhythm section, featuring the powerful Walter Page on bass; rhythm guitarist Freddie Green, who even though he rarely soloed, brought both depth and breadth to the overall "feel" of the rhythm; and the dynamo, drummer Jo Jones, who was known, among other things, for his incredible looseness and his uncanny ability to swing mightily, yet at a relatively low volume. Basie himself held sway at the piano; however, even though his style was minimal, he always managed to find the right notes and chords to play at the right tempo. Together, the Basie rhythm section was known for having a light touch while being extremely propulsive.

One element that made the Basie band unique was the fact that it had almost no written music on the bandstand. At that time, the disastrous economic situation all but prohibited most bands in Kansas City from hiring arrangers to create a "book" of pieces that the band could perform. Instead, the band played mostly "head arrangements," that is, a series of musical motifs or "riffs" learned by ear by all members in each section. These "arrangements" got their name from the fact that the riffs were created "off the top of one's head"—in other words, right there, on the spot. We have already described an example of this performance style in the description of the Gerry Mulligan Concert Jazz Band's Village Vanguard performance.

Kansas City did not feel the full weight of the Great Depression as did other cities and towns around the country. In the late 1920s through the '30s, the Pendergast regime's tight grip on the city kept it from imploding economically. It also provided dozens of places that musicians could unpack their horns and play, even if it was for a substandard wage or even no wage at all. The town never seemed to sleep, and musicians like those in the Basie band would often play until sunup (or even through the morning, if you factor in "breakfast dances"). The jazz lovers and those fans who loved to dance were equally enthralled by the music and the party atmosphere.

Interlude VI: Goin' to Kansas City

In the liner notes to one of his earlier recordings, valve trombonist and composer Bob Brookmeyer remembered Kansas City this way:

> When I was one of the youngest jazz fans in the country, my dad and I would cheat the parson on a Sunday or two and stay by the radio to wait for the 15 minutes of Basie. . . . Then too, Basie would be through town at the Tower theatre five, six times a year and I got to be a real pro at forging passes from school to catch three shows and two bad westerns before there would be some salt from the home kitchen.

When I was old enough to sneak into the night clubs and dives where the good bands played, it was always the same feeling, to my heart anyway. Smooth, rich, deep, mellow, like a fine cigarette.

While Count Basie's band played head arrangements almost exclusively, they didn't name each head arrangement played, primarily because there were so many of them. Basie's famous "One O'Clock Jump" was so named because at one of the frequent radio broadcasts the band played, the host asked Basie the name of the arrangement they were going to play. Because the arrangement was named "Blue Balls," Basie knew that he couldn't identify the song as such on the air. So when he saw that the wall clock said 1:00, he informed the host that the song was called "One O'Clock Jump." And the rest is history. . . .

The swing era produced many other fine big bands that have not been profiled here. Clarinetists Artie Shaw and Woody Herman both led exceptional ensembles. Drumming masters Chick Webb and Gene Krupa had great bands as well. Saxophonist Charlie Barnet had an excellent band, as did the Dorsey Brothers, Tommy and Jimmy. Add to these the many big bands across the country that didn't receive the same level of recognition outside of their own cities and towns. The public loved jazz, and they loved to listen and dance to the sounds of the big bands. Jazz had truly become a popular music on a national level.

The demise of the swing era came about after World War II for a number of reasons, both economic and stylistic. There were problems that festered between the musicians' union and the radio networks, which brought about a recording ban in 1942 that, in effect, crippled the recording industry and specifically the big bands that relied partly on their recordings for revenue. Stylistically, other forms of music began to attract the public's attention. Rhythm and blues caught hold, as did folk and country music. Everyone wanted to capture the attention of the listening public, and one result was that swing lost a fair portion of its audience to other types of music.

However, big bands continued to survive in the late 1940s and '50s, most notably the bands of Dizzy Gillespie, Woody Herman, and Stan Kenton. Gillespie's band and the later editions of Herman's "Thundering Herd" were steeped in the bebop tradition, featuring bop soloists and rhythm sections within the big-band structure. Both Gillespie and Herman led exciting, high-energy bands that featured prominent soloists, sparkling section work, and skillful arrangements. Gillespie also displayed a love of Latin music and often augmented his band with the great Cuban conga drummer, Chano Pozo.

Stan Kenton was unique among big-band leaders in the late 1940s and '50s, in that he led bands that were often much larger than the standard 14- to 16- piece band. Kenton was also unique in that he evolved independently in California, outside the sphere of influence of Ellington, Basie, or any of the other big bands that had come before him. He hired a staff of arrangers such as Bill Holman, Pete Rugolo, Johnny Richards, and Bob Graettinger, who created often extravagant, multidimensional musical compositions and arrangements that were quite diverse. He also hired the best musicians that the West Coast had to offer, including the alto saxophonist Art Pepper, the trombonist Frank Rosolino, the trumpeter Maynard Ferguson, and the drummer Shelly Manne. What began as a big dance band became, under Kenton's leadership, something entirely different—something more akin to Duke Ellington's approach to the large ensemble as a concert vehicle.

The Kenton Innovations in Modern Music projects were thematically interesting. For example, one album was called *Cuban Fire*, which attempted to capture the feeling of Latin music in a jazz setting. Another was called *Adventures in Time*, which featured pieces written in odd meters, much like what Dave Brubeck and his quartet did with *Time Out* and its successor, *Time Further Out*. Still another project was called *Adventures in Jazz*, which featured the writing and playing of trombonist/drummer Dee Barton, among others. Other *Adventures* albums included *Adventures in Blues* and *Adventures in Standards*, and there were also concept albums for *West Side Story*, *Kenton/Wagner*, and *City of Glass*—and even a rather dismal project called *Kenton/Ritter*, which offered the almost surrealistic, otherworldly pairing of the Kenton orchestra and cowboy singing star Tex Ritter.

Kenton favored expanded brass, woodwind, and percussion sections, depending upon the nature of the project. On a number of recordings, he augmented his brass section with four "mellophones," a French horn–like instrument, and he often had his woodwind players "doubling" on other, more exotic woodwinds like the bass clarinet, the oboe, or the bass saxophone. Often, he utilized entire percussion sections in addition to the drum set player. In all of these instances, Kenton may have sought to expand the tonal palette of his bands, in accordance with the needs of each recording.

Did the ends justify the means? It depends on who you ask. Kenton fans saw him as ahead of his time—a band leader who always went his own way to create music that was truly unique and timeless. Kenton's critics, on the other hand, found his music pretentious, overblown, and extremely frilly. They also saw him as someone who arrogantly created his own "tradition," while ignoring the legacy of the great bands that came before him.

Interlude VII: Where Is Jazz Going?

One unique personal experience points not so much to Kenton's smugness as it does to his sense of humor: I was a student enrolled in the summer program at the Cincinnati Conservatory of Music in the early 1960s, and I had the opportunity to hear Kenton's band at a concert in a local amusement park. After the concert, a group of us star-struck fans were gathered around the maestro, hanging on his every word, when someone asked him, "Mr. Kenton, where is jazz going?" to which he replied, "Well, from here, we go to Cleveland." I was too young and naïve to know whether or not he was kidding . . .

To best evaluate Kenton's multidimensional approaches to big-band music, a listener would have to spend some time with it. In any case, listen and decide if you like what you're hearing, if it resonates for you. That is always the bottom line.

The mid-1950s and '60s saw big bands evolving in different, yet stimulating directions. While it may be safe to say that small groups dominated the jazz scene during those decades, it is also reasonable to suggest that big bands were alive and well, although in far smaller numbers than during the swing era.

Baritone saxophonist and sometime pianist Gerry Mulligan, while known primarily as the leader of innovative small bands, was also at the helm of one of the most unusual big bands in the history of jazz. Built around his pianoless quartet, Mulligan's 13-piece Concert Jazz Band was capable of swinging softly like the best of Count Basie's big bands but was also adept at more adventurous music. Blessed with gifted writers and arrangers such as Bob Brookmeyer, Gary McFarland, and George Russell, and with outstanding soloists such as saxophonist Zoot Sims, trombonists Willie Dennis and Brookmeyer, and trumpeters Clark Terry and Conte Candoli, as well as Mulligan himself, the New York–based Concert Jazz Band produced some of the most creative big-band music of the time. Between 1960 and 1964, the Concert Jazz Band recorded a handful of records for the Verve label before disbanding. It became economically impossible to keep the band together, and Mulligan decided to throw in the towel, even though the Concert Jazz Band was both critically acclaimed and very popular among small- and big-band listeners alike.

Another big band that garnered much critical praise in the '60s was the Thad Jones–Mel Lewis Jazz Orchestra. Comprising some of the leading studio and jazz musicians in New York City, the band made quite a sensation at its inception in 1965 at the Village Vanguard, with Jones playing cornet and conducting, and Lewis holding it all together behind the drums. Thad Jones was one of the Detroit-born Jones brothers—one of the most celebrated families in jazz history. His younger brother Elvin was a mainstay in John Coltrane's classic quartet during the '60s and is considered one of the premier jazz drummers of all time. Older brother Hank continues to be one of the most respected pianists in jazz and has recorded an enormous body of work, both as a sideman and as a leader. Thad Jones was a triple threat in that he was a gifted soloist and composer/arranger who created music that was innovative and swinging at the same time.

Mel Lewis was simply one of the best big-band drummers in the history of the music. Lewis performed and recorded with the big bands of Kenton, Mulligan, McFarland, Brookmeyer, and a multitude of others. He was known affectionately as "The Tailor," because of his ability to fuse all of the sections of a big band together into a unified body. Lewis was an affable, opinionated man who understood and respected the entire breadth and depth of his instrument and always knew the right thing to play at the right time, while either prodding a soloist or fueling the ensemble. He was one of the undisputed masters of the art of big-band drumming.

The Jones-Lewis band was what was often called "a musician's band" in that it attracted the attention of many musicians in the community, who would come out and listen to the music on the band's regular Monday nights at the Village Vanguard, or whenever else they appeared in concert, either in New York or elsewhere across the country or in Europe. Nearly all members of the band were distinctive soloists, and the band's repertoire of original compositions and creatively arranged standards attracted a sizable audience. Even though Jones passed away in 1986 and Lewis in 1990, the band—now known as the Vanguard Jazz Orchestra—continues to hold sway almost 30 years later on Monday evenings at the Village Vanguard.

While he actively led his own big bands only sporadically, it should be noted here that pianist/composer/arranger Gil Evans was one of the most masterful and innovative of all composers and arrangers. His early association with trumpeter Miles Davis on the aforementioned *Birth of the Cool* sessions, as well as his later collaborations with Davis for Columbia Records, revealed him to be a unique visionary in the world of jazz composition and orchestration. While his later work for large ensemble was quite interesting and certainly different conceptually than the music of other big bands, Evans's shimmering and evocative writing style never shone more brightly than it did on recordings by Miles Davis, like *Miles Ahead*, *Sketches of Spain*, and *Porgy and Bess*.

A number of today's big bands manage to draw from the past without replication of earlier approaches to composing or performing. Three of the best of these ensembles to be discussed are interrelated, in that the leaders of two of them are protégés of the third.

Bob Brookmeyer, about whom we've read frequently in this book, was a marvel. His long career—better yet, his path, if you will—led from boyhood Saturday matinees to hear the Count Basie Band in Kansas City, to his early work as pianist with the Claude Thornhill band in the '40s, to his long relationships from the 1950s through the '80s with jazz luminaries Gerry Mulligan and Stan Getz, Jimmy Giuffre, Thad Jones and Mel Lewis, Clark Terry, and many others. In addition to being the acknowledged master of the valve trombone (see chapter 8) and one of jazz's most recognizable soloists, Brookmeyer evolved over the last 30 years into a formidable composer, arranger, and band leader. His final ensemble, called the New Art Orchestra, is still based in Europe, and has been together since 1997. Composed of young players from Germany, America, Belgium, Norway, and the Netherlands, the 18-piece orchestra is an absolutely fearless bunch who is able to play any music Brookmeyer composed for them. At times they can sound like a wind ensemble, and at other times like a brass chorale—and of course they know how to swing. The New Art Orchestra remains a willing and valuable testimony to Brookmeyer's genius and his visionary and adventurous writing.

Interlude VIII: New Love

Jazz musicians are often a romantic lot—but instead of flowers and candy as ways of affirming love and affection, we attempt to offer heartfelt feelings through the melodies and harmonies we write, through the solos we create on the spot, and through the way we are able to make our respective instruments speak through us and for us. Oftentimes if you experience a chill walking up and down your spine when you are listening to a musical performance, chances are good that there has been a deeply affecting—yet unnamable—transaction between you and the artist making the music.

Sidney Lanier suggested that music is "love in search of a word." Perhaps a prime example of this is the New Art Orchestra's sensitive performance of a Bob Brookmeyer composition called "New Love."

This piece never gets very loud. It sounds almost like a series of sighs and whispers. The orchestra literally breathes together, and the entire effect creates quite a lush and romantic atmosphere. This is one of those pieces of music that may remind you of a time when you first fell in love, or when you've shared a moment or two of pure beauty with another person. Whether Brookmeyer intended that or not remains to be seen. As listeners, we bring all sorts of personal experiences to the act of getting inside whatever it is we are listening to. That's one of the joys of music! So let's explore this piece in a little more detail:

"New Love" begins gently with a synthesized keyboard playing a simple melody, which is first echoed by a flute and an English horn, and then restated by the bass and the brass section. It moves lazily along, with all of the wind instruments weaving in and out of one another, playfully tossing the original melody back and forth between brass and woodwind sections, until the tenor saxophone soloist (Nils van Haften) surfaces from the sea of sound. He enters softly and delicately and shares his "story" with us. Some of what he is playing at this point is actually interpreted from the musical notes on the page, while some of his solo is completely improvised and is basically an emotional reaction to the other musicians' written parts. Ultimately, he improvises completely and offers us a very personal, loving statement of the song's melody, all the while gently cushioned by the rest of the orchestra. The piece ends quietly with a brief piano passage, which just seems to evaporate into the musical mist created by the composer.

Maybe a first love is like that sometimes, too—fleeting, impermanent, yet etched forever in our memories.

Brookmeyer was also well known as a brilliant teacher and an inspiring mentor. It is no accident that two of his finest students lead their own accomplished and critically acclaimed ensembles. Maria Schneider, a native of Windom, Minnesota, studied with Brookmeyer after moving to New York City in the mid-'80s. Schneider is a petite, willowy redhead whose appearance belies her great power as both a composer and as a band leader. After graduating from the University of Minnesota, and further studies at the University of Miami and Eastman School of Music (where she earned a master of music degree in jazz writing and contemporary media), she relocated to New York and sought out Brookmeyer for further composition studies. The two became close friends, and Schneider counts her studies with Brookmeyer and her three-year apprenticeship with Gil Evans as two of the most important associations in her growth as a musical artist.

Schneider has continued her evolution as a composer and in recent years has received two Grammy Awards for her brilliant recording *Con-*

Figure 6.3.   The Maria Schneider Orchestra. Courtesy of David Kaufman.

cert in the Garden and for her composition "Cerulean Skies." She is also a commissioned composer and has written pieces for various jazz ensembles, symphony orchestras, and dance companies. Her own ensemble is made up of gifted New York musicians who interpret her music with energy, imagination, and great skill.

Another fine musician who was mentored by Bob Brookmeyer is drummer and composer John Hollenbeck. As an instrumentalist, Hollenbeck is by turns imaginative, fiery, delicate, and always in the moment. He is also deeply rooted in cutting-edge, exploratory music, whether playing in Brookmeyer's New Art Orchestra, his own Claudia Quintet, or with various large ensembles, including Jazz Bigband Gras, a group of Austria's finest jazz musicians.

As a composer, Hollenbeck, like Maria Schneider, received a grant to be able to study with Brookmeyer in the mid-1990s. His approach to composing is without boundaries and is far reaching in its scope. Hollenbeck has been the recipient of many prestigious commissions, residencies, and fellowships and has been recognized worldwide as an accomplished composer, band leader, and instrumentalist. In 2007, he was awarded a Guggenheim Fellowship. His music is attractive, yet uncategorizable, employing unconventional combinations of instruments, including cello, synthesizers, unusual percussions, and the human voice. With the latter, he has formed a fruitful and productive relationship with vocalist Theo Bleckmann, who is one of the most original and exciting singers creating music today. He is featured on Hollenbeck's critically acclaimed recording, *Joys and Desires*, along with Jazz Bigband Gras. As an example of the Hollenbeck imagination, "The Bird with the Coppery Keen Claws," the first track of *Joys and Desires*, opens with a trombonist playing a musical phrase repeatedly, accompanied by various members of the band whistling and playing what sounds like bird calls. The effect is at once sweet and mysterious, and the composition becomes a journey that is almost irresistible and joyful. Hollenbeck's music is so varied and cliché free that a listener should always expect the unexpected when listening to it.

Brookmeyer, Schneider, and Hollenbeck are three band leader/composers who represent the past, present, and future of large-ensemble music, all at once. Schneider and Hollenbeck, following in Brookmeyer's footsteps, draw from the well of tradition, synthesize it with feelings of the moment, and create music that looks squarely into the future. It is engrossing and stimulating music and shows listeners that big-band music is not a thing of the past, but a gateway to all possible futures.

7

HORN OF GABRIEL

The Trumpet

I was minding my own business when something says to me, "you ought to blow trumpet," and I have just been trying ever since.

—Miles Davis

The trumpet is to jazz what a star quarterback is to a football team. Always the most visible (or in the case of music, audible), the trumpeter often leads the charge, whether in a small group or a big band. Trumpeters in jazz ensembles have, more often than not, been the ones given the honor of playing the melody of a song, rather than one of its inner harmonies—a job usually assigned to other wind instruments. This is not to say that trombones or saxophones are not just as important as the trumpet—just as a tight end would be to football or a shortstop would be on the baseball diamond. To the contrary, the roles played by these and other instruments help to provide a firm foundation for the trumpet as it glides over the total ensemble sound. In any case, everyone works together for the good of the whole, whether it is on the bandstand or the sports team.

Interestingly enough, the first trumpets used as jazz instruments were not really trumpets at all, but cornets. The cornet was used most frequently in both brass bands and early jazz groups as well. All in all, it has a sound that is less brilliant and piercing than the trumpet—sort of like the difference between hard edges and soft, rounded surfaces. Almost all of the early players—men such as Buddy Bolden, Freddie Keppard, King Oliver, Bix Beiderbecke, and of course, Louis Armstrong—played the cornet. In fact, it was Armstrong who in 1928 switched over to the trumpet, preferring the more cutting, powerful sound of the instrument over the more rounded and burnished tone quality of the cornet.

To be able to distinguish between the trumpet and the cornet visually, have a look at both instruments on Google Images.

SOME TOOLS OF THE TRADE

In order to broaden the tone colors that could be extracted from either instrument, early trumpeters/cornetists used a variety of devices placed in the bells of their horns. These objects are called "mutes" and might be anything from ashtrays and paper bags to toilet plungers and aluminum foil, each of which is capable of producing a distinctly different sound. To see how sounds can be changed or muted, take a comb and cover it with some tissue or wax paper. Then hum a note through the paper-wrapped comb. You will likely produce a "buzzing" version of whatever note you've hummed through your homemade kazoo. Mutes operate on the same principle, in that they take whatever column of air comes through the horn and change its characteristics. Some commercially produced horn mutes are shown in figure 7.1.

Since the early days of jazz in New Orleans, brass players have always broadened their sound palettes through the use of mutes or muting devices. The New Orleans cornetist and band leader King Oliver lamented that even though muting the cornet was something he claims to have invented, he never made any money from it, since he didn't know how to patent his invention. Whether or not that story is true, the fact remains that Oliver and other early brass players used a variety of muting devices to get their instruments to "growl," to sound tinny and nasal, or to produce a "wa-wa" effect. These effects have been used through the generations as jazz trumpeters continue to explore the many sound-altering devices available to them. Most notable, of course, is Miles Davis, whose Harmon muted trumpet became a signature sound for trumpet players everywhere.

Figure 7.1.   Trumpet and cornet mutes.

"POPS"

While the trumpet and/or the cornet took the melody lead in many early jazz groups, it was really not considered a "solo" instrument until Louis Armstrong came on the scene. Since that time, it has been an indisputable fact that "Satchmo" (short for Armstrong's original nickname of "Satchel mouth") was one of the first true jazz soloists and probably the biggest influence for all succeeding generations of jazz trumpeters. As one of the two undisputed fathers of jazz trumpet (and cornet) playing—Bix Beiderbecke being the other—Armstrong was also affectionately called "Pops." Before he came on the scene, most early jazz focused upon ensemble playing with short solo statements surfacing in the midst of a lot of collective improvising. Armstrong was certainly among the first of the early jazz musicians to actually create extended solo space, in lieu of the more traditional approach of the day, which was where everyone would often solo simultaneously. In fact, you can hear what might well be the first of his astonishing recorded solo flights on a track by his Hot Five, called "West End Blues." Opening with a remarkable unaccompanied solo, he follows with the melody of the song in a slow tempo, supported by the band; then the trombonist plays a little variation, after which Satchmo returns to duet vocally with the clarinetist. An unaccompanied piano solo by Earl "Fatha" Hines follows and leads in to Armstrong's solo, which is arguably one of his most remarkable, both technically and in terms of sheer feeling.

While numerous biographies and critical studies have been published about Louis Armstrong over the years, three books stand out for the new listener to investigate. The first two are written by Armstrong himself: *Satchmo: My Life in New Orleans* (Prentice Hall, 1954) and *Louis Armstrong in His Own Words: Selected Writings* (Oxford, 1999). The third is a recent and highly regarded biography by critic Terry Teachout, simply called *Pops* (Houghton Mifflin Harcourt, 2009). All three books, as well as other notable volumes, not only present a picture of a great musician but also serve as a window in time, allowing us to step into the early years of jazz and life in New Orleans, Chicago, and New York, as we move with Satchmo from poverty and destitution through his long and amazing journey to worldwide fame and adoration.

BIX

It has been mentioned in an earlier chapter (and will undoubtedly be repeated several more times before you reach the back cover of this book) that no two jazz musicians on the same instrument sound exactly alike, nor are their approaches to rhythm and improvisation identical. In other words, put six trumpeters in a lineup and have each of them play "St. Louis Blues," and see if any two of them sound or "feel" exactly alike in their approach to the song's melody. Chances are that you will find that the sound and feeling each trumpeter produces—just like the human voice—will vary among all six players.

When listeners—especially those who are new to jazz—think of the first great jazz trumpeter, they immediately defer to Louis Armstrong, and rightfully so, since his influence as a technical virtuoso, as an astonishing soloist, and as a true jazz vocalist is far reaching. However, we can't really attribute all of this greatness to Armstrong alone. Satchmo might well be quick to tell us that Bix Beiderbecke was equally inventive and influential in the early days of jazz.

Leon Bismark "Bix" Beiderbecke was born in Davenport, Iowa, in 1903 and was completely self-taught on the cornet. He also was a proficient pianist and composed a small number of pieces for that instrument. Bix lived a short, difficult life (he died in 1931), yet he was romanticized as a brilliant, out-of-control jazz genius who, as a result of his battle with alcoholism, left us at a much-too-young age. The movie *Young Man with a Horn*, as well as the novel upon which it was based, was inspired by Bix's tragic life. Both book and film unwittingly created a stereotype of the tragic, self-destructive jazz musician that has been expanded to include such prominent figures as saxophonist Charlie Parker and trumpeter Chet Baker.

Unfortunately, this stereotype remains with us today and has expanded beyond jazz into other creative areas as well, including rock music (Kurt Cobain), art (Jean-Michel Basquiat), and literature (Jack Kerouac), leading us to believe erroneously that the lives of many artists are short, painful, and ultimately, tragic. Even though Bix's life certainly was not an easy one, it was not by any means an existence to which musicians of every era aspired, including Beiderbecke's contemporary, Louis Armstrong.

Bix's cornet sound and his approach to improvisation were unique and completely different than Armstrong's. Whereas Satchmo's sheer technical brilliance and his unabashed exuberance produced solos of great power, Beiderbecke's were less "raw" sounding and more cerebral in nature, owing largely to the fact that Bix was influenced not so much by the African American blues tradition as by European classical music, specifically the works of French impressionist composers such as Debussy and Ravel. In short, whereas Satchmo was "hot," Bix was "cool," and his thoughtful, almost introverted approach was one that would influence jazz musicians in future generations such as Chet Baker, saxophonists Lee Konitz and Paul Desmond, and even Miles Davis, in his late 1940s and '50s period.

SWING-ERA TRUMPETERS

Combining Satchmo's sheer power and sense of swing and Bix Beiderbecke's thoughtful and inventive improvisations, the trumpeters who flourished during the swing era were responsible for keeping the instrument in the jazz spotlight, mostly in big bands. For example, Count Basie's band liberally featured trumpeters Harry "Sweets" Edison (one story has it that he was so named because of his love of sweets) and Buck Clayton, both of whom were consistently excellent as soloists and team players in Basie's trumpet section. Both men played lyrical, songlike solos and emphasized creativity in improvisation over sheer technical wizardry.

Duke Ellington was also generous in spotlighting many of his musicians prominently in his compositions. Among the trumpeters he featured were Bubber Miley in the pre-swing era of the 1920s, Cootie Williams and Rex Stewart in the '30s and '40s, Ray Nance in the '40s and '50s, and Clark Terry throughout the '50s. All of these men were unique stylists who helped mold the identity of the Ellington orchestra at various times over a 40-plus-year span. Miley, for example, was the master of the "wa-wa" effect, which was essentially to put a straight mute in his horn and at the same time move a plunger back and forth to create a distinctive wa-wa sound. Later on, Cootie Williams used a plunger to create a talking, growling sound, almost like the human voice. Rex Stewart, who played the cornet more than he did the trumpet, also developed a vocal-sounding technique; however, he did so by depressing the valves of the instrument only halfway down, rather than the full distance, thereby creating compressed sound and, as a result, some startling vocal effects. And Ray Nance and Clark Terry embodied these and other techniques that came before and synthesized them into their own personal styles throughout their long and illustrious careers. Terry in particular forged a deeply personal style that combined astonishing technique with an extroverted sense of humor—qualities that make him instantly recognizable to this day.

The powerhouse trumpeter Roy "Little Jazz" Eldridge worked with many large and small swing bands and was known for his raw, passionate, inventive improvisational style and his good humor. He did some of his best work with tenor saxophonist Coleman Hawkins as well as the big band of drummer Gene Krupa.

We spoke earlier about how musicians who play the same instrument—in this case, the trumpet—often sound completely different from one another, even though their instruments are basically almost identical in construction. In the case of the trumpet or cornet, the size of the mouthpiece, the diameter of the bore, the size of the bell, and so on constitute minimal structural differences. So how is it possible, then, that five trumpet players who play basically the same instrument are able to sound so different from one another? You have to factor in the amount of air pushed through all of that piping, the blowing and tonguing techniques developed by the player, and the accuracy with which he or she

depresses the valves. But there's another factor that is not as easily identifiable. It occurs during the improvisation being created on the spot and
has to do with factors that are more emotional or spiritual than they are
technical. Remember, jazz comes from the heart as well as the mind. The
former gives the musician an opportunity to express his or her feelings,
whereas the latter provides the technique to be able to communicate
these feelings to the listener.

Interlude I: Little Jazz, Big Sound

Summer 1959: It's 2 a.m. in New York City and you find yourself having
a nightcap at an after-hours club in Midtown. The group on stage is made
up of real jazz heavyweights, including the great Coleman Hawkins (who
has often been called "the father of the tenor saxophone" but is known
more affectionately among his colleagues as "the Hawk"), and the swinging
rhythm section of guitarist Barry Galbraith, pianist Dick Hyman, bassist
Milt Hinton, and drummer Cozy Cole.

The group is midway through their second set and working over a tune
called "Sunday," when all at once, "Little Jazz" himself, trumpeter Roy Eldridge (see figure 7.2), bursts through the club's swinging doors, trumpet
in one hand, horn case in the other. Small in stature but big in personality
and masterful musicianship, he sports a straw fedora and an ear-to-ear
grin, and he exchanges enthusiastic welcomes with the guys on stage.

Naturally, he is welcomed to the bandstand immediately. Little Jazz and
the Hawk are no strangers to sharing the stage. They worked together with
many different swing-oriented aggregations and were well known throughout the world as a very distinctive front-line duo. And even though he was
considered a trumpeter whose roots were in the swing era, Little Jazz was
a significant influence upon later brassmen like Dizzy Gillespie.

Wasting no time, Little Jazz jumps in after the Hawk's solo and creates
even more excitement. If you had to use some adjectives to describe his
trumpet sound, some of these might include raspy, powerful, human-like,
gutsy, intense, and above all, swinging. Little Jazz rears back, aims his
trumpet upward, and unleashes a stream of notes, covering the full range
of his instrument, from lowdown bluesy growls, to piercing, high-pitched

Figure 7.2. Roy "Little Jazz" Eldridge. Courtesy of the William P. Gottlieb Collection.

wails—he says it all through his horn. And no one speaks the language better or in a more personal and exuberant way. The rhythm section rattles and rolls underneath him, dotting his i's and crossing his t's.

People are clapping along and dancing wherever they can find space on the small dance floor. Because the guys on stage are having such a good time, the vibe is infectious and the audience feels it, too. The joint is definitely jumpin', and the warm summer night just got a little warmer.

THE BOPPERS: TRAGEDIES AND TRIUMPHS

There were many wonderful trumpet players who came out of the bebop era, including Theodore "Fats" Navarro and Clifford Brown—both of whom left us much too early, as a result of very different circumstances. Navarro was a formidable technician and creative spirit; yet, like Bix Beiderbecke, his life was cut short in his 20s by a series of tragic events— in this case, heroin addiction and tuberculosis. Even though his star shone only briefly on the horizon, Navarro exerted a tremendous influence upon other trumpet players, notably the brilliant Clifford Brown. In fact, Fats and "Brownie" are considered by many listeners and critics to be the trumpeters who forged the hard bop style of playing. Clifford Brown's life ended tragically in his 25th year as a result of an early-morning traffic accident—a tremendous loss to the jazz community. Fortunately, both Fats and Brownie, in particular, left a legacy of recordings that have proven to be enjoyed among listeners and inspirational for generations of jazz trumpeters to follow, including Lee Morgan, Kenny Dorham, Blue Mitchell, and many others.

Naturally, when we talk about the history and appreciation of the trumpet and its role as an instrument used in jazz, we pay homage to one of the true giants of any era—John Birks "Dizzy" Gillespie (see figure 7.3). Dizzy was not only a master musician and innovator, but he also helped to create the image of jazz musician as "hipster." Actually, the persona was originally created by tenor saxophonist Lester "Prez" Young a number of years before the advent of bebop (more about Prez a few chapters from now).

Dizzy was the epitome of hipness. His beret, his Van Dyke (as seen in figure 7.3, under his chin), and his often outlandish mode of dress made him an instantly recognizable figure among musicians and audiences. Diz always presented his music with a real joie de vivre and was well loved by listeners around the globe throughout his long and distinguished career. While stylistically he was definitely unique, Dizzy combined Louis Armstrong's exuberance and humor with Roy Eldridge's intensity and power. And he, along with alto saxophonist Charlie Parker, pianist Thelonious Monk, drummer Kenny Clarke, and a few others, pioneered the new form of jazz known as bebop, creating a vital new language that continues to influence generations of jazz musicians to this day.

Figure 7.3. Dizzy Gillespie. Courtesy of the William P. Gottlieb Collection.

Interlude II: Groovin' High with Dizzy

During the school year in 1964, a group of five or six of us jazz wannabes from the University of Miami went to a local Liberty City club called the Sir John Knight Beat to see Dizzy Gillespie and his quintet play. The Sir John was a venue that booked jazz stars as well as local talent, and arranging for Dizzy Gillespie to appear there was a real coup for the club and a special treat for Miami jazz fans. I had been to live jazz concerts only a dozen or so times, and only a handful that featured nationally and internationally known talent, so this was a special treat for me—to see Dizzy Gillespie up close and personal, and in a nightclub setting rather than on the concert stage.

We arrived at the club early enough to get a great table almost in front of the bandstand. To be that close to a jazz legend was almost unbeliev-able, especially when you're an aspiring young drummer whose hopes and dreams are all about playing with guys like Dizzy Gillespie. The quintet entered the room and filed onto the bandstand, which was really not a bandstand at all, but a carpeted area only a few feet away from the first semicircular row of tables. I don't remember who the bassist was, because I was so focused on the other guys: Rudy Collins on drums, Lalo Schifrin on piano, James Moody on alto and tenor saxes, and of course, Dizzy Gil-lespie on trumpet. This was like dying and going to jazz heaven!

The lights came down and the next hour flew by like minutes. The music was exhilarating and the soloists were amazing, particularly Dizzy and Moody, both of whom played jaw-dropping solos throughout the set. In between songs, Dizzy was the congenial host and a really funny guy. I remember that Moody was his straight man and stood there stone-faced as Dizzy toyed with him—much to the delight of everyone in the room.

When the set was over, Dizzy visited with members of the audience and eventually wound up at our table. He seemed delighted to know that we were college musicians who were in the UM jazz program. When it came my turn to talk to him, I mentioned that I was the drummer in the school big band and that I also played in several small groups in club settings. With that, Dizzy invited me to come back the next day for the Sunday matinee and to sit in with his group. Needless to say, I was speechless except to say "Thank you." For the rest of the night, I was in a daze, imagining myself up there on the stand playing "Groovin' High" with Dizzy and Moody. It was almost too much to bear and I couldn't wrap myself around it. To this day, it remains the most exciting and terrifying musical invitation I've ever had.

I woke up the next morning sweating, and it was not because of the Miami heat. It was only about four hours until the matinee set at the Sir John and my chance to play with two of jazz's greatest musicians. I had an entire flock of butterflies in my stomach, and when my parents wanted to know why I was acting so edgy, I was unable to explain, since neither of

Figure 7.4.   Dizzy Gillespie and the author (age 17). Courtesy of the author.

them had any idea who Dizzy Gillespie was in the first place. So I offered no explanation, other than that I was worried about an upcoming test or something equally inane.

The long and the short of it was that after vacillating about going to the club, I opted not to go. I figured that Dizzy was just being kind and didn't really think that I would actually show up, drumsticks in hand, ready to burn up the stage with my fiery drumming. On some level, I knew that I was nowhere near ready to play with those guys, and that if that's what I truly aspired to do, I would have to practice a whole hell of a lot more to even begin to approach that level of mastery.

But to this day miles and years later, I still wonder what it would've been like to play "Groovin' High" with one of the greatest icons in jazz, and certainly one of its finest trumpeters.

MILES AND MILES OF MILES!

There are really no words adequate to describe the phenomenon of Miles Davis. For many of us, his contributions to jazz stand as almost immeasurable, and his influence from generation to generation, beginning with the bebop era, has been immense. Miles never sat still. He was always interested in moving forward and exploring new forms of musical expression. Among his many accomplishments, Miles Davis

- Played alongside bebop innovator Charlie Parker in the mid-'40s
- Was instrumental in creating the genre known as "cool" jazz with arranger Gil Evans, on the *Birth of the Cool* recordings in the late '40s
- Recorded and released *Kind of Blue* (1959), which is considered to be one of the greatest jazz recordings of all time, which introduced "modal" improvisation (basing solos on musical scales or "modes," rather than chords)
- Led two of the most famous and influential small groups in jazz history in the '50s and '60s, featuring such jazz icons as saxophonists John Coltrane and Wayne Shorter, pianists Red Garland and Herbie Hancock, bassists Paul Chambers and Ron Carter, and drummers Philly Joe Jones, Jimmy Cobb, and Tony Williams

- Was the featured soloist, beginning in the late '50s, on a series of classically influenced orchestral recordings composed and/or arranged by Gil Evans (*Miles Ahead, Sketches of Spain, Porgy and Bess,* and *Quiet Nights*)
- Pioneered jazz-rock fusion in the mid-'60s through the mid-'70s, with the creation and release of recordings like *Filles de Kilimanjaro, In a Silent Way,* and the marathon *Bitches Brew* sessions of the late '60s
- Returned to playing and recording in 1981 after a six-year hiatus, leading a variety of jazz-rock bands throughout the '80s
- Fused jazz with hip-hop music, recording the album *Doo-Bop* with hip-hop artist Easy Mo Bee in early 1991, less than a year before his untimely death

It's easy to see the amazing trajectory of Miles Davis's career by examining his enormous recorded output, from his earliest recordings with Charlie Parker through his final recordings released after his death in 1991. Here's how I introduce Miles Davis to my Jazz Experience classes: I begin with Miles's recording of "Bye, Bye Blackbird," which was recorded by his first great quintet in the mid-'50s. Besides asking the class to note that he is using a Harmon mute to give the trumpet a compressed, metallic sound,

Figure 7.5.   Miles Davis with Charlie Parker, 1947. Courtesy of the William P. Gottlieb Collection.

I also ask my students what kind of "feeling" or "vibe" Miles might be creating during his solo. The answers I get usually include "cool," "laid back"—and one student suggested the color blue, rather than a feeling (Miles might have liked that).

In terms of his sound and approach, Miles was less influenced by powerful trumpet players like Louis Armstrong, Roy Eldridge, and Dizzy Gillespie than he was by pianist Ahmad Jamal's subtle improvisations and his use of simplicity and space between phrases; by his friend and mentor Clark Terry's elegant improvisations on both trumpet and fluegelhorn; and possibly even by Bix Beiderbecke's introverted approach to playing the cornet in the early days of jazz. Miles often played in a spare, economical, and perhaps romantic way. This is not to say that he couldn't play intense, white-hot solos when the occasion called for it, as evidenced by his classic quintet recordings in the 1950s and '60s or his fusion recordings that came afterward. Miles Davis could do anything; however, he is probably best remembered for his "sound" and the feeling that that sound gave many of his listeners, particularly on ballads.

Interlude III: Blue in Green

One evening, in the second of our two discussions about the importance of Miles Davis, I tried an experiment with my Jazz Experience students: I dimmed the house lights to the point of semidarkness, and asked that they be completely quiet. At that point, I played Miles's recording of "Blue in Green," one of the ballads from Miles's classic recording *Kind of Blue*.

As the track played, you could have heard a pin drop in that room. Forty-two people were completely absorbed in the listening process, even as the final notes of Bill Evans's piano and Paul Chambers's bowed bass faded into the air. Now this was pretty amazing, especially since the class was made up of a really diverse group: all ages, ethnicities, and musical interests. Yet, there they all were—completely speechless, even in the seconds after "Blue in Green" ended. The silence was broken by a sigh from one end of the room and what sounded like a sob from the other. After a moment, I asked my students to describe how the music made them feel, or what thought it brought to mind. Here were some of the responses:

Loneliness
Sadness over losing someone or something
Longing for something or someone
Two people holding each other close, dancing under a starry sky
The moon setting over the Pacific Ocean
A first kiss
Saying goodbye to someone

The students were fascinated and moved by the music and how it made them feel; even those whose musical orientation was purely rock or hip-hop. Miles Davis brought all of us squarely into that moment in time and space when music transfixes us and transports us all to places we've never been, either in our hearts or imaginings. Such is the power of music—and of Miles Davis.

And so, as part of the jazz experience, I encourage YOU, dear reader, to try this at home. Download "Blue in Green" onto your mp3 player, put on your headphones, sit back in the dark, or, better yet, somewhere under a starry sky, and immerse yourself in blues and greens. This will be where the jazz experience and the life experience become inseparable.

When pianist Keith Jarrett was playing in one of Miles Davis's bands in the '70s, he had occasion to ask the trumpeter why he never played ballads anymore. Miles replied that he no longer played ballads because he loved them too much. That may seem like a strange answer, yet Miles staunchly refused to revisit his earlier successes or musical endeavors; he preferred instead to move only forward into other realms of musical expression. Perhaps that is one of the reasons that Miles Davis will always be considered as one of jazz's true giants.

UNSUNG HEROES OF THE TRUMPET

While Dizzy, Clifford Brown, and Miles Davis certainly made their mark as world-class trumpeters in the bebop era and beyond, there were many other fine jazz stylists who are worth listening to as well. While not one of those three, Lee Morgan (1938–1972) was certainly one of the most individualistic of all. His brassy, exuberant, swaggering sound graced many fine recordings by Art Blakey and the Jazz Messengers, and he played on the legendary *Blue Train* sessions—John Coltrane's only album on the venerable Blue Note label. It was also on this label that Morgan recorded many of his finest records as a leader, including *The Sidewinder*, one of the earliest and most successful examples of playing jazz with a boogaloo beat.

Whereas Lee Morgan was on one side of the coin, trumpeter/fluegelhornist Art Farmer (1928–1999) was on the flip side. Farmer's sound, as compared to Morgan's, was like the difference between a butterfly and a bee. His tone was light and airy, and his solos songlike and lyrical. Farmer was one of the earliest of trumpeters to liberally use the fluegelhorn, and at one point, he abandoned the trumpet altogether in favor of the larger and mellower-sounding horn.

Deserving much more recognition than he ever received, Kenny Dorham (1924–1972) combined Morgan's energetic playing with Farmer's singsong lyricism. He was also a fine composer whose compositions (like the jam session favorite "Blue Bossa") are favorites in the jazz repertoire. One little known fact about Dorham was that he was also a good singer. His vocal album *This Is the Moment* (Riverside Records) surprised a lot of listeners and critics alike and added another dimension in which listeners could appreciate his gifts.

Like those mentioned thus far, Clark Terry is completely in a class by himself and is instantly recognizable to many experienced jazz listeners. A virtuoso on both the trumpet and the fluegelhorn and a product of the rich St. Louis, Missouri, music scene, Clark has been active in jazz for over seven decades. He has been extremely well recorded and has been one of the most beloved of all jazz artists, with over 900 recordings to his credit, as well as memorable musical associations with Count Basie, Duke Ellington, Quincy Jones, Dizzy Gillespie, Thelonious Monk, Bob Brookmeyer, Gerry Mulligan, Sarah Vaughan, Ella Fitzgerald, and countless others. Clark is also an NEA Jazz Master and a legendary jazz educator. And as if that weren't enough, he is also a wonderful blues singer and—like Louis Armstrong—a great scat singer. Listen to his recording of "Mumbles," and you will see what I mean. It is infectiously funny, swinging, and is all Clark. At this writing, Clark is 92 years young and still making his wonderful presence known as one of jazz's true treasures. I worked with Clark years ago in Washington, D.C., and got to witness his genius, humor, and great humanity, up close and personal on the bandstand. If there is an essence to our music, it is certainly well represented by Clark Terry.

Trumpeters Blue Mitchell (1930–1979) and Donald Byrd (1932–2013) both recorded extensively as leaders for both Blue Note and Riverside records in the late '50s through the '60s. Both trumpeters were also very much in demand on the New York jazz scene. Mitchell was a mainstay for a number of years in the Horace Silver Quintet, and Byrd played with everyone from John Coltrane to Thelonious Monk. Each man's approach to playing was similar to the other; both were inventive and thoughtful soloists whose body of recorded work was consistently excellent.

Three forward-thinking trumpeters on the scene beginning in the late '50s were Booker Little, Don Ellis, and Don Cherry. While all three were grounded in the language of bebop, each man was a restless and creative seeker of new ways to approach composition and improvisation—in other words, to expand the vocabulary and language of jazz. Booker Little (1938–1961) was a gifted composer and a unique soloist whose graceful, flowing, melodic improvisations made him easily identifiable among his peers. Unfortunately, Little died of uremia in his midtwenties, and was never able to reach his full potential as one of jazz's truly original trumpet stylists.

When one thinks of Don Ellis (1934–1978), the word "fearless" comes to mind. Never one to play it safe stylistically, Ellis was deeply influenced by the avant-garde composer John Cage and others who broke away radically from both 20th-century classical and jazz conventions. Late in his career, Ellis also led one of the most exciting and original big bands in jazz history. Utilizing three bass players and three drummers, Ellis wrote impossibly complex music that utilized odd rhythms and fiery ensemble passages and featured a number of fine soloists, including Ellis himself.

Finally, Don Cherry (1936–1995) was perhaps the most original and innovative trumpeter of his generation. A member of Ornette Coleman's groundbreaking quartet in the late '50s, Cherry played pocket cornet (a miniature cornet) and was equally skilled in playing bebop and avant-garde jazz. It's also important to note that Cherry was one of the first American jazz musicians—if not the first—to embrace the music of other cultures and blend it with jazz improvisation, often to stunning effect. In addition to the pocket cornet, Cherry studied and performed on a variety of exotic instruments like wooden flutes and a stringed instrument native to Mali, called a douss'n gouni. In retrospect, it is appropriate to suggest that Don

Cherry was one of the first American practitioners to integrate what we now call "world music" with jazz, initiating a many-faceted hybrid music that continues to evolve to this day in many places in the world.

Another fine trumpeter worthy of mention, who like Lee Morgan was an alumnus of Art Blakey's Jazz Messengers, as well as a Blue Note artist, was Freddie Hubbard (1938–2008). He was a superb technician hailing from Indianapolis, and his solos were fiery and adventurous. It's also important to note that his breadth of experience was impressive. In addition to his many fine recordings as a leader for Blue Note, Impulse, CTI, and other major jazz record labels, Hubbard recorded with saxophonists Sonny Rollins, John Coltrane, Ornette Coleman, and Eric Dolphy.

One of the most influential trumpeters for generations of trumpet players to come was Woody Shaw (1944–1989), who hailed from a small town in North Carolina. While Shaw was well grounded in the bebop tradition, his interest in classical music, as well as Indian, Japanese, and Indonesian music, propelled him into a lifelong exploration of how best to utilize all that he was hearing into his own compositions and improvisations. Shaw also expressed an interest in avant-garde jazz, no doubt stemming in part from his early association with multi-instrumentalist Eric Dolphy (who will be discussed in several other chapters of this book). In addition to his many recordings as a leader, Woody Shaw also recorded with many great musicians, including Dolphy, Art Blakey's Jazz Messengers, fellow trumpeter Freddie Hubbard, tenor saxophonist Joe Henderson, and pianists Horace Silver and Chick Corea.

THE NEXT GENERATION: HORNS OF PLENTY

As you can see, in jazz's 100-year history, there has never been a shortage of great jazz trumpeters. The post-bop generation proves to be no exception. First and foremost in terms of national and international visibility is New Orleans–born Wynton Marsalis. A prodigious musician even as a teenager, Wynton grew up as a member of an extraordinarily talented musical family. His father Ellis is an accomplished pianist, and his brothers, most notably saxophonist Branford, are all excellent jazz musicians. Wynton is also a Pulitzer Prize–winning composer and a fine classical trumpeter as well. His approach to jazz is steeped in tradition, and he is not afraid to integrate one genre of music with another. For example, one of his most recent recordings pairs him with country music legend Willie Nelson, while another finds him engaged in classical duets with soprano Kathleen Battle and keyboardist Anthony Newman. His sheer breadth of musical experiences and interests is quite impressive, and he currently brings all of these into play as the artistic director of Jazz at Lincoln Center in New York City.

Other great trumpeters, while not as widely recognized as Wynton Marsalis, are nonetheless consummate artists. Randy Brecker is one of the inner circle of post-bop trumpeters who has the technique and imagination to play beautifully in any setting, from acoustic jazz to rhythm and blues to fusion jazz. He has been a consistently in-demand player since arriving on the New York scene in 1966, and he has lent his considerable abilities to a wide variety of groups, including the one he co-led with his late brother, the brilliant saxophonist Michael Brecker. Randy is also a prominent jazz educator and has offered master classes at colleges and universities throughout America.

Wallace Roney was a protégé of Miles Davis and is another excellent trumpet stylist worth hearing. Mentored by Davis, Roney was invited by the great trumpeter to perform with him shortly before his death in 1991, at the Montreux Jazz Festival. After Miles's passing, Roney toured with Wayne Shorter, Herbie Hancock, Ron Carter, and Tony Williams—all members of Miles's second great quintet—and recorded the Grammy-winning *A Tribute to Miles* with them. He also performed and recorded with two legendary master drummers: Art Blakey and Tony Williams. Since that time, Roney has been very prolific as a leader and has also lent his talents to a wide variety of musicians and singers. For an extensive and very interesting profile of Wallace Roney, search Google for writer Stanley Crouch's essay in the September 24, 2000, edition of the *New York Times*.

A peer of Wallace Roney who has also received much well-deserved acclaim is trumpeter Roy Hargrove. Born in Waco, Texas, in 1969, he began playing trumpet in the fourth grade and ultimately continued his studies at Berklee College of Music in Boston and the New School in Manhattan. Hargrove recorded his first solo project for the RCA/Novus label at the age of 21 and has recorded many CDs since that time.

If one had to pick adjectives to describe Hargrove, they might include these: restless, curious, imaginative, and limitless. He has not ever limited himself to one genre of jazz or, for that matter, to any musical genre. For example, one of his CDs pairs him with some of jazz's greatest saxophonists

(*With the Tenors of Our Time*), and another finds him leading a Latin jazz group called "Crisol," featuring some of Cuba's finest musicians (the Grammy-winning Habana). As if this weren't enough, Hargrove also leads a big band, as well as a group called "The RH Factor," which blends jazz with contemporary hip-hop and R & B.

On his website, Hargrove offers some insight into his approach to the art of presenting jazz and the challenge of connecting with his audiences: "What do we have to offer in the world of jazz today? It's about being innovative, which is cool. But innovation right now will come in music that's swinging and feels good. It's meaningless if it doesn't make you feel something."

There are many other accomplished trumpet players who have established themselves both nationally and globally. A short list of these include Americans Terrell Stafford, Tim Hagans, Terence Blanchard, Tom Harrell, and Clay Jenkins; Italian-Swiss trumpeter Franco Ambrosetti; Poland's Tomasz Stanko; Italy's Enrico Rava; Cuba's Arturo Sandoval; and Germany's Till Bronner. All are creating music that is very much worth experiencing, so don't hesitate to listen to samples of their music on amazon .com as well as on their respective websites.

A LITTLE PRELUDE TO THE FUTURE

Jazz musicians don't become "established" overnight. Putting their music out there for the listening public takes a lot of work. All of the trumpeters profiled thus far put in a lot of time and effort to present their music—in both the recording studio and on the bandstand. In the best possible cases, they are supported in their efforts by record labels, which take care of product distribution, promotional materials, and sometimes even tour and concert bookings.

This next group of trumpeters represents not only what's happening today in the world of jazz trumpet playing, but each also validates the potential of a healthy future for newer players on every instrument. In fact, the following brief comments and observations apply to younger musicians mentioned in every instrumental chapter, as well as many other players from previous generations:

Because times are changing as this is being written, jazz musicians who are working to present their music do not often have the benefit of "industry support," largely because the music industry itself is undergoing tremendous changes. With the advent of the Internet, we have seen the demise of large record stores such as Tower Records and Virgin Records, as well as a decrease in CD sales and a significant increase in the sale of downloaded music from a variety of online sources. As a result of these and other factors, musicians are now responsible for subsidizing, recording, editing & mixing, manufacturing, distributing, and promoting their music—and making the listening public aware of their existence! This is an enormous task for jazz musicians to take on, largely because jazz is not pop music and is not too often bolstered by corporate machinery, personal representation, and lots of hype.

INTO THE FUTURE:
DISCOVERING THREE NEW TRUMPET VOICES

Obviously, this listing—like others in this book—is not all inclusive. The idea is to point new listeners in the right direction: to visit the artists' websites, sample and download their music, contact them with questions or comments, and in general, get to know them better as both musicians and people. Many jazz musicians, younger and older, are very approachable and quite accommodating in this regard.

Here are profiles of three trumpeters who, by virtue of their musicianship and respective (and very different) musical visions, are moving jazz trumpet squarely into the 21st century:

Trumpeter Dave Douglas knows all about "pointing listeners in the right direction." Even though he really doesn't qualify as a "new face" in jazz (he's been active on the jazz scene in New York since the mid-'80s), Douglas has achieved prominence in the contemporary, "postmodern" jazz world for two reasons: his abundant musical abilities and his understanding of ways in which to harness the power of the Internet to promote his music. As a result, he has earned praise both nationally and globally, and he has won many awards for his contributions to the music, including the prestigious Guggenheim Fellowship in 1995.

It was also during that same year that Douglas launched Greenleaf Music, his own record label and website, to promote his and others' musical projects, including recordings, concert presentations, and tours. He currently leads a number of ensembles, each quite different from the other, and he is also a commissioned composer for ensembles, both small and large.

As a trumpeter, Douglas's playing is steeped in a number of traditions. His sound is bold and bright and is somewhat reminiscent of both Don Ellis and Booker Little. Even so, he is his own man stylistically and is comfortable in any setting from post-bop and avant-garde to chamber music and music for film. He is also an affable and accessible man who appreciates and values his listening public, as evidenced by his website and his accessibility to fans and, in this case, authors!

Like Dave Douglas, trumpeter Ralph Alessi has become a mainstay on the New York scene. A highly individualistic improviser, Alessi is the son of classical trumpeter Joe Alessi and opera singer Maria Leone. As his website indicates, "Ralph himself freelanced as a classical player as he was coming up through the ranks." Indeed, the classical influence seems to pervade his sound and approach on the instrument. Alessi favors a pure sound and long tones, although his command and execution of rapid and complex lines is very much in evidence throughout his recorded work. Also, one quality that makes him easily identifiable is his command of the trumpet's lower register. Alessi can move from the dark bottom of the horn through a rich, buttery middle register, then up to crystal clear sonorities in a heartbeat, creating solo statements that are both intriguing and exciting.

Like trumpeters Terrell Stafford, Clay Jenkins, and others, Ralph Alessi is committed to music education, as evidenced by his past and present involvement with a variety of reputable colleges and universities, including Eastman School of Music and New York University. He is also the founder and guiding light of the School for Improvisational Music, a nonprofit organization based in Brooklyn.

Cornetist Graham Haynes comes from noble jazz lineage. His father is the legendary drummer Roy Haynes, whose illustrious career has spanned over 65 years and whose virtuosity has enabled him to make music with Lester Young, Charlie Parker, Sarah Vaughan, Thelonious Monk, John Coltrane, and countless others. Suffice it to say that the younger Haynes has grown up in a musical environment perhaps second to none.

Even so, Graham Haynes has forged his own very musical path. Like Dave Douglas and Ralph Alessi, Haynes is a multidimensional artist and, judging by his recorded work and live performances, an infinitely curious man. He is not only a fine musician but also a composer and producer, and his areas of interest and experience beyond jazz include classical, electronic, and world music. For example, Haynes spent a considerable amount of time in the late '80s studying African, Arabic, and South Asian musical forms, and the next decade found him exploring the synthesis of jazz, electronic, and world music, with contemporary hip-hop. Somehow he has managed to integrate these into the jazz milieu without sacrificing the integrity of any of them.

As a cornet and fluegelhorn player, Haynes's sound is sometimes reminiscent of Miles Davis, particularly from the latter trumpeter's "electric" period when he was enhancing and extending the sound of the instrument with the aid of synthesizers and other sound reinforcement devices. Another Haynes influence would perhaps be Don Cherry, whose love of multicultural musical explorations was inspiring to a lot of musicians looking for ways to expand their approaches to jazz.

Dave Douglas's, Ralph Alessi's, and Graham Haynes's musical frontiers are quite broad, which means that we as listeners can expect much more exciting and provocative music from them in years to come. Even so, there are still other fine trumpeters who are worth your time: Ingrid Jensen from the Pacific Northwest is a beautifully evocative player who leads large and small ensembles and performs both nationally and internationally; Steven Bernstein is a denizen of New York and a wildly eclectic and energetic band leader, composer, arranger, and soloist on both the trumpet and its cousin, the slide trumpet; and finally, Ambrose Akinmusire from Oakland, California, is a trumpeter of immense imagination, skill, and potential. His 2011 Blue Note release, *When the Heart Emerges Glistening*, received rave reviews from all corners of the jazz world, and his is a name to watch in coming years.

In summary, today's trumpeters carry on the legacy of the great players who came before them; yet, while each has a firm grasp of the jazz tradition, all continue to offer us glimpses of jazz's future—a music without boundaries. Stay tuned!

Getting Personal with Dave Douglas

What advice would you offer a new listener who will be experiencing your music for the first time, either in concert or via one of your recordings?

Drop your preconceptions about the artist and the music. Listen for fresh combinations of melody, harmony, rhythm, timbre, and density, and a variety of connections to tradition, innovation, and community. By community I mean WHO is playing and WHERE their sound emanates from, and how that impacts the musical results. Accept that the joys of the music may come in unexpected ways. Or not. Allow yourself to be moved. Search for the story in the music.

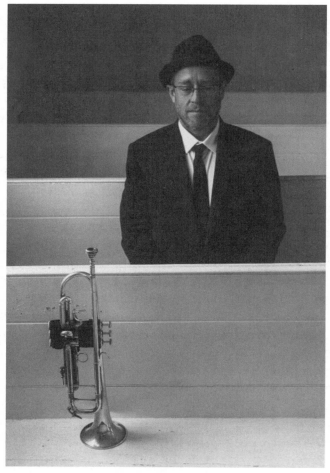

Figure 7.6.   Dave Douglas. Courtesy of Austin Nelson.

What would be the first recording of yours that you would recommend for an initial listening experience and as a good introduction to your music?

In Our Lifetime, by the Dave Douglas Sextet, written and recorded thinking of the great trumpeter and composer Booker Little. Booker Little had a short and brilliant career, playing with Max Roach, Eric Dolphy, and Sonny Rollins and re-cording a series of visionary sextet pieces before tragically succumbing to uremia at the age of 23 in 1961.

SELECTED TRUMPETERS' WEBSITES

Louis Armstrong: www.satchmo.net
Bix Beiderbecke: www.bixsociety.org
Dizzy Gillespie: www.dizzygillespie.com
Miles Davis: www.milesdavis.com
Freddie Hubbard: www.freddiehubbardmusic.com
Woody Shaw: www.woodyshaw.com
Randy Brecker: www.randybrecker.com
Wynton Marsalis: www.wyntonmarsalis.org
Wallace Roney: www.wallaceroney.com
Nicholas Payton: www.nicholaspayton.com
Terence Blanchard: www.terenceblanchard.com
Dave Douglas: www.greenleafmusic.com
Ralph Alessi: www.ralphalessi.com

RECOMMENDED READING

Sandke, Randy. "The Trumpet in Jazz." *The Oxford Companion to Jazz*. Ed. Bill Kirchner. New York: Oxford UP, 2000. Print.
Yanow, Scott. *Trumpet Kings*. San Francisco: Backbeat Books, 2001. Print.

Bix Beiderbecke

Sudhalter, Richard M., Philip R. Evans, and William Dean-Myatt. *Bix: Man and Legend*. New Rochelle: Arlington House, 1974. Print.

Miles Davis

Carr, Ian. *Miles Davis: The Definitive Biography*. New York: Thunder's Mouth Press, 1998. Print.
Davis, Miles, with Quincy Troupe. *Miles: The Autobiography*. New York: Simon & Schuster, 1989. Print.
Troupe, Quincy. *Miles and Me*. Berkeley and Los Angeles: U of California P, 2000. Print.

Dizzy Gillespie

Gillespie, Dizzy, and Al Fraser. *To Be or Not to Bop: Memoirs by Dizzy Gillespie*. Garden City: Doubleday, 1979. rpt. Cambridge: Da Capo Press, 1985. Print.

Lee Morgan

McMillan, Jeffery S. *DelightfuLee: The Life and Music of Lee Morgan*. Jazz Perspectives Series 12. Ann Arbor: U of Michigan P, 2008. Print.

Clark Terry

Terry, Clark, and Gwen Terry. *Clark: An Autobiography*. Berkeley and Los Angeles: U of California P, 2011. Print.

8

RASPY, GASPY, SMOOTH, AND SILKY

The Trombone

When I first saw a trombone, it looked like the instrument no sane person would want to play, so I immediately found my niche.

—Delfeayo Marsalis

The trombone seems to have forever been the butt of jokes among musicians. For example, in the world of classical music, there is some dispute
as to whether Richard Strauss or Richard Wagner offered this advice to
orchestra conductors: "Don't look at the trombone players—you will only
encourage them." Or this old joke:

Question: How do you get a trombone to sound better?

Answer: Run over it with a truck.

Along with musical instruments like the tuba, the banjo, and particularly
the accordion, the trombone has been the recipient—or some would say,
the victim—of a lot of degrading humor. Why this should be is anybody's
guess; however, all of the lampooning is usually generated as good fun
among musicians and not as proof positive of the instrument's inferiority.
Quite the opposite; the trombone is the instrument whose sound quality,
range, and resonance are the most similar to the human voice.

A LITTLE TROMBONE HISTORY

Tracing the origins of the trombone is an interesting journey. The first trombones were called "sackbuts," which translates loosely as to "push" and to "pull"—what a slide trombonist does when pushing the slide away, then pulling it back toward the horn. These sliding instruments relied upon a number of different slide positions to change notes and pitches. The first ancestors of the slide trombone came into existence sometime in the 13th century and became more prominent in the 14th century when they were employed in church ensembles and wind bands. Ultimately, the trombone found its way into orchestras, brass choirs, and of course, jazz bands.

Early in its history, the trombone appeared in a variety of forms. The two we see and hear most often today in orchestral music and jazz are the tenor trombone and its slightly larger cousin, the bass trombone; however, many early ensembles also included soprano trombones and alto trombones, both of which still appear from time to time in orchestras throughout the world.

Another member of the trombone family is the valve trombone, which utilizes trumpet-like valves rather than a slide. If you had short arms and couldn't reach any of the outlying positions on the slide trombone, then the valve trombone would be a lot more negotiable. Valve trombones made their first appearance in the 1800s in Europe and gained prominence in America during the Civil War. In the early days, one would see and hear them in military brass bands, territory bands, marching bands, and later, in jazz bands.

In the earliest forms of jazz, the trombone—like the tuba—was usually relegated to a supporting role. Whereas the tuba, banjo, and drums played the rhythm, the trombone often provided a "middle voice"—that is, the harmony and a countermelody in support of the cornet (which played the melody) and the clarinet (which provided the "obbligatos" or musical commentary above the cornet lines). The trombone, by its very vocal nature, often also produces sounds we think of as human sounds. So in an early jazz setting, it was not unusual to hear growls, raspy slides moving from one note up or down to the next, and an assortment of bleets and smears underneath any given melody, fast or slow.

THE TAILGATE TROMBONE

The colorful history of the trombone in jazz begins with what was (and is still) called "tailgate" trombone. In the early days of the music, jazz bands would often pile onto the back of wagons, and later flatbed trucks, and would rumble down the street and provide live music for the townsfolk, usually in order to promote a dance or a seasonal celebration. Because of the nature of his instrument, the trombonist needed a lot of room to extend his slide so as not to hit another musician with it; so, as a result, he was relegated to sitting on the back of the vehicle, out of harm's way, where he could extend the slide as far as necessary—hence, the name "tailgate."

EARLY 'BONES

There were a few really notable trombone players in the early days of jazz. Among the earliest and most memorable were Kid Ory and Miff Mole. Edward "Kid" Ory was born in 1886 in Louisiana and began to make a name for himself in his mid-'20s. Ory was a fiery player whose solos were filled with growls, smears, and a rough and earthy quality that was joyous and infectious. Ultimately, Ory migrated to Chicago to join cornetist King Oliver's band. It was in that band that he worked with Louis Armstrong and began what was to become a long relationship with the great trumpeter, playing in both Armstrong's Hot Five and Hot Seven groups.

Irving "Miff" Mole may well be jazz's first great white trombonist. A contemporary of Ory, Mole approached the trombone in a completely different way, emphasizing technique rather than boisterousness, smoothness over rawness. He had an exceptional range from high to low notes and could execute difficult melodic patterns flawlessly. As a result of his technical abilities, Mole became one of jazz's first "studio" trombonists; that is, he worked in studio bands for a number of radio stations, as well as for NBC. He was also a significant influence upon a number of trombonists to come, most notably Tommy Dorsey and Jack Teagarden. Both Dorsey and Teagarden would go on to achieve legendary status as well, the former as a big band trombonist/leader and the latter as another of jazz's early trombone greats.

Tommy Dorsey, like Miff Mole, was an impressive technician and an excellent soloist; however, he organized a big band and gradually moved away from jazz and into the realm of commercial music, with his most famous hit being a ballad called "I'm Getting Sentimental over You," which featured his silky smooth trombone voice, recognizable even today. Even though he made a stylistic shift from jazz into commercial dance music, Dorsey populated his band with great jazz musicians such as drummer Buddy Rich, trumpeter Charlie Shavers, and clarinetist Buddy DeFranco, all of whom he featured over the years of the band's existence.

Jack Teagarden as a trombonist is the stuff of legend. Born in 1905 in Vernon, Texas, and raised in Oklahoma, Teagarden, or "Big T," one of the nicknames he was eventually called, received his first trombone at age seven and a scant nine years later auditioned for and won a place in the Peck Kelley band. His style was markedly different than other so-called

Figure 8.1.   Jack "Big T" Teagarden. Courtesy of the William P. Gottlieb Collection.

Dixieland trombonists, since it was smoother and more harmonically advanced. And there was nothing rough or raspy about his approach to the instrument. As a child, Teagarden was exposed to Negro spirituals and country blues—two genres of music that helped define his approach to the trombone's sound and to soloing. Certain critics have called Teagarden the "King of the Blues Trombone," as a result of these rural influences.

Along with his technical prowess on the horn, Teagarden—like Louis Armstrong—was an exceptional jazz singer. His style was easygoing and deceptively lazy sounding, even though his phrasing, pitch, and delivery were near perfect. In fact, in 1947 Teagarden was invited by the great trumpeter to be a part of his group, and for four years, they played, sang, and toured together. Satchmo indicated more than once that Teagarden was his favorite trombonist. A number of their performances may be seen on various sites on the Internet, including YouTube.

SWINGIN' 'BONES

As the swing era blossomed, so, too, did the work of a number of trombonists, who helped increase the visibility of the trombone in both large and small jazz groups. These men (and later, women) began to free themselves from the confines of Dixieland ensemble playing and raucous solo styles, and they began redefining their roles as both soloists and as members of big-band brass sections.

For the most part, swing-era trombonists had to be much better equipped than their predecessors in order to meet the musical challenges of the day. Whereas one of the roles of early jazz trombonists was to add to improvised ensemble passages, swing-era trombonists—as part of, say, a big-band trombone section—needed not only to be able to play improvised solos and read music, but also had to have the ability to blend with the two or three other trombonists in the section in order to achieve a "group" trombone sound. This meant playing in tune and reading the notes accurately and in unison with the other members of the section. Consequently, many swing-era trombonists—as well as other brass and woodwind players—brought many new skills to the jazz band that were previously unnecessary.

A classic example of this new breed of trombonists was Duke Ellington's most famous trombone section, pictured in figure 8.2.

Figure 8.2. Duke Ellington's trombones. Courtesy of the William P. Gottlieb Collection.

Each of the Duke's trombonists had a distinctive style. "Tricky Sam" Nanton was an earthy soloist whose exuberant, no-holds-barred style was immediately recognizable by fans of the Ellington band. With a musical background that was colored by the blues, "Tricky" was among the first jazz brass players to completely personalize the use of the common toilet plunger to create sounds that approximated the human voice. He would move the plunger toward and away from the bell of the horn in such a way as to sound like muttering, growling, and even laughing. Nanton would go on to influence scores of trombonists in what is definitely a warm and human approach to the instrument.

In contrast to Nanton, Lawrence Brown had a silky tone and was known for both his beautiful ballad playing and his gentle, sensitive accompaniments behind Ellington's various vocalists. But Brown could also "put the pots on" when a song called for it. His technique, especially at lightning-fast tempos, was astounding, and he made technically difficult solo passages sound effortless. Brown was also the section leader of the Ellington trombone section, and he played lead trombone on many Ellington compositions.

In addition to Nanton and Brown, Juan Tizol rounded out the trombone section. Unlike either of his section mates, Tizol played the valve trombone rather than the slide horn. While he was never really featured as a jazz soloist, Tizol was valued by Ellington for the written passages he was able to play that couldn't be executed on the slide instrument. In fact, Duke liked to write Tizol parts that could be voiced with the band's saxophone section, thereby creating a totally unique sound, rather like throwing something unexpected into a stew and making it even tastier as a result. In addition to his playing abilities, Tizol was also a noted composer and arranger and penned two of swing's most popular compositions: "Caravan" and "Perdido."

The swing era also produced a number of other fine and distinctive trombone stylists, each of whom is worth a listen. Unfortunately, we don't have enough space here to discuss each one; therefore, you may wish to explore these men and their music via both Google and YouTube: Jimmy Harrison, J. C. Higginbotham, Dicky Wells, Vic Dickenson, Trummy Young, and Bill Harris. Each had a personal and distinctive vocabulary and helped lay the foundation for future generations of trombonists.

BEBOP 'BONES

When we discussed bebop in chapter 3, we suggested that this new form of post-swing jazz lost a significant number of listeners because the music was not really intended for dancing. This was evidenced by the tendency for bebop musicians to play complex melodies and harmonies, often at breakneck tempos—much faster than any dancer could ever hope to negotiate. The reason for these new complexities was not to alienate either listeners or dancers, but as a way for musicians to challenge their individual technical skills and imaginations. Nowhere was this more of a challenge than in the case of the slide trombone, whose very construction was not geared for articulating fast passages using only a slide to do so. Unlike trumpet players, who use valves, or saxophonists, who instead of valves use keys, slide trombonists had only the use of their lips and the slide positions common to the horn. Consequently, the transition to bebop was much more technically difficult.

While there were some swing-oriented trombonists like Bill Harris and Lawrence Brown who could play very fast tempos on those occasions when they were called upon to do so, there were many more who had neither the technical skills nor the inclination to play fast tempos, largely because much swing music was played at slower, more danceable tempos. However, as is true with any art form, musicians are often very adaptable when it comes to expanding their musical horizons. Like other instrumentalists, trombonists were also interested in plumbing the depths of bebop. Two of the earliest and best bop trombonists were J. J. Johnson and Kai Winding. Johnson, often called the father of modern jazz trombone, hailed from Indianapolis and became a vital part of New York's famed 52nd Street scene, playing with the combos of Charlie Parker, Dizzy Gillespie, and many other early beboppers. He exerted a tremendous influence upon trombonists for generations and still does so today, even after his death in 2001. Winding, originally from Denmark, played mainly with big bands, including those of Benny Goodman and Stan Kenton, and was present on Miles Davis's historic *Birth of the Cool* sessions in the late '40s.

The amazing thing about Johnson and Winding is that even though they came from very different geographic and musical backgrounds, they developed very similar styles, completely independent of each other. Both had a big, warm sound and could execute complex improvisations at any tempo. Johnson, in particular, was incredibly facile, and like all great musicians, he made playing his instrument seem effortless.

Ultimately, it seemed only natural that the two should form a quintet that would showcase their individual and collective abilities. Their group—frequently known as the Jay and Kai Quintet—was popular among jazz fans in the '50s and kept the bebop fires burning into the next decade and even beyond via reissues from record companies like the excellent Mosaic Series.

Figure 8.3.   J. J. Johnson. Courtesy of Jack Vartoogian / FrontRowPhotos.

Figure 8.4. Frank Rosolino (left) and Don Menza. Courtesy of Rose Menza.

While there have been many fine trombonists who played in the bebop idiom, Frank Rosolino, Curtis Fuller, and Bob Brookmeyer stand out for a variety of reasons.

Frank Rosolino was an exciting, extroverted player whose virtuosity was almost frightening. He played the trombone in a manner that often defied the conventional limits of the instrument. His range, particularly in the upper register of the horn, was stratospheric, and his sense of swing was unparalleled. He was also a true jazz vocalist and scat singer, whose wordless solos matched the musical intensity of his trombone solos.

Interlude I: Yo-Yo

That was Frank's nickname, and it seemed to fit him to a T. A yo-yo was something we kids always had fun with, and when most of us reminisce about yo-yos, we think of good times. Having fun and playing great jazz sum up what Rosolino meant to those of us who knew the great trombonist and were fortunate enough to be on the bandstand with him.

My exposure to Yo-Yo came about in the late '70s. I had relocated to Los Angeles and was making an effort to become a part of the sprawling jazz scene, even though I knew only a handful of L.A. musicians. It was definitely an uphill climb, given that there were so many great jazz players living there; yet, I was determined to at least give it a shot and test the waters.

One day, I got a call from a friend, a great drummer named Dick Berk, who told me he was under the weather and couldn't make his gig that evening, and that he wanted me to sub for him. I was so hungry to get some exposure that I would've played in a circus band at that point. I gladly accepted the gig and asked for the particulars. Dick told me to be at a club called the Baked Potato, ready to play at 9:00 p.m. Then he sprung it on me that I'd be playing with Frank Rosolino. "You mean *the* Frank Rosolino?" I said. Dick just laughed and thanked me for helping him out.

I couldn't believe it. I used to sit in my room and play along with Frank Rosolino records. Now I was going to be on the same stage with the man, trying to keep up with his phenomenal energy. I got to the club extra early and set up the drums. The other guys ambled in close to starting time, and Rosolino came in last. Inside of a minute he unpacked his trombone, counted off a brisk tempo, and off to the races we went. No warm ups, no talk throughs; just BOOM! Straight out of the gate! I held on for dear life, my right hand bouncing off the cymbal at warp speed, as though it had a life of its own. I think that sheer nervous energy got me through that first tune, and the rest of the evening as well. Yo-Yo smiled a lot that night—although in retrospect, I don't think I ever saw him get angry or even frown. He always seemed to be up, and ready with a humorous story. And he played that way, too—joyously and with every bit of the energy I remembered from his records. We became friends after that night, and I used to go over to his house and jam with him and other great musicians on those hot, dry California days. It was nirvana, and he seemed to really enjoy those afternoons. Unfortunately, tragedy struck hard for Frank and his family. I still play the recordings now and then, often as a reminder to myself that one of the reasons we play this music is for the pure joy of pushing the notes out into the air and bouncing them back and forth between us, telling our stories until it's time to go . . .

Curtis Fuller has often been wrongly described as a disciple of J. J. Johnson. While there is a similarity in their sound, Fuller is very much his own man. A native of Detroit—a hotbed for jazz talent like bassist Paul Chambers and the musical Jones family (pianist Hank, cornetist Thad, and drummer Elvin)—Fuller came to national prominence after moving to New York City in the '50s. Fuller was a featured player on John Coltrane's legendary Blue Note recording, *Blue Train*, in 1957 and became a familiar fixture on many other jazz records at the time. While he was a member of a number of notable jazz groups beginning in the mid-'50s, Fuller became a household name among seasoned jazz fans as a member of Art Blakey's Jazz Messengers, as well as a leader in his own right, during the next decade.

As a trombonist, Curtis Fuller has been praised for his very relaxed and smooth sound and tremendous command of his instrument. In every musical situation from Coltrane to Blakey, he was the perfect foil in that his solos—even over complex chord changes—were models of cool control. Fuller could also solo with the same relaxed approach at ridiculously fast tempos, as evidenced by his amazing solo on the title track of his 1973 album, *Crankin'*.

He went on to play with Count Basie's band in the '70s and, after resolving some medical issues, has continued to play and record today with many notable jazz groups. It's been said that Fuller, like his solos, is a relaxed and affable man—always the professional as well as a model of solid artistry.

Bob Brookmeyer (see figure 8.5) has been considered by many critics and fans alike to be the undisputed master of the valve trombone. He became well known originally through his work as both a trombonist and as a composer/arranger in the 1950s and '60s with saxophonists Stan Getz and Gerry Mulligan. Brookmeyer's style is almost uncategorizable, in that he draws from numerous musical sources. For instance, even though he has acknowledged a debt to trombonists Bill Harris and Brad Gowans (the latter a valve trombonist from the ranks of traditional jazz musicians), Brookmeyer was mightily influenced by tenor saxophonist Lester "Prez" Young, whose long, flowing melodic solos were models of spontaneous invention. He was also influenced as a whole by the Kansas City jazz scene of the 1930s and '40s and most notably by the freewheeling yet disciplined swing of the Count Basie band, whom he saw numerous times when his father took him to matinee concerts at the local theater.

Perhaps Brookmeyer's best-loved period, stylistically, was from the late '50s through the '60s, when his solos, though couched in the language of

Figure 8.5. Bob Brookmeyer. Courtesy of and copyright Herman Leonard Photography, LLC.

both swing and bebop, became quite "vocalized." He was a funky, puckish soloist who through the use of half-valve effects (depressing the valve only halfway down) could approximate the sound of the human voice. It was not unusual to hear a Brookmeyer solo punctuated with growls, smears, roars, and whinnies—much like some of the trombonists from earlier eras. It was a totally unique approach and breathed life into the instrument in a way that was unique, resonant, and very attractive to his listeners.

Never one to sit still stylistically, however, Brookmeyer continued to grow as an improviser. Abandoning his funkier inflections, he began developing and refining a new musical vocabulary, one that was more melodically and harmonically advanced. Still drawing from the past, his solo lines became smoother, yet more abstract. Even so, Brookmeyer's tremendous sense of swing and his wonderful sense of humor were very much a part of his playing well into the new millennium, until his passing in late 2011. Fortunately, his many recordings keep him front and center; they have introduced his playing and writing to a whole new generation, and will doubtless do so for generations to come.

Interlude II: An Odyssey of Friendship

I first heard valve trombonist Bob Brookmeyer when I was in my mid-teens. My family and I were in Jacksonville, Florida, visiting some relatives, and while out walking around town one day, I happened into a record shop and bought an album by baritone saxophonist Gerry Mulligan and the Concert Jazz Band. To make a long story much shorter, I brought the record back to my cousin's house, took it out of its glossy black sleeve, and plopped it onto the phonograph. The first cut I heard was one of those finger-snapping things that sort of chugged along like a big old Hudson Hornet, lumbering from side to side, rooty-tooting down the street. The piano and tenor solos were good, but sort of unmemorable; however, after the tenor solo, there was a funky, raspy, downright greasy trombone solo that changed how I would hear and play music over the next 50 years. It wasn't a slide trombone solo, even though initially I knew it was some sort of trombone. This was a different breed of animal—one that wheezed, bleated, belched, farted, yowled, and groaned. This was down and dirty, and somehow I knew in my underdeveloped teenaged brain that this was the real deal. This was my first exposure to the genius of Bob Brookmeyer.

Now, even an uneducated green-gilled teenager like me back then could figure out that Brookmeyer didn't play slide trombone. He played the valve trombone, which has always been considered the illegitimate step-child of the more conventional slide instrument.

But it wasn't only the valve horn that caught my attention. It was the way that Bob Brookmeyer was playing it that completely turned me around. By using certain valve techniques, Brookmeyer could bend and twist notes. He could actually sing the same note he was playing into the horn and make the note being played sound wet and raspy, like a bull elephant with a cold. Sometimes he would not play a note at all, but just move the valves and breathe through the horn, sending a column of air loudly out of its big brass bell. All of these techniques made the valve trombone sound incredibly like a living, breathing thing—a gruff, yet fundamentally primordial voice that dug down deep into something I could not even begin to identify. It sang and resonated. It mesmerized. It incandesced brilliantly, like a dizzying mix of silver, gold, and copper stars blanketing the 'glades at midnight, and like a full, hot Florida sun at midday.

Even though I was a young and somewhat overzealous jazz drummer, I wanted to be as soulful and hip as Brookmeyer. Whoever said that imitation is the sincerest form of flattery would've been amused at just how much I embodied that statement. I cut my hair in an ivy-league style like Brookmeyer's. I dressed in that early '60s New York hip couture like he did. I even tried to effect his mannerisms. It was quite ridiculous, really; it was idol-worship at its most chronic. When no one was home, I would crank up the volume on the stereo in my room and play air trombone to Brookmeyer's solos, bending forward and arching backward, swaying from side to side, like an old Hassidic rabbi singing and praying on the Sabbath. I was pretty far into it after school one day, when my father (who came home early that afternoon) opened the door and leaned in to ask me to turn the music down. Catching me in a particularly dramatic pose, as I pointed my air trombone toward the ceiling at the zenith of the solo, my father looked at me with bewilderment before closing the door, leaving me to feel like someone who just got caught with his hands deep in the cookie jar. What does one say at a time like that? In my house the exchange probably would've gone something like this:

Oops. . . . Excuse me, Dad, I was pretending to be Bob Brookmeyer.

Who? Bob who?

Brookmeyer. The famous jazz valve-trombonist. You know, the guy who plays with Mulligan and Getz and . . .

A jazz musician? A jazz musician? This is your hero? What happened to Mickey Mantle, Sandy Koufax, President Kennedy? A ball player I understand. A president I understand. Even Jimmy Hoffa I understand. But a jazz musician? Is this Brookmeyer Jewish, at least?

Given the circumstances in my house, had this been a real scenario, I probably would've lied and said yes. And somehow, at least for a little while, that would've made it all right. But my father merely closed the door behind him, leaving me to the demons of self-doubt who pointed at me and shouted, "Weird! Weird! Weird!" before I chased them away with a swat of my invisible horn.

I finally met Brookmeyer in the mid-'70s, about a month after I moved to Los Angeles from the East Coast. We became immediate friends and musical associates, jamming, rehearsing, and playing local jazz joints. Those were rough years for Bob, since he was battling alcohol addiction— a battle he eventually won. After a time he began the long and arduous journey back to music and life, and his rebirth as both man and artist.

In the late '70s, Bob moved back to New York City and rejoined the vigorous Manhattan jazz scene. Even so, he returned frequently to the West Coast, and we played some successful and inspiring club gigs and concerts. In the mid-'80s, he called from New York and said, "I think it's time we did a record together." And so, a dream came true for me. We recorded *Oslo* for Concord Records in September 1986. Every minute in the studio with Brookmeyer was like magic, and his disciplined and focused approach to recording was inspiring and challenging. We went into the studio again in 2000 and coproduced a beautiful recording called *Stay Out of the Sun* for Challenge Records, further documenting our lifelong friendship.

Brookmeyer regained his stature as a well-respected jazz soloist, composer, and teacher both here in America and in Europe. And our relationship continued to flourish, even though we didn't play together nearly as much as we used to. But when we had the opportunity to make music together, it was always as though we never stopped. It was always very personal music, filled with joy and humor and even a touch of sadness. I continued to dot Bob's i's and cross his t's, and he continued to turn around and smile at me when we moved along through the music on the same wavelength: the teenaged kid from Miami and the suave, world-class hipster from New York–cum–Kansas City. The stuff dreams are made of.

Other fine bop-oriented trombonists worthy of mention here are Jimmy Cleveland, Jimmy Knepper, Garnett Brown, Julian Priester, Grachan

Moncur III, Carl Fontana, Willie Dennis, Frank Rehak, and Bob Enevold-
sen—all consummate musicians who deserve to be heard.

BEYOND BEBOP: TROMBONISTS HERE AND NOW

While the number of prominent post-bop jazz trombonists has not increased as much as in other instrument categories (as in saxophonists and
trumpeters), there continue to be admirable players on the trombone horizon in the 21st century.

Among the established pacesetters—that is, trombonists who have given
the horn new voice and energy beyond bebop—four names stand out:

Roswell Rudd has been active on the avant-garde scene for decades and
continues to literally breathe new life into the world of trombone playing.
Active initially as a Dixieland musician, Rudd seemingly skipped the swing
and bebop schools and moved directly into what was then called "the new
thing." He came to prominence in the mid-'60s New York avant-garde
scene with a number of distinctive groups: the New York Art Quartet (with
altoist John Tchicai) and ensembles with prominent postmodern tenor
saxophonist Archie Shepp and soprano saxophonist Steve Lacy, who, like
Rudd, moved from Dixieland directly to postmodern jazz. He also was the
recipient of a Guggenheim grant for composition and has been involved in
a variety of scholarly endeavors as well.

Rudd's style is a wonderful and lusty mix of both early and free-style jazz
improvisation. His sound is big and brash, much like the early tailgaters,
yet he excels at playing music that has no chord changes and sometimes no
discernable tempos either. His solos are, more often than not, exuberant
and filled with smears, roars, and sweeping glissandos—that is, slides up
and down the horn. In recent years, Rudd has investigated world music
and has performed and recorded with musicians from Africa and Mon-
golia, among others. Plainly put, he is one of those continually evolving
musicians who refuses to be compartmentalized in one genre or another.

George Lewis is another trombonist whose intellect and curiosity have
led him to explore other musical terrains besides any one school of jazz.
A graduate of Yale University with a degree in philosophy, Lewis was one
of the original members of Chicago's famous AACM (Association for the
Advancement of Creative Music) in the early '70s and has been active on
the experimental music scene, especially in the areas of electronic music

and interactive computer systems, which allow the computer to instanta-neously "dialogue" with an improvising musician. Lewis has held a profes-sorship at Columbia University and the University of California at San Diego, and was the recipient of a MacArthur Fellowship in 2002. He has played with a wide variety of jazz artists, ranging from Count Basie and Gil Evans to musician/composer Anthony Braxton and performance artist/composer Laurie Anderson.

The late German trombonist Albert Mangelsdorff (figure 8.6) was truly a wonder among his peers. He was, in every sense of the word, a pioneer among trombonists and, in a larger sense, the world of jazz.

Mangelsdorff explored two relatively uncharted areas in the jazz world: first, he was the first jazz trombonist to develop the use of "multi-phonics." By singing a note while playing another note on the trombone, Mangelsdorff could create two or more pitches at one time. Extending and refining this technique further, he found that it was possible to play additional notes si-

Figure 8.6. Albert Mangelsdorff. Courtesy of Illo Mangelsdorff.

multaneously as well. The end result was that Mangelsdorff could play the equivalent of chords on the trombone—much like a pianist or guitarist might be able to do on their respective instruments. The end result was astounding and has been documented on Mangelsdorff's many recordings.

The other area for which Albert Mangelsdorff was justly well known was solo playing—that is, playing solo concerts without the aid of a supporting group or even a rhythm section. Imagine a concert where a horn player comes out on stage and captivates an audience with several hours of solo playing. Not an easy feat, especially on an instrument like the trombone with its relatively limited range, at least compared to other wind instruments. However, Mangelsdorff was the consummate musician, and his innovative use of multi-phonics, combined with his creative imagination, gave him the ability to sustain the solo art and, in the end, make it ultimately an enthralling listening experience.

While Ray Anderson is the youngest of the four, he is by no means less respected or less vital in the evolution of the 21st-century jazz trombone. Like Roswell Rudd's, Anderson's sound harkens back to the trombone styles of the 1920s and '30s. He shares a special kinship with early masters such as Kid Ory and "Tricky Sam" Nanton who, as mentioned earlier, had big, fat, robust approaches to the slide horn. The difference is that Anderson is not a revivalist. He does bring the neo-primitive sound of the instrument into a wholly modern setting and has recorded with a wide variety of avant-garde, rhythm and blues, and even mainstream jazz and fusion groups.

One of the frustrating things about writing a jazz book is that there just is not enough room to offer substantial profiles of the many fine musicians who grace the jazz scene today. So the best we can do is to suggest that the reader seek out and explore the music of all of the trombonists profiled, as well as these fine players: the stunning Poll winner Wycliffe Gordon; the consistently excellent post-bopper Steve Davis; two forward-thinking sonic explorers, Josh Roseman and Jeb Bishop; and three creative and versatile sliders, Delfeayo Marsalis, Robin Eubanks, and Steve Turre. All are definitely worth spending some time with.

Getting Personal with Roswell Rudd

What advice would you offer a new listener who will be experiencing your music for the first time, either in concert, on YouTube, or via one of your recordings?
It's good to take stock once in a while, and you've provided me with incentive.

**Figure 8.7. Roswell Rudd.
Courtesy of Patrick Hinley.**

The sound just keeps on coming through me, so I've devoted my life to perfecting the art of getting it the rest of the way, that is, into you, the listener. But this is not a one-way street. Please open yourself and use all your perceptions to get INSIDE THE SOUNDS and enjoy the ride!

What would be the first recording of yours that you would recommend for an initial listening experience, and as a good introduction to your music?

First recording? First accessible/articulate recording in terms of composition-arrangement-performance I'd have to say is probably *Flexible Flyer* (Arista Freedom, 1974), with the great [singer] Sheila Jordan.

SELECTED TROMBONISTS' WEBSITES: FROM THEN 'TIL NOW

Note: Only official sites are listed. Use Google for all others.

Jack Teagarden: www.jackteagarden.info
Bob Brookmeyer: www.bobbrookmeyer.com
Roswell Rudd: www.roswellrudd.com

Ray Anderson: www.rayanderson.org
Wycliffe Gordon: www.wycliffegordon.com
Jeb Bishop: www.jebbishop.com
Delfeayo Marsalis: www.delfeayomarsalis.com
Steve Turre: www.steveturre.com

RECOMMENDED READING

Berrett, Joshua, and Louis G. Borgois III. *The Musical World of J. J. Johnson.* Lanham: Scarecrow Press, 2001. Print.

Schuller, Gunther. "The Trombone in Jazz." *The Oxford Companion to Jazz.* Ed. Bill Kirchner. New York: Oxford UP, 2000. Print.

Smith, Jay, and Len Guttridge. *Jack Teagraden: The Story of a Jazz Maverick.* Cambridge: Da Capo Press, 1988. Print.

9

REEDS AND DEEDS I

The Tenor Saxophone

> If you like an instrument that sings, play the saxophone. At its best, it's like the human voice.
>
> —Stan Getz

In truth, a study of the woodwind family—like some of the other instruments used in playing jazz—could easily fill the pages of an entire book. As a matter of fact, there have been numerous volumes that have focused solely upon woodwind instruments, their history, construction, and uses. Likewise, much has been written about men and women who, over the years, have mastered saxophones, flutes, and clarinets in both the classical and jazz worlds. So then, what we'll do here in these first two woodwind chapters is have a look at the tenor and alto saxophones and their place in jazz, as well as some little profiles of those jazz musicians who are notable for their excellence as players of each of the two saxophones discussed. Chapter 11 will focus upon two other saxes often used in jazz: the soprano and the baritone; and finally, chapter 12 will continue our look at woodwinds, but will focus upon three of the non-saxophone woodwinds: the flute, the clarinet, and the bass clarinet.

THE SAXOPHONE: A LITTLE HISTORY

The saxophone has been part of our musical palette in one form or another for at least 150 years. In the grand scheme of things, that's not really a long time when you consider that many other instruments came into existence much earlier. The primary force behind the saxophone's development was a musician and instrument maker named Antoine-Joseph (Adolphe) Sax—hence, the name of the horn. Sax, whose father was also an instrument maker, actually made his first instrument at the tender age of six! Eventually, Sax saw the need to create a woodwind instrument that would fill a tonal void that he saw existing between brasses, strings, and other woodwinds such as clarinets and flutes. Specifically, Sax felt that there was a need to develop an instrument that retained the power of a brass instrument, yet would still be a woodwind instrument—one that operated on the principle of a vibrating reed; in other words a brass horn that utilized keys and keypads and, most importantly, a mouthpiece that would accommodate a single reed. As a result, the first saxophone was born in 1841. The next year, Sax moved to Paris, where he created a variety of saxophones in different keys and pitches—14 in all. He was responsible for the saxophone's assimilation into military bands, orchestras, and eventually into dance bands and jazz bands. Ultimately, the saxophones that have been the most commonly used in modern-day ensembles are the tenor, alto, baritone, and soprano saxes. Let's have a look at each of these as well as some of the great players—past and present—who set standards of excellence for each instrument from decade to decade.

SETTING THE STANDARD: TWO TENOR SAXOPHONE GIANTS

It's hard to imagine how the tenor saxophone would have evolved in jazz without the presence and innovations of either Coleman Hawkins (figure 9.1) or Lester Young (figure 9.2). Both men were brilliant soloists and complete masters of the horn; however, stylistically, they are like night and day.

Figure 9.1. Coleman "Hawk" Hawkins. Courtesy of the William P. Gottlieb Collection.

Figure 9.2. Lester "Prez" Young. Courtesy of the William P. Gottlieb Collection.

Interlude I: The Hawk and the President

The Hawk talks and his voice sounds deep and gruff like heavy-gauge sandpaper. If he were a road, he'd be bumpy. There is also boisterousness and brightness when he fashions his words, phrases, and sentences. Sort of like a guy telling you a story and enjoying the way he's telling it.

When Prez speaks, his voice sounds *smoooooth* like satin and the words just seem to roll off his tongue in a fashion that is comfortable and cushy, like riding in the back seat of a '57 Cadillac Eldorado convertible on a cool, clear night on the Pacific Coast Highway.

The Hawk serves a meal through the horn! A thick, juicy porterhouse cut with all the trimmings and a pint of Foster's finest. Hold the dessert, please; just bring on two fingers of Remy and a Montecristo.

Prez is the breeze, not the wind. Prez is pastel pink and cerulean blue on the soft canvas of dawn or early dusk. Prez is crème brûlée and sassafras tea with a dollop of lavender honey. But Prez is also Kansas City and all-night cutting contests where he holds the horn high and sideways, the notes sliding out into the smoky air, sending the challengers scurrying to the exits, cases in hand.

While Coleman Hawkins has often been anointed as the father of the tenor saxophone, I would suggest that Lester Young shares that title with him, largely in terms of the amount of influence both men had—and still have—over generations of tenor saxophonists. In fact, one might say that most swing, bebop, and post-bop tenor players owe an enormous debt to one or the other. Without Hawkins, there would be no Sonny Rollins, Dexter Gordon, Johnny Griffin, John Coltrane, Joe Henderson, Wayne Shorter, or David Murray, to name only a few. And without Prez, there would've been no Paul Quinichette, Stan Getz, Al Cohn, Zoot Sims, Buddy Collette, or Jimmy Giuffre.

Fortunately for us, both Hawkins and Young live on through their many recordings. The Hawk can be heard in a wide variety of musical settings, from his exciting work with the Fletcher Henderson Orchestra in the early days of jazz, through his later performances such as those matching him with tenorist Sonny Rollins. Prez's recordings with iconic singer Billie Holiday, Count Basie, and many of his own groups are all classics and are well worth experiencing for his sheer relaxed virtuosity and great sense of swing.

A word of caution: don't ever fall into the trap of believing or suggesting that Coleman Hawkins was a better musician or soloist than Lester Young—or vice versa. It would be like suggesting that an apple pie is somehow better than a blueberry pie, when in fact, it's not better—only different. In fact, this is often good advice when discussing any two players of the same instrument. Saying that one player is somehow better than the other is a waste of energy, when both players may have something that is uniquely theirs to offer the listener. And as we have said and will continue to say throughout this book, jazz has always been and continues to be rich with stylistic diversity.

THE TENDER BRUTE: BEN WEBSTER

We can't talk about tenor saxophonists without paying homage to Ben Webster, another of the true giants of the instrument. Unlike Hawk or Prez, Webster—who was affectionately known as "Brute" or "Frog"— didn't create a major style of saxophone playing. He came out of the

Coleman Hawkins school of very muscular playing, and he could burn the house down on up-tempo numbers like "Cottontail," which he recorded with Duke Ellington's orchestra. Perhaps his Hawkinesque approach to the tenor on these fast tunes is where Webster got the nickname "Brute." However, this same man became one of jazz's most memorable interpreters of the ballad form. An admirer of alto saxophonist Johnny Hodges, Duke Ellington's star soloist, Webster claimed that Hodges was an enormous influence on him, particularly the way the latter played ballads. As a result, there were two sides to Ben Webster: the rough-and-tumble swinging soloist and the beautifully warm and tender ballad soloist. Webster had a breathy, romantic sound on the slower pieces, and when you watch him play ballads (thanks to video preserved on YouTube and commercial DVDs), it almost looks as if he is kissing the mouthpiece of the horn. He tilts his head and plays wonderfully rich and heartfelt phrases that seem to float in the air for a moment or two before evaporating into memory.

COOL SOUNDS: STAN GETZ

Stan Getz has a sound that has been compared to the feel of velvet between the fingers. His sound was straight out of the Lester Young school: cool, calm, and collected. But make no mistake: Getz—like Prez—could swing the doors off a barn.

First gaining the public ear as a member of clarinetist Woody Herman's big band, Getz recorded a memorable version of "Early Autumn," a lovely song by Ralph Burns, Woody Herman, and Johnny Mercer that featured his light and airy sound. That recording helped put Getz on the map. In the early '50s, he also recorded "Moonlight in Vermont" and other songs from the American Songbook, on an album with guitarist Johnny Smith that became one of the top albums of 1952. This recording further helped secure Getz's place among the great tenor saxophonists in the jazz canon.

In the early '50s, Getz formed a memorable quintet with valve-trombonist Bob Brookmeyer that showcased the warm sound of the two horns in a way that listeners found most appealing. Getz and Brookmeyer reunited in 1961 to record one of the most beautiful yet underrated albums of his career, simply called *Recorded Fall 1961* (Verve Records). And it was around that time that he also recorded a critically acclaimed album with

Figure 9.3. Stan Getz with granddaughter Katie. Courtesy of Beverly Getz.

strings, called *Focus*, which is still considered one of the loveliest and most innovative saxophone concept albums ever recorded.

Getz was also well known for his contribution to the merging of jazz and the Brazilian music called "bossa nova," which was brought to his attention by guitarist Charlie Byrd. For example, when you listen to the most famous version of "The Girl from Ipanema," the saxophonist is Stan Getz.

Not one to sit still in any one style of jazz, Getz went on from the late '60s until his death in 1991 to record with many fine modern jazz musicians in a variety of settings, each one different but all with that "sound" that brought him to prominence at the very beginning of his long and illustrious career.

SAXOPHONE COLOSSUS: SONNY ROLLINS

When I was in India at an ashram, my teacher told me, "When you are
playing your horn, that's meditation." And that is a way of worship.

—Sonny Rollins

Sonny Rollins began his lifelong love affair with the saxophone at age 14,
and we listeners are the beneficiaries of this tenor saxophonist's 50-plus-
year reign as one of the music's most imaginative and exciting players.
Inspired by many of his predecessors—most notably Coleman Hawkins—
Rollins began to catch the listening public's ear in the 1950s, performing
and recording with the likes of trombonist J. J. Johnson, trumpeter Miles
Davis, and pianist Thelonious Monk; however, many critics and listeners
believe that his best work of that decade began in 1955 when he joined the
Clifford Brown–Max Roach quintet. Brown, as you may remember from
a previous chapter, was a brilliant young trumpeter whose tragic death in
1956 was a major loss to the jazz world, and coleader Max Roach was a
fiery and intensely creative drummer whose concepts helped extend the
vocabulary of jazz drumming for generations to come.

After Brown's untimely death and the dissolution of the quintet, Rollins
went on to record a series of landmark discs, including a phenomenal two-
volume live set from New York's famous Village Vanguard, which featured
him in a pianoless trio setting with only bass and drums accompaniment.
He was also the first to utilize that saxophone in a completely unaccompanied setting as well.

However, as prolific as Rollins was during that period, he became disenchanted with the jazz scene and, specifically, was uneasy with the amount
of praise that was being heaped on him by the critical press. As a result, he
removed himself from the public eye completely in 1959 and retreated to
his home on the Lower East Side of New York, to rethink and expand his
approach to the music as well as his improvisational skills. It was during
this period that Rollins would practice the saxophone late into the evening
and early-morning hours on the nearby Williamsburg Bridge. He also immersed himself in the study of Eastern philosophies as well as yoga, and
he continued to develop his interest in music from the Caribbean Islands,
from which his family immigrated before his birth in New York City.

Figure 9.4. Sonny "Newk" Rollins. Courtesy of Chuck Koton.

Sonny explains his hiatus from the public eye as follows:

> I was getting very famous at the time and I felt I needed to brush up on various aspects of my craft. I felt I was getting too much, too soon, so I said, wait a minute, I'm going to do it my way. I wasn't going to let people push me out there, so I could fall down. I wanted to get myself together, on my own. I used to practice on the Bridge, the Williamsburg Bridge because I was living on the Lower East Side at the time. (www.sonnyrollins.com/bio)

Perhaps because of his self-imposed exile as well as his regular solitary visits to the Williamsburg Bridge, Rollins developed and continued to refine his explorations into unaccompanied solo saxophone performance. Once he resurfaced in the public eye (and ear) in 1961, his solo presentations ultimately became an essential part of his performances. If there was anyone up to the demanding challenge of a solo saxophone setting, it was Sonny. He had—and has—a way of taking a song apart and exploring every nook and cranny of its melody, harmony, and rhythm. The nation bore witness to his solo virtuosity on September 24, 1979, when Rollins appeared on *The Tonight Show* and played a lengthy solo piece as guest host Bill Cosby looked on in awe.

Sonny's ultimate return to the jazz scene back in 1961 was an auspicious one. The effects of his retreat were indeed favorable, in that he was playing with renewed energy and was more creative and inspired than ever. He made some remarkable recordings for RCA that featured guitarist Jim Hall, trumpeter Don Cherry, drummer Billy Higgins, and bassists Henry Grimes and Bob Cranshaw. And he continued his explorations into uncharted territory, among them a soundtrack album for the popular film *Alfie*.

Today, Sonny Rollins is in his early 80s and is as vital and inspired as ever. May he continue to enrich the lives of old and new listeners for years to come!

A LOVE SUPREME: JOHN COLTRANE

> To be a musician is really something. It goes very, very deep.
> My music is the spiritual expression of what I am—my faith, my knowledge, my being.
>
> —John Coltrane

> To me, John Coltrane was like an angel on earth. He struck me that deeply.
>
> —Elvin Jones

Earlier in this book, we talked about the art of jazz as a means of self-expression—that what a jazz musician creates in that singular moment on the bandstand or concert stage is often something unique and deeply personal. As a listener, how much you are able to receive that "creation" depends largely upon what you expect to derive from an evening of "live"

Figure 9.5. John Coltrane. Photofest.

jazz. As we know, earlier jazz styles such as Dixieland and swing often had entertainment as their primary focus. More specifically, jazz was great as accompaniment to imbibing in alcohol and partying and, of course, was very popular among dancers. As we also know, much of jazz's entertainment value diminished with the advent of the bebop era, when musicians began to think less about entertaining their audiences and more about sharing their music with them as an art form.

If jazz is indeed about offering one's feelings through the music, then it's here that we must spotlight the music and genius of John Coltrane. Someone once likened Coltrane to a brilliant comet that raced across the sky from one end of the horizon to the other—and then burned out all too soon. This is an accurate analogy when you consider that the saxophonist's recordings—

many of which exerted a tremendous influence on generations of musicians and listeners—span a period of only a dozen years (1955–1967). That's all the more amazing when we also consider that during those few years, Coltrane's approach to the music changed radically a number of times.

John Coltrane, or "Trane," as he is known, perceived music making as something akin to a religious experience, something deeply spiritual that transcended ego or entertainment. Coltrane's commitment to his music and its place in the world was total, and he was always seeking new ways to expand the language of the saxophone as well as to broaden his approach to composition and improvisation.

But early in his musical career, this was not the case. Like so many others of his generation, Coltrane was addicted to heroin and alcohol, and these dependencies nearly destroyed his career. However, in 1957, upon realizing that he had reached rock bottom, Trane returned to his family home in Philadelphia and sequestered himself in his room for a period of one to two weeks, during which he fasted and subsisted only on the barest necessities. As a result, he kicked his heroin habit and, shortly thereafter, eliminated his alcohol dependency. It was also at that time that he found renewed strength in spirituality—a devotion that would remain deeply embedded in his being and music for the rest of his life. Coltrane passed his credo on to other musicians through an interview with critic Ira Gitler in the December 1958 issue of *DownBeat*: "Live cleanly. . . . Do right. . . . You can improve as a player by improving as a person. It's a duty we owe to ourselves."

As a musician, Coltrane was a virtuoso, a saxophonist whose skill was unquestionably amazing in every regard. His command of the instrument—his tone, his attack, and the sheer, stunning speed of his execution—would influence saxophonists for generations to come.

Stylistically, Trane moved quickly through a number of distinct periods:

In the mid-'50s, Coltrane's solos were remarkably agile and dynamic. Even though playing in a bebop context (notably with Miles Davis), Trane's work was complex, many noted, and vigorous.

Toward the end of the '50s, Coltrane began experimenting with complex chord changes and, as a result, composed and performed pieces like "Giant Steps," which sent many musicians scurrying to their practice rooms in an attempt to understand and be able to follow this complex multichordal path.

As a result of participating on Miles Davis's landmark *Kind of Blue* in 1959, and influenced by the trumpeter's use of "modes" (examining the notes in a scale, rather than each note in a chord, as in traditional bebop), Coltrane entered his "modal" period. He wrote songs in this modal fashion and even took popular tunes such as Rodgers and Hammerstein's "My Favorite Things" and reconstructed the solo space in a way that allowed him maximum freedom of expression, using just the barest of modal guidelines. It was a year or so after *Kind of Blue* that Coltrane formed the first edition of his "Classic Quartet," which ultimately featured pianist McCoy Tyner, bassist Jimmy Garrison, and the volcanic drummer Elvin Jones. It was with this group in the final weeks of 1964 that Coltrane recorded his spiritually conceived masterpiece and also one of the greatest of jazz recordings of all time, *A Love Supreme*.

Coltrane's final period was one of relentless exploration. He abandoned much that came before and pursued freedom from both harmony and conventional swing rhythms. He also delved further into avant-garde and world music, assimilating Eastern and African influences into his performances. He disbanded the classic quartet and enlisted the aid of more avant-garde musicians, including his wife, pianist Alice Coltrane, and drummer Rashied Ali, as well as a second saxophonist, Pharoah Sanders. The later Coltrane groups often played music that was searingly intense and, to many listeners, seemed to border on a kind of controlled chaos.

John Coltrane died in 1967. Many listeners and students of his music believe that his final exploratory phase was, like his other stylistic periods, merely a stop along the way. Many conjecture about what his direction might have been and where his musical journey might have led him, had he lived beyond his 40 years. While no one really knows the answer, one thing is for sure: Coltrane would have continued what was, for him, a lifelong quest to find truth and beauty in his music and to be able to communicate those essences to his many listeners. In this, Coltrane was more than successful, as his music continues to resonate deeply for many listeners today. As Grammy-winning jazz record producer Michael Cuscuna so aptly put it: "I often wonder if he ever realized what he did for me or any of the other hundreds of thousands of fans that he had on the planet. By reaching inside himself, he reached inside all of us."

BEYOND COLTRANE:
ALBERT AYLER, ARCHIE SHEPP, PHAROAH SANDERS

Not only did John Coltrane influence future generations of saxophonists and other instrumentalists, but there were three distinct, forward-thinking tenor players he admired and was certainly affected by, to varying degrees. Each has developed a highly individual style, and two of the three also performed with Trane at various times in his final stylistic period, from the mid- to later '60s.

Albert Ayler was truly a wonder and most certainly an American original. Drawing from the rich folkloric music of the Pentecostal church, nursery rhymes, and early prejazz sources such as marches and patriotic hymns, tenor saxophonist Ayler, along with his brother Donald on trumpet and a who's who of avant-garde improvisers, created an entirely new and powerful hybrid music. His recorded performances often exhibit a happy, childlike quality that is irrepressible. That's not to say that his music was undemanding. Often an Ayler performance would evolve into a form of collective improvising that could be dissonant and ultimately off-putting unless you spent some time with it. And if you did, the rewards could be exhilarating. The man had a big, fat, dramatic saxophone sound as well as his own vocabulary—one that has not been replicated since his untimely death in 1970. Even though it was recorded almost 50 years ago, the music of Albert Ayler still offers the curious listener a uniquely solid mix of Americana and forward-thinking "jazz."

Another tenor saxophonist who synthesized the past—this time, the rich traditions of his instrument—in a totally unique way was Archie Shepp. Utilizing the deep, rich tone of past saxophone masters such as Coleman Hawkins and Ben Webster, and juxtaposing a huskiness reminiscent of the great tenor sax bluesmen, honkers, and shouters such as Arnett Cobb, Eddie Lockjaw Davis, and Red Prysock, Shepp moved the past squarely into the present by retaining that saxophone sound in an altogether modern free-jazz setting. Thoroughly schooled in the entire spectrum of jazz and other forms of African American music, Shepp brought his tremendous breadth to the beginnings of the free-jazz movement, recording and performing with such icons as pianist Cecil Taylor and fellow saxophonist John Coltrane, as well as many other notables in the avant-garde world. In addition to being a musician, Shepp is also an author, playwright, teacher, and social critic, and he remains a vital and enduring force in music today.

When John Coltrane invited Pharoah Sanders to sit in with his group in the mid-'60s, the entire complexion of the band changed. Coltrane much admired the raw aggressiveness and energy that Pharoah brought to the group. Sanders's sound was enormous, and his attack blistering. At times, he sounded as though he was screaming through the saxophone as he moved from the lower depths of the horn into the extreme upper register. The effect was, to many listeners, jarring and unsettling; however, it complemented Trane's own approach and the vision he had for his new group perfectly.

After Coltrane's passing in 1967, Pharoah played for a time with his widow, pianist/harpist Alice Coltrane, and ultimately embarked on a life-long journey that has encompassed all manner of musical endeavors. The ensuing years found him redefining and expanding his approach to playing and composing, all of which have included a variety of spiritual and ethnically diverse elements. Pharoah, along with trumpeter Don Cherry, was among the first to deeply explore and blend world music into his own musical oeuvre. The spiritual element added grace and a marked lyrical quality to his efforts, which differ significantly from his earlier work with Coltrane, even though Trane's pervading influence is still very much present in all of Pharoah's work. Perhaps as a result, he has developed a large following over the years; listeners seem to connect with his music on a very deep emotional level that has little to do with Coltrane-inspired nostalgia, and more to do with the sincerity, the energy, and the gentleness that he seems to exude at every performance.

Interlude II: A Week with Pharoah

The voice at the other end of the line said something like, "Hi, this is Pharoah Sanders. I'd like you to work with me at the Jazz Bakery [a prominent jazz venue in Los Angeles] next week." To put it mildly, I was stunned. This was a legendary figure who not only played with Trane but also was one of the music's mightiest tenor players.

What do you do when you get a call like that? The first thing you do is walk around in disbelief. The second thing you do is start practicing immediately!

As it turned out, Pharoah's longtime pianist William Henderson had recommended me for the gig, and Pharoah accepted his judgment. He was my guiding light throughout that week, and his encouragement and great playing provided both inspiration and confidence.

Playing with Pharoah Sanders, looking back on it, was probably as close as I would come to playing with Coltrane himself. In the past I had been fortunate enough to play with Art Davis, one of Trane's favorite bassists. I even had the opportunity to hold one of Coltrane's first soprano saxophones, thanks to woodwind wizard Bennie Maupin, to whom Trane bequeathed the instrument. But that one week with Pharoah was the icing on the Coltrane cake.

Every night was heaven. The group was amazing and the music exhilarating—but it was Pharoah himself who conjured up pure magic from the first moment of music to the last.

It was like being in the middle of a maelstrom—a hurricane! One minute, the notes swirl around you at 100 miles an hour; the next, you are feeling this incredible peace there in the eye of the storm. Never had I played with someone so intense, yet at the same time so beautifully serene. The man sang songs through the horn and transcended the music itself. Something special was happening on the stage and in the audience every night. Pharoah Sanders lifted us all up and brought us deeply into ourselves—musicians and listeners alike.

Looking back on those nights, I can't remember the songs we played or some of the other particulars of the gig. What I can remember is the audiences rising to their feet and offering standing ovations every night. And I can remember my wife, Kathleen, coming up to me after one of our sets, tears in her eyes, not saying a word. She didn't have to.

Figure 9.6. From left to right, the author, Trevor Ware, Dwight Trible, William Henderson, and Pharoah Sanders. Courtesy of the author.

CARRYING THE TORCH

Other fine tenor saxophonists who have continued the explorations of Ayler, Shepp, and Sanders include David Murray, who—along with Pharoah Sanders—has an abiding interest in multicultural approaches to improvised music as well as the jazz tradition; Peter Brötzmann, an uncompromising and electrifying player who is very much a part of the international avant-garde scene; and the late David S. Ware, an early protégé of Sonny Rollins, who developed into a powerful and emotional player, well grounded in all forms of improvised music but especially active in free jazz. All are worth investigating for the richness and depth of their music.

However, a word of caution: question your notions of whatever "beauty" in music might be, and suspend hasty judgments. Free jazz deserves the fairness of repeated listening and a really open mind. These musicians—and indeed many of the preceding ones presented—will challenge you. In the end, exposure to their music will only sharpen your skills in experiencing jazz of all kinds.

ODYSSEY OF ISKA: WAYNE SHORTER

One of the most distinctive voices in modern jazz, Wayne Shorter is like a chameleon. He blends into any musical setting with ease, yet has the gift of being able to maintain his truly original sound and identity in any musical environment, from groups led by jazz masters Art Blakey and Miles Davis to world-class singers Joni Mitchell and Milton Nascimento and guitarist Carlos Santana; and with the stellar groundbreaking jazz-fusion group Weather Report, which he cofounded with another Miles Davis alumnus, keyboardist Joe Zawinul.

Shorter, like all of the great saxophonists profiled thus far, has always been a total individualist. His sound is smoky and mysterious and draws from the traditions of the early masters, the beboppers, and of course, John Coltrane. He came into prominence in 1959 with Art Blakey's Jazz Messengers and began establishing himself as a force to be reckoned with as both an instrumentalist and a composer. A number of years later, in 1964, he became a member of Miles Davis's second great quintet—one of the most celebrated small groups in jazz history—all the while making superlative records as a leader for the Blue Note label. While Shorter is

Figure 9.7. Wayne Shorter. Courtesty of Jack Vartoogian / FrontRow-Photos.

a brilliant saxophonist on both tenor and soprano saxes, he is equally well known as one of jazz's most revered composers. Compositions such as "Footprints," "Fall," and "Nefertiti," to name only a few, are very much a part of the standard jazz repertoire in many of today's jazz ensembles all over the world.

Shorter's Blue Note recordings just before he began his 15-year association in 1971 with Weather Report further demonstrated his interest in free jazz, most notably the organized chaos of *The All Seeing Eye* and the Miles Davis–influenced *Super Nova*. And his records after the dissolution of Weather Report revealed his ongoing interest in all kinds of music, including Brazilian, European classical, Latin, and Caribbean styles. His ongoing relationship with keyboardist Herbie Hancock, his old bandmate from the Miles Davis days, continues to be fruitful in a number of different settings, from duets to larger ensembles.

As he enters octogenarian status, Wayne Shorter continues to move forward, playing new and exciting music and reconstructing older pieces in brilliant new ways. His current quartet features three younger virtuosos (pianist Danilo Perez, bassist John Patitucci, and drummer Brian Blade) who are not only moved by Shorter's music but have also inspired the saxophonist to produce some of his best playing in a career that has spanned over a half century.

MAINTAINING THE STANDARD: THREE INFLUENTIAL STYLISTS

The best jazz musicians are true individualists, no matter the era. While there are many wonderful players creating jazz today, only a handful can be described as completely original in terms of both their sound on the instrument and their approach to creating improvisations. Each of the following three saxophonists are among the most original tenor saxophone voices in modern jazz:

Line up 100 tenor saxophonists and place Joe Henderson in that lineup. Now ask each one to play the first four bars of any melody you choose. If you had been a fan of Henderson's playing as so many listeners and musicians have been, you would have been able to pick him out easily, because his sound and technique are inimitable. His dark, rich, full-bodied tone, combined with his sense of rhythm and complete command of his instrument, made him distinctive among the many fine players out there.

Henderson recorded as a leader and as a participant (often called a "sideman") on many memorable Blue Note recordings in the 1960s. His first solo outing, titled *Page One*, received a great deal of critical acclaim, as did his subsequent releases on the label. Henderson was considered a "musician's musician" back in those days. Guitarist John Scofield put it this way:

> Joe Henderson is the essence of jazz. He embodies all the elements that came together in his generation: the mastery of hard bop and the avant-garde. He can play . . . abstractly without getting away from the roots. He can play a blues the way [bluesman] Joe Turner would sing it, and then play the fastest, craziest, most angular atonal music you've ever heard. Who, on any instrument, plays better, more interestingly, and with more bite than Joe Henderson? He's my model in jazz. (Berendt and Huesmann, 326)

Henderson could fit into any setting, and the minute he'd take a solo, he was able to put his own personal stamp on it, completely free of musical phrases or sounds (often called "licks") played by other musicians. You'd even be hard-pressed as a listener to find Henderson repeating his own musical phrases—combinations of notes he might have used in another of his solos.

In the '90s, Henderson finally received the positive recognition he had deserved all along, and his recordings often became instant classics in the jazz world. All the while, until his death in 2001, Joe Henderson remained true to himself and to his music. Truly one of our great jazz treasures.

Interlude III: A Cup of Joe

Meet Joe Lovano. Maybe you've heard the expression "a regular Joe"? If you haven't, it means a down-to-earth, friendly guy—someone you'd enjoy sitting with at 2 a.m. in the Tic-Toc Diner in Jersey, quaffing coffee and eating a piece of black-bottom pie. Lovano's that type of guy. Animated, spirited, and deeply passionate about a variety of subjects, not the least of which is music. "I live in the world of music," he told me the other night, "and I've had really fortunate and incredible experiences playing in some incredible bands with others who also draw from the world of music that fuels their ideas."

Figure 9.8. Joe Lovano. Courtesy of Jimmy Katz.

As regular a guy as he is, Joe is internationally recognized as one of the most accomplished and identifiable of all contemporary tenor saxophonists. He is one of the most respected players as well, and he has won polls and graced the covers of all the major American jazz magazines. Following his own path, Lovano has clearly absorbed the entire history of the saxophone, from the early masters such as Lester Young, Coleman Hawkins, and Ben Webster, through bebop pioneers like Charlie Parker and Sonny Rollins, and on through modern masters John Coltrane and Ornette Coleman. Yet even with this great lineage of influences, Joe is still very much his own man. His big, smoky, dusky sound is also full and round, and he makes some of the incredible things he plays sound almost effortless.

Born into a musical family in Cleveland in 1952, Lovano began playing the alto saxophone at age five and, after a while, moved to the tenor sax, the instrument that his father, Tony "Big T" Lovano, and several of his uncles played. By the time he was old enough to drive, young Joe was a member of the musicians' union and was already playing professionally. His formal studies took him to Berklee College of Music, and his informal studies took place on the bandstand with many fine musicians, including organists Brother Jack McDuff and Dr. Lonnie Smith, among other notables. After moving to New York in the mid-'70s, he worked and recorded with many famous jazz artists—far too many to mention here!

Joe is a creative musician not only of great depth but of equally astonishing breadth as well. His innate sense of curiosity about a wide range of music has led him down some very interesting paths, from unique explorations
of Charlie Parker's music to the music associated with Enrico Caruso and
Frank Sinatra; from orchestral collaborations with composer-conductor
Gunther Schuller to timeless meetings with jazz masters Hank Jones and
Paul Motian; and these examples just scratch the surface! He has currently
been leading a quintet of young players, including the Cuban and American drummers Francisco Mela and Otis Brown III and the amazing bassist
and vocalist Esperanza Spalding.

Joe and his partner, Judi Silvano—a fine vocalist and all-around aes-
thete—enjoy a long-standing musical association as well as a full, rich life
at home in New York State, where they enjoy landscaping and gardening.
In fact, the first in-depth conversation we ever had was not about music at
all; it was at Birdland, the famous Manhattan jazz venue, where this giant
of jazz and I compared the joys and frustrations of owning and using lawn
tractor mowers. Like I said—"a regular Joe."

Michael Brecker, the last of our three saxophonists in this category, continues to exert a strong influence upon legions of tenor saxophonists. The
winner of every conceivable award and much international recognition, Michael was indeed a shining star who breathed a different kind of life into the
tenor saxophone—a life that was to be cut painfully short by bone marrow
disease complicated by leukemia. Fortunately, he left a body of recordings
that continue to inspire many jazz musicians, in addition to saxophonists.

Like others we've introduced in this chapter, Michael explored other
genres of music besides straight-ahead, bebop-based jazz. In addition to
being greatly influenced by John Coltrane, Michael seemed also to inter-
nalize the music of a number of soulful rhythm and blues reedmen, such
as Junior Walker and King Curtis. As a result of these and other influences, he synthesized a very original and recognizable style—one that was
grounded in astonishing technique and seemingly limitless imagination.

After studying at Indiana University, Michael, along with his equally
gifted trumpet-playing brother Randy, moved to New York City, where
they played with a variety of groups and cofounded Dreams, one of the

first and most memorable jazz-rock fusion groups, in 1970. A number of years later, they went on to form the Brecker Brothers, an innovative, high-energy ensemble whose recordings garnered immediate praise from all corners of the jazz community.

Michael was the "compleat musician." He was at home in any musical situation and recorded with jazz, rock, and popular music giants as diverse as Herbie Hancock, Chick Corea, James Taylor, Joni Mitchell, Paul Simon, Frank Sinatra, Bruce Springsteen, and many others. However, at his core, Michael was a jazz musician who was committed to being the best he could be. He recorded album after album, all of which garnered praise and a variety of honors. As a result, he was and still is a major influence among both established and up-and-coming saxophonists.

One of the last groups Michael played in was the Saxophone Summit, which featured the incredible three-saxophone frontline of Brecker, the previously profiled Joe Lovano, and the extraordinary Dave Liebman as the third saxophonist. So much virtuosity on the same stage! Fortunately for the listener, the group recorded the critically acclaimed CD *A Gathering of Spirits*, which features all three saxophone giants at the peak of their powers.

Michael became ill in 2004 and succumbed to his illness in January of 2007; however, before he passed away, Michael summoned enough strength to complete his last album with an all-star group. His playing, even under debilitating circumstances, was nothing short of amazing. Fittingly enough, this last recording was titled *Pilgrimage*, which means a long journey, usually to a sacred place. Michael Brecker's musical journey may have been just that. . . .

AND THE LIST GOES ON

When it comes to great tenor saxophonists, past and present, the list sometimes seems endless! Consequently, there is just not enough space in a guidebook like this one to profile them all. However, here are some other great players worth your time: Dexter Gordon, Hank Mobley, Benny Golson, and James Moody! These gentlemen are all products of the bebop era, yet each one has a distinctive sound and style. Gordon was an expatriate in Europe for many years, but returned to the United States and enjoyed new acclaim as both a saxophonist and as an Academy Award nominee for his performance in Bertrand Tavernier's deeply moving jazz movie, *Round Mid-*

night. Mobley logged in quality time with both Art Blakey and Miles Davis. Likewise, Golson—also a fine composer—was a member of one of Blakey's most popular editions of the Jazz Messengers; and Moody, in addition to his own many fine groups, worked extensively with Dizzy Gillespie.

Also: Clifford Jordan, Jimmy Heath, George Coleman, and Charlie Rouse! Again, from the bebop era, but each one unique in his own way. Jordan performed and recorded extensively with the volatile and brilliant bassist/composer Charles Mingus. Heath, along with his equally gifted brothers Percy (bass) and Albert "Tootie" Heath (drums), recorded in many great settings, often together with their own Heath Brothers group. Coleman, like Hank Mobley, played with Miles Davis after John Coltrane's departure, and his powerful, muscular tenor sound graced a number of Miles's memorable mid-'60s recordings. Rouse, for years, was the lone saxophone voice in the Thelonious Monk Quartet, although he led a number of his own groups before, during, and after his long tenure with the legendary pianist.

Three other bop-oriented saxophonists who deserve mention are the underrated Warne Marsh and two powerhouses: Don Menza and Pete Christlieb—all denizens of the West Coast. The late Warne Marsh was a student of the legendary pianist Lennie Tristano, whom we will discuss in the chapter about the piano. His tenor sound was reminiscent of Lester Young's; however, his approach to improvisation was quite modern, particularly his work with Tristano and alto saxophonist Lee Konitz.

Although Don Menza hails from upstate New York, he has spent many years living and working in California. Menza's credentials are impressive as both a saxophonist and as a composer and arranger. He has performed and recorded with his own small groups and big band and was also a key member of the big bands of drummers Buddy Rich and Louie Bellson. Menza is a fiery soloist whose influences include both his friend Sonny Rollins and Stan Getz.

Pete Christlieb is a native of Los Angeles and one of that town's preeminent tenor saxophonists. His body of experience includes stints with the big bands of Woody Herman and Count Basie, as well as extensive work in the L.A. studios. Like Menza, Pete is an energetic, exciting player. In fact, being on the bandstand with them both is akin to holding two tigers by the tail!

Among the post-bop tenor players, in addition to Wayne Shorter, Dave Liebman is at the top of the list. While certainly an acolyte of John Coltrane, Liebman has gone well beyond carrying that single mantle, exploring all manner of music and constantly challenging himself to a lifetime of musical and personal growth. Originally earning his credentials with Elvin Jones and Miles Davis, Liebman is an intense, vital, and enduring presence in the jazz world, both as a player and as an educator. We'll visit him in more depth when we focus upon the soprano saxophone in the next chapter.

Other fine tenor saxophonists in this category who are worth investigating include Bob Mintzer, Rick Margitza, George Garzone, Branford Marsalis, Joshua Redman, Ravi Coltrane, Chris Potter, and Poland's Piotr Baron. Among the newer voices on the instrument are Chris Speed, Tony Malaby, Ralph Bowen, and Donny McCaslin.

Suffice it to say that the tenor saxophone has maintained a long and honorable existence in the jazz world. The many great tenor players discussed on these pages are certainly worth your time. And thanks to technology, all you need to do to experience their music is to fire up your computer, surf some of the websites noted in this book, sit back, and enjoy.

Getting Personal with Joe Lovano

What advice would you offer a new listener who will be experiencing your music—or jazz in general—for the first time, either in concert, on YouTube, or via one of your recordings?

[You have] to realize that to go hear jazz—or classical music of some kind— you're not going into a room to have a party. You're going there to listen; and you're going into an environment that you might not have ever been in before. For someone to go into an environment and maybe have to pay a cover charge to go in, and not talk, and sit and listen—you have to have a certain attitude about that.

You know, people go to the opera, people go to see modern dance or the ballet. There's a certain attitude about where they're going and why they want to be there. They want to be enlightened; they want to be taken out of their "groove" and into some other place; and that's really what jazz music is all about . . . coming and listening and being drawn in and taken somewhere.

What is the responsibility of the jazz musician in implementing this process?

Musicians have a responsibility also to reach out to an audience. You can't play "at" your audience, you know. You want to involve them somehow. You do that with your sound . . . and your repertoire. You plan. You do that with communication on the bandstand—a joyous communication that is not only inviting for the listener, but it's like . . . contagious. They feel a part of what you're doing.

It's about the truth and the passion!

What would be the first recording of yours that you would recommend for an initial listening experience and as a good introduction to your music?

I would want someone to hear my current recording—to hear what I'm doing right today and that, hopefully, would make them want to do more research and discover where I've been on my previous recording that led me to today's moment. [So] instead of starting earlier on and making their way to where I am now, start where I am now. Maybe you'll come and hear me tomorrow night somewhere and that's what I'm playing.

Any final thoughts?

When the music touches you, when you go hear people . . . you don't remember every little thing, but you remember the whole experience.

SELECTED TENOR SAXOPHONISTS' WEBSITES: FROM THEN 'TIL NOW

Note: Only official sites are listed. Use Google for all others.

Sonny Rollins: www.sonnyrollins.com
Stan Getz: www.stangetz.net
John Coltrane: www.johncoltrane.com
Wayne Shorter: www.wayneshorter.com
Albert Ayler: www.ayler.co.uk
Archie Shepp: www.archieshepp.net
Joe Lovano: www.joelovano.com
Michael Brecker: www.michaelbrecker.com
Dave Liebman: www.daveliebman.com
Ravi Coltrane: www.ravicoltrane.com
Joshua Redman: www.joshuaredman.com
Branford Marsalis: www.branfordmarsalis.com
Chris Potter: www.chrispottermusic.com
Donny McCaslin: www.donnymccaslin.com
Chris Speed: www.chrisspeed.com
Tony Malaby: www.tonymalaby.net

RECOMMENDED READING

John Coltrane

Kahn, Ashley. A Love Supreme: *The Story of John Coltrane's Signature Album.* New York: Viking Press, 2002. Print.

Porter, Lewis. *John Coltrane: His Life and Music*. Ann Arbor: U of Michigan P, 1998. Michigan American Music Series 2. Print.

Ratliff, Ben. *Coltrane: The Story of a Sound*. New York: Farrar, Straus & Giroux, 2007. Print.

Stan Getz

Gelly, Dave. *Stan Getz: Nobody Else but Me*. San Francisco: Backbeat Books, 2002. Print.

Coleman Hawkins

Chilton, John. *Song of the Hawk: The Life and Recordings of Coleman Hawkins*. Ann Arbor: U of Michigan P, 1990. Michigan American Music Series 5. Print.

Sonny Rollins

Blumenthal, Bob, and John Abbott. *Saxophone Colossus: A Portrait of Sonny Rollins*. New York: Abrams Books, 2010. Print.

Wayne Shorter

Mercer, Michelle. *Footprints: The Life and Music of Wayne Shorter*. New York: Jeremy P. Tarcher–Penguin Books, 2004. Print.

Ben Webster

Büchmann-Moller, Frank. *Someone to Watch over Me: The Life and Music of Ben Webster*. Ann Arbor: U of Michigan P, 2009. Jazz Perspectives Series 16. Print.

Lester Young

Daniels, Douglas Henry. *Lester Leaps In: The Life and Times of Lester "Pres" Young*. Boston: Beacon Press, 2002. Print.

10

REEDS AND DEEDS II

The Alto Saxophone

The alto saxophone is smaller than the tenor but larger than the soprano. Its overall sound also falls in between those two horns. The history of the alto saxophone is fairly similar to that of the tenor sax, except that the alto has been utilized more extensively in classical music than the larger horn. However, both the alto and tenor saxophones were prominent in both marching bands and, of course, jazz bands.

The alto players we'll discuss in this section fall into roughly four categories: (1) the early notables, (2) Charlie Parker and his disciples, (3) Lester Young–influenced altoists, and (4) the postmodernists.

In each section below, the headings contain some reference to food. I hadn't thought initially about comparing two such seemingly different things as alto saxophonists' playing styles and a variety of gastronomical tastes. However, these metaphors and similes seem to work in the case of many of the musicians we'll meet in this section. I have used these kinds of comparisons in my Jazz Experience classes to great effect, since students seem to be an eternally hungry bunch. See how they work for you as we visit alto-land.

WHIPPED CREAM ON A HOT FUDGE SUNDAE: JOHNNY HODGES AND BENNY CARTER

No one ever forgets a great hot fudge sundae: the chilled metal tulip cup, the double scoop of rich French vanilla ice cream, topped with a generous portion of thick hot fudge. A mountain of fresh whipped cream, some minced nuts, and a maraschino cherry adorn the top. The real thing!

If you think of the sweet confection described above—or better yet, if you are indulging in that guilty pleasure—then there is no better time to be listening to both Johnny Hodges and Benny Carter, arguably the first two great alto saxophonists in jazz history. Each man had a distinctive sound that was rich, sweet, and pure—and swinging.

Johnny Hodges (see figure 10.1) was most closely affiliated with Duke Ellington's orchestra for over 40 years. He was Duke's "lead alto voice,"

Figure 10.1. Johnny "Rabbit" Hodges. Courtesy of the William P. Gottlieb Collection.

which means that when you listen to the Ellington saxophone section, the lead horn you may be hearing is, more often than not, alto saxophonist Johnny Hodges. He was not only a great lead player but also a magnificently elegant soloist. All one need do is listen to the Ellington opus, "I Got It Bad and That Ain't Good" to savor Hodges's genius. He slides up to notes like a fresh cool breeze over the ocean on a day in early summer. His sound was not only very rich and sensuous but also quite powerful. Couple these characteristics with a crystal pure tone, and you have the musical essence of the man.

In addition to Hodges, Benny Carter was the other great pre-bebop alto saxophonist, and like Hodges, his saxophone sound was also rich and lustrous. Carter was also an accomplished trumpeter—an unusual second instrument for a reed player—as well as an excellent composer and arranger. Compared to Hodges, Carter's sound was lighter and airier, and unlike Hodges, his tone had almost no vibrato, or wavering in pitch. Carter moved to California, where he became an in-demand presence as an arranger and composer in Hollywood TV and movie studios.

CITRUS TWIST AND BIRD CALLS:
CHARLIE PARKER AND HIS DISCIPLES

Orange juice, lemonade, limeade—all coolness that can make mouths pucker and awaken the taste buds more than a little. Imagine biting into a piece of tangerine: cool, juicy, and slightly tart with a hint of sweetness—or a piece of real key lime pie, that first bite a sensual alarm clock!

The above descriptions are an amalgamation of "taste-related" student responses when comparing alto saxophonists Charlie Parker, Jackie McLean, and others to the two earlier alto voices profiled initially above. Sometimes we can better understand the differences in sound and style among players, by comparing them to nonmusical things like colors and foods. In the case of the alto saxophone, this works really well in my Jazz Experience classes. After all, one can experience life via any of the five senses, and this is only too true in the world of music, where all of these can come into play at any given time. That we can relate the sound of a saxophone to the senses of sight, sound, taste, smell, and touch is one of the beauties of living art.

Charlie "Bird" Parker (figure 10.2) redefined the role of the alto saxophone—and to a large extent, all saxophones—in terms of both sound and style. Unlike Hodges and Carter, Parker's sound was less sweet and his approach to soloing was less laid back and more aggressive and daring. He was relentlessly committed to mastering his instrument as well as bebop, the new language that he and trumpeter Dizzy Gillespie were largely responsible for creating in the early 1940s. In fact, their quintet became the talk of 52nd Street in New York, during the early days of bebop.

Figure 10.2. Charlie Parker. Courtesy of the William P. Gottlieb Collection.

In the words of the brilliant alto saxophonist and National Endowment for the Arts (NEA) Jazz Master Phil Woods:

> Bird and Diz? Yin and Yang! Diz told me when . . . he heard Bird, he realized that was the articulation. It was the epitome of improvisatory rhythm, harmony, and melody. Mother Nature knows how to do it. What a fortuitous time in America. World War II was over and the artists exploded like land mines.

There has been much written about Bird both as a major figure in jazz and as a person: biographies, documentaries, and even a full-length feature film by Clint Eastwood. So how do we describe a jazz giant in a small space such as this one? Bird was an anomaly—that is, he was a study in contradictions. He could be kind and generous, or he could be the exact opposite. He was intellectually engaging, yet he could also be irrational and erratic. His life was one of both brilliance and chaos, both personally and professionally. Two reasons for such opposites were undoubtedly his dysfunctional upbringing and his addiction to heroin from a very early age. That he was able to create such vital and world-changing music with the specter of drug addiction hanging over him was absolutely amazing.

As Joachim Ernst-Berendt suggests in *The Jazz Book*, "[Parker] led many lives, each intensely and to the hilt: intellectual, drug addict, philosopher, playboy, responsible father of a family, ladykiller." (2009, 116)

Charlie Parker died at the age of 35 on March 12, 1955, laughing at a joke while watching the *Tommy Dorsey Show* on television. His autopsy revealed the body of a much older man, due to his excessive alcohol and drug abuse. While his untimely death was a tremendous loss to the music world, his legacy has lived on for many, many jazz musicians on every instrument for over a half century, and it is safe to say the Bird's flame still burns brightly today and shows no sign of ever diminishing. As the saying goes . . . "Bird lives!"

As mentioned above, Charlie Parker influenced many musicians on every instrument. Of course, he had countless disciples among saxophone players. On the alto saxophone—Bird's own instrument of choice—there were some players who really stood out among the throngs of acolytes. One such notable was Jackie McLean, who, while influenced wholly by Parker's aggressive approach to soloing, forged his own unique style, which is instantly recognizable today. His tone was a bit off-pitch and tended to be a little sharp (as opposed to flat); however, it was not objectionable in any way and was overshadowed by his blues-drenched phrases and intense emotionality. "Jackie Mac," as he was known by his friends and fellow musicians, was one of the young musicians Parker took under his wing back in the 1940s. In fact, Bird would occasionally send McLean on gigs if he knew he would be late or unable to show up, for one reason or another. Jackie McLean went on to play with the brilliant, volcanic bassist Charles Mingus, as well as an early edition of Art Blakey's Jazz Messengers, and he subsequently recorded with both of them as well as with Blue Note artists such as trumpeters Lee Morgan and Donald Byrd and tenor saxophonists Sonny Rollins and Hank Mobley. Later in his career, McLean's own records became more daring and exploratory, due largely to his interest in avant-garde jazz and the music of such forward-thinking figures as Ornette Coleman and John Coltrane. McLean maintained that the transition from bebop to the avant-garde was not out of the realm of possibility, as long as musicians were willing to move ahead and not get stuck in any one style.

For the remainder of his career, McLean not only stayed active as a vital jazz artist, but he also moved into the realm of education. In 1967 he worked in the prison system as a counselor and as a music teacher. A year or so later, McLean embarked upon a career in college teaching at the University of Hartford in Connecticut, where he established the university's African American music program, later renamed the Jackie McLean Institute of Jazz. Subsequently, he and his wife Dollie created a community-based foundation in Hartford, dedicated to nurturing fine arts (including jazz) in that city's impoverished African American community. Jackie McLean died in 2006, and while his distinctive alto saxophone voice was stilled, we listeners are fortunate to have access to a wonderful 30-minute documentary by Ken Levis, *Jackie McLean on Mars*, as well as the many fine recordings that amply document his 50-plus-year jazz journey.

Another alto saxophonist whose roots were watered by Charlie Parker was Phil Woods. Like McLean, Woods's bright, forceful sound and aggressive approach was deeply influenced by Bird, even though he was perhaps more deeply influenced by the early masters Benny Carter and Johnny Hodges. Whereas Jackie McLean's sound was a little more raw and slightly out of tune—not bad qualities, by any means, just different—Woods's alto voice is shining and brilliant. It's almost like comparing a 75-watt light bulb with a fluorescent bulb. Both shine brightly in different ways. You can see that comparing these two fine players using mere words is highly insufficient. Hearing is believing!

A product of Springfield, Massachusetts, Woods began his 70-year love affair with the saxophone at age 12, studying both formally and with teachers such as the innovative pianist Lennie Tristano. Eventually, Woods enrolled at the Juilliard School of Music and began his lifelong trek as one of jazz's most recognizable alto voices. While definitely considered one of Charlie Parker's acolytes, Woods became much more than an imitator. His rich and lively sound and his spirited solos brought him much well-deserved recognition on the New York jazz scene, beginning in the mid-'50s. Woods's alto voice graced the bandstands and recordings of some of jazz's best-known figures, including Dizzy Gillespie, Thelonious Monk, Quincy Jones, Gerry Mulligan, Bob Brookmeyer, Benny Goodman, Buddy Rich, Clark Terry, and many others. He has also led his own stellar small bands, including his present group, which has been performing for almost four decades. And his association with the core of that unit—bassist Steve Gilmore and drummer Bill Goodwin—began roughly a decade before that! Not an easy task, keeping a group together and working for that period of time; however, Woods has managed what many musicians know to be almost impossible. Having a stable working band is a dream for many musicians, but it has been a reality for Woods.

Among his many accomplishments (including his famous solo on Billy Joel's hit single "Just the Way You Are"), three-time Grammy winner Woods cofounded the Celebration of the Arts (COTA) Festival over 30 years ago in Northeast Pennsylvania and was also instrumental in creating CampJazz, the annual summer COTA camp for young musicians, which has in recent years produced a hotbed of jazz talent.

A third distinctive alto saxophonist to emerge from the "Charlie Parker School" was Julian "Cannonball" Adderley. Originally from Tampa, Florida, Adderley was on a completely different career track, having begun his musical career as a band director in a Fort Lauderdale high school in the late 1940s. He relocated to New York in the mid-'50s, intent upon continuing his music studies; however, as fate would have it, he began sitting in at clubs like the Café Bohemia and, as a result, the talk on the street was that he was the new heir apparent to Charlie Parker—flattering, although it was not really a reputation Adderley cared to cultivate. In reality, although he was certainly influenced by Bird, he was in no way an imitator, let alone "the New Bird," as the press touted him. In fact, Cannonball's style was also influenced by Benny Carter, who, as we know from earlier in this section, came on the scene earlier than Bird.

Cannonball's clear and rich tone and his joyous approach to soloing did, in fact, draw a lot of attention on the New York scene in the mid-'50s; so much so that in 1957 Miles Davis invited him to join his quintet, creating the amazing frontline of the trumpeter, John Coltrane, and Adderley. Cannonball stayed for two years, long enough to be an integral part of Davis's legendary *Kind of Blue* recording, arguably one of the most important jazz records of all time.

After his stint with Miles, Cannonball re-formed an earlier quintet that featured his brother Nat on cornet. This group recorded a superior live album that firmly established its presence on the national jazz scene, but more important, it introduced the listening public to a new form of jazz that drew from the groove-oriented gospel music often heard in churches and at revival meetings. As a result, the Adderley quintet became one of the leading exponents of what came to be known as "soul jazz," whose funky, infectious grooves and catchy melodies captivated audiences for the rest of Adderley's career.

One of the most endearing things about Adderley, aside from his consummate musicianship, was his ability to relate to listeners at concert and club gigs. Always the gracious host, Cannonball announced each song, introduced the members of his group, and would even tell a story or two, either about the music being played or about a particular band member. As a result, Cannonball had a way of making audiences feel valued and very much a part of the experience. The jazz world lost Cannonball Adderley in 1975 at the much-too-young age of 47, yet his exuberant and earthy alto saxophone voice continues to attract listeners even today.

While McLean, Woods, and Adderley are considered three of Bird's major disciples, there were many other fine alto saxophonists who fell under Parker's spell and who deserve mention here as well. Charles McPherson, Lou Donaldson, Art Pepper, Sonny Criss, Frank Strozier, Sonny Stitt, and Gigi Gryce are among the most prominent. All are worth spending time with as you progress through the royal lineage of Bird-influenced players.

COTTON CANDY: THE COOL ALTOS

Lighter than air. We were never really sure what it was made of. All we knew was that its superfine pink or light blue angel hair seemed as if it would float away if we opened our hands and let it go in the evening breeze at the carnival. And we would always remember the feeling of how it tasted as it dissolved quickly on our tongues. Semisweet . . . fleeting like a puff of smoke . . . but so firmly etched into memory.

To be clear at the outset of this section, it should be known that descriptions like "lighter than air," "sweet," and "fleeting" are not meant to be negative descriptions of a sound. A "lighter" sound does not make a musician—in this case, an alto saxophonist—less vital or less important than his or her more "muscular"-sounding counterparts. Indeed, this small group of saxophonists—most of whom were influenced more by the breezy sound of Lester Young's tenor saxophone—were and still are among the most innovative of musicians to come out of the bebop era.

The place to begin here is with Lee Konitz, who is indisputably one of the most original voices on the alto sax. Born in Chicago, Illinois, in October 1927, Konitz was an integral part of two important pieces of jazz history. First, he was a participant in the legendary Miles Davis *Birth of the Cool* sessions in 1949–1950. As discussed earlier, these were the recordings that ushered in the cool jazz movement, which took root mostly on the West Coast in the early '50s. And second, as a teenager Konitz was a student—and later a musical colleague—of the important pianist and teacher Lennie Tristano, whose advanced harmonic concepts became very significant to jazz in the late '40s.

Konitz's style to this day retains the airiness of tenor saxophonist Young and less of the bite of Charlie Parker's sound. Furthermore, early on he played with little or no vibrato—in other words, without the "quavering" sound often associated with singers and instrumentalists of any era or style of music. Later, as he matured, Konitz became even more expressive as a soloist, unleashing long and fluid musical statements as effortlessly as water flowing in a stream.

One unique characteristic of Lee Konitz has been his career as a "freelance" jazz artist—that is, one who did not spend much of his long career as a member of one or two particular groups. On the contrary, in his 60-plus years on the jazz scene, Konitz has appeared in many different kinds of musical situations, from solos and duos to big bands and even string quartets. The man has an insatiable curiosity and refuses to sit still in any one musical setting. Even as an octogenarian, Konitz continues to place himself in challenging musical situations, often with much younger players. Yet he has always managed to remain himself throughout, and his unique solos continue to delight and amaze listeners from around the world.

Another musician who falls into this category of altoists is Paul Desmond. Unlike Konitz, Desmond played in a variety of conventional settings before settling into a lifelong musical partnership with pianist Dave Brubeck—one that brought them both worldwide acclaim as half of the Dave Brubeck Quartet.

One of the characteristics that set Desmond apart from many other jazz artists is his "lyricism"—that is, his ability to make his improvisations sound like little songs that we might be able to sing along with after hearing one of his recorded solos a few times. In fact, "lyric" or "lyrical" means "song-like." Desmond had that singsong quality in his playing. Not a flashy or showy player, he constructed his solos honoring the melodies upon which they were based and did so in a relaxed, thoughtful, and altogether appealing manner. As far as his sound goes, Desmond—always the sublimely witty sophisticate—likened it to a dry martini.

Desmond's relationship with Brubeck began in 1951 and lasted until 1967. It should be noted that the Dave Brubeck Quartet was one of the most commercially successful jazz groups in history and, back in the day, captivated audiences from college students to older jazz fans. In fact, the quartet toured constantly, playing in colleges, clubs, and concert halls both here and abroad. They even played in orchestral settings, for example, with the New York Philharmonic (under the baton of Leonard Bernstein) and appeared a number of times on television.

The Brubeck Quartet scored a major commercial success with their album called *Time Out*, which they recorded for Columbia Records in 1959. In fact, the album was the first jazz recording to sell one million copies worldwide—an absolutely unheard-of feat for any jazz album at that time. Perhaps the most popular track on *Time Out* was "Take Five," an odd-rhythm tune written by Desmond as basically throwaway, in case they had space on the disc for an additional song. Little did anyone know that it would be one of the two most popular tracks on the album (the other being another odd-meter tune, "Blue Rondo à la Turk").

In the five years before his death in 1977, Desmond played and recorded in a variety of settings, notably with guitarist Jim Hall (with whom he began his association in 1959), trumpeter Chet Baker, baritone saxophonist Gerry Mulligan, Canadian guitarist Ed Bickert, and the Modern Jazz Quartet, among others. It's interesting to note that when Desmond left the Brubeck Quartet in 1967, he retired from playing for three years, intending to fulfill his dream of becoming a writer. Unfortunately for him (and for us), that dream was never fully realized, although some of his writings were preserved in *Take Five: The Public and Private Lives of Paul Desmond*, Doug Ramsey's remarkable biography of the saxophonist; however, fortunately for jazz listeners everywhere, Desmond returned to playing in 1970 and brought his considerable talents back into the limelight for the remainder of his life.

Three other fine West Coast–based alto saxophonists whose cool-tinged work deserves to be heard include Gary Foster, for years an in-demand L.A. studio musician who also happens to be an exemplary jazz musician and multi-instrumentalist. His melodic approach to the instrument has been likened to Lee Konitz's fluid style and pianist Lennie Tristano's unique method of improvising. Two others were Art Pepper, a slightly harder-toned, adventurous player whose personal excesses and tragic life were the subject of *Straight Life*, a beautiful yet painful book written by the late saxophonist and his wife, Laurie; and finally, Bud Shank, who, like Pepper, had a wonderfully bright, cool style that graced many jazz groups, beginning in the '50s and continuing until his passing in 2009. In addition to being a versatile musician (recording with artists as diverse as Brazilian guitarist Laurindo Almeida and Indian sitar virtuoso Ravi Shankar), Shank was also a fine flutist whose solo on the Mamas and the Papas' hit song "California Dreamin'" reached the ears of an entirely new generation of listeners in the '60s and '70s.

SPICY AND SPELLBINDING: ORNETTE COLEMAN, ERIC DOLPHY, ANTHONY BRAXTON

Hot peppers . . . nature's wake-up call! While there are many varieties of spicy peppers, there are really only two kinds: those that create instant fire on the palate and the others that sneak up on you and set you aflame after a moment of false security, when complacency ("This isn't so hot") is replaced by the feeling that you've just set your tongue on fire.

Avant-garde jazz—and specifically in this case, alto saxophonists—can be like that, too. Some hit you right away with a fiery barrage of notes and rhythms, while others sort of sneak up on you and lead you into the stratosphere. In either case, keep your ears and your mind open and enjoy the offerings of these distinctly different artists as they explore uncharted territories in jazz.

When alto saxophonist Ornette Coleman burst upon the scene at New York City's legendary Five Spot Café with his revolutionary quartet in 1959, he redefined both the sound and the approach to soloing of the alto saxophone in jazz, and he moved it beyond the realm of any of the previous approaches presented so far. In fact, Coleman was the major force behind the avant-garde movement in jazz, discussed in an earlier chapter. His quartet, which featured trumpeter Don Cherry, bassist Charlie Haden, and drummer Billy Higgins, astounded audiences during their months-long engagement at the club and created quite a stir during that time. Many listeners such as conductor/composer Leonard Bernstein, Modern Jazz Quartet pianist/composer John Lewis, and author Norman Mailer championed Coleman's abstract but blues-drenched playing, as well as his jumpy, colorful compositions and the free soloing of each member of his group. But others were put off by this new music, claiming that Coleman was "shucking and jiving" on his instrument, and that he didn't know how to play jazz. Even Miles Davis at the time said that Coleman was "psychologically screwed up inside," a comment he later recanted.

No longer shackled by traditional chord changes that have been so much a part of jazz (the group didn't use a chordal instrument like the piano or guitar), Ornette's vision was that each soloist was totally free to follow his own imagination. And hovering over all of it was Coleman's bright and edgy white plastic alto saxophone.

Ornette was born in Fort Worth, Texas, in 1930, and began his musical journey on the tenor saxophone. He played with a variety of rhythm and blues bands and traveled around Texas and neighboring states as well. After he was assaulted and his tenor was reputedly thrown off a hill, Ornette switched to the alto saxophone. His travels as a road musician eventually landed him in Los Angeles, where, after a considerable period of time, he finally found a small group of musicians who shared his creative spirit of adventure and were totally committed to his musical vision. In the late '50s Ornette and his group recorded *Something Else* for Contemporary Records, to both critical acclaim and disdain. There didn't appear to be a middle ground. However, as time passed, more and more listeners, musicians, and even critics were attracted to his music. After many groundbreaking recordings, Ornette Coleman went on to win the Pulitzer Prize for his 2007 recording *Sound Grammar*—years and miles from the alienation he suffered as a result of following his highly personal quest for musical freedom. And even now, as an octogenarian and a musical icon,

Figure 10.3.   Ornette Coleman. Photofest.

Ornette stands as a role model for maintaining courage and conviction as a creative artist. And his earthy, bluesy alto saxophone sound continues to be immediately recognizable and revered across generations of listeners.

Eric Dolphy was a wonder, a triple threat. A virtuoso in every sense of the word, Dolphy played alto saxophone, flute, and bass clarinet with equally stunning skill and imagination, and had the gift of a totally unique approach on all three instruments. We'll revisit Dolphy as both a flutist and a bass clarinetist in later chapters, but we will discuss him here as an alto saxophonist.

"Joy" is a word that comes to mind when you listen to Eric Dolphy. More specifically, exuberant joy; sort of a "whoop-de-do!" kind of energy. "Happy chaos" might be more accurate still.

Sometimes listening to one of Dolphy's frenetic flights on the alto was akin to holding a tiger by the tail—almost too much energy and fire. But at the end of the day, these are only rather limp words written to describe something that should be heard firsthand.

One thing is for sure: Eric Dolphy had his own vocabulary. He had a way of improvising that was all his own. Even though he was a thoroughly schooled musician, Dolphy found ways of speaking through his horn that melded bebop with startling, speech-like cadences and rapid-fire runs from the bottom to the top of his instrument. Unlike Ornette Coleman, whose roots were firmly planted both in rhythm and blues and chord-free music, Dolphy's approach began in the bebop tradition and became outward bound very quickly. In fact, *Outward Bound* was the title of his very first record as a leader for the Prestige label in 1960. Additionally, like Coleman, Eric was a thoughtful composer whose melodies were both abstract and swinging. His charismatic, extroverted playing caught the attention of drummer Chico Hamilton, who helped bring Dolphy to prominence. Within a short period of time, he began his famous association with bassist Charles Mingus and also joined John Coltrane's classic quartet as a foil to Coltrane's own volcanic horn playing. His career was on a definite upward trajectory. Unfortunately, Dolphy, who was a diabetic, left us after only 36 years, the result of what may have been a misdiagnosis at the beginning of a gig in Berlin in June 1964.

One of the goals of this book is to present many of the musicians discussed on these pages as human beings as well as artists—to enable you to see them as real people and not just as creative types removed from the rest of us, by nature of their brilliance. In the main, these were often just plain folks who happened also to be gifted musicians. As an example, Eric Dolphy completely belied the stereotype of the brilliant yet drug-addled and altogether self-destructive jazz musician. Here is a eulogy that was written for Dolphy by record producer George Avakian in *Jazz Magazine*, shortly after his death:

> Perhaps the most important thing about Eric was that he was a fine person, a gentle gentleman of a man, a person whose curiosity about everything led him into every kind of social milieu and whose warm friendliness made him welcome. . . . In the end, every man is seen as a human being. Brilliant musician that he was, Eric was still greater as a person. He was thoughtful, gracious, and genuinely interested in others. . . . He knew how to enjoy what came his way, and how to give in return. (14)

Eric Dolphy's star still shines brightly for those in the jazz world who know his playing, thanks largely to his recorded output. It's safe to say that there has really not been anyone like Dolphy to come along since his passing. Yet even though his influence is still felt today among many musicians, the listening public is largely unaware of Dolphy and his significant contributions to jazz. It's time for that to change, and with your help, we can make that happen.

Interlude I: Eric Dolphy Day

This was to be a special day here in Los Angeles—one that should have been celebrated by lots of jazz musicians and listeners alike. Thanks to virtually no media coverage and no apparent support from any immediately recognizable source, Eric Dolphy Day in South Central L.A. went almost completely unnoticed. Dolphy, the seminal innovator and universally acknowledged woodwind master, died at the much-too-young age of 36 back in 1964—a tremendous loss to the jazz world. In his all-too-brief career, Dolphy played and recorded with John Coltrane, Charles Mingus, Chico Hamilton, Ornette Coleman, and many other great musicians. His wondrously free alto saxophone, flute, and bass clarinet solos were (and are) immediately recognizable, and his legendary virtuosity is remarkable.

So with all that being said, where was everybody yesterday, as the new $5 million Denker Community Center was being renamed the Eric Allan Dolphy Memorial Center? Where was everybody when some great musicians performed, or when Clora Bryant, Dr. Art Davis, and other legends of the Central Avenue jazz scene that gave us Eric Dolphy stood up to share personal anecdotes and memories about Dolphy that very few musicians and fans are rarely, if ever, privy to? Those who composed the small audience yesterday were most appreciative, and the vibe in the gymnasium where this beloved event took place was a sort of microcosm of the way it should have been with an audience 10 times its size.

A larger question that looms over all this is, if the jazz community didn't know about the Eric Dolphy Day celebration, why didn't it? On the other hand, if it did, then where was everybody? How can we expect the perpetuation of this music if we ourselves don't support it? Is it that we leave that to someone else who, in turn, leaves it to us? If that's the case, then nobody shows up and you have a pitifully small but spirited audience, reaping the treasures of some excellent musicians and some fine poets and artists as well. Commitment to change and change itself begins with each of us in our communities. Want to preserve America's only true art form? Then, whenever you can, support jazz and the many gifted musicians, poets, and artists who give so much of themselves to both music and audience. Jazz, after all, is about filling up an empty world with the sustenance of song and spirit. That's what Eric Dolphy was all about—as both a man and as an artist. And it's up to each and every one of us who love this music and who cherish freedom of expression to help keep the lamp of jazz lit and burning.

Like Eric Dolphy, Anthony Braxton seems almost uncategorizable—perhaps more so, in that Braxton is known as both a player and as an extremely prolific composer, author, and teacher. As an alto saxophonist, he has likewise redefined the sonic limits of the instrument, adding percussive effects, impossible tonal leaps from the top to the bottom of the instrument (similar to Dolphy's work, but perhaps even more extreme), and a crazy quilt of unorthodox, cliché-free runs and phrases. He has also expanded his highly original concept to include a variety of unconventional woodwind instruments, including the sopranino saxophone, the bass saxophone, and the dragon-like contrabass clarinet.

Over the years, Braxton's recorded and live outputs have been nothing short of amazing in their sheer quantity and variety. He was one of the first improvisers to develop the unaccompanied solo performance, an extremely challenging milieu for any improvising artist. He also has played and recorded in duo settings, and he has composed music for and performed in all other manner of small-group settings, as well as larger ensembles, from tentets to larger groups, to three orchestras performing simultaneously. Recently, Braxton composed and recorded an opera called *Trillium R*, as well as a theater piece called *Composition 173*, written for musicians and actors. Braxton has been awarded numerous grants, including the MacArthur Fellowship (often called the "genius grant"), all of which have enabled him to further explore and expand the boundaries of composition and improvisation.

As an author, Braxton has sought to introduce his varied musical and philosophical approaches and materials in extensive writings, including a three-volume set of his thoughts called *Tri Axium Writings*. He has also explored world music, including Native American, African, and Persian sources, and has pioneered a musical form he calls "Ghost Trance." He presents these and other concepts at Wesleyan University, where he is a tenured professor, teaching courses focusing upon not only his original music, but also on electronic and computer-generated music, and even sources as varied as contemporary classical and medieval music. All in all, he is a tremendously gifted altoist, multi-instrumentalist, composer, author, teacher, and thinker. It's reasonable to think of Anthony Braxton as a true renaissance master.

TENDING THE FIRE: THREE RECENT VOICES: KENNY GARRETT, TIM BERNE, RUDRESH MAHANTHAPPA

While there are some remarkable alto saxophonists on the scene today, three in particular stand out, in terms of each one's approach to the instrument, and to their distinctive qualities as soloists and musical visionaries. A few words about each of these fine players are in order:

Kenny Garrett first came into prominence as a five-year member of one of Miles Davis's later electric bands, even though before Miles, he played for a number of years with the Duke Ellington Orchestra led by Duke's son, Mercer. A native of Detroit, Garrett recorded his first CD as a leader in 1984 and has recorded at least a half-dozen CDs since. He has also been featured on many other CDs with high-profile artists such as Chick Corea, Joe Henderson, Freddie Hubbard, Herbie Hancock, and many others. Garrett's 1997 CD *Songbook*, featuring his own compositions, was nominated for a Grammy Award.

In terms of his approach to playing, Garrett's credo, according to his website, urges listeners not to pigeonhole him into a stylistic corner. In his own words, Kenny says:

> Once you try to define me, that's where problems begin because I'm not doing just one thing. I do straight ahead [post-bop]. I also do funk, classical, and many other things. Don't look for me to sound like my last record. I'm shifting—following what my spirit feels. (www.kennygarrett.com)

One thing that does remain constant in all of his music is Garrett's unmistakable alto saxophone sound. Part hard-bop, part R & B, part Coltrane— Garrett has fused these and other stylistic influences together into a highly original and much-imitated sonic gumbo. His playing is at once soulful and spiritual, rooted in the blues, yet very modern. Hearing is believing.

Tim Berne seems always to be on the cutting edge of new musical avenues, particularly when it comes to very modern improvisational music. A product of what he calls "a perfectly normal childhood" growing up in Syracuse, New York, Berne entered the music world by way of basketball and college. He bought an alto saxophone from a fellow student, largely because he liked the sound of the instrument and wanted to learn how to play it. While he did listen to a variety of music, Berne's initial love of Stax Rhythm & Blues artists like Sam and Dave and Gladys Knight and the Pips influenced both his style and approach to playing, early on. However, when at one point he heard the music of avant-garde reedman Julius Hemphill, a whole new world opened up to him—one that would change the course of his relationship with the alto and would challenge and ultimately reinvigorate his views about creating music. Ultimately, Hemphill became Berne's mentor and opened up an entirely new world to the young altoist, offering him stimulating perspectives on music, spirituality, and even business-related dimensions such as recording and promoting one's music.

Musically, Tim Berne has performed and recorded with his own groups and has written music for both small and large ensembles. He has also received commissions to help support his creative efforts, from many organizations such as the New York State Council on the Arts and the British Arts Council. Berne's playing reflects both his love of tradition and his quest for new musical avenues of expression. His saxophone sound is bright and clear, and his solos are remarkably free of clichés. All in all, Berne remains one of jazz's freshest and most original newer voices.

There has been an ongoing—and completely inaccurate—notion in jazz that only American musicians can play jazz with any degree of authenticity; specifically, that to be a great jazz artist, one has to have been born here in America. Many fans had often been led to believe this idea by the critical press, other listeners, and occasionally by musicians themselves. It was a common belief that musicians who were born (or whose parents were born) in Europe, the Middle and Far East, South America, and other countries could simply not play the music at the level established by American jazz musicians. As we shall discover in a later chapter, this is a patently ridiculous belief; and as you will discover here, this silliness can be completely dispelled by listening to the phenomenal Rudresh Mahanthappa. Ironically, Rudresh was born, not in India, but in Italy, and he was raised in Boulder, Colorado. He earned bachelor's and master's degrees from Berklee College of Music and DePaul University, respectively, and teaches at New York University. In an all-too-brief nutshell, Rudresh's music synthesizes traditional South Indian music—which honors his ancestry—with much of the music he grew up listening to in Colorado. The end result is original and intense, yet also exuberantly happy and exciting. Astonishingly enough, Rudresh leads at least seven different groups, from duos to larger ensembles, all featuring his intricate but spellbinding compositions and, in the words of the *New Yorker*, "his visceral tone and grab-you-by-the-collar attack." In recent years, the jazz community, the critical press, and the listening public have recognized this major artist, and as a result, Rudresh has received a coveted Guggenheim Fellowship, as well as grants from Rockefeller Center and Chamber Music America, among others. He has also won many polls as both an alto saxophonist and as a composer. Yet, at the root of this rather large and impressive tree, Rudresh's credo has remained the same, as stated on his website: "To address what it is to be Indian-American by digesting Indian music on my own terms." Listen, and prepare to be exhilarated!

AND THE LIST GOES ON . . .

Other fine alto saxophonists worthy of mention include bop-oriented players such as Frank Strozier, Lou Donaldson, and Charles McPherson; post-bop altoists James Spaulding, Bunky Green, and Steve Wilson; R & B–influenced figures such as David Sanborn, Hank Crawford, and Grover Washington Jr.; and finally, the ultramodern Oliver Lake, Julius Hemphill, Marion Brown, Steve Coleman, Marty Ehrlich, Greg Osby, Steve Lehman, and David Binney.

Getting Personal with Rudresh Mahanthappa

What advice would you offer a new listener who will be experiencing your music for the first time, either in concert or via one of your recordings?

My primary advice to the listener is to have an open mind. It sounds so contrived, but many audiences come to my music with preconceptions about what they are going to hear. Try to shed the expectation of hearing something blatantly Indian or exotic or "avant-garde." My ancestry plays a significant role in my music but is by no means the only influence. Charlie Parker, YES, Grover Washington Jr., and Busta Rhymes (to name a few) equally inform my work. After all, I am an '80s child of Indian immigrant parents who was raised in Boulder, Colorado.

Figure 10.4. Rudresh Mahanthappa. Courtesy of Mark Duggan.

Try to enjoy the music and don't concern yourself with "understanding" it. Contrary to popular belief, enjoyment and engagement are indeed the deepest, perhaps most important, levels of understanding. The passion, energy, introspection, and message will all shine through if one allows.

What would be the first recording (or two) of yours that you would recommend for an initial listening experience and as a good introduction to your music?

I find myself most proud of my recent work. I would recommend my latest album *Samdhi* as a first recording to check out. For me, it's the most seamless expression of who I am and where I come from. Musically, it's the jazz-rock fusion album that I've wanted to make since I was in high school!

For a second album, I choose *Kinsmen*. This album was a dream come true for me, as I was able to collaborate with the great Kadri Gopalnath, the pioneer of the saxophone in Indian classical music. This album highlights where jazz and Indian music intersect and diverge in meaningful and beautiful ways, thus putting forth a timeless story and eloquent intercultural dialogue.

SELECTED ALTO SAXOPHONISTS' WEBSITES: FROM THEN 'TIL NOW

Note: Only official sites are listed. Use Google for all others.

Benny Carter: www.bennycarter.com
Charlie Parker: www.cmgww.com/music/parker
Phil Woods: www.philwoods.com
Cannonball Adderley: www.cannonballadderley.com
Paul Desmond: www.puredesmond.ca
Art Pepper: www.artpepper.net
Bud Shank: www.budshankalto.com
James Spaulding: www.speetones.com
Ornette Coleman: www.ornettecoleman.com
Oliver Lake: www.oliverlake.net
Anthony Braxton: www.tricentricfoundation.org
Kenny Garrett: www.kennygarrett.com
Tim Berne: www.screwgunrecords.com
Rudresh Mahanthappa: www.rudreshm.com
Steve Coleman: www.m-base.com
Steve Wilson: www.stevewilsonmusic.com
Greg Osby: www.gregosby.com
Marty Ehrlich: www.martyehrlich.com
David Binney: www.davidbinney.com

RECOMMENDED READING

Benny Carter

Berger, Morroe, Edward Berger, and James Patrick. *Benny Carter: A Life in American Music*. 2 vols. Lanham: Scarecrow Press, 2002. Print.

Ornette Coleman

Wilson, P. N. *Ornette Coleman: His Life and Music*. Berkeley: Berkeley Hills Books, 1999. Print.

Paul Desmond

Ramsey, Doug. *Take Five: The Public and Private Lives of Paul Desmond*. Seattle: Parkside Publications, 2005. Print.

Eric Dolphy

Simosko, Vladimir, and Barry Tepperman. *Eric Dolphy: A Musical Biography and Discography*. Rev. ed. Cambridge: Da Capo Press, 1996. Print.

Lee Konitz

Hamilton, Andy. *Lee Konitz: Conversations on the Improviser's Art*. Ann Arbor: U of Michigan P. 2007. Print.

Jackie McLean

Ansell, Derek. *Sugar Free Saxophone: The Life and Music of Jackie McLean*. London: Northway Publications, 2012. Print.

Charlie Parker

Reisner, Robert, ed. *The Legend of Charlie Parker*. Cambridge: Da Capo Press, 1979. Print.
Russell, Ross. *Bird Lives: The High Life and Hard Times of Charlie (Yardbird) Parker*. Cambridge: Da Capo Press, 1996. Print.

11

REEDS AND DEEDS III

Highs and Lows—The Soprano and Baritone Saxophones

After the tenor and alto saxophones, the other two horns that are most common in the jazz world are the soprano and baritone saxes. In this chapter, we'll focus upon both and introduce you to the acknowledged masters on each horn, as well as some voices that certainly deserve wider recognition. Finally, we'll have a look at a few of the newer soprano and baritone saxophonists emerging on the scene today.

THE SOPRANO SAXOPHONE

> I heard Sidney Bechet play a Duke Ellington piece and fell in love with the soprano saxophone.
>
> —Soprano saxophonist Steve Lacy

The soprano saxophone comes in two shapes: the straight horn and the curved horn. Essentially, these are the same instrument, albeit with two different shapes. Soundwise, the soprano saxophone is pitched higher than the alto and, by all accounts, is a bit more difficult to play in tune. Also, like the other saxes we've discussed so far, each of the notable soprano players profiled in this section have markedly different sounds from one another. The instrument can sound full and rich and can cut through the tonal density of an entire big band's horn section (brass and reeds); or it might sound thin and nasal—almost oboe-like in tone and texture—depending on who is at the blowing end. Its sound is distinctly identifiable, and it has become "the other horn" played by many jazz tenor and alto saxophonists.

THE PIONEERS: SIDNEY BECHET, STEVE LACY, JOHN COLTRANE

Another thing that makes the soprano saxophone distinctive is its history. Unlike the tenor saxophone in particular, the soprano does not really have an expansive history in terms of the sheer number of notable players in each of jazz's eras. While sopranos were around as far back as the mid-1800s, the first real jazz soprano saxophonist was New Orleans's Sidney Bechet, who came to the instrument as a clarinetist. He began his recording career in 1921, and his first known recordings on soprano saxophone came two years later in 1923. It's fair to say that Bechet put the soprano saxophone on the map. However, the curious thing is that after Bechet, there were only a handful of saxophonists or clarinetists who followed suit and played the small horn on a regular basis. One such notable figure was Johnny Hodges, Duke Ellington's lead alto saxophonist, who played the instrument for a while but ultimately gave it up for a variety of reasons.

Sidney Bechet was a powerful player on both the soprano sax and the clarinet. When you listen to his recordings, the first thing that might impress you would be his big, passionate sound and his use of vocal effects that, at times, replicated the human voice. Another thing that makes Bechet easily identifiable is his wide vibrato—that is, the wavering quality of his sound. While these characteristics apply to both of his instruments, it is Bechet's soprano saxophone playing that qualifies him as one of jazz's early icons. He remained active in both Europe and America until his passing in 1959. Many listeners and musicians continue to believe that he stands shoulder to shoulder with Louis Armstrong as one of the fathers of the music.

Oddly enough, the soprano saxophone was not played often in the context of either the swing or bebop eras. One reason for this might have been that the small horn was—and often still is—notoriously hard to play in tune. Before any set of music, most horn players get their tuning note from the piano or guitar, which helps them play in tune with other members of the group; in other words, everyone's B-flat is in tonal accord with each other—hence, no sour notes. However, the soprano saxophone, even after tuning, often falls out of tune and becomes either "sharp" (slightly above everyone else's same note) or "flat" (slightly below). This lack of tonal reliability in the soprano may have been one of the reasons it was not used in the woodwind sections of swing-era big bands. Another reason might have been that swing bands often used clarinets (certainly in the case of the bands of clarinetists/band leaders Benny Goodman and Artie Shaw) as lead instruments, and didn't consider the soprano as a suitable replacement in the reed section. There were, however, some band leaders such as Charlie Barnet and Georgie Auld who played the instrument in front of their respective orchestras in the mid-'40s, possibly as a replacement for the clarinet. Both men were saxophonists rather than clarinetists, so it's possible that using the soprano saxophone was a substitute for the latter horn and an attempt to emulate the more popular bands of Goodman, Shaw, and even Jimmy Dorsey.

As infrequently as it was used in the swing era, the soprano saxophone was practically nonexistent in the bebop era of the '40s and '50s. With few exceptions, saxophonists preferred the tenor and alto and even the baritone saxes for recording and performance. The soprano was once again left out in the cold. Reasons for this remain unclear to this day, but one suspicion is that most bebop saxophonists fell under the spell of Charlie Parker (alto saxophonist) and Coleman Hawkins, Lester Young, and Ben Webster (tenor saxophonists)—none of whom played the soprano saxophone.

So then, after Sidney Bechet, the next great soprano saxophonist was Steve Lacy (see fig. 11.1). Interestingly enough, Lacy emerged not from a bebop background, but from traditional jazz circles. Even though his early performances were with Dixieland groups led by such early jazz legends as Pee Wee Russell and Henry "Red" Allen, he assimilated quite effortlessly into the modern jazz world. One of Lacy's first notable modern jazz recordings was with composer/arranger Gil Evans's 10-piece group in 1957. *Big Stuff* featured Lacy along with altoist Lee Konitz, bassist Paul Chambers, and a host of other New York notables. He also performed and recorded with the brilliant avant-garde pianist Cecil Taylor around that time. Lacy was, along with Anthony Braxton and England's Evan Parker, one of the first saxophonists to perform and record improvised solo pieces, that is, totally unaccompanied musical excursions that were created on the spot, with no preconceived guidelines or parameters—just Lacy and the soprano, nothing more. The fact that he was able to completely captivate and hold the rapt attention of a listening audience was nothing short of amazing, and a true testimony to his artistic abilities.

However, before that time and throughout his life, Lacy maintained an ongoing interest in the music of pianist/composer Thelonious Monk. Although he played with Monk on occasion and recorded with him in large ensembles, Lacy never recorded in a small-group setting with the pianist; in any case, he recorded many of Monk's quirky and altogether intriguing compositions on quite a few of his recordings, including the wonderful *Reflections* for Prestige Records.

Lacy had a full and rich sound, perhaps as a result of his early experiences with Dixieland groups, as well as the influence of Sidney Bechet. Like the great soprano sax pioneer, Lacy played the small horn in tune, and his solos were models of both creative logic and passion. He was

Figure 11.1. Steve Lacy. Courtesy of Gilles Lahuerte.

also unafraid to experiment and extend the breadth of the conventional sound of his instrument beyond the normal notes and tones we might hear coming out of a saxophone. So then, a solo by Lacy might include chirps, electronic-sounding beeps, low-pitched guttural noises, and many other mind-bending effects, mixed in with the traditional sound of the soprano.

In addition to his many musical explorations, Lacy maintained an interest in the visual arts as well as spoken word performance. He collaborated with painters, dancers, and writers—poets in particular, including Robert Creeley, with whom Lacy recorded numerous times. Perhaps as a result of his brilliant performances, his wide-ranging interests, and what appeared to be an insatiable curiosity, Lacy was awarded a prestigious MacArthur Fellowship in 1992.

Steve Lacy went on to record many albums both here and in Europe, where he eventually relocated. He lived in Paris from 1970 until 2002, when he returned to the United States to accept a teaching position at the New England Conservatory of Music. Unfortunately, Lacy passed away in 2004, a victim of cancer. Fortunately for us, he left an enormous body of recorded work, which continues to expand and challenge our listening skills today in a most interesting and pleasurable way.

Even though Steve Lacy was the first to play and record the soprano saxophone in a modern jazz setting, it is John Coltrane (see figure 11.2) who many musicians and listeners believe has been its main proponent. Such a debate is irrelevant for a number of reasons. First of all, in the big picture, Lacy was exclusively a soprano saxophonist, while the smaller horn could be said to be Coltrane's second instrument, after the tenor sax—the primary horn of the two, even today. Secondly, both men had highly individual approaches to the soprano, and both were incomparable improvisers. Neither was better than the other. In fact, in the world of jazz, we shouldn't really think of one great player being superior to another; better we should listen to both and then decide which of the two resonates with us the most. Such an approach to listening opens up an entire world of exploration for any open-minded jazz fan.

Coltrane, according to a number of reports, may have started playing the soprano sometime early in 1959, notably in the jazz club at the Sutherland Hotel in Chicago. He definitely played it at Manhattan's Jazz Gallery in 1960, especially on a medium-tempo standard called "I Can't Get Started." A bootleg recording of some if not all of this gig exists and may well be the only known performance of that venerable old tune to feature Trane on soprano.

Figure 11.2. John Coltrane. Photofest.

It was that same year that Coltrane went into the Atlantic Records studio to record his now famous album *My Favorite Things*. The title cut—a
song from Rodgers and Hammerstein's Broadway show *The Sound of Music*—was the first formal outing for Trane on the soprano sax and was so
popular that it began appearing on jazz juke boxes everywhere. In fact, it
was one of the most requested tunes in the Coltrane repertoire throughout
the rest of his career. He eventually followed his version of "My Favorite
Things" a year later with his take on the old folksong "Greensleeves," then
some years later with a similar take on "Chim Chim Cheree," a tune from
the musical *Mary Poppins*. Perhaps it was Coltrane's desire to try to follow "Favorite Things" with a similar soprano saxophone feature song that
would once again become a "hit" in the public ear. Unfortunately, neither

of the follow-up tunes caught the fans' attention, and as a result, Trane moved on to other explorations.

John Coltrane's sound on the soprano saxophone had sort of a Middle Eastern, Asian, and Catalan inflection to it—definitely reminiscent of several reed instruments like the shawm, the zurna, and the shenai. Coltrane's interests included studies of Eastern philosophies and, undoubtedly, the music of many countries in the East, Middle East, and other regions of the world, including Africa, Spain, and others. All of these influences existed in Coltrane's music, and the soprano saxophone was an ideal instrument with which to express and expand these influences. One need only listen to Coltrane's recording of his composition "India" (on Impulse Records) to get a sense of his involvement in world music in the early '60s.

AFTER TRANE: WAYNE SHORTER AND DAVE LIEBMAN

Like Coltrane, the next two soprano saxophonists began as tenor players and added the soprano well into their careers. Wayne Shorter (see figure 11.3) is the first of these and has had a long and distinguished history, as we discovered in the chapter on the tenor saxophone. However, his "voice" on the soprano is one of the most recognizable in all of jazz and pop music. It is so similar in some ways to his tenor saxophone style: an angular, swirling, often mysterious approach that always seems to spiral into beautifully constructed, instantaneous melodies. Shorter began recording on the soprano as a leader and as sideman with Miles Davis in late 1968, and he played it exclusively in early 1969 on Davis's legendary recording *In a Silent Way*, one of the first of the master trumpeter's recordings to successfully fuse jazz with rock. However, the musical bombshell really exploded later that summer when Miles recorded *Bitches Brew*, the gold standard for many jazz fusion recordings to follow. On that project, Shorter played soprano exclusively. Other Shorter-led recordings followed during and after that time, all of which featured both his tenor and soprano saxophones. All show his brilliance, both as a player and as a composer—perhaps one of the greatest living composers in the world of modern jazz.

Much of the '70s and '80s found Wayne Shorter and keyboardist/composer Josef Zawinul recording and performing with their group Weather Report. Again, Shorter's soprano sax was liberally featured throughout the band's many recordings. Shorter also played the smaller horn on recordings by singer-songwriter Joni Mitchell and Steely Dan, among others.

Figure 11.3. Wayne Shorter. Courtesy of Chuck Koton.

One notable recording and DVD featuring Shorter was a live concert in Japan in 1987, which paid tribute to John Coltrane. The setting was an unusual quintet that featured Shorter as one of two soprano saxophonists, the other being Dave Liebman, who happens to be the next great soprano saxophonist we will profile in this section. *DownBeat* had this to say about Liebman:

> His . . . style, as identifiable as a human voice in its emotional tone and dramatic role playing, may in a given solo, conjure up anguish, ecstasy, anger, fear, hilarity, or haughtiness. Liebman's music is storytelling of a very high order—form, content, accent, color, and mood are all in place, on cue.

Although his first instruments were piano and clarinet, Liebman eventually gravitated toward the tenor saxophone; in 1980 he put the tenor aside to concentrate completely upon the soprano saxophone. It is altogether true that Liebman, like Coltrane, Wayne Shorter, and Steve Lacy, has one of the most recognizable voices on the instrument. Of the four, however, Liebman has the most distinctively "human" quality in both his sound and his approach to interpreting and soloing in any musical context whatsoever. In Liebman's hands, the soprano saxophone loses its identity as a metal instrument and comes alive as if it were a living, breathing thing. Certainly, the same can be said of Coltrane, Lacy, and Shorter, but to my ear, it is Liebman who is able to coax a more immediate "humanity" out of his horn. On his website, Liebman describes how he came to play the soprano saxophone:

> The truth is that I came upon the soprano saxophone by chance. After exclusively playing the tenor from age twelve, I began my relationship with the soprano when landing my first full time job as a musician in 1970 with one of the early pioneering fusion bands, Ten Wheel Drive. This was an important step in my life, not only because of the soprano (although in the final analysis that was the most enduring aspect of that gig), but due to the fact that this band placed all the musicians on salary, meaning this was a full time job. Up to that time, I played mostly on weekends and at summer resorts throughout high school and college, enabling me to earn some extra cash money. But by the time I graduated from New York University in 1968 with a degree in American history, I had already decided that I was going to give music a chance but only on my terms. In other words, no more dance music at weddings or the like, only music where there was improvising in a jazz concept. In Ten Wheel Drive I was the only reed player along with several brass, a standard rock rhythm section and a lead singer named Genya Ravan who was very much in the Janis Joplin mode. In any case, I was required to play tenor and baritone saxophone, flute and soprano. So upon completing the audition and being hired, I immediately went to 48th Street in Manhattan where all the music stores are located and bought my first Selmer soprano saxophone with a hard rubber mouthpiece.

And more directly, in terms of his relationship to the soprano:

> So when I began to play the soprano in 1970, I had no direct link to anyone playing it, nor did I consider it a serious instrument for myself. Little did I know what the future would hold for me. . . .

[As a tenor saxophonist] I couldn't see myself looking at the end of a rainbow forever. How could I ever leave my mark on the tenor? It seemed impossible. The soprano was untouched outside of Lacy, Trane, and Shorter. There was room at the top and in 1980, I made the move. ("My Journey with the Soprano Saxophone," Education section www.daveliebman.com)

Liebman's "future" included musical associations with Coltrane's majestic drummer, Elvin Jones, as well as jazz icon Miles Davis and dozens of other prominent jazz artists. All in all, Liebman has recorded over 350 LPs and CDs as a leader and countless more as a "sideman" (a participant).

As a human being, Dave Liebman is energetic, passionate, endlessly curious, and totally committed to jazz—as both a player and as a teacher. As the former, he won both the *Jazz Times* and *DownBeat* polls in 2011 as best soprano saxophonist, and in that same year was named by the National Endowment for the Arts as one of its Jazz Masters—the highest award for exemplary contributions to the music by a living artist. In addition, Liebman has garnered many other awards worldwide, including the prestigious Ordre des Arts et des Lettres from France.

Totally committed to the flourishing of jazz, Liebman has been extremely active as a teacher as well. He founded the International Association of Schools of Jazz, an organization whose goal is to bring both teachers and students together from around the world to share ideas about teaching and playing. His website is one of the most comprehensive sites ever created by a musician and is a forum for his and others' thoughts about the music, as well as a resource for listeners, researchers, and fellow musicians. Liebman has authored dozens of books, articles, and audiovisual aids for both teachers and students, and he continues to expand his efforts as both artist and teacher. His autobiography, *What It Is: The Life of a Jazz Artist*, is an immensely interesting window into one of jazz's most energetic and enigmatic figures—both as an artist and as a human being, devoted to family, friends, students, and listeners alike.

AND THE LIST GOES ON . . .

Even though Lacy, Coltrane, Shorter, and Liebman may be considered the four most influential voices on the soprano saxophone, there are other fine players out there worthy of your time: Englishman Evan Parker has been perhaps one of the most influential players on the European avant-garde scene for some time now and has developed a highly personalized style. While he plays the tenor saxophone as well, he is best known for his stellar soprano work.

Another UK artist, John Surman, while known primarily for his work on baritone saxophone, is also a superlative and highly expressive soprano player. Both he and Parker are adept at what's called "circular breathing," which is the unusual technique of continuous breathing without having to take a breath. The end result is incredible, in that you never see or hear the performer stop to breathe at the end of a phrase.

Jane Ira Bloom plays the soprano exclusively (as did the late Steve Lacy, profiled earlier in this chapter) and is known for her beautiful full sound and fluid phrasing. Like all of the aforementioned soprano players, Bloom has crafted a highly individualized approach to the instrument, giving her a style that is easily identifiable, once you spend some time with her recordings.

Unlike Bloom and Lacy, many of today's notable soprano saxophonists are, in reality, tenor or alto saxophonists who double on the smaller horn as a second instrument. Even so, these are all fine players whose technical and creative skills exist at a very high level. Of particular interest are Norwegian Jan Garbarek, and Americans Steve Wilson, Greg Osby, Branford Marsalis, Chris Potter, and Sam Newsome. Finally, there are avant-garde multi-instrumentalists like Anthony Braxton, Roscoe Mitchell, and Vinny Golia, all of whom include the soprano saxophone among the many woodwind instruments they play.

THE BARITONE SAXOPHONE

Like the baritone voice, this majestic saxophone can fill an entire room with a big, bountiful sound! It is the lowest-pitched of the four saxophones we have examined. The baritone saxophone has for years been the essential low voice in the sax section of the best big bands in jazz. Yet, in addition to its standing as an indispensable voice in the ensemble, the baritone (or "bari," as it is often called) is also a sensational solo instrument. Let's have a look at some of the masters of the instrument.

THE FOUNDATION: HARRY CARNEY

Quite simply, Harry Carney is the gold standard to which most baritone saxophonists aspire. "Harry's sound was as large as a big band," indicates modern bari player Hamiet Bluiett. Indeed, Carney played with such power and yet such beauty that he was an essential force—indeed, the anchor—in any situation in which he participated.

What is also extraordinary about Carney is the lifelong relationship he had with the great Duke Ellington. Carney joined the Ellington band as a teenager in 1926 and stayed with every edition of it until Ellington passed away in 1974—a musical and personal relationship that lasted almost 50 years. Five months after Ellington's death, Carney too died; it was almost as though the Duke and his orchestra were Carney's raison d'être.

It's been said by jazz writer Joachim Ernst-Berendt that Carney was to the baritone saxophone what Coleman Hawkins was to the tenor sax: sheer power, beauty, and exuberance. Listen to Carney's masterful solo on Ellington's composition "Warm Valley," for example, to appreciate his virtuosity. In sum, Harry Carney's positive musical attributes created the standard to which many baritone saxophonists have aspired over the decades.

MULLIGAN STEW: GERRY MULLIGAN

Gerry Mulligan came on the scene in the late 1940s as both a writer and a baritone saxophonist. Commissioned to write an original composition for drummer Gene Krupa's big band, Mulligan flexed his muscles with a "chart" (meaning a composition or arrangement of someone else's song) called "Disc Jockey Jump," which became instantly popular. Mulligan was also an indispensable part of the *Birth of the Cool* recordings of Miles Davis toward the end of the decade. Mulligan was among the first bebop players on the instrument (along with Serge Chaloff). His sound, while not as enormous as Harry Carney's, was more akin to tenor saxophonist Lester Young's somewhat lighter approach. Even so, Mulligan could swing relentlessly. His small groups were often pianoless quartets that featured Mulligan's baritone, opposite either trumpeter Chet Baker or valve trombonist Bob Brookmeyer, buoyed along by bass and drums. The effect was often light and airy, due in no small part to Mulligan's writing and his superlative and lyrical soloing. He carried the small-group approach forward into his Concert Jazz Band by using his quartet as the nucleus of the larger ensemble. As a result, his baritone saxophone and Brookmeyer's trombone were the most prominently featured instruments of that exciting ensemble.

MADE IN DETROIT: PEPPER ADAMS

The first bari player to distinguish himself from either the Harry Carney or Gerry Mulligan sound and style was Pepper Adams. A product of the Motor City, Adams fell under the spell of tenor saxophonist Coleman Hawkins and, as a result, had a uniquely aggressive way of playing the horn that made his intense soloing stand out among his peers. He co-led a hard-bop quintet with trumpeter Donald Byrd and recorded a number of fine discs in the '50s and '60s for Blue Note Records and other labels. Adams was also a superlative section player, and his baritone graced the big bands of Stan Kenton, Thelonious Monk, and the Thad Jones–Mel Lewis Orchestra.

THE SPIRIT OF ST. LOUIS: HAMIET BLUIETT

Although he is now in his 70s, Hamiet Bluiett is one of the most versatile and modern of all baritone saxophonists. A product of East St. Louis (actually a small community just north of it called Brooklyn, Illinois), Bluiett began his lifelong relationship with the baritone at the age of 10. He was also musically active in the navy (where he predominantly played the clarinet), as well as at Southern Illinois University.

Harry Carney was a major early influence upon Bluiett, who heard the great saxophonist with Duke Ellington's orchestra. When you hear Bluiett play, there shouldn't be any doubt that the influence of Carney looms large, even today. Bluiett's sound is big and his tone is dark, yet rich in texture.

After his stint in the navy, Bluiett returned to St. Louis and helped found the Black Artists' Group, an organization dedicated to encouraging and fostering creative African American contributions to music, dance, theater, poetry, and film. In late 1969, he relocated to New York City and a few years later cofounded the World Saxophone Quartet, along with Oliver Lake and Julius Hemphill. The WSQ was and is an enormously versatile and enjoyable group, and to experience their music is an absolute delight. When listening to any of this group's recordings, you will hear the tremendous contributions of Hamiet Bluiett, from the bottom up!

AND THE LIST GOES ON . . .

. . . and includes bop virtuosos such as Cecil Payne, Nick Brignola, and Ronnie Cuber; modernists John Surman, Gary Smulyan, and Scott Robinson; and avant-garde multi-instrumentalists who play the baritone sax among their arsenal of woodwinds, including Vinny Golia, Fred Ho, and the late and brilliant Curt McGettrick. Actually, these last two categories show how inaccurate it can be to "label" players as proponents of one school or the other. For instance, Surman seems to transcend all schools, as did McGettrick. Both men have at their core the deep tradition of the instrument, with Harry Carney at the root of the tree.

The baritone saxophone, like the soprano, does not have the long and expansive tradition that is characteristic of the tenor and alto saxophones; yet both are vital voices in the jazz world and have become essential contributors to all facets of the music.

Getting Personal with Dave Liebman

What advice would you offer a new listener who will be experiencing your music for the first time, either in concert, on YouTube, or via one of your recordings?

First of all, don't let the intensity throw you off. Coltrane was and is my model in many ways, and intensity was one of his many trademarks. (Believe it, I do enjoy playing slow and soft music as well.) A short guide for enjoying my music: listen for shapes rather than specific melodic lines; for color/texture in addition to the sound of the horn. Imagine the rhythms I play that often "bounce" off the pulse as small detours one might take while walking in a park, exploring something of interest off the given path. Listen to the "conversation" with the other musicians. Most of all, try to hear and imagine the story that I tell . . . that's the most important aspect of music to me. Be patient, listen again a few times, and try to be open to the vibrations.

What would be the first recording of yours that you would recommend for an initial listening experience and as a good introduction to your music?

The Loneliness of a Long Distance Runner is probably impossible to get, but in any case it is a solo soprano saxophone recording I did around my 40th birthday in

Figure 11.4.   Dave Liebman. Courtesy of Matt Vashlishan.

1986. The title (taken from a book and film) and the compositions are metaphors for the personal and intense inner voyage that artists of all stripes go through. I like programmatic writing, meaning an image inspires a musical sound. Some of the titles of the tracks are "Personal Best," "Against the Wall," "Breakaway," "Alone," and "Victory/Defeat." The entire recording is only soprano sax, which at that time I played exclusively (putting the tenor down for a 15-year period). There are seven sopranos overdubbed, for example, at one point. As well, it is among the most hard-core composing I have done for a recording. The music was dedicated to an artist I consider one of the best examples of a long distance runner, soprano sax master Steve Lacy.

SELECTED SOPRANO SAXOPHONISTS' WEBSITES: FROM THEN 'TIL NOW

Note: Only official sites are listed. Use Google for all others.

Sidney Bechet: www.sidneybechet.org
Steve Lacy: www.stevelacymusic.org
Dave Liebman: www.daveliebman.com

Evan Parker: www.evanparker.com
Jane Ira Bloom: www.janeirabloom.com

Please note that while many other fine saxophonists play the soprano saxophone, it is often not their primary instrument. The above list includes only those who have been known primarily for their work on the soprano saxophone.

SELECTED BARITONE SAXOPHONISTS' WEBSITES: FROM THEN 'TIL NOW

Note: Only official sites are listed. Use Google for all others.

Gerry Mulligan: www.gerrymulligan.com
Pepper Adams: www.pepperadams.com
Hamiet Bluiett: www.hamietbluiett.com
John Surman: www.johnsurman.com
Ronnie Cuber: www.ronniecubermusic.com
Gary Smulyan: www.garysmulyan.com

RECOMMENDED READING

Soprano Saxophone

Bechet, Sidney. *Treat It Gentle: An Autobiography*. 2nd ed. Cambridge: Da Capo Press, 2002. Print.
Liebman, Dave, with Lewis Porter. *What It Is: The Life of a Jazz Artist*. Studies in Jazz 66. Lanham: Scarecrow Press, 2012. Print.
Liebman, Dave. "My Journey with the Soprano Saxophone." daveliebman.com. n.d. Web. 2 Nov. 2011.
Weiss, Jason, ed. *Steve Lacy: Conversations*. Durham and London: Duke University Press, 2006. Print.

Baritone Saxophone

Klinkowitz, Jerome. *Listen—Gerry Mulligan: An Aural Narrative in Jazz*. New York: Shirmer Books, 1991. Print.

12

REEDS AND DEEDS IV

Top and Bottom Woodwinds—
The Clarinet, Flute, and Bass Clarinet

Each of these three instruments has played an integral role in the evolution of jazz music. The clarinet was one of the first instruments used in jazz music and continued to be a major voice in the music through the swing era. Even though its popularity waned considerably with the advent of bebop and later forms of jazz, it is making a small but surprising comeback. The C-flute and the bass clarinet, while at the opposite ends of the sound spectrum, share some common traits. Unlike the clarinet, their histories in jazz have been fairly recent, and both were categorized initially in the jazz world as "miscellaneous instruments," particularly in jazz polls. However, both the C-flute and the bass clarinet have come into their own as jazz voices, so we have included them here.

THE CLARINET: JAZZ'S LICORICE STICK

Clarinet, *n.* An instrument of torture operated by a person with cotton in his ears. There are two instruments worse than a clarinet—two clarinets.

—Ambrose Bierce, *The Devil's Dictionary* (1906)

The Foundation

Often, when we think about the clarinet in terms of jazz, it is common to think of its role primarily in the music's early years. Originally, it provided an essential voice in Dixieland, along with the front line of cornet and trombone. There were some great New Orleans clarinetists who helped solidify the instrument's place in jazz history, including Alphonse Picou, George Lewis, Johnny Dodds, Jimmy Noone, and Sidney Bechet. All were there at the beginning, and each had a distinctive style; some like Noone played with a softer, more subtle tone, while others like Dodds—a master of the chalumeau, or lower register of the clarinet—were more visceral and aggressive in their approach to both the instrument's sound and to soloing. And then there was Sidney Bechet (see figure 12.1), whose impassioned playing and fast, emotional vibrato made him instantly recognizable on both clarinet and soprano saxophone.

Figure 12.1. Sidney Bechet. Courtesy of the William P. Gottlieb Collection.

While it is clear that the clarinet was a shining star in the world of early jazz, it was also an important voice in swing music, even though its role changed considerably. For one thing, it often became the lead voice in the woodwind sections of big bands like those of Jimmy Dorsey, Artie Shaw, and Benny Goodman, whereas in Dixieland jazz, the clarinet maintained a more subservient role to the trumpet or cornet. In other words, the clarinetist in early jazz embellished the melody as opposed to stating it, a role more defined by brass players like King Oliver, Louis Armstrong, or Bix Beiderbecke.

Certain clarinetists bridged the gap between early jazz and the swing era. Barney Bigard was a versatile clarinetist who straddled the stylistic fence between early jazz and swing. A native of New Orleans, Bigard came up in that city's musical tradition and was comfortable in the Dixieland idiom. However, in the late '20s he began a 15-year association with Duke Ellington's Orchestra, playing mostly clarinet and occasionally the tenor saxophone. He went on to play with Louis Armstrong and his All Stars for almost a decade, and he spent much of the rest of his life in California, touring and working in the studios.

After Bigard left Ellington, he was replaced by another fine clarinetist, Jimmy Hamilton, who stayed with the Ellington orchestra for the next 25 years. Hamilton, who also played tenor saxophone, had a soft, precise tone and an impressive technique instantly recognizable to Ellington fans.

One clarinetist who transcended labels was Pee Wee Russell, who, though born in the first decade of the 20th century, played not only with early jazz bands and Chicago's Austin High Gang (see chapter 3) but also with jazz icon Thelonious Monk. Toward the end of his life, Russell led a pianoless quartet with valve-trombonist Marshall Brown, bassist Russell George, and drummer Ronnie Bedford. Their repertoire included pieces by Monk, John Coltrane, and saxophonist Ornette Coleman. While his style often seemed fragile, Russell's solos were always inventive and maintained a voice-like quality that won him a loyal following, even beyond his passing in 1969.

Two for the Road: Benny Goodman and Artie Shaw

The two clarinetists we often think of in conjunction with the swing era—without much hesitation—are Benny Goodman and Artie Shaw. We've already been introduced to these two fine musicians as band leaders, but not as clarinetists. There continues to be an ongoing debate among diehard swing fans as to which was the better instrumentalist. Some self-styled "experts" say that while Shaw had better technical proficiency, Goodman swung harder. And others maintain the exact opposite. The bottom line is . . . who cares? Both could swing relentlessly, both played in tune and had admirable facility, and both were excellent soloists. Listen to Goodman and Shaw and make up your own mind. That's what's really important here; not some other person's opinion. You may just wind up liking both clarinetists equally.

Two More for the Road: Jimmy Dorsey and Woody Herman

We can also throw another name into the mix: Jimmy Dorsey. He and his trombonist brother Tommy formed the Dorsey Brothers orchestra in the '30s, but Tommy departed in the middle of the decade and Jimmy continued to lead the orchestra alone. Even though Dorsey wasn't really in the same league as Goodman or Shaw—especially since he played alto saxophone as well as clarinet—Dorsey was a fluid craftsman on both instruments and as an alto player was reputed to have been a favorite of Charlie Parker.

Toward the end of the swing era, one more big-band clarinetist-leader came into prominence and kept his bands working, on and off, through the '50s and into the three decades that followed. Woody Herman was a fine musician and an energetic and imaginative organizer. While he was known primarily as a clarinetist, Herman also played alto and soprano saxophones. He often called his groups "herds" and, over a 40-year span, populated his bands with world-class musicians. As a result, the music garnered many fans—and not just the dancing crowd. Listeners came to hear the music and to thrill to the virtuosity of first-tier players as well as the leader's impassioned playing. Unlike Goodman and, to a lesser extent, Shaw, Herman was interested in exploring other types of music, from classical (Igor Stravinsky wrote "Ebony Concerto" for him) to bebop, to rock music.

Yesterday's Keepers of the Flame

As we mentioned earlier, even though the clarinet was most prominent in early jazz and the swing era, its popularity began to diminish with the birth of bebop. However, there were a number of clarinetists who continued, over the decades that followed, to keep the voice of the instrument alive. Among the most notable—and certainly the most enjoyable—of these were Bob Wilber, Kenny Davern, and Pete Fountain. Wilbur and Davern were also accomplished soprano saxophonists and for a time had a group they called "Soprano Summit." Fountain, a New Orleans native son, recorded over a hundred albums as a leader and has, over the years, been immensely popular among a wide cross section of the listening public, especially in the '60s and '70s.

As bop began to take hold, there were a few clarinetists who embraced the new music. Tony Scott and Buddy DeFranco were two reedmen totally immersed in the new language, and both worked to assimilate Charlie Parker's fluency and creativity on the clarinet. It should be noted that while they each played other woodwinds, they focused much of their work on the clarinet.

If anything, Jimmy Giuffre was different than anyone who came either before or after him. A contemporary of DeFranco and Scott, Giuffre had a sound and approach derived less from Charlie Parker's and more rooted in Lester Young's airier tone and long, swooping phrases. Add to that the fact that Giuffre's sound was darker than many other clarinetists, and you have a clarinetist who was totally unique. Giuffre also played tenor and baritone saxophones and exhibited the same dusky sound on those instruments. He led a memorable series of drummerless trios in the late '50s, especially one with guitarist Jim Hall and valve trombonist Bob Brookmeyer—and a few years later, other even more adventurous units with musicians like pianist Paul Bley and bassist Steve Swallow.

Today's Keepers of the Flame

Today's clarinetists are an interestingly diverse bunch. All are wonderful musicians who have chosen markedly different yet fascinating paths. Ken Peplowski continues to be a keeper of the flame for swing jazz and is one of the best of our neoclassicists. Eddie Daniels has an absolutely beautiful sound and is one of the most lyrical of all contemporary clarinetists. Grammy winner Paquito D'Rivera was born and raised in Cuba but has lived in the United States since the 1980s. In addition to clarinet, he plays alto and soprano saxophones, and he has been an integral part of many great jazz groups over the years. He can play bebop, classical music, and

Latin jazz with equal skill and has become much loved by a wide cross section of audiences.

Anat Cohen was born in Tel Aviv, Israel, and, like D'Rivera, has an abiding interest in a wide range of musical genres, including swing and straight-ahead jazz, Brazilian music, Argentine tango, and various forms of Afro-Cuban music. She is equally formidable on both clarinet and the tenor saxophone, and she has won numerous prestigious awards from national jazz magazines such as *DownBeat* and organizations such as the Jazz Journalists Association.

Looking Ahead

The clarinet is alive and well utilized in avant-garde jazz and spontaneous music settings as well. Perhaps the first truly significant clarinetist in the area was the late John Carter, who, together with Ornette Coleman and trumpeter Bobby Bradford, led a number of vibrant and adventurous ensembles beginning in the mid-'60s. He continued his work as both a clarinetist and composer, with Bradford and others, until his passing in 1991. In addition to his ensemble work, Carter was an accomplished unaccompanied soloist. A consummate artist and teacher, he set the tone for generations of clarinetists to come.

Another important modern clarinetist is Perry Robinson, who has played and recorded with many of America's and Europe's finest forward-thinking players. An eclectic and interesting player, Robinson has lent his considerable talents to all manner of musical settings, from a modern world music trio and an improvisational jug band to the Three Generations of [Dave] Brubeck Ensemble. Robinson's style is well rounded and malleable, which suits him well, when it comes to playing in both traditional and avant-garde settings.

It's obvious when you look at the recordings of clarinetist and saxophonist Don Byron that he, like Robinson, is an explorer of the first order. Musical categories mean nothing to him, and every Byron project is different from the last. From gospel to funk to Latin to classical to Lester Young to music for piano and voice to arias to klezmer to . . . infinity and beyond. To experience Don Byron is to experience music on many levels, often simultaneously. This is where words become inadequate. Explore Byron's website (listed at the end of this chapter) and expect the unexpected.

There are two other modern clarinetists who are well worth experiencing. Multi-instrumentalist Marty Ehrlich is an alumnus of the New England Conservatory and a master woodwind wizard. A virtuoso on clarinet, bass clarinet, alto saxophone, and other woodwind instruments, Ehrlich has been on the cutting edge of creative music for quite some time. He has been a recipient of a prestigious Guggenheim Fellowship, as well as a number of other grants and awards. Ehrlich's rich, full sound on all of his instruments is one major characteristic of his virtuosity. His clarinet playing in particular is rich, woody, and very attractive, regardless of which of the many musical genres he wishes to explore. His website, like Don Byron's, is a journey unto itself and very worth the trip!

Chris Speed, like Ehrlich and Byron, is a sonic traveler of the first order. A veteran of New York's youthful "Downtown Scene," Speed is also a first-rate clarinetist as well as an exceptionally good tenor saxophonist. He plays both instruments with equal ease and skill, and he has been a force behind some very intriguing and exciting recordings—both his own and with other excellent musicians like drummer Jim Black and trumpeter Dave Douglas. Speed has also created his own recording label, Skirl Records, which focuses upon contemporary improvised and composed music—both his own projects and the work of others.

FLUTE SALAD

The flute is not an instrument with a good moral effect. It is too exciting.

—Aristotle, *Politics*

Pioneers and Pace Setters

Of the flute and the bass clarinet, the flute has the longer history in jazz. Its use can be traced back to the late '20s and early '30s; yet it was played in jazz settings somewhat infrequently, possibly because it couldn't compete with other instruments in terms of projecting its sound. In other words, put a flutist alongside a trumpeter or a saxophonist, and chances are good that you may not hear the flute at all. However, with the advent of sound amplification such as microphones, and eventually amplifiers, the flute came into its own, both in ensemble and solo work.

While most big bands in the swing era through the early '50s didn't have flute soloists, there was one musician who became the first prominent flutist to be featured consistently in a large-ensemble setting. Frank Wess joined the Count Basie band in 1953, where he was featured on both tenor and alto saxophones, as well as flute. It was through his 11-year association with Basie that Wess became one of the first true solo flutists in jazz. After Basie, Wess continued both large- and small-band activities and was eventually awarded the National Endowment of the Arts Jazz Masters' Fellowship in 2007. At age 90, Wess is still very much a part of the jazz scene and is much beloved by musical colleagues and legions of listeners. His flute sound has always been pure and rich, and his sense of swing, consistently appealing.

Four other flutists who came into the public eye and ear during the '50s were Yusef Lateef, Bud Shank, Sam Most, and Herbie Mann. Multi-instrumentalist Yusef Lateef was one of the first musicians on any instrument to express an interest in the music of Asia, Africa, and other places in the world. Not only does Lateef play the C-flute, but he also plays a wide variety of other members of the world flute family; Lateef also plays the tenor saxophone, as well as the oboe. It is on this last instrument that Lateef achieved worldwide recognition as one of the first true jazz oboe soloists.

Bud Shank was known as a spirited and passionate alto saxophonist, based on the West Coast. He was a fine flutist as well and recorded on the instrument in both large- and small-group settings. He recorded some particularly good sessions with another fine saxophonist, Bob Cooper, who—like Lateef—also played oboe. In fact, in 1956 Shank and Cooper recorded an album called *Flute 'n' Oboe*, which is still a breath of musical fresh air, even today. Shank was a joy to make music with, and he never sounded less than excellent, both in his live performances and on his many recordings.

Sam Most has frequently been called the father of jazz flute. Many critics and seasoned listeners agree that Most is one of the first—if not the first—creative jazz masters of the flute. Most was also the first jazz flutist to master the art of "overblowing"—that is, to sing or hum into the flute while playing it, thereby creating a dual sound of voice and flute in unison. He was also called the father of bebop flute, because his solos were often solidly created in the bebop tradition.

Figure 12.2. Frank Wess on the Jazzmobile, Rochester, New York, 1977. Courtesy of Tom Marcello.

Interlude: "Most Is the Man!"

Sam Most entered his eighth decade in this world in 2010 and, until his death in 2013, played as aggressively as he did 50 years ago. Whether you were in the audience or on the bandstand with Sam, you were assured of having a good time. Sam Most was a virtuoso who was all about high creative standards, and as a person, Sam was an absolute "mensch"—that is, he was a decent, positive, jovial guy who had the gift of instant likability. I played in a small band that Sam co-led with his brother, the clarinetist Abe Most. It was a happy little aggregation and was quite adept at bringing smiles to the faces of listeners, bartenders, and waiters and waitresses everywhere. Sam was a classic example of joy in music and could swing the doors off a barn. Sam and I, for reasons I don't exactly remember, got to talking one night about the joys (and heartburn agonies) of Jewish food, particularly a buckwheat and noodle dish called "kasha varnishkes." And from then on, when we would see each other, Sam would point to me and say the name of that dish and then give a good laugh. For a man who had truly been one of a handful of musicians who put the flute on the jazz map, Sam was extraordinarily humble. It would never dawn upon him to think of himself as more than a guy who happened to really enjoy playing music. As his fans were so apt to say—particularly at concerts that featured both Sam and another pace-setting flute legend, Herbie Mann—"Most is the man!" whereas Mann's fans would counter with, "Mann is the most!"

Like Sam Most and the others discussed thus far, Herbie Mann also brought the flute into the consciousness of the listening public in the '50s and beyond, perhaps even more so, given that Mann experimented with many musical styles in order to provide interesting frameworks for his performances and recordings. Mann crossed all sorts of genre boundaries and lent his considerable talent to Brazilian music and other styles of Latin music, as well as jazz-rock fusion, rhythm and blues, country music, reggae, and even disco music. This, of course, didn't exactly endear Mann to the critics, who cried "Sellout" and "Shallow." However, Mann's skillfulness as a musician, as well as his ability to put together unlikely groups of musicians

Figure 12.3. From left to right, Henry Mancini, Sam Most, the author, and Tom Warrington in Los Angeles, California, in the early 1980s. Courtesy of Fernando Gelbard.

from many genres, transcended the criticism and won him a great many listeners and fans. Needless to say, it also boosted his record sales and his marketability. And like Yusef Lateef, Mann could also be considered as one of our first true practitioners of world music, even though his forays into global styles often had a commercial dimension to them.

Other fine flutists who gained prominence on the instrument in the '50s and '60s were Buddy Colette (a fixture on the legendary Central Avenue jazz scene and an in-demand studio musician thereafter), Paul Horn (who recorded several popular records in the '70s featuring solo flute improvisations in India's Taj Mahal), Jeremy Steig (a brilliant flutist who has experimented with a variety of acoustic and electrified sounds), James Spaulding (an inventive and fiery alto saxophonist whose beautiful flute work was also critically acclaimed), Joe Farrell (known equally for his work on saxophones and flute), and James Moody (long a member of one of trumpeter Dizzy Gillespie's best small groups).

When a seasoned jazz listener thinks of avant-garde flutists, there are two who frequently come to mind. Eric Dolphy, in addition to being an exciting and innovative presence on alto saxophone and bass clarinet, was also a remarkable flute player. It has been said that when he lived at home with his family in Los Angeles, he would practice the flute in his backyard and would attempt to incorporate birdsong into his flute solos. He also had an abiding interest in contemporary flute music and was influenced significantly by the Italian virtuoso Severino Gazzelloni. Dolphy's flute solos are breathtakingly inventive and take the instrument to another level. In contrast to his work on alto saxophone and bass clarinet, his flute playing had a light and airy tone and he played with tremendous facility; his solos are as fresh today as they were right up to his untimely death in 1964.

Like Dolphy, James Newton expanded the language of the flute considerably. Unlike the other fine flutists mentioned thus far, who all doubled on other instruments, Newton is unique in that flute is his main instrument. To call him a virtuoso flutist is an understatement, because he has mastered so many unusual aspects of the instrument. In addition to the overblowing technique mentioned earlier, Newton also developed the ability to play multi-phonics—producing as many as three or four notes at the same time, much like playing a chord on the piano or guitar. The resulting sound is astonishing, coupled with the clear and powerful tone of Newton's flute. His work is well represented on his wonderful duo recordings with pianist Anthony Davis, as well as his solo flute work on a tour-de-force recording called *Echo Canyon*, recorded in the place of the same name, in New Mexico.

No survey of the jazz flute would be complete without introducing flutist Hubert Laws to new listeners. One thing that sets Laws apart from the other fine jazz flutists presented here has been his extensive background in a variety of genres. He earned his degree at Juilliard School of Music in New York City, where he studied with the eminent classical flutist Julius Baker. As a result, Laws is a very accomplished classical player, in addition to being equally at home playing jazz, rhythm and blues, contemporary pop, fusion, and other styles of music. His CTI recordings in particular show all the dimensions of his versatility and virtuosity, yet there are at least 20 CDs under Laws's name that showcase the art of the flute in many settings.

One of the settings in which the flute has become especially prominent has been in a variety of jazz-fusion genres. First and foremost, the flute has always held an esteemed place in Latin music—notably Cuban and Puerto Rican music—and eventually, in Latin jazz fusions as well. One of the most respected Latin-American flutists is Puerto Rican–born Nestor Torres, whose astonishing work with the famed percussionist Tito Puente, pianist Herbie Hancock, trumpeter Arturo Sandoval, vocalist Gloria Estefan, and many others in both Latin and jazz circles earned him a well-deserved place among Latin jazz soloists. A true master of the instrument, Torres has often been called a virtuoso by musicians and listeners alike.

Dave Valentin, born in New York City and of Puerto Rican descent, is another accomplished and well-recorded flutist whose Latin jazz work has earned him a respected place in the hierarchy of both Latin and contemporary jazz flutists. A student of Hubert Laws, Valentin—like Nestor Torres—spent time playing with Tito Puente, as well as many other prominent figures on the New York City Latin jazz scene, and was ultimately signed by pianist/composer Dave Grusin to the GRP label, where he produced a series of crossover recordings that were well received by both Latin and contemporary jazz listeners. He can also be heard to good advantage with the Caribbean Jazz Project, with whom he has recorded some very exciting Latin jazz music.

AND THE LIST GOES ON . . .

There are many other masters of the jazz flute today who are worth noting here. Tenor saxophonist Lew Tabackin has one of the most individual sounds on the instrument and often plays it with his trio, composed only of acoustic bass and drums. Dave Liebman, while known primarily as a virtuoso on the tenor and soprano saxophones, is also an accomplished flutist and has recorded on the C-flute, the alto flute, and a variety of wooden flutes. In the world of contemporary jazz-rock flutists, Bobbi Humphrey and Steve Kujala are two of the best. Finally, among those attempting to expand the possibilities for the flute in new and daring musical settings are Robert Dick, Ali Ryerson, Jamie Baum, and 2012 *DownBeat* poll winner Nicole Mitchell. Their intriguing musical journeys continue to unfold before our very ears!

In addition to the C-flute, other members of the flute family have been featured in jazz settings, even though we don't profile them on these pages. The alto flute, bass flute, and even the tiny piccolo have been featured in live and recorded performances, and they should be explored and enjoyed by all jazz flute fans.

THE BASS CLARINET: ENTER THE DRAGON

It gives people the feeling that someone's blowing on part of a tree.

—David Murray

The bass clarinet has had a relatively short history in the jazz world; how-ever, its major proponents have been responsible for putting it on the musical map in a memorable way. Even so, the bass clarinet cannot claim one or more central figures in its early history who were responsible for an entire school of playing—like Louis Armstrong did for the trumpet and Coleman Hawkins and Lester Young did for the tenor saxophone. The bass clarinet was used rarely in early jazz and didn't really become visible (or more precisely, audible) until Harry Carney began playing it in Duke Ellington's orchestra—occasionally as a soloist, but mostly to give the woodwind section a broader set of tonal colors, much as a painter would want to do on a canvas.

The Major Voice: Eric Dolphy

The musician who really put the bass clarinet front and center was the bril-liant and innovative multi-instrumentalist Eric Dolphy. In Dolphy's hands, the bass clarinet sounded as though it was a living, breathing thing. While Dolphy could exact a beautiful tone from the instrument, particularly on ballads, it was his medium and up-tempo playing that captured his amaz-ing abilities. A Dolphy bass clarinet solo on any given composition might swoop down to the darkest regions of the instrument and soar back up to the instrument's upper register in a matter of seconds. He also brought a genuine vocal quality to the bass clarinet, replete with shrieks and cries, hollers and laughter, moans and groans, and other lifelike sounds. This was never gimmickry on Dolphy's part. It was, for him, purely a matter of self-expression—in essence, speaking his mind through his horn. Nowhere was this more obvious than Dolphy's work with bassist Charles Mingus, with whom he played from 1960 until his untimely death in Europe in 1964.

Indeed, the best way to hear Dolphy—and to see him play—is with Mingus. In 1960, Mingus recorded an album for Candid Records called simply *Charles Mingus Presents Charles Mingus*, which features an aston-ishing speech-like duet between the bassist and Dolphy on bass clarinet.

Figure 12.5. Bennie Maupin. Courtesy of Ewelina Kowal.

Figure 12.4. Eric Dolphy. The Frank Driggs Collection.

This is as close as two instrumentalists come to emulating human voices—it begins as a rather civilized "conversation" and deteriorates quickly into a full-blown "argument." Speaking solely through their instruments, Mingus and Dolphy are truly amazing. The bass has an air of superiority as it scolds the bass clarinet. The latter begins responding in a quiet way but soon explodes, and as the minutes pass, the two "voices" devolve into a full-blown shouting and screaming match, before moving back into the theme of the song they are playing. This has to be heard to be believed. Only two virtuosos like Mingus and Dolphy could have pulled this off.

Fortunately for us, there is video footage of Dolphy with both Mingus's and John Coltrane's groups, both on commercially available DVDs, as well as on YouTube. For instance, on the Mingus DVD Dolphy plays a stunning bass clarinet solo on Duke Ellington's famous opus, "Take the A-Train." It is amazing to watch him make it look so effortless. And through it all—as well as any other music he ever played—Eric Dolphy never failed to swing mightily, shake our very foundations, and transport us into the stratosphere!

Keeper of the Flame: Bennie Maupin

Dolphy set the bar very high for bass clarinetists to come, and no one has met that challenge as memorably as Bennie Maupin. He came to the attention of the listening public mostly as a tenor saxophonist on recordings by trumpeters Lee Morgan and Woody Shaw; pianists McCoy Tyner, Andrew Hill, Horace Silver, and Chick Corea; and other high-profile players. However, it was his bass clarinet playing that attracted the attention of Miles Davis, who was in the midst of an enormous period of transition, moving from the post-bop style to a more electric rock sound. Miles loved Bennie's dark-hued bass clarinet sound and invited him to participate in the now legendary *Bitches Brew* sessions. Many critics agreed that Maupin's atmospheric bass clarinet backgrounds helped give those sessions their unique quality. Maupin also appeared in a similar role on Davis's *Big Fun*, *Jack Johnson*, and *On the Corner*.

But Bennie's musicality goes much beyond his time with Miles Davis. Following his association with the trumpeter, Maupin was a charter member of two notable groups led by keyboardist and Davis alumnus Herbie Hancock. The first, Mwandishi, was a brilliantly conceived, ahead-of-its-time sextet that created and recorded some beautiful and mystical music in the early '70s; and the second Hancock group, called the Headhunters, was formed after the demise of Mwandishi in 1973, and was steeped in both jazz and funk. Of the two groups, the Headhunters was far more commercially successful and easily adaptable to radio airplay. Bennie Maupin's bass clarinet, as well as his saxophones and flutes, was the one constant in both groups.

Maupin's life took some very interesting turns beyond these two fine groups. He took some time off from playing in public and returned to college in Southern California, where he earned his degree and studied composition with Lyle Murphy, a true American original and one of jazz's overlooked and underappreciated geniuses. During this time away from public jazz performances, Bennie practiced, studied with Murphy, and even played B-flat clarinet in the college chamber orchestra. Soon after college graduation, Bennie and I met and began a 20-plus-year relationship that has yielded some uniquely beautiful music.

Maupin's exquisite sound and total command of the bass clarinet from the bottom to the top of its range continue to be impressive today. He can be heard to great advantage with his American group, the Bennie Maupin Ensemble, as well as his Polish quartet. In both groups Maupin plays not only the bass clarinet, but also tenor and soprano saxophones, alto flute, and piano.

And the List Goes On . . .

While Dolphy and Maupin are historically the best known of all jazz bass clarinetists, there are others who are also quite accomplished on the instrument. Foremost among these are David Murray and France's Michel Portal. Murray, a warm, engaging, yet adventurous tenor saxophonist, carries over these characteristics into his bass clarinet playing, adding a touch of Dolphy into the upper reaches of his horn. Unlike Dolphy, Maupin, and Murray, Portal comes to the bass clarinet directly from the B-flat clarinet, rather than from a saxophone. Perhaps as a result, his "sound" on the bass clarinet seems more akin to its smaller cousin.

Other fine bass clarinetists playing today include the multi-instrumentalists Marty Ehrlich and Charles Pillow (New York), Louis Sclavis (France), Willem Breuker (Holland), Piotr Baron (Poland), and Michael Pilz (Germany). And mention should be made of two other multi-instrumentalists: Anthony Braxton, who—among the many woodwinds he has mastered—plays the contra-bass clarinet, which is capable of producing incredible low pitches; and Joe Lovano, who has recorded and performed on the warm and woody alto clarinet, rarely played in jazz settings. With players like these, as well as Dolphy, Maupin, Murray, and Portal, the organic and wonderfully warm and deep sound of the bass clarinet continues to appeal to both players and listeners alike, and will no doubt expand your horizons as a listener, if you take the time to explore and sample their musical wares.

Getting Personal with Bennie Maupin

What advice would you offer a new listener who will be experiencing your music for the first time, either in concert, on YouTube, or via one of your recordings?

I've given your questions some serious thought, and as simple as the questions are, it's a challenge to answer them.

I would never offer any advice if not directly asked to do so. If somehow that question did come up, my only advice would be to listen with an open spirit and enjoy the experience of hearing the musical dialogues between the outstanding musicians that I've had the pleasure of recording and performing with.

Repeated listening of recordings provides an excellent opportunity to listen deeply. However, I believe a live concert is always the most direct way to be introduced to my musical thinking. Being in the moment with live musicians is unique and truly heartfelt.

What would be the first recording of yours that you would recommend for an initial listening experience and as a good introduction to your music?

Most certainly *The Jewel in the Lotus* (ECM Records) would be the first, as it is my very first recording as a leader. Second would be my 2006 recording *Penumbra* (Cryptogrammaphone Records). Both of these projects are a good introduction to my work.

SELECTED CLARINETISTS' WEBSITES: FROM THEN 'TIL NOW

Note: Only official sites are listed. Use Google for all others.

Sidney Bechet: www.sidneybechet.org
Benny Goodman: www.bennygoodman.com
Buddy DeFranco: www.npr.org/programs/jazzprofiles/archive/defranco.html
Eddie Daniels: www.eddiedanielsclarinet.com
Paquito D'Rivera: www.paquitodrivera.com
Don Byron: www.donbyron.com
Marty Ehrlich: www.martyehrlich.com
Anat Cohen: www.anatcohen.com
Chris Speed: www.chrisspeed.com

SELECTED FLUTISTS' WEBSITES: FROM THEN 'TIL NOW

Note: Only official sites are listed. Use Google for all others.

Frank Wess: www.frankwess.org
Sam Most: www.sammost.com
Hubert Laws: www.hubertlaws.com
Jamie Baum: www.jamiebaum.com
Ali Ryerson: www.aliryerson.com
Nicole Mitchell: www.nicolemitchell.com

SELECTED BASS CLARINETISTS' WEBSITES: FROM THEN 'TIL NOW

Note: Only official sites are listed. Use Google for all others.

Eric Dolphy: www.ericdolphy.net
Bennie Maupin: www.benniemaupin.com
Gunter Hampel: www.gunterhampelmusic.com

Don Byron: www.donbyron.com
Marty Ehrlich: www.martyehrlich.com
Charles Pillow: www.charlespillow.com

RECOMMENDED READING

Clarinet

Bechet, Sidney. *Treat It Gentle: An Autobiography*. 2nd ed. Cambridge: Da Capo
   Press, 2002. Print.
Firestone, Ross. *Swing, Swing, Swing: The Life and Times of Benny Goodman*.
   New York: Norton, 1993. Print.
Lees, Gene. *Leader of the Band: The Life of Woody Herman*. New York: Oxford
   UP, 1995. Print.
Nolan, Tim. *Artie Shaw, King of the Clarinet: His Life and Times*. New York:
   Norton, 2010. Print.

Flute

Westbrook, Peter. *The Jazz Flute*. Berkeley: Berkeley Hills Books, 2003. Print.

13

I GOT RHYTHM I

The Piano

To me, the piano itself is an orchestra.

— Cecil Taylor

If I didn't make it with the piano, I guess I would've been the biggest bum.

—Thelonious Monk

I never had much interest in the piano until I realized that every time I played, a girl would appear on the piano bench to my left and another to my right.

—Duke Ellington

The history of jazz really does begin with the piano. While brass bands were certainly a part of events like parades, funerals, family and community celebrations, and the like, the music itself—that is, the rags, cakewalks, and other forms of syncopated dance music that was jazz in its nascence—came from the pianists who composed, arranged, and performed the earliest jazz. We spoke in chapter 3 briefly of Jelly Roll Morton, who retained the syncopations of ragtime and built solos into the mix, thereby creating a hybrid that might well be the beginnings of jazz in its most elemental form, which included both syncopation and improvisation.

The purpose of this chapter is to offer new (and even not-too-new) listeners a look at some of the finest keyboard players in jazz's 100-plus-year history. The emphasis here is on the word "some," because to attempt much more than that would necessitate writing another book, one exclusively about jazz pianists. And frankly, that's already been done quite well by writers like Robert Doerschuk (88: *The Giants of Jazz Piano*) and Alyn Shipton (*A Handful of Keys: Conversations with Thirty Jazz Pianists*). So hopefully, this chapter will serve as a diving board into the jazz piano pool and all of the rich diversity it has to offer.

JELLY ROLL MORTON: "THE INVENTOR OF JAZZ"?

Jazz has always been populated by some really flamboyant characters, and history tells us that Jelly Roll Morton was definitely one of them. He was a pool shark, was always sharply dressed, carried a pistol much of the time, and wore a diamond embedded in one of his front teeth. He was also one of jazz's earliest and best pianists, and he was certainly an innovator in his time. Morton excelled at composing and playing ragtime, which, as we know, was a large part of jazz's beginnings. This style of music, while also played by brass bands and marching bands, emanated from the piano; however, since pianists couldn't readily march down the street, rags were often rewritten or "transcribed" for wind instruments.

Morton came up playing in the brothels in New Orleans, and ultimately he played in New York, Chicago, Washington, D.C., and Los Angeles, among other cities. Even though he was a fine composer and pianist, he was also very forthright about his abilities and innovations—to the point of sounding like a braggart. For instance, during an interview with *DownBeat* magazine, he claimed to be the creator of jazz: "New Orleans is the cradle of jazz, and I, myself, happened to be the creator in 1902." When discussing styles of jazz, he was also reputed to have said: "Kansas City style, Chicago style, New Orleans style—hell they're all Jelly Roll style."

The irony of Jelly Roll Morton is that as much as he would exaggerate and inflate his claims and accomplishments, Jelly was a consummate musician. In the words of clarinetist Omer Simeon, "[Jelly] would back up everything he said by what he could do."

WHAT *IS* STRIDE PIANO PLAYING?

In order to understand what stride piano playing is, we will first need to understand that to stride means "to walk a regular, steady course or pace." In chapter 2, when we were discussing syncopation and pulse, we spoke of the regularity of rhythm we create as we walk down the street. This steady walking pace can be called "striding."

Stride piano styles were born and came of age in New York City in the '20s. Stride pianists in those early days of jazz often played by themselves, and so they had to state the melody of the song with their right hand and create the rhythmic momentum in their left hand, as though they were playing with a tuba player and a drummer.

Now, if you think of playing "Yankee Doodle" on the piano by stating the melody with your right hand on the keys, and simultaneously using your left hand in tempo to play both the bass notes on beats 1 and 3 and the correct chords on after-beats 2 and 4 in each measure, then you have a pretty good idea of the technical challenges facing a stride pianist.

To see a great re-creation of a Fats Waller stride piano solo, go to You-Tube and look up "Jim Hession"; more specifically, search for the following: "Jim Hession/Minor Drag/Harlem Fuss/Fats Waller/stride." Hession is a marvelous pianist, and the camera wisely focuses on his hands throughout the entire piece. This is two-fisted jazz piano playing at its best, and you can actually experience stride piano playing through this video in order to help you understand its sound and feel. Prepare to be amazed!

THREE EARLY GIANTS: JAMES P. JOHNSON, FATS WALLER, WILLIE "THE LION" SMITH

No conversation about great jazz pianists would be complete without acknowledging three absolute masters. Without their contributions, we might not be where we are today in the evolution of jazz piano.

James P. Johnson was one of the greatest of all early jazz pianists and is often called "The Father of Harlem Stride Piano." Classically trained, Johnson was the major innovator of the stride style and moved beyond the confines of ragtime by combining elements of European classical music with the syncopated rhythms of the rags that had been popular in the early part of the 20th century.

Johnson, along with Jelly Roll Morton and other early pianists, recorded his original compositions on "piano rolls," which were originally paper rolls with perforations that were ordered on the paper according to the composition's notated structure and then "read" by player pianos—not piano players! Johnson's most famous compositions, including "The Charleston," "Carolina Shout," and "You've Got to Be Modernistic," were "recorded" onto rolls and were and still are often studied by aspiring stride pianists, who slow the player piano's mechanism down in order to learn the composition in its entirety.

Perhaps Johnson's most famous student was Thomas "Fats" Waller, who achieved much success by combining a ferocious stride piano style with his humorous compositions and vocals. Many of Fats's songs were about having fun ("The Joint Is Jumpin'") or even poking fun ("Your Feet's Too Big"). Two of his most famous and beloved songs were "Ain't Misbehavin'" and "Honeysuckle Rose" (Waller's music and Andy Razaf's great lyrics).

Fats Waller was a phenomenon in every way. At five feet ten inches, he weighed around 300 pounds. He developed a persona that couldn't help but put a smile on the face of all who experienced one or more of his performances. He was a natural comedian and would offer commentary simultaneously while rendering a song. One of his most famous remarks came after the final notes of "Your Feet's Too Big," when he sighed and said somewhat philosophically, "One never knows, do one?"

Whether singing, performing solo, or with one of his small bands, Waller was a wonder. Fortunately, there are some videos available on YouTube and elsewhere that will enable you to experience Waller's magic as both pianist and entertainer.

His full name was William Henry Joseph Bonaparte Bertholoff Smith, but Willie "The Lion" Smith is the name he preferred to be known by. He was a contemporary of both Johnson and Waller and was, in his way, as colorful a character as Waller. He was an imposing-looking man, almost always wearing his derby hat and smoking his ever-present cigar—and always ready to do battle at the keyboard by taking on all would-be stride pianists. There have been various stories about how Smith became "lionized," and certain accounts dispute others. However, one thing is for sure: when the Lion entered the room at one of Harlem's rent parties and you were sitting at the piano getting ready to play, you'd best be at the top of your game—because if you were not, the Lion would let you know that you weren't "up to snuff."

The Lion was a masterful ensemble player, in addition to being a fine so-loist. He maintained a group he called "The Cubs" and worked with them and other small bands over the years. He was also a masterful composer, although his compositions never achieved the commercial popularity of Waller's material. Smith played his music throughout the decades and lived a long life. Just a few months before his passing in 1973 at age 75, he played a concert in New York. By all accounts, it was a great swan song for a great musician.

FLYING FINGERS: ART TATUM

As National Public Radio's John Burnett tells it: "The great stride pianist Fats Waller famously announced one night when [Art] Tatum walked into the club where Waller was playing, 'I only play the piano, but tonight God is in the house.'"

Figure 13.1. Art Tatum. Courtesy of the William P. Gottlieb Collection.

Tatum has been called one of the greatest of all jazz pianists. He executed impossibly difficult keyboard passages with uncanny accuracy and lightning speed. Amazing, when we consider that Tatum was practically sightless from birth and learned to play the piano initially by ear. Many say that his best work was as a solo pianist—indeed, Tatum seemed to prefer that format, even though he did record with his trio (bassist Slam Stewart and guitarist Tiny Grimes), as well as other ensembles. Not intentionally, Tatum bested many a pianist during informal competitions, or "cutting contests," as they were often called. As his reputation grew in Harlem and elsewhere, Tatum was the object of much praise and awe on the part of both musicians and listeners. His roster of fans outside of the jazz world grew as well and included George Gershwin, Oscar Levant, and classical pianist Vladimir Horowitz, to name only a few.

Tatum himself looked up to fellow pianists Fats Waller and Earl "Fatha" Hines, particularly the latter, who had begun to break away from the stride tradition by playing more single lines of notes—almost hornlike—rather than chords. This approach would continue to grow and develop with the advent of bebop; however, Tatum had begun experimenting along these lines quite some time before the birth of bebop. This was ironic, since once bebop took hold, Tatum's audiences shifted away from his style of playing into the more modern realms of the new music of Charlie Parker and Dizzy Gillespie.

While the stride piano style was exciting and had its own infectious groove, it was not what we would call "swinging." Pianists who may have come from the stride era yet moved effortlessly into a smoother, more flowing way of playing included Teddy Wilson, Duke Ellington, Count Basie, and Nat "King" Cole. Tatum, on the other hand, remained firmly entrenched in his unique style—and was a brilliant musician who transcended the piano itself and moved into the higher realms of virtuosity, where he remains to this day.

TWO OUTSTANDING FEMALE PIANISTS: MARY LOU WILLIAMS AND DOROTHY DONEGAN

While instrumental jazz was decidedly a man's world back in its early days, two female pianists emerged as distinctive voices on the instrument. The first of these was Mary Lou Williams. A pianist whose career spanned decades and moved from playing stride piano, swing, bebop, and even avant-garde jazz, Williams seemed insatiably curious. She didn't merely stay rooted comfortably in one style of playing or another, but challenged herself to explore all approaches to the jazz art. As the music continued to evolve, so did she. Williams also became known as a fine arranger and composer. She was often accused of not embodying one style or another, which was, to her way of thinking, a compliment. Williams felt that not being pigeonholed as this or that kind of pianist freed her up to explore, experiment, and innovate—all of which she certainly did.

The other pianist, while not as revered or as creative as Mary Lou Williams, certainly made her mark as a jazz pianist, largely because of her energetic, powerful approach to performing. To call Dorothy Donegan a jazz pianist is not really enough. She was, in fact, a true performer and entertainer as well. Although she played in different musical combinations,

Figure 13.2. Mary Lou Williams. Courtesy of the William P. Gottlieb Collection.

her real forte was solo piano. Like Art Tatum, Donegan was an entire orchestra unto herself, creating dazzling virtuosic displays from the low to
the high end of the keyboard. However, whereas Tatum's touch was light
and his articulations incredibly accurate, Donegan's approach was much
heavier and more dramatic, with less of an intellectual, creative emphasis
and more of an intensely physical one.

Interlude I: Thunder!

At first, Dorothy Donegan scared the hell out of me. I had been hired as a
last-minute sub for the regular drummer in a Miami Beach nightclub. His
job as part of the house rhythm section was to accompany all of the singers and performers who came through town from New York, Chicago, and
other big cities, to entertain the locals as well as the tourist crowd. I was
probably the only drummer he could get on such short notice. He knew I
was green behind the gills with only a little experience playing for singers
and acts; however, I was probably his last best hope to cover the gig in his
absence.

I was to play for singer Dakota Staton, who at that time was enjoying
success as a jazz singer and a recording artist for Capitol Records. She was
beautiful, gracious, and a wonderful song stylist in the manner of Sarah
Vaughan and Dinah Washington. Sharing the bill with Staton was someone
named Dorothy Donegan, whom I hadn't heard of until that night, when
the bassist said something to me like, "Don't let her intimidate you." Hearing those words intimidated me, and I found myself with sweaty palms and
a lot of apprehension. At the verbal rehearsal, Donegan, who was a large,
imposing woman, said only a few words: "Just follow me." I thought about
those words all the way through Dakota Staton's laid-back, swinging set.

After a brief intermission, it was Donegan's turn in the spotlight. From
the first note, she got everyone's attention. Right out of the gate, she exuded
power and a kind of "my-way-or-the-highway" confidence that let the bassist
and me know that she meant business and we had better be there for her on
every moment of every tune. Not only was Dorothy a pianistic powerhouse,
but, my God, she was fast and loved to play tempos at breakneck speed. I
hung on for dear life, and several times during those terrifying moment she

looked over at me and smiled, as if to say, "I bet you never heard a woman play like this." Frankly, I had never heard anyone play like that!

When the set was over, I was drenched in sweat and felt about 20 pounds lighter. Looking back on it, I must have passed some kind of test, because she thanked me and shook my hand. Her grip was harder than my father's.

HOW DID BEBOP AND STRIDE PIANO PLAYING DIFFER?

Unlike the stride style of playing, which emphasized the importance of the role of the left-hand bass (beats 1 and 3) and after-beat notes (on 2 and 4), bebop had no such constraints, since there were almost always a bassist and a drummer present in the piano-bass-drums rhythm sections that were typical of bebop groups from their beginnings. The bop pianists often used their left hands to play a song's chords or its altered chords; all the while, the right hand was free to solo in the bebop idiom.

RHYTHM-A-NING: THELONIOUS MONK AND BUD POWELL

We can't begin talking about the evolution of bebop piano styles without beginning with two giants: Thelonious Monk and Bud Powell.

There have been many books, essays, and articles written about Thelonious Monk (see figure 13.3). There are videos of his performances, as well as documentaries, notably *Straight, No Chaser*, executive producer Clint Eastwood's lovely tribute to Monk. There is even an institute named in his honor, which continues to be a training ground for aspiring and gifted young jazz musicians.

So what was it that made Monk so special? One thing was that he was an important figure in and a major contributor to the birth of bebop. He was there when and where it all began: at Minton's Playhouse in New York City, along with Charlie Parker, Dizzy Gillespie, and Miles Davis, as well as pianist Bud Powell, bassist Tommy Potter, and drummers Kenny Clarke and Max Roach, among others.

Figure 13.3.   Thelonious Monk. Courtesy of the William P. Gottlieb Collection.

Even though Thelonious Monk was part of that important jazz revolution, he brought something to the musical table that was and would forever be completely unique. He was inimitable, both as a pianist and as a composer. Monk followed his own path, and while he may have been overshadowed in the early days of bebop by those more visible revolutionaries mentioned above, the man and his music became an American institution—so much so that Monk appeared on the cover of *Time* in February 1964. However, the picture that the mainstream media painted of Monk was that of an eccentric, left-of-center, rather distant man—in short, an oddball. It was an unfair and largely inaccurate portrayal of someone who merely viewed life and music through a different set of lenses—and followed that path unflaggingly throughout his career.

When we consider Monk's greatness, we need to do so from two distinct perspectives: as a pianist and as a composer. Monk the piano player was well schooled early on in gospel music, as well as in the stride style of piano playing. His breadth and depth of experience prepared him for his immersion in jazz in the early '40s with his own small bands. As a "bebop" musician, Monk developed a completely unique playing style. Instead of trying to emulate the long, fluid multi-noted solos of a Dizzy Gillespie or a Charlie Parker, Monk's solos were sparse and economical, yet at the same time intriguing and ear catching, with their little twists and turns into unknown musical territories and otherworldly terrains. As a result, his solos left considerable space for the bassist and the drummer to add rhythmic comments between his phrases. And when Monk engaged one or more horn players, he would often "lay out" (cease playing completely) in order to let them solo with just bass and drums. Perhaps the most exciting instances of this unique approach occurred in his quartets: the electrifying late '50s group with saxophonist John Coltrane and Monk's long-standing foursome with saxophonist Charlie Rouse. During those pianoless moments, Monk would be so lost in the music that he would often get up from the piano bench and do a little dance—sort of a "soft shoe," punctuated by gentle 360-degree spins. Then, at a point usually right before his own solo, Monk would slide back onto the piano bench and jump into the music.

Interlude II: The Dancing Monk

One night at New York's legendary Village Vanguard proved to be my front-row seat to Monk, the pianist, the composer—and the dancer.

I was visiting the city and went to the Vanguard with my cousin especially to experience Monk and his music. I had only recently begun to listen to his records and was especially attracted to his quirky piano playing with its jagged edges and its jabs, bobs, and weaves. Monk the pianist would sneak up on you like a great boxer—and when you were least prepared for it, he'd bop you in the nose with some unexpected note, chord, or rhythmic figure.

That night, while Charlie Rouse was soloing on one of Monk's medium-tempo tunes, the pianist got up, one-quarter of a lit cigarette between two fingers of his right hand, and proceeded to trip a little light fantastic fairly close to where we sat. While Rouse built up a good head of steam, Monk danced a little closer to our table, cigarette burning dangerously close to his fingers. Seeing this, I moved the ashtray close to the edge of the table in case Monk needed a place to put the cigarette out. Not more than two or three feet in front of us, Monk did a little pirouette, his cigarette hand extended in our direction. My heart stopped. I moved the ashtray a little closer and Monk extinguished the butt . . . on the table, before moving back to the piano bench and beginning his solo—all without missing a beat. I was in the presence of greatness.

Monk the composer was as original as Monk the pianist. Like Charlie Parker, he could take a song like the old standard, "Just You, Just Me," and—keeping the song's original chord changes—substitute a melody of his own. In this case he called his composition "Evidence" or "Justice," the latter being a bit of wordplay, based upon the song's original title. So "Just You, Just Me" became "Just us" or "Justice." However, even if you knew the former song's melody, you'd have difficulty finding any semblance of it at all in "Evidence," the melody of which is really just a series of short, spaced-out jabs of notes scattered throughout the length of the song.

Stylistically, Monk's music falls into many different categories. Some of his songs use melodic repetition as a vehicle, so you might hear the simple melody of "Raise Four" or "Friday the Thirteenth" repeated numerous times before the solos. Other songs like "Skippy" or "Trinkle Tinkle" are impossibly hard to play in that each song contains long, complex groupings of notes that take some serious practice to be able to play correctly on any instrument. At the other end of the musical spectrum, Monk's ballads are beautifully expressive. His most famous ballad, and an important part of any serious jazz musician's repertoire, is "Round Midnight," which is also a favorite among jazz vocalists. Finally, some of Monk's work defies categorization. There has never been anything quite like "Brilliant Corners," a march-like song that has an air of the sinister about it. There is "Boo-Boo's Birthday," a bright, childlike piece that Monk wrote for his daughter's birthday. And of course there are the swingers: compositions like "Rhythm-a-ning" and "Straight, No Chaser," that were reflections of the bebop era, as seen through Monk's eyes.

Monk is definitely worth spending some time with via the many YouTube videos, DVDs, and CDs of his performances, as well as via Robin D. G. Kelley's exhaustive biography, *Thelonious: A Life*, which is a wonderfully readable book and a perceptive, intimate portrait by a Monk scholar and eminent jazz writer. Whether it be in his solo, quartet, or big-band performances, Thelonious Monk was an American original and continues to be celebrated as such. New listeners are heartily invited to join in the celebration!

Thelonious Monk was close friends with the other great pianist to emerge from the bebop era: Bud Powell was "yin" to Monk's "yang." It's not exactly that the two men were musical opposites; both were major innovators in jazz, particularly in the expanding role of the piano in this new music. However, where Monk scattered small clusters of notes here and there in his solos and played sparsely (to great effect) throughout many of his performances and recordings, Bud Powell played long, brilliantly fluid bebop lines, unbroken by very many silences. It seems as if he rarely took a breath! If you listen to Charlie Parker's solo on his composition "Ornithology" and you follow Bird's solo with Bud Powell's solo from one of his trio recordings, you will find very little difference in their solo styles. Powell absorbed much from Bird—to the point where he was truly the first pianist to emulate Bird's multi-noted approach to soloing. It's fair to say that Powell played piano much the same way a great horn player would play a solo in the bebop idiom.

Unfortunately, Powell lived a relatively short life—one that was complicated by serious mental health issues, alcoholism, and narcotics abuse. He endured hospitalizations, electro-shock therapy, and other nightmares and made a number of comebacks, only to be crushed under the weight of his personal and physical problems. Bud Powell passed away in 1966 at the age of 41. Like Charlie Parker and, later, John Coltrane, Bud Powell was like a comet arcing brilliantly across the sky for a mere moment, before disappearing into history. And his legacy continues to burn brightly whenever someone discovers Powell's genius for the first time. His music—at its best—is filled with a richness that waits only for us to discover it.

THEORY AND PRACTICE:
A FEW WORDS ABOUT LENNIE TRISTANO

Pianist Lennie Tristano was an enigmatic individual and a musical vision-ary whose influence has never been fully appreciated by the listening pub-lic, who—thanks to those in the critical press who either overlooked or ignored him—have no idea of who he was, nor what his accomplishments were. Tristano was one of the first, if not the first, jazz musician to intro-duce the avant-garde school of playing to musicians and listeners alike. In 1949, Tristano recorded two pieces that had no preconceived form at all. The group, which included alto saxophonist Lee Konitz and tenor saxophonist Warne Marsh, created the music on the spot, without any planning as to melody, harmony, or rhythm. Tristano's innovations in free music came about almost a decade before Ornette Coleman introduced the freedom principle with his pianoless quartet. In addition, Tristano's written compositions were often made up of long, sinewy phrases, almost as if J. S. Bach had written them himself. He came to New York in the late '40s largely as a player, and he performed with the likes of Charlie Parker and Dizzy Gillespie; however, as the years passed, Tristano played less and less and concentrated upon teaching his theories more. He opened a school for jazz in the early '50s, which lasted about five years, and after that time taught privately. His students, admirers, and fans included Bill Evans, Charles Mingus, and Warne Marsh, as well as many other musi-cians who passed through his music studio. Principles from the Tristano school are still being taught today, at the college and university level. Per-haps we are just now catching up to and appreciating Tristano's unique-ness. In any case, his music is complex but, in the end, fully accessible for old and new jazz listeners alike.

AN EMBARRASSMENT OF RICHES

As a pianistic pioneer, Bud Powell influenced a great many fine pianists and still does so today. Back in the mid- to late '40s, during that vibrant and fertile time of transition from swing to bebop, Monk intrigued more musi-cians than he actually influenced, largely because of his uniqueness as both pianist and composer. However, Powell's horn-like approach to soloing seemed to be very attractive to other pianists, who found his innovations to be attractive and accessible, if not always technically achievable. And to be sure, jazz has never seen a shortage of fine pianists.

Among those who got Powell's—and to a greater extent, bebop's—message were Oscar Peterson, whose ferocious sense of swing and explosive cascades of notes created sheer excitement in the community of musicians and listeners; Tommy Flanagan, Barry Harris, Walter Bishop Jr., Horace Silver, Harold Mabern, Bobby Timmons, Cedar Walton, and George Wallington, all of whom evolved into fluent interpreters of the new music, both as accompanists and soloists in the great bop bands that began to appear with the birth of bebop; Red Garland, a major innovator of what is called the "block chord" approach to soloing (where both hands play chords in a solo, not just the left hand accompanying the right), whose rich harmonies and relaxed delivery were an integral part of Miles Davis's first great quintet; Ahmad Jamal, whose sparse elegance and economy exerted a tremendous influence upon the solo style of trumpeter Miles Davis, who even credited Jamal publicly as one of his important influences; Erroll Garner, a totally different kind of pianist, whose elegant inventiveness and love affair with the melodies of songs, more so than with their improvisational possibilities, gave him perhaps more commercial appeal than other players, even though he was an adept improviser; and finally, Hank Jones, brother of drummer Elvin and trumpeter Thad, who was one of jazz's preeminent pianists, and whose tasteful, swinging brilliance graced many records—both his own and others'—and whose performances delighted countless listeners until shortly before his passing at age 91.

SEVEN STEPS TO HEAVEN: THE PIANISTS OF MILES DAVIS

We already know that Miles Davis was a major force in jazz for almost five decades and was at the forefront of bebop, cool jazz, orchestral jazz, postbop, and jazz-rock fusion. We also know that Miles nurtured musicians who would go on to create their own innovative music after leaving his group. Miles's band, like those of drummer Art Blakey and pianist Horace Silver, was an incubator that produced major talent, especially pianists.

While there were other pianists who played with Miles off and on throughout his career, there are seven who stand out, not only for the level of their musicianship, but also for their ultimate contributions to the music, made largely during or after their tenure with the trumpeter.

The first two of these are Red Garland and Wynton Kelly. Garland, as noted in the previous section, was a member of Davis's first great quintet, along with saxophonist John Coltrane, bassist Paul Chambers, and drummer Philly Joe Jones. Garland, Chambers, and Jones became known at that time as one of the premier rhythm sections in jazz. Garland's chordal elegance and his ability to play consistently excellent solos, bolstered by Chambers and especially the fiery Jones, brought him much critical praise.

Wynton Kelly replaced Garland when the latter decided to leave the Davis quintet to pursue other musical interests. He stayed with Miles for four years, from 1959 to 1963, and added a soulful voice to the rhythm section, as well as an infectious, finger-snapping groove. By this time, drummer Jimmy Cobb replaced Philly Joe Jones, and the Kelly-Chambers-Cobb rhythm section became a cohesive unit—so much so that they worked together after their stint with Miles, most notably with guitarist Wes Montgomery. Kelly also continued his musical relationship with Jones and recorded a series of swinging small-group albums with both Jones and Chambers as his section mates.

There is a quote by Miles Davis at the beginning of one of the early chapters of Keith Shadwick's 2002 biography of Bill Evans, which describes the pianist's playing quite perceptively: "The sound Bill got was like crystal notes or sparkling water cascading down from some clear waterfall" (Shadwick, 61).

Just as Fats Waller, Art Tatum, Thelonious Monk, and Bud Powell changed the face of jazz piano playing in their times, so, too, did Bill Evans forever alter the way we hear the piano and perceive its role in the jazz world. Rather than coming out of the blues, gospel, or early jazz traditions, Evans brought elements of European classical music into the mix. For example, if you listen to Maurice Ravel's Piano Trio in A Minor and follow that with any number of Evans's trio performances, you may hear some distinct similarities in the way the music flows and in the emotional depth of the harmonies. The other side of that coin was Evans's tremendous sense of swing—undoubtedly as a result of Bud Powell's influence.

You don't have to be an expert or even a seasoned listener to know how certain music makes you feel. Often when new listeners who say that they like Bill Evans's music are asked why they like it, the answers usually revolve around the words "romantic," "peaceful," "swinging," and "full of real feeling." However, the most intriguing response among my own students has always been something like this: "I honestly don't know exactly how to

Figure 13.4. Bill Evans. Photofest.

put it into words. Bill Evans just seems to put me in touch with something deep inside that I can't put a name to. Something really personal. . . ."

Indeed, part of Evans's magic is the depth of feeling in his playing, as well as his choice of musical settings. Here are some of the characteristics that made him so special:

His Sound

Evans's "touch" was light and sensitive, yet aggressively swinging. He always managed to get to the "essence" of whatever song he was playing, his interpretations enhancing rather than detracting from it.

Evans understood the importance of the relationship between sound and silence. He would often let a note or chord hang in the air and dissipate into silence, before continuing to play. This is an approach that many master poets use when setting up their poems visually, in order to create a certain feeling.

He would use the piano's "sustain" pedal to allow a note or chord to ring for a long time. This technique was very much in evidence on his trio recordings and his remarkable duo recordings, especially those with guitarist Jim Hall.

Evans was a master of what is known as the "locked hands" approach, which has a pianist playing chords with both hands, close together on the keyboard, giving a song a certain thickness it would not ordinarily have with single-note statements created by only one hand.

His Groups

Solo: Evans's first solo outing on record in 1963 (*Conversations with Myself*) was, by definition, a "group recording," since he recorded piano solos, then overdubbed his "conversations" with the originals, on two additional tracks. The album won a Grammy the following year, and Evans went on to record several more albums in a similar vein.

Duo: Three notable duos, all critically praised for their great beauty. The first duo with equally sensitive guitarist Jim Hall yielded two lovely albums: *Undercurrent* and *Intermodulation*. The second series paired Evans with bassist Eddie Gomez for several recordings, beginning with *Intuition*. The third duo collaboration was with singer Tony Bennett, which resulted in two inspired albums, *The Tony Bennett–Bill Evans Album*, released in 1975, and *Together Again*, in 1977.

Trio: This was easily the most memorable of all the pianist's chosen settings for his music. Ostensibly, the most well-known and beloved of Evans's threesomes included the virtuoso bassist Scott LaFaro and drummer Paul Motian. The group existed from the end of 1959 until the middle of 1961, when LaFaro was killed in an automobile accident. The true essence of this trio lay in its ability to create and sustain three-way musical "conversations." The result altered the course of piano trio music in jazz for decades to come. Other fine Evans working trios included bassists Chuck Israels, Eddie Gomez, and Marc Johnson; and drummers Larry Bunker, Marty Morell, Eliot Zigmund, and Joe LaBarbera.

Larger Groups: These included, most famously, Evans's tenure with the Miles Davis sextet; many other pre-trio recordings with Lee Konitz, Chet Baker, Tony Scott, George Russell, and many others. Later, quartet and quintet recordings with Cannonball Adderley, Freddie Hubbard, Kenny Burrell, Toots Thielemans, and others.

Another of Miles Davis's pianists who went on to well-deserved fame after leaving Miles was Herbie Hancock. There are two words that come to mind when describing him: "virtuosity" and "versatility." Like many of the pianists already introduced, Hancock is a complete virtuoso. At age 11 he debuted playing one movement of a Mozart piano concerto with

Figure 13.5.   Herbie Hancock (left) and Chick Corea. Photofest.

the Chicago Symphony Orchestra at one of their Young People's Concerts. He seemed, as he continued his musical studies, to be able to adapt to any type of music—a characteristic that has served him well throughout his long and successful career. The years have shown Hancock to be a creative artist who has set the standard for excellence, both as a pianist and as a composer.

That Herbie Hancock is versatile is obvious once you look at the breadth of his discography. On *Takin' Off*, his first recording as a leader in 1962, Hancock includes a diversity of sounds and feelings, including a jazz waltz, some soulful "grits 'n' gravy" originals, a wonderfully mysterious song called "The Maze," a duet for Hancock and tenor saxophonist Dexter Gordon called "Alone and I," and finally a song called "Watermelon Man" that has since become an important part of the repertoire of many bands—jazz and otherwise. This first effort by Hancock gives us a preview of the versatility that was to be a staple part of his musical life over the years.

In 1963 Hancock auditioned for and got the gig with Miles Davis and became a member of one of the most startling and revolutionary rhythm sections in the history of jazz. Miles's "Second Great Quintet" came into existence in 1964 and featured saxophonist Wayne Shorter, Hancock, bassist Ron Carter, and the then 16-year-old wunderkind Tony Williams on drums. Their first studio effort in 1965 was called *E.S.P.* and was the first of a series of incredibly exciting and ear-opening albums. Hancock's work in this group, from recording to recording, showed tremendous growth as both a soloist and an accompanist. The group lasted until 1968. Even though Hancock left to pursue his own musical path, he did record with Davis on subsequent projects, as the trumpeter began moving into the realm of jazz-rock fusion.

One of the first and still one of the most intriguing and daring Hancock projects was a sextet formed in 1970 called "Mwandishi," which featured the three-horn front line of Bennie Maupin (woodwinds), Eddie Henderson (trumpet/fluegelhorn), Julian Priester (trombone), and a rhythm section consisting of Hancock, bassist Buster Williams, and drummer Billy Hart. Eventually, synthesizer player Patrick Gleeson was added to the lineup and appeared on the group's second recording, *Crossings* (the first was self-titled). The music—mostly by Hancock and Maupin—was mysterious, atmospheric, and subtly rhythmic—all at the same time. The group recorded two albums and disbanded in order that Hancock might pursue a funkier approach to jazz-rock. Retaining Maupin on woodwinds,

Hancock formed a group called the Headhunters, which recorded its first project in 1973. Featuring players like Maupin, bassist Paul Jackson, drummers Harvey Mason and Mike Clark, and percussionist Bill Summers, this band successfully fused jazz and funk, and would define one of the directions Hancock has taken over the years. The word "one" is stressed here because Hancock continues to immerse himself in a wide and impressive variety of musical endeavors, including a number of concept recordings honoring the music of other artists, from the Gershwins and Joni Mitchell to artists representing pop, hip-hop, and world music. Even so, he still returns in numerous ways to his jazz roots by recording and performing with many of today's leading jazz artists. Herbie Hancock is truly a man for all seasons.

After Miles disbanded his second great quintet, he formed a third quintet, which featured hold-over Wayne Shorter, pianist Chick Corea, bassist Dave Holland, and drummer Jack Dejohnette. The music was dense and very challenging; Corea played electric piano on this band, which contributed to the deliberately dark and murky sound Miles seemed to be looking for. Corea first recorded with Miles in 1968 and the subsequent year toured with the third quintet. Corea was also present on three of Davis's landmark recordings: the eerily beautiful *In a Silent Way*, the pioneering jazz-rock fusion recording *Bitches Brew*, and *Live at the Fillmore*.

The late '60s and early '70s also found Corea recording what has become a piano trio classic. *Now He Sings, Now He Sobs* featured bassist Miroslav Vitous and drummer Roy Haynes. Many musicians and listeners alike believe it to be one of the greatest modern jazz trio records ever made. Corea is in top form, and Haynes and Vitous are responsive, supportive, and daring in their accompaniment and solos. Corea also formed another unit around that time called "Circle"—this one more avant-garde in its approach to group improvisation. As a trio, it included Corea's Miles Davis section mate, bassist Dave Holland, and drummer Barry Altschul. As a quartet, Circle added avant-garde woodwind player and composer Anthony Braxton. This was a time of much experimentation in jazz, and Circle was representative of a lot of the musical explorations taking place back then.

Like Herbie Hancock, Chick Corea was also interested in fusing elements of jazz and rock, except that in his case, Corea also added the component of Latin music into the mix. He utilized elements of Spanish and Brazilian music in his compositions—perhaps even more so than rock influences. The first edition of his fusion group, Return to Forever, featured Joe Farrell on flute and, occasionally, saxophone; Stanley Clarke on bass; Brazilian percussionist Airto Moreira on drums; and his wife, Flora Purim, on vocals. Later editions of RTF included Clarke, drummer Lenny White, and either guitarist Bill Connors or Al DiMeola.

Corea further explored fusion's possibilities with a series of amazing studio recordings featuring an all-star cast of contemporary jazz artists like saxophonist Michael Brecker and drummer Steve Gadd. He also recorded memorable duos with Herbie Hancock, long-time duet partner vibraphonist Gary Burton, and banjoist Bela Fleck.

Corea's other endeavors have included his Elektric Band and his Akoustic Band, the core of which originally included bassist John Patitucci and drummer Dave Weckl. While the personnel for the Elektric Band changed numerous times, the trio with Patitucci and Weckl remained constant.

His recent live two-CD set, with Bill Evans alumni bassist Eddie Gomez and the late drummer Paul Motian, moves both backward in time and forward as they explore Evans's timeless compositions. Corea had this to say about his admiration of Bill Evans: "Bill's contribution to the world of music and aesthetics is unable to be measured. Those he inspired know. I personally have learned a great deal from him!"

There have been many more recordings that point to an incredible diversity in Corea's musical life, and yet the one constant that remains through all of it is the pianist's energetic and joyous approach to making the music come alive.

Austrian-born Joe Zawinul came to international prominence in 1961 as a member of the very popular Cannonball Adderley Quintet. His gospel-tinged composition "Mercy, Mercy, Mercy" became a hit for the group and ultimately a staple in the soul jazz repertoire for jazz groups everywhere.

However, it was Zawinul's brief association with Miles Davis, during the trumpeter's transitional phase from straight-ahead jazz to jazz-rock in the late '60s, that brought him further into the jazz limelight—this time as a composer more so than as a player. Zawinul, drawing from the folkloric elements of his Austrian youth, composed the beautiful, ethereal title track of Davis's landmark recording *In a Silent Way*. Many jazz historians and seasoned listeners consider this Davis album one of the best of all his fusion works. Zawinul was also an active participant on the trumpeter's seminal *Bitches Brew*, as a player rather than as a composer. All things considered, Zawinul was an integral part of the birth of this new hybrid music, which would attract many listeners and enrage other, more traditionally minded jazz fans.

It was Zawinul's relationship with Davis saxophonist Wayne Shorter that was truly history in the making. The two had spent some time discussing the possibility of a band that would build upon what Miles Davis had created—yet present the music in a different and unique light. Their proposed group would avoid the traditional jazz format of stating a musical theme or melody, following it with individual solos, and returning to the melody to end the performance. Zawinul and Shorter envisioned a band where there would be no solos in a conventional sense; instead, the players would make musical statements that would weave in and out of one another, thereby creating a "group solo" on any given composition. Zawinul's and Shorter's creative ideas became reality when in 1970 they formed Weather Report, one of the most memorable of true fusion groups in the jazz-rock genre. Zawinul's compositions, as well as his immersion into the world of synthesizers and electronics, were an important component in the band's development and longevity, well into the '80s. And as a result of his creative energies in the use of electronic keyboards, Zawinul won the *DownBeat* magazine poll in that category over two dozen times.

Zawinul's interest in world music and jazz-rock was a key factor in his forming a group known as the Zawinul Syndicate, which he led in its various incarnations from 1988 until his death in 2007.

Unlike Hancock, Corea, and Zawinul, pianist Keith Jarrett did not follow the fusion road and had no abiding interest in using fusion-oriented electronic keyboards in either his compositions or performances. With the exception of his work on electric piano and organ with Miles Davis in the early '70s, Jarrett simply devoted his full attention to playing the acoustic instrument in all jazz and classical settings, both live and in the studio.

Another element that makes Keith Jarrett unique among this group of pianists is his dual skills as both a jazz and classical pianist. He is equally at home in both worlds and has recorded prolifically in both arenas.

Furthermore, of all the fine pianists introduced in this chapter, Jarrett has been the most prolific in terms of his output as a solo artist. His solo concerts have often been stream-of-consciousness affairs, wherein he sits down at the piano and simply begins to play—with little or no preconception of what he's going to play. Occasionally, he'll play a song, either a standard from the Great American Songbook or one of his original compositions, but such is a rare occurrence. The amazing thing about Jarrett is that he is able to sustain interest—both his own and that of his listeners—when performing these long improvisational journeys. Of his many solo recordings, *The Köln Concerts* (ECM) stands out as a particularly attractive introduction to his work. There are touches of blues, gospel, and country music present in addition to jazz. To call this music anything but solo improvisation is to shortchange it. Jarrett covers a lot of ground as a solo pianist, and in experiencing his music, listeners must not approach it with any preconceptions whatsoever. Expect the unexpected, and be patient as the music unfolds before your eyes and ears.

Here is an interesting note about one of his solo recordings that is atypical of his usual approach—but first, some background: In the late '90s, Jarrett was diagnosed with chronic fatigue syndrome, a debilitating illness that severely curtails many kinds of physical activities, including the strenuousness that goes along with touring and playing concerts regularly. During that difficult recovery time at home, Jarrett was able to record a special album—sort of a love letter to his wife. He called it *The Melody at Night, with You*, and it was made up of all ballads, including some unlikely choices like "My Wild Irish Rose," a number of which a Jarrett fan would have never associated with his usual output.

Interlude III: Facing Jarrett

There have been a lot of stories about Keith Jarrett that portray him as someone who does not suffer fools very well—a temperamental artist who can be painfully blunt and will even put the brakes on during a concert if there is any kind of distraction, from a cell phone ringtone to talking in the audience. I didn't really know much about any of those things firsthand; however, I was about to meet the man and was very much on my best behavior.

I was invited by his drummer, Jack Dejohnette, to the green room backstage after a Jarrett trio concert. There was the usual crowd of well-wishers and press folks, and after being there for a few minutes, I found myself standing within earshot of Jarrett as a fan approached him with the offering of an original composition he thought might interest the pianist. Before the young man got half a sentence out, Jarrett politely interrupted by thanking him but declining the offer, saying that he already had a room full of such pieces that he would probably never get to play. Visibly embarrassed, the young man smiled wanly and excused himself.

Jarrett stood there alone for a minute or two, and I got the sense that people were afraid to approach him, lest they say something they might regret. So I took my shot. I approached him and introduced myself and thanked him for his beautiful solo album, *The Melody at Night, with You*, saying what simple pleasures it brought into our home, and how much my parents enjoyed hearing the old songs again. A smile spread across Jarrett's face, and he described how the recording came to be. If I remember correctly, I recall him saying that he and his wife had secured the microphones, after which he sat down and played (and recorded) the music pretty much at one sitting. The product of that inspiration was the lovely solo album he and Manfred Eicher brought into the world.

He smiled again and looked at me and said, almost conspiratorially, that the mics were still there in their original places near the piano, awaiting the return of the muse of inspiration. So far, Jarrett said almost wistfully, she hadn't made a return visit.

Jarrett has recorded in other configurations in addition to his solo performances. His duo partners have included drummer Jack Dejohnette and bassist Charlie Haden—and, from the world of classical music, recorder virtuoso Michala Petri.

Jarrett's trio recordings and performances revolved around two distinguished groups. The first, which was formed in the early '70s with bassist Charlie Haden and drummer Paul Motian, explored everything from free jazz to gospel-tinged music to their readings of certain rock and folk songs. They ultimately expanded to a quartet, adding saxophonist Dewey Redman, and occasionally added extra percussion and guitar. Jarrett also played soprano saxophone and percussion during these years. The second trio is a true testimony to both longevity and the kind of creative nirvana that can be reached if a group has staying power—and this one certainly does. As of the year 2013, the Standards Trio will have been together for 30 years. Jarrett, along with bassist Gary Peacock and drummer Jack Dejohnette, formed this group in 1983 at the suggestion of ECM producer Manfred Eicher, with the initial purpose of revisiting and reconstructing standard songs from the Great American Songbook. This trio has been extremely well documented, both on CD and video, and are a joy to experience. The high level of communication is very evident throughout each performance, and these three men form a living, breathing entity, much in the manner of Bill Evans's first and last trios.

Finally, mention must be made of Jarrett's European quartet, which was active from the mid- to late '70s and featured saxophonist Jan Garbarek, bassist Palle Danielsson, and drummer Jon Christenson. This group recorded a number of fine albums for the ECM label and was quite different from Jarrett's American quartet in both repertoire and overall sound, especially Garbarek's immense and resonant sound on both tenor and soprano saxophones as distinguished from Redman's warmer and more burnished tone.

In the final analysis, it's safe to say that all of the pianists who passed through Miles Davis University "graduated with honors" and forged jazz immortality for themselves. Those who are still with us continue to move forward, as Miles himself always did, exploring new paths of expression and in some cases "putting new wine in old bottles."

CHASIN' THE TRANE: TWO COLTRANE PIANISTS

While there were certainly some fine pianists who played and/or recorded with John Coltrane, such as Tommy Flanagan, Wynton Kelly, Cedar Walton, and Steve Kuhn, the focus here will be upon the two who played and recorded with him from the early '60s until his death in 1967. The first of these is McCoy Tyner, who formally joined Coltrane's quartet in 1960. At that time Coltrane was seeking a "sound" that would truly be in line with his ever-evolving musical vision. Prior to McCoy, Steve Kuhn, an excellent pianist in his own right, played in the quartet, along with bassist Steve Davis and drummer Pete LaRoca. It wasn't quite what Trane needed for his music, and that realization hit home when McCoy played with the group. There was something about McCoy's way of accompanying, chording, and soloing that Trane found to be compatible with the direction in which he seemed to be headed. Eventually, bassist Jimmy Garrison and drummer Elvin Jones joined Tyner in the rhythm section, to create what we now call Coltrane's "Classic Quartet," arguably one of the finest small groups in modern jazz history.

Tyner's full-bodied chordal approach, his visceral, percussive style of comping, and his exciting solo work became fully realized in the Coltrane quartet. His especially thick chords gave the group a great deal of depth, and made each performance sound more orchestral. A great way to experience Tyner's musical power would be to watch the DVD *John Coltrane Live in '60, '61, and '65*, which is part of the Jazz Icons Series produced by Mosaic Records and Reelin' in the Years Productions. Experiencing an entire performance of any given song by the quartet will help you understand the importance of Tyner's role in the group. His accompaniment as well as his solos helped build a remarkable amount of intensity throughout each of the selections.

Tyner's recorded output since Trane's passing in 1967 has been enormous. Even though the saxophonist's influence is always present, McCoy Tyner has explored many different avenues of expression, including the music of Latin American, Middle Eastern, and African cultures, injecting

Figure 13.6. McCoy Tyner. Courtesy of John Abbott.

each piece with his fiery virtuosity and always putting his personal imprint on everything he does.

Alice McLeod Coltrane, a highly skilled pianist, organist, and harpist, was Trane's wife as well as his last pianist. She was classically trained and studied the keyboard works of many of the masters. Ms. Coltrane was also conversant with liturgical music and served as keyboardist for her church choirs. Her musical path led her to jazz, and she became a known jazz performer on the jazz scene in her native Detroit and eventually in New York. She married John Coltrane in 1965 and replaced McCoy Tyner in the Coltrane group the following year.

Even though she was a very good bebop player, Ms. Coltrane's approach to playing in her husband's group was much more meditative—that is, she responded to the free form, tempoless rhythm flow created by bassist Jimmy Garrison and drummer Rashied Ali by playing piano chords that would float underneath the horn solos, laying down a carpet of sound that helped anchor the improvisations and give the music more depth. Her own solos reflected a beautifully light touch. Even as the horns swirled around her like a hurricane, Alice Coltrane was the eye at the center of the storm and seemed to maintain a focused calm throughout even the most impassioned horn solos.

This sense of calm also manifested itself in Ms. Coltrane's life. There is no doubt that she shared an interest in spirituality and Buddhism with her husband, and that this interest and further immersion in spiritual matters further defined her path. Her recorded work after Trane's death in 1967 reflected her growing spiritual devotion, and she further cultivated her interest in creating more meditative music. Five years after Trane's death, she moved to Southern California and became even more involved in Buddhist teachings. She eventually took a Buddhist name and became the spiritual director of an ashram (a Buddhist spiritual and cultural center) in Malibu. Alice Coltrane passed away—or as she might have said, "left the body"—in 2007, 40 years after her husband's death. She is buried next to her John in Pinelawn Cemetery in Farmingdale, New York.

DESTINATION OUT: CECIL TAYLOR AND PAUL BLEY

As "free" or avant-garde jazz began to flourish from the early '60s through the balance of the decade, it would be good to remember that this new and daring music had its humble beginnings with pianist Lennie Tristano in the late '40s; however, the two musicians who integrated the piano more fully into the free-jazz setting were Cecil Taylor and Paul Bley.

Taylor is a free-jazz institution and a role model for many artists, not just jazz musicians. In this age of canned, processed, homogenized music, dance, and other arts, he is a beacon of light. While Taylor began his career as a "jazz" pianist in the early '50s, playing with well-known swing musicians like saxophonist Johnny Hodges and trumpeter Oran "Hot Lips" Page, he began exploring other avenues of musical expression that, once understood and refined, might help him capture and solidify what he was hearing in his head. By the middle of the decade, Taylor was leading a quartet with soprano saxophonist Steve Lacy that was expanding the limits jazz had imposed upon itself rhythmically, melodically, and harmonically. This kind of radical transition was not well received—just as bebop was not looked upon favorably by more than a few swing-era musicians and listeners. Yet Taylor was not going to look back—only forward. In fact, one of his early albums was called *Looking Ahead*.

Throughout the remainder of the '50s, Taylor continued his quest and refused to compromise his music by watering it down or making it sound more traditional in any way. That meant that gigs were slow in coming, and at times were not available at all. Taylor did anything he could to survive economically, just so he didn't have to prostitute himself by performing in a fashion that removed him from what he felt was his true calling and essence. This meant a tremendous amount of scuffling and sacrifice.

All the while, Cecil Taylor was working with like minds and creating improvised music on his terms. And it's been like that ever since, although the listening public has been catching up with him in recent years.

Taylor's style is quite percussive (the piano is, after all, a bona fide percussion instrument) and listening to one of his long, intense sets of music can take your breath away. He rages at the piano, and his energy level is nothing short of amazing. He throws clusters of notes into the air and follows them with others. He plays all 88 keys with great force and passion. Many listeners say that the music becomes trancelike; others say it's just noise. Listeners who wish to really experience Taylor's music should see him in a concert setting, watch one of his videos, or buy or download one of his recordings. Then sit and listen to a little each day until you've heard the entire recording. This will be a challenge, given how radically different Taylor's piano solos are. But sometimes we are rewarded if we put some effort into the craft and art of truly listening. Taylor, now in his 80s, is here to help us do just that.

Paul Bley has approached free music in a different way—one that, in a sense, is somewhat more traditional in terms of rhythm. Whereas much of Cecil Taylor's music is rarely undergirded by conventional tempo and rhythm, Bley often uses that as a starting point—a diving board from which to plummet into the abyss of music without limitations. Also, Bley's touch is much less percussive than Taylor's. There are times listening to Bley that it sounds as though a mouse is skittering across the keys. Bley has always maintained a sense of the playful. His is avant-garde music that can be highly unpredictable and can take a listener on a camel ride one minute and on a rocket ship the next.

Like Taylor, Paul Bley began in more or less traditional settings. In the early to mid-'50s, he performed with Charlie Parker, Lester Young, and Ben Webster, to name a few, and began an association with bassist Charles Mingus, who, along with drummer Art Blakey, appeared on his first album, *Introducing Paul Bley*.

Later in the decade, Bley would hire Ornette Coleman's quartet (with Don Cherry, Charlie Haden, and Billy Higgins) to record a quintet album. A few years later, in the early '60s, Bley would tour and record with tenor saxophonist Sonny Rollins. The recording featured another titan of the tenor sax, Coleman Hawkins. There was also a stint with clarinetist Jimmy Giuffre's drummerless trio, with Bley and bassist Steve Swallow as the other two members.

When the avant-garde music began to gain a foothold, Bley formed one of the classic free-form piano trios with bassist Steve Swallow and drummer Barry Altschul. Their classic mid-'60s ESP-Disk has been reissued in recent years in CD format, bringing new clarity to their crystalline creations.

Fortunately, Bley has been extremely prolific and versatile. He has used synthesizers and other electronics, making them the focal points of some recordings, and has recorded in more traditional settings with a variety of trios playing both standards and songs from other repertoires as well. He has recorded solo projects, duo encounters, and quartet and quintet outings, and has cowritten an autobiography with David Lee (*Stopping Time: Paul Bley and the Transformation of Jazz*, 1999, Vehicule Press) and a book of conversations with Norman Meehan (*Time Will Tell*, 2003, Berkeley Hills Press)—and all in all, over 100 recordings by one of modern music's most imaginative and creative pianists.

GETTING ORGAN-IZED

While this chapter is about the piano and its important role in jazz, some mention here—with all due respect—must be made of the organ and its place in the music. Of course, the organ was initially used as a church instrument, in both the classical and liturgical music worlds. Since the music of the church—particularly the African American Baptist church—was one of the elements that combined with blues and folk music to help form early jazz, it is conceivable that the organ would be one of jazz's keyboard voices in addition to the piano.

Fats Waller was an accomplished organist, as was Count Basie, who learned to play the instrument under Waller's tutelage. Other early organists were Wild Bill Davis and Milt Buckner.

The man who really put organ on the jazz map, however, was Jimmy Smith, whose exciting, soulful, blues-drenched playing influenced future generations of organists. Legend has it that pianist Smith switched over permanently to the organ after hearing Wild Bill Davis, sometime in the early '50s. Smith soon became the premier jazz organist, recording as a leader and with many of the great hard bop musicians of the day, mostly for Blue Note Records. His music encouraged foot tapping and hand clapping and, generally, a party atmosphere. Others who followed in Smith's footsteps were Brother Jack McDuff, Baby Face Willette, and Big John Patton.

The first organist to move away from the soul-groove jazz feel was Larry Young (Khalid Yasin), who, even though he could play in the soul-groove idiom, took a more adventurous road—one that was Coltrane influenced. In fact, the drummer on several of Young's Blue Note recordings in the mid-'60s was Coltrane drummer Elvin Jones. Khalid went on to create brilliant music as part of Lifetime, with drummer Tony Williams and guitarist John McLaughlin.

Another accomplished jazz organist who must be mentioned here is Dr. Lonnie Liston Smith, who has traversed a number of stylistic musical terrains in his 40-year career, from playing piano with singer Betty Carter and drummer Max Roach, to playing keyboards with Pharoah Sanders, and later, with his own groups. Smith is at home playing soul music, free music, fusion music—whatever interests him at the time. And he does it all quite well.

Among newer players of the next generation are the funky, swinging Joey DeFrancesco Jr., who has absorbed the work of both Jimmy Smith and Larry Young into his own style; the versatile Larry Goldings, a pianist and organist who is at home with James Taylor as much as he is with the trio of Jack Dejohnette and John Scofield; and two very forward-thinking players, Jamie Saft and Sam Yahill, both of whom are pushing past the boundaries of the instrument toward new sonic frontiers.

AND THE LISTS GO ON . . .

Thus far in this chapter, we've focused upon or mentioned 39 pianists who have been integral to the development of various eras of jazz. As mentioned elsewhere, this jazz companion is meant to get new listeners started on the road to discovery and to perhaps fill in some gaps for more seasoned listeners. Also, it's meant to offer a few personal thoughts by some well-known musicians (written especially for this book and presented here for new listeners), and finally, to offer some of my personal anecdotes and stories to help portray jazz people as real people!

All well and good . . . *but*, in the world of jazz pianists in particular, there is no way to include profiles of everyone whose work—past and present—has been really praiseworthy or is just now beginning to shine brightly on the horizon of jazz's future. So, with that in mind, the following mini-profiles of selected pianists, as well as listings of excellent keyboardists, have been included in a number of categories, with the understanding that many of these fine and versatile players might very well exist in more than one listing.

JAZZ WITHOUT BORDERS

There have been many great jazz pianists from around the world who either relocated to the United States or continue to live and work in their countries of origin. Among those in the first group, one particular standout is New Zealand's Alan Broadbent, who is a formidable pianist, composer, arranger, and conductor. Broadbent came to the United States at age 19 to study at the renowned Berklee College of Music, and supplemented his time by also studying in New York with the legendary Lennie Tristano. Broadbent is a superlative pianist who prefers solo and, particularly, trio formats as vehicles for expression, although he is also well known for his work with the bassist Charlie Haden's Quartet West.

Other notables who relocated to America to live and work have included Kei Akagi, Masabumi Kikuchi, and Hiromi Uehara (Japan); Karl Berger (Germany); Milcho Leviev (Bulgaria); Renee Rosnes (Canada); Jean-Michel Pilc (France); Michel Camilo (Dominican Republic); Danilo Perez (Panama); Tamir Hendelman (Israel); Tigran Hamasyan (Armenia); and Gonzalo Rubalcava (Cuba).

Among the pianists who live outside of the United States and are internationally known for their creative output are Misha Mengelberg, Kris Goessens, and Jasper van't Hof (Holland); Bobo Stenson, Bengt Hallberg, and the late Esbjörn Svensson (Sweden); John Taylor, Keith Tippett, and Stan Tracey (United Kingdom); Joachim Kuhn, Wolfgang Dauner, and Alexander von Schlippenbach (Germany); Stefano Bollani, Enrico Pieranunzi, Giorgio Gaslini, and Dado Moroni (Italy); Michal Tokaj, Adam Makowicz, and Piotr Orzachowski (Poland); Martial Solal, Michel Grallier, Christian Jacob, Jacky Terrason, and René Utreger (France); Abdullah Ibrahim (South Africa); Ivan Farmakovsky and Simon Nabatov (Russia); and Tete Montoliu and Chano Domínguez (Spain).

YOU'VE HEARD THEIR NAMES, BUT DO YOU REALLY KNOW THEIR MUSIC?

Beyond their hit records, Dave Brubeck ("Take Five") and Ahmad Jamal ("Poinciana") have had a lot more to offer—both venerable grand masters of jazz piano. Jamal is in his 80s, and Brubeck passed away in December 2012 at the age 91. Jamal puts his unmistakable personal stamp on everything he plays. He remains one of the most interesting and elegant of pianists. Brubeck, in addition to being declared a "Living Legend" by the Library of Congress, has been a major innovator and maintained a busy performance schedule in both jazz and classical settings until his death.

"TDWR"

. . . which simply means "Talent Deserving Wider Recognition," a term *DownBeat* magazine used in its yearly jazz polls, for up-and-coming artists worth hearing. This little section will introduce you to some terrific pianists who are on the scene today but, for one reason or another, are not as well known as they should be to jazz fans. Each continues to be a vital part of the jazz experience.

Established masters include Kenny Barron, Stanley Cowell, Ran Blake, Don Friedman, Hal Galper, Phil Markowitz, Geri Allen, Marc Copland, Cedar Walton, JoAnne Brackeen, Richie Beirach, Bill Mays, and Billy Taylor.

"Youngish Lions" haven't been around quite as long as many of the established masters above, but they certainly have the staying power that is achieved only by being a long-standing active member of the jazz scene. This group includes Uri Caine, Joey Caldarazzo, Brad Mehldau, Larry Goldings, Eric Reed, Alan Pasqua, Billy Childs, Danny Grissett, David Hazeltine, Frank Kimbrough, Lynne Arriale, Geoff Keezer, Jim Ridl, and Bill Carruthers.

"Lion Cubs" are the best hope for preserving the voice of the piano in jazz. They are our preservers of tradition, yet many are also explorers of uncharted territories—our adventurers on the edges of the musical known. The future of jazz piano is literally in good hands with the likes of Jason Moran, Myra Melford, Kevin Hayes, Matthew Shipp, Vijay Iyer, Craig Taborn, Taylor Eigsti, Robert Glasper, Kris Davis, Bobby Avey, and Fabian Almazan.

All of these listings can be daunting; however, exploring and ultimately experiencing new music and musicians is a gradual, and even lifelong process. So take your time!

Maybe a great place to begin your explorations might be by visiting Marian McPartland's innovative radio show, *Piano Jazz*, on National Public Radio (NPR). Marian McPartland, in addition to being a fine pianist herself, has done the most to introduce the world to many great jazz pianists. On her show McPartland interviewed many jazz pianists from all eras and played in-studio duets with most of them. *Piano Jazz* was the longest-running cultural program on National Public Radio; after over 30 years as its host, McPartland stepped down in November 2011. The show itself will continue with reruns and archived segments, however, and even though McPartland will be missed, the new format will basically remain the same, with perhaps more emphasis on featuring pianists such as those mentioned above, whose work merits further attention through national exposure.

So how best to preserve the heritage of a century of jazz piano playing? Of course, we have CDs, MP3 downloads, DVDs, YouTube, iTunes, and the rest; all are helpful. However, you are a crucial component in the mix. All of these media are literally at your fingertips.

The piano train leaves the station in a few minutes. Climb aboard and enjoy the ride.

Getting Personal with Alan Broadbent

What advice would you offer a new listener who will be experiencing your music (in either the solo or trio format) for the first time, either in concert, on YouTube, or via one of your recordings?

The key to listening to a Beethoven symphony, to looking at a Picasso painting, to observing a Gehry building, to reading a sonnet, is to understand on some basic level the structure upon which these works of art are formed. This enhances our appreciation and gives us a deeper understanding and experience. So, too, with improvised jazz. It's important to get a sense of the structure upon which the improvisation is based. That's why great jazz composers such as Monk, Clifford Brown, Sonny Rollins, Dizzy, and Bird, to name but a few, chose simpler song forms to build their compositions. This certainly makes it easier for us listeners to follow along. Most standard songs have the structures of AABA or ABAB, each section usually of eight bars in length, or the simpler 12-bar blues form. Of course there are many variants of these, but having that basic sense of the song enables us to enjoy the variations and new melodies the improviser is creating. The next hurdle is to follow the pattern of harmonies in each of the repeated sections, but with listening practice this can be accomplished. To listeners not experienced in jazz or any music without words, it sounds like a lot of gibberish. Now, instead of hearing mysterious doodlings of notes going up and down, the listener can discern the ebb and flow of the improviser's melodies, however complicated, over the basic harmony and the form. This is why, when I compose a jazz tune, I'm very conscious of creating something that is easily comprehensible upon first hearing.

Figure 13.7. Alan Broadbent. Courtesy of Juan Carlos Fernandez.

That way, no matter how complicated the improvisation, with concentration I can follow along and be in the moment with the improviser. But jazz has an element no other music can lay claim to. The feeling (what Lennie Tristano called a life force) of swing, without which, as Duke Ellington said, it don't mean a thing. But that's another chapter.

What would be the first recording of yours that you would recommend for an initial listening experience and as a good introduction to your playing?

My trio album *Personal Standards* (1992) contains my compositions which include all of the forms mentioned above. It's now hard to find, but similar CDs are available. *Pacific Standard Time* and *Live at Giannelli's Vol. 1* include a mixture of known standard songs and my compositions.

SELECTED PIANISTS' WEBSITES: FROM THEN 'TIL NOW

Note: Only official sites are listed. Use Google for all others.

Fats Waller: www.fatswaller.org
Thelonious Monk: www.monkzone.com
Bud Powell: www.budpowelljazz.com
Oscar Peterson: www.oscarpeterson.com
Horace Silver: www.horacesilver.com
Ahmad Jamal: www.ahmadjamal.net
Dave Brubeck: www.davebrubeck.com
Bill Evans: www.billevanswebpages.com
JoAnne Brackeen: www.joannebrackeenjazz.com
Herbie Hancock: www.herbiehancock.com
Chick Corea: www.chickcorea.com
Joe Zawinul: www.zawinulmusic.com
Keith Jarrett: www.keithjarrett.org (unofficial site)
McCoy Tyner: www.mccoytyner.com
Alice Coltrane: www.alicecoltrane.org
Paul Bley: www.improvart.com/bley/
Alan Broadbent: www.alanbroadbent.com
Marc Copland: www.marccopland.com
Renee Rosnes: www.reneerosnes.com
Uri Caine: www.uricaine.com
Brad Mehldau: www.bradmehldau.com
Jason Moran: www.jasonmoran.com
Vijay Iyer: www.vijayiyer.com
Myra Melford: www.myramelford.com

RECOMMENDED READING

General Reading

Doerschuk, Robert. *88: The Giants of Jazz Piano*. San Francisco: Backbeat Books, 2001. Print.

Lyons, Len. *The Great Jazz Pianists: Speaking of Their Lives and Music*. Cambridge: Da Capo Press, 1989. Print.

Shipton, Alyn. *Handful of Keys: Conversations with Thirty Jazz Pianists*. New York: Routledge, 2004. Print.

Jelly Roll Morton

Pastras, Phil. *Dead Man Blues: Jelly Roll Morton Way Out West*. Berkeley and Los Angeles: U of California P, 2001. Print.

Reich, Howard, and William Gaines. *Jelly's Blues: The Life, Music, and Redemption of Jelly Roll Morton*. Cambridge: Da Capo Press, 2003. Print.

Fats Waller

Waller, Maurice, and Anthony Calabrese. *Fats Waller*. New York: Music Sales Corp., 1997. Print.

Art Tatum

Lester, James. *Too Marvelous for Words: The Life and Genius of Art Tatum*. New York: Oxford UP, 1995. Print.

Mary Lou Williams

Dahl, Linda. *Morning Glory: A Biography of Mary Lou Williams*. New York: Pantheon Books, 1999. Print.

Teddy Wilson

Wilson, Teddy, with Arie Ligthart and Humphrey Van Loo. *Teddy Wilson Talks Jazz*. New York: Continuum Books, 2001. Print.

Bud Powell

Paudrais, Francis. *Dance of the Infidels: A Portrait of Bud Powell*. Trans. Rubye Monet. Cambridge: Da Capo Press, 1998. Print.

Thelonious Monk

Kelley, Robin D. G. *Monk: The Life and Times of an American Original*. New York: Free Press, 2009. Print.

Bill Evans

Pettinger, Peter. *Bill Evans: How My Heart Sings*. New Haven: Yale UP, 1998. Print.

Dave Brubeck

Hall, Fred M. *It's about Time: The Dave Brubeck Story*. Fayetteville: U of Arkansas P, 1996. Print.

Cecil Taylor

Mandel, Howard. *Miles, Ornette, Cecil: Jazz beyond Jazz*. New York: Routledge, 2008. Print.

Paul Bley

Bley, Paul, and David Lee. *Stopping Time: Paul Bley and the Transformation of Jazz*. Montreal: Vehicule Press, 1999. Print.

Herbie Hancock

Gluck, Bob. *You'll Know When You Get There: Herbie Hancock and the Mwandishi Band*. Chicago: U of Chicago P, 2012. Print.

14

I GOT RHYTHM II

The Acoustic and Electric Basses

The bass, no matter what kind of music you're playing, it just enhances the sound and makes everything sound more beautiful and full. When the bass stops, the bottom kind of drops out of everything.

—Charlie Haden

Bass players are a breed unto themselves! Depending on who you talk to, many jazz musicians believe that bassists are at the heart of the rhythm section; that they—along with drummers—are the engine that gets the car moving. Like the guitar, the acoustic or "upright" bass was not the first bass instrument used in early jazz. Whereas the guitar was preceded by the banjo, the string bass was the natural successor to the tuba, which was a mainstay in early jazz bands. This might have been because the early jazz bands evolved from the parade, carnival, and street bands—all bands that played and marched or walked at the same time. These mobile ensembles used to play at all manner of celebrations from weddings to funerals to a variety of celebrations such as Mardi Gras and All Hallows' Eve. As they eventually morphed into jazz bands, the tuba went along for the ride and provided the "bottom" in early jazz groups, just as it had in the street and parade bands. As bands moved into the swing era, the contrabass or string bass became the norm, rather than the tuba. As the music gave way to swing (and later, to bebop), the sound of the tuba became antiquated and out of place in this new jazz sound and style. It was soon replaced by the more subtle sound and pulse of the string bass. And ultimately, with the advent of rock and roll, the string bass was joined, and in some situations replaced by, the electric bass. In any case, the string bass has for years served as the backbone of the rhythm section. Without the pulse a bassist can provide, the groups—large or small—may seem shallow sounding, grooveless, and adrift.

IN THE DOG HOUSE

That's just one of the nicknames that exist for the string bass—probably because like the vintage doghouse, it, too, is constructed out of wood. It has also been called the stand-up bass (because many bassists play it in a standing position), the upright bass (because the instrument itself is played in an upright position), and the bass violin or bass fiddle (because, after all, it is the largest member of the violin family!). One of the earliest string bassists was New Orleans's Pops Foster, who played with many of the great early jazz legends like Louis Armstrong and Sidney Bechet. Foster would pluck the bass (the technical term for this is "pizzicato"), play it with a bow (which is also called "arco" playing), or even "slap" the bass (pulling the strings outward on the first and third beats—the beats on which a tuba would normally play—and letting them slap back on the second and fourth "backbeats," giving the bass rhythm a more percussive feel). While this style of playing created a buoyant and happy rhythm, it soon fell out of fashion, when swing bass players abandoned the slap and began playing four equal beats in each measure of music. This soon came to be known as the "walking bass" feel, because it emulated the feeling of walking down the street. So the next time you are walking for any period of time, as you move evenly from one foot to the other, you are doing what bassists everywhere often do on their instruments—walking. . . . You use your feet; they use their strings, which resonate roundly and warmly against the wood.

TOWER OF POWER: WALTER PAGE

Swing-era bassists didn't have the benefits of the amplifiers used several decades later by their successors. That meant that they had to rely on physical strength and endurance in order to rise above woodwind and brass sections, as well as drummers, in big bands. One bassist in particular who rose mightily to the challenge was Walter Page, who was nicknamed "Big 'Un," because he was large and powerfully built. He exuded the same kind of power as a bassist, and together with drummer Jo Jones, guitarist Freddie Green, and pianist Count Basie, was at the core of "The All-American Rhythm Section," which drove the Basie band and gave it the mighty sense of swing that made it legendary. In Jo Jones's words from his book *Rifftide*:

> We were not coming to New York unless Big 'Un come. Without Mr. Walter Page, you wouldn't have heard of Basie, Jimmy Rushing, Hot Lips Page, Lester Young, Charlie Parker, nor myself. (95)

TWO FOR THE ROAD:
JIMMY BLANTON AND OSCAR PETTIFORD

If we were to trace the beginnings of the bass as a solo instrument, we would probably start with Jimmy Blanton. Many modern bassists believe that Blanton was the first true jazz soloist on the instrument. Blanton's improvisations were not confined to the instrument's lower register; rather, they were often hornlike and quite melodic in nature. Blanton's primary association was with Duke Ellington, whom he began working with in the late '30s, in both small- and large-group settings. Ellington recognized and valued Blanton's unique approach to the bass as solo instrument as well as time keeper, and he began featuring the bassist in a variety of Ellingtonian settings. Unfortunately, tuberculosis took Jimmy Blanton at the age of 23; yet he exerted great influence upon many bassists in his brief but shining career, and continues to do so today.

Oscar Pettiford was a natural heir to Blanton and was also the logical choice to succeed him in Ellington's orchestra. He was also important, not just because of his enormous musicality or his association with Ellington, but also because he was instrumental in moving the acoustic bass from the swing era into the newer, more adventurous realm of bebop. Pettiford was also distinctive because he further developed Jimmy Blanton's ideas of bass as a solo instrument, by creating unaccompanied bass solos as well as bop-oriented tunes that featured the bass. One such composition was

Pettiford's "Trichotism," which is, to this day, a piece that tests any bassist's technical skill and imagination.

Bill Crow, himself an outstanding bassist—and author of two marvelous books about the jazz life—has this to say in *From Birdland to Broadway* about Oscar Pettiford's brilliance—and his occasional volatility:

> Oscar's bass playing was a great ornament to the New York jazz scene in the 1950s. He had a big sound and a tremendous technique, especially for those days of unamplified basses and gut strings. The first time I saw him in person . . . Oscar announced that he would play "Stardust" as an unaccompanied bass solo. . . . Halfway through the verse of the tune, Oscar suddenly stopped and grabbed the microphone.
>
> "Quiet!" he bellowed furiously. The noisy conversation in the club stopped as if it had been switched off.
>
> "I've been working on this damn song for three years!" shouted Oscar. "The least you can do is shut up for five minutes while I play it!"
>
> Scowling with menace, he began the tune again and played brilliantly. There wasn't a peep out of the audience until he finished. (155–56)

THE JUDGE: MILT HINTON

Milt Hinton has often been called the "Dean of the Bass." His timekeeping was impeccable, and he was extremely versatile—enough so that he became a very in-demand session musician in New York and one of the greatest of jazz bassists as well. Fortunately for us, Hinton is well represented on many, many big-band and small-group recordings, made from the early swing era until the time of his death in 2000. He has been called one of the most recorded jazz musicians in history and has played and recorded with many of its major figures, including Duke Ellington, Dizzy Gillespie, John Coltrane, Coleman Hawkins, and Billie Holiday, to name only a few. In addition, Hinton, who was also known affectionately as "The Judge," recorded and played with nonjazz artists such as Barbra Streisand, Bette Midler, and Paul McCartney.

In addition to being a great bassist, Hinton was also a gifted photographer and, fortunately for us, took over 60,000 fine—and often candid—photographs of many great jazz artists at work and play. His work has been exhibited in galleries and in several spectacular books: *Bass Line: The Stories and Photographs of Milt Hinton* (Temple University Press,

Figure 14.1.   Milt Hinton in the recording studio. Courtesy of the Milton J. Hinton Photographic Collection.

1988) with David G. Berger; and *Over Time: The Jazz Photographs of Milt Hinton* (Pomegranate ArtBooks, 1991). Hinton was the recipient of many awards, both as a musician and a photographer, including eight honorary doctorates and an NEA Jazz Master Award. A documentary of his life was made two years after his passing, called *Keeping Time: The Life, Music, and Photographs of Milt Hinton.* His was a life well lived, and his artistic gifts continue to inspire and resonate for musicians, listeners, and art lovers alike.

MR. TIME: RAY BROWN

If that nickname ever truly existed, we would have to bestow it upon Ray Brown, whose gifts as a "timekeeper" and bass soloist have assured him an honored place in any jazz hall of fame.

When jazz musicians use the expression "time," they are referring to the pulse of the music. So if one musician says about another musician, "he has good time," then what that probably means is that the other musician has a good, steady rhythm—one that doesn't speed up or slow down unintentionally; it locks into a groove and stays right there, unwavering and swinging. There is a funny story about one of jazz's master drummers, Philly Joe Jones, which goes something like this:

Philly Joe hired a certain young bassist to play an engagement at a New York jazz club. When the bassist asked him how much the gig paid, Philly Joe told him he would be earning $125 for the week. As the week wore on, the bassist, probably out of excitement for getting to play with one of jazz's greatest drummers, pushed the beat to the point of rushing and getting ahead of the rest of the band. Even though Philly Joe repeatedly called this to his attention, the bassist became more and more anxious—to the point where his rushing became even more problematic with each passing night. There was just no way of holding him back!

At the end of the week, Philly Joe paid each guy in the group his $125. When he came to the young bassist, he handed him a fifty, a twenty, and a five.

"Thank you, Mr. Jones," said the bassist, "but I thought this gig paid $125. You gave me only $75."

"It did, and I did," Jones said wryly, "but I fined you $50 for speeding."

So you may well be asking, what does this little story have to do with Ray Brown? History has it that Ray Brown was the perfect timekeeper. It is said that he could elevate any rhythm section to the point where it would be swinging like there was no tomorrow. His walking bass sound and feel gave him a "presence" on the bandstand that was indisputable. And his solos were exuberant and joyous and demonstrated his great facility on the instrument.

Like his contemporary Milt Hinton, Brown was not only a great jazz artist but was also quite versatile, and as a result, he graced many a studio session with his gifts. And like Hinton in New York, Ray Brown was one of the most in-demand bassists on the studio music and jazz scene in Los Angeles from the 1960s through the end of the century. He worked with a great many jazz stars, including the legendary Duke Ellington, pianist Oscar Peterson, trumpeter Dizzy Gillespie, vibraphonist Milt Jackson, saxophonist Ben Webster, and guitarist Joe Pass. The roster of singers Brown performed and recorded with was equally impressive and included Frank Sinatra, Tony Bennett, Sarah Vaughan, Ella Fitzgerald, and Nancy Wilson.

MINGUS AH-UM: THE VOLCANIC CHARLES MINGUS

Jazz has always been peopled by very interesting and individualistic artists—one-of-a-kind men and women whose artistic, and often personal, lives went completely against the grain. We need only to point to a few of jazz's more famous individualists—saxophonists Lester Young and Charlie Parker, pianist Thelonious Monk, trumpeter Miles Davis, vocalist Billie Holiday, and of course, Louis Armstrong, Duke Ellington, John Coltrane, and many others. One name we haven't mentioned is another of jazz's great figures—and certainly, along with Monk, Miles, Dizzy, Prez, and Bird, one of the most colorful: the brilliant bassist and composer Charles Mingus.

Powerful, emotional, eccentric, melodramatic, and at times difficult, Charles Mingus was totally committed to the music, as well as to what might be called its transformative power—the ability to educate and inspire listeners from all walks of life. More specifically, Mingus never separated his music from the culture and society in which he lived. Like so many other African American artists, he was moved by the resiliency of black Americans

Figure 14.2. Charles Mingus, New York City, 1976.
Courtesy of Tom Marcello.

in the face of outright racism, and he was outraged by the levels of inequality that came with racial prejudice. All of this was and is reflected in his
many musical compositions, his virtuosity as a bassist, and his skills as a band
leader. His was a powerful and unique presence in every way.

Born in Arizona and raised in the Watts section of Los Angeles, Mingus gained his early experience in a wide variety of musical situations,
including the traditional jazz band of trombonist Kid Ory, the big band of
vibraphonist Lionel Hampton, and particularly the trio of vibraphonist Red
Norvo; however, Mingus also played with some superlative bebop groups,

especially a super quintet that included saxophonist Charlie Parker, trumpeter Dizzy Gillespie, pianist Bud Powell, and drummer Max Roach—all icons of the bebop revolution.

The interesting thing about Mingus—indeed, the thing that makes him stand out as one of the great jazz musicians of our time—is the fact that he refused to be compartmentalized in one style or another. In other words, we can't comfortably classify him in one particular approach to jazz. His musical and cultural interests and passions were extremely diverse and were reflected in his music. As you explore Mingus's world, you will hear gospel, flamenco, avant-garde, bebop, cumbia, and classical influences—and sometimes you will hear more than one of these influences in the same song. His recording *Tijuana Sketches* is a classic melding of jazz and Spanish/Mexican music. His gospel-tinged compositions such as "Better Get It in Your Soul," "Lord, Don't Let Them Drop That Atomic Bomb on Me," and "Eat That Chicken" all reflect the breadth and intensity of the African American Baptist church. As mentioned earlier, Mingus was also very aware of the racial problems that existed in the country at that time and accordingly took aim at those who perpetuated racism at every level. Two of his most famous compositions in this area were "Fables of Faubus" (named after Arkansas governor Orval Faubus, who in 1957 defied the Supreme Court and blocked the integration of Little Rock's Central High School) and "Meditations on Integration." The Faubus piece—particularly the 1960 version on Candid Records—features a Mingus poem and has to be experienced firsthand. Its satirical and angry tone and march-like cadence has Mingus singing and speaking the words and his drummer, Dannie Richmond, responding. The music is free and uncluttered and moves from stately and magisterial through avant-garde, bebop, and the blues—all in a little over nine minutes! This piece, like so many other Mingus masterworks, is buoyed by his powerful, percussive bass playing.

As a composer, Mingus was the recipient of two Guggenheim Fellowships, as well as grants from the National Endowment for the Arts and the Smithsonian Institute. Mingus's compositional brilliance reached its zenith with a posthumously discovered work called *Epitaph*, an epic large-ensemble composition over two hours in length, which received its premiere in New York City, 10 years after Mingus's death, in 1989.

Just as bassist Milt Hinton expanded his artistry to photography, Mingus had a passion for writing words, and he was an excellent writer. His autobiography, *Beneath the Underdog*, was first published by Knopf in 1972 and reprinted by Pantheon Books in 1980, a year after his passing. It is, like his music, simple and complex at the same time, yet imminently readable, and provides us with a window into the heart of a man whose life was filled with both frustration and exuberance of spirit. His wife, Sue Graham Mingus, has been a mighty force in continuing the Mingus legacy and has also authored *Tonight at Noon: A Love Story* (Da Capo Press), a beautiful and often poignant book about him as a husband, as a creative artist, and as a force of nature.

THE BLINK OF AN EYE: SCOTT LAFARO

In the world of jazz, as we have discovered by reading about major artists who passed from this life much too soon—like trumpeter Clifford Brown and saxophonist John Coltrane—sometimes a flame will burn brightly for a moment or two before flaring out prematurely and becoming the stuff of legend. For "Brownie," it was a mere four or five years; for Trane, it was around twelve. This was also tragically true in the case of the brilliant, inno-

Figure 14.3.   Scott LaFaro. Courtesy of Helene LaFaro Hernandez.

vative bassist Scott LaFaro (1936–1961), who, although he was with us in the jazz world for only a brief six years, made a major impact upon bassists for the next 50 years and continues to do so today, thanks to his recorded work.

To say that LaFaro was an astonishing bassist is an understatement. When he first arrived on the scene in 1958 with pianist Victor Feldman's trio, he amazed both musicians and listeners alike with his absolute control, dexterity, and most of all, his virtuosic soloing. Many bassists could not believe their ears. Here was a young man who, after playing the bass for only a few short years, could not only excel at playing any groove, but could also solo in a whole new way, with articulation and phrasing that was previously characteristic only of horn players, guitar players, and pianists. There was seemingly nothing that LaFaro couldn't do.

Perhaps his most famous and endearing musical relationship began in 1959, when he joined pianist Bill Evans and drummer Paul Motian in a trio that was to become one of the best-loved small groups in jazz. It was truly a different kind of trio—one in which the bassist and drummer took a more active role, rather than the more traditional approach of bass and drums merely supporting the pianist during the latter's solos. These men were carrying on a three-way "conversation" in their improvisations, and as a consequence, the Bill Evans Trio illuminated the meaning of the word "democracy" when applied to music. In other words, Evans, LaFaro, and Motian were equal partners in the creation of their musical interpretations, tossing the ball back and forth, and elevating the "call and response" approach so firmly embedded in the music to new and exciting levels of performance and creation. Many listeners and critics believe that none of this would have been possible without the presence of LaFaro, who almost single-handedly liberated the bass from being a mere supporting voice to one that was far more interactive.

The end of Scott LaFaro's life came in the form of an automobile accident that took place in the early hours of July 6, 1961, a short time after his historic performances with the trio at New York's Village Vanguard. He was only 25 years old. Fortunately for us, those performances were captured by Riverside Records and stand today as masterpieces of creative interplay and as living legacies for Bill Evans, Paul Motian, and Scott LaFaro, who, even 50 years after his death, continues to be a profound influence upon bassists and a source of musical wonder to seasoned and new listeners alike.

TWO MODERN MASTERS: CHARLIE HADEN AND RON CARTER

In addition to Scott LaFaro, there are two other bassists who have been important to the development of the role of the bass in modern jazz: Charlie Haden and Ron Carter. Both were contemporaries of LaFaro. Admittedly, there have been other fine players as well who have helped set the course of modern jazz bass playing from the '60s forward. Among these, we would have to list Eddie Gomez, whose facile, imaginative playing with Bill Evans, Chick Corea, and others is worth hearing. Dave Holland is yet another fine bassist who first came to prominence with the Miles Davis groups of the late '60s and whose evolution as a leading bassist in the jazz world is indisputable; however, Haden and Carter set the stage for the next generations of bassists, and we shall focus a bit upon them here.

Charlie Haden has always been one of jazz's true individualists. Born into a musical family in Shenandoah, Iowa, in the late '30s, Haden was an active participant in the family's radio show, which focused upon country and folk music—influences that have remained a very important part of the bassist's music, both composed and improvised.

As opposed to the breathtaking virtuosity of his contemporary Scott LaFaro, Haden has always been a master of understatement. He has also shown us that in order to be a virtuoso, one doesn't have to exhibit astonishing technique. If anything, Haden is what we might call a "quiet master," in that he values the nuances that can come with the silence between notes. In other words, he might play a low G on the bass and let the note ring through the air until it evaporates, creating a beautifully flowing sound and feeling; which is not to say that he can't swing, because he is extremely adept at providing a strong, solid pulse—one that is capable of lifting any soloist to new heights.

Haden began his jazz journey in the late '50s in Los Angeles, playing with many of the city's best jazz musicians; however, it was his work with pianist Paul Bley and, to a larger extent, with saxophonist Ornette Coleman that brought him to national prominence in the jazz world. In particular, the revolutionary Coleman recordings, *The Shape of Jazz to Come* and *This Is Our Music*, introduced the listening public to Coleman's pianoless quartet, which featured Haden as one of its four principal voices.

Fruitful and imaginative collaborations followed in the late '60s with pianist Keith Jarrett in mostly trio and quartet settings, once again with Haden's bass as one of the essential components. Haden's dark, sometimes melancholy sound beautifully complemented Jarrett's powerful, imaginative soloing; drummer Paul Motian's sensitive underpinnings; and in the quartet setting, Dewey Redman's warm and full-bodied tenor saxophone work.

Haden also was the force behind the Liberation Music Orchestra, a large ensemble he led in 1969 and again throughout the '90s and into the new millennium. The group was composed of a mix of veterans and younger players, and Haden composed and arranged music that ran the gamut from folk songs and world music to music of a decidedly more political nature. The entire mix of music and musicians was an exhilarating one, to say the least, and is as timeless today as it was when first conceived.

The same holds true of many of Haden's other projects, which include a wide variety of ensembles, including one of his most beloved groups, Quartet West, which is composed mainly of pianist Alan Broadbent, saxophonist Ernie Watts, and a variety of excellent drummers. The music is wide ranging, always interesting, and includes Cuban love songs, standards from the Great American Songbook, original compositions, and so much more. In that group, as well as in the beautiful duo recordings he made with fellow Midwesterner, guitarist Pat Metheny (*Under the Missouri Sky*) and pianist Hank Jones (*Steal Away* and *Come Sunday*), Haden has returned to his roots—folk songs, gospel music, and hymns. These examples are only the tip of a very large iceberg of an enormously prolific and gifted musician. Arguably, there is something in Charlie Haden's music for everyone; and at the core of all of it is the Haden bass—deeply resonant and extraordinarily moving.

In 2012, Charlie Haden received the Jazz Masters Award from the National Endowment for the Arts, for a lifetime of achievement as a jazz artist. These words are excerpted from his acceptance speech: "I learned at a very young age that music teaches you about life, because when you are in the midst of improvisation, there is no yesterday and no tomorrow—there is only the moment you are in" (www.charliehadenmusic.com).

Just as we perceive LaFaro and Haden as complete individualists, we must also say the same of Ron Carter (see figure 14.4), whose equally beautiful sound and approach to the bass become instantly identifiable, the more we experience his music. Carter, along with Milt Hinton and several others, has been one of the most recorded bassists in jazz history, with over 2,500 recordings to his credit. Experienced as both a classical and jazz musician, Ron Carter brings a certain uniqueness to the jazz world. He is highly adaptable to any musical situation and sounds completely at home in any setting.

Figure 14.4.   Ron Carter. Courtesy of Beti Niemeyer.

Carter hails from Michigan and spent his formative years in Detroit, before moving to New York in the late '50s, where he earned his bachelor's and master's degrees in music from the Eastman School of Music and the Manhattan School of Music, respectively. He first came to the attention of both critics and jazz fans in the early '60s through his work with the pianist

Jaki Byard and, most notably, in his association with multi-reed virtuoso Eric Dolphy. Carter also recorded at that time on cello as well as the bass, and he became widely known as one of the first—if not the first—jazz cellist. The cello recordings are called *Where* (under Carter's name) and *Outward Bound* (under Dolphy's) and are considered classics even today, a half century after their initial release on Prestige/New Jazz Records. Other early recordings included work with saxophonist Coleman Hawkins, valve trombonist Bob Brookmeyer, and pianist Red Garland.

However, it was Carter's association with Miles Davis that brought him worldwide acclaim. As a member of Miles's second great quintet, he introduced an approach to bass playing that has set a certain stylistic standard that has become integral to the instrument's history. Rather than play only a walking groove like his predecessors, and in lieu of creating the kind of musical conversation Mingus had with Eric Dolphy or LaFaro sustained with Bill Evans, Ron Carter—to quote his website—"uses gonglike tones and glissandos [sliding up or down to a note] in his work. Once his exclusive trademark, these sounds have now become part of every modern bassist's vocabulary" (www.roncarter.net).

It is exactly this technique, combined with Tony Williams's elastic and spontaneous drumming and Herbie Hancock's in-the-moment approach to both accompanying and soloing, that defined the quintet's free-form musical approach. Considered one of the greatest small groups in jazz, the Miles Davis Quintet of the mid-'60s was certainly innovative in its approach to group performance and improvisation, thanks in part to Ron Carter's willingness to explore new approaches to rhythm section playing with his section mates. Rhythm section players are still trying to catch up to the innovative approaches developed by Williams, Hancock, and master bassist Carter.

ELECTRIFYING!: THE ELECTRIC BASS IN JAZZ

The electric bass, also called the bass guitar, was actually invented sometime in the 1930s; however, it did not meet with any enthusiasm until it was redesigned and marketed by Leo Fender in the early '50s. Even then, jazz bassists didn't really favor the instrument over the acoustic bass, mostly because the sound of the electric instrument lacked the full, dark, woody timbres that came to be associated with the bass violin. Perhaps the first bassist to embrace the electric bass in jazz was Monk Montgomery, who played it in the '50s with a group called the Mastersounds. Eventually, he became part of a very popular family group called the Montgomery Brothers, which featured him and his brothers, guitarist Wes and vibraphonist-pianist Buddy Montgomery. Aside from Monk Montgomery, there were few other electric bassists playing jazz at that time.

The electric bass didn't really take hold until the jazz-rock fusion era began in the late '60s and early '70s. At that point, many bassists added the electric bass or, in some cases, abandoned the acoustic instrument altogether in favor of it. While there have been many fine electric bassists on the jazz scene, there are three who stand out in particular:

Steve Swallow began his career as an acoustic bassist who became well known for his work with jazz greats such as clarinetist-saxophonist Jimmy Giuffre, pianist Paul Bley, and trumpeter Art Farmer, among many others. In 1970 Swallow made the switch to the electric bass and has not returned to the acoustic instrument since that time. The electric bass has also been called the "bass guitar," and in Swallow's hands, it really does sound like a bass guitar, in that he plays the instrument in a very guitar-like fashion. While his walking bass groove is solid and is informed by his years as an acoustic bassist, Swallow's improvisations often sound like guitar solos, played an octave lower than the guitar—very un-basslike, yet very unique, melodic, and inventive. Swallow is also a prolific composer who writes ear-catching compositions with titles like "Ladies in Mercedes," "I Think My Wife Is a Hat," and "Babble On."

Unlike Swallow, Jaco Pastorius (see figure 14.5) didn't transition from acoustic to electric bass, but came to the instrument from the drums, which he gave up after sustaining a sports injury. Much as Scott LaFaro revolutionized the approach to acoustic bass playing and influenced generations of bassists, Pastorius did much the same thing on the electric bass. His sound on the instrument was like no other: a wide, expansive, almost dreamlike sound at times, yet at other times, a bright, sometimes trebly quality, usually at medium to fast tempos, either in the jazz or jazz-rock idiom. This latter quality can be heard in abundance on *Bright Size Life*, guitarist Pat Metheny's debut album for the German ECM label. In addition to Metheny and drummer Bob Moses, Jaco is heard liberally throughout the disc in both supportive and solo capacities, and his work here is a textbook source of study for electric bassists everywhere.

Figure 14.5.   Jaco Pastorius. Courtesy of Donna Ranieri.

Interlude I: Experiencing Jaco

One of the best experiences a young jazz musician can have is to be mentored by other more experienced players. Growing up in Miami, many of us aspiring swingers had what we used to lovingly call "The University of Ira Sullivan," so named because Ira—trumpeter, saxophonist, flutist, drummer, jazz legend, you name it—really took us all under his wing, by sharing his knowledge and his love of jazz with guys like us who really wanted to play at that level, but needed the opportunity to experience the music firsthand by being on the bandstand with him. Ira would play with his group five or six nights a week at a little jazz joint called the Rancher Lounge in North Miami, usually from 9:00 p.m. to around 1:00 a.m. and would invite us college kids to "sit in" after that. He and his group were a patient, amiable lot and really helped us along in our struggles to be better than we were at that time.

I moved to Washington, D.C., after University of Miami studies and would return home every so often. Whenever I did, I'd find out where

Sullivan and his quintet were playing and would hang out to hear some great jazz and soak up the inspiration that inevitably came with it. One night when I dropped by the club, the band was getting ready to begin its second set, but there was a noticeable difference in personnel. The regular bassist was nowhere to be found, and in his place there on stage was this scruffy little kid with an electric bass. Electric bass in a jazz group? For me, that was sacrilege! Worse still, this guy didn't look like a jazz musician was supposed to look (you can see how my mind worked in those days). He had stringy, unwashed hair; he was barefoot and wore old blue jeans and—get this—a white T-shirt with his own picture on the front. The audacity! The nerve! I was prepared not to like this guy under any circumstances. All of that changed the minute Ira counted off the first tune. This kid—Jaco Pastorius was his name—was right in there, playing these intensely beautiful walking bass lines, locking in tight with the drummer to create an exciting, pulsating cushion of rhythm that propelled Ira and guitarist Joe Dioro into the stratosphere. And when it came time for his solo, Jaco astonished everyone. He sounded like a flamenco guitarist and a great jazz soloist all rolled into one. And to add to the excitement (and to my confusion), he jumped up and down during his solo, as though he were playing with a rock group. The entire set was a true jazz experience. The more I listened to this group, the more I was moved by the joy with which they communicated with each other and with us—and the more I understood that old saying "You can't judge a book by its cover." I had to rethink that statement in terms of both the use of the electric bass in jazz as well as the "look" and behavior of the amazing young man who was playing it. Little did I know that I was watching jazz history unfold before my eyes.

Jaco Pastorius went on to become one of the best known and most imitated electric bassists in both the jazz and rock worlds. Most notably, he joined the group Weather Report in 1976 and stayed until 1981. During that time, he composed music for the group and helped define its sound and direction. It was also around that time that he began working with singer-songwriter Joni Mitchell, and his atmospheric electric bass sound on Mitchell recordings such as *Hejira*, *Mingus*, and *Don Juan's Reckless*

Daughter added a beautiful depth and lent an immediately identifiable sonic quality to her work at that time.

Unfortunately, Jaco fell on bad times and circumstances in the mid-'80s, which ultimately cost him his life in 1987 and robbed the contemporary jazz world of a major talent. In his liner notes to a 2000 reissue of *Jaco Pastorius*, the bassist's first recording as a leader, Pat Metheny sums up Jaco's contributions in a most succinct and perceptive way:

> Jaco restructured the function of the bass in music in a way that has affected the outcome of countless musical projects to follow in his wake—an innovation that is still being absorbed by rhythm section players to this day. He showed the world that there was an entirely different way to think of the bass function, and what it meant. For this alone, Jaco would earn a major place in the pantheon of jazz history.

The year 1971 introduced bassist Stanley Clarke to the jazz world. Moving from Philadelphia to New York, Clarke made a name for himself initially as an acoustic bassist, playing with the likes of pianist Horace Silver and saxophonists Stan Getz, Dexter Gordon, Joe Henderson, and Pharoah Sanders, to name only a few. A master of both the acoustic and electric basses, Clarke joined forces with pianist Chick Corea in 1972 to form one of the first jazz fusion groups, "Return to Forever." The group went through a number of iterations, with Clarke and Corea being the constants. Initially, Clarke played acoustic bass in Return to Forever, but ultimately moved over to the electric bass early in the group's evolution. Clarke's electric sound is completely different than either Swallow's or Jaco's, and encompasses more R & B and funk feels, although he is equally at home in a straight-ahead jazz setting. He has also experimented with and personalized his use of other kinds of basses, including the piccolo bass and the tenor bass, in order to expand the range of his sound. Clarke continues to tour and record today with both the reunited Return to Forever and his own groups.

FACES OF THE BASSES: THREE RECENT VOICES

There have been many wonderful and distinctive bassists like Jerome Harris, Drew Gress, William Parker, and Mark Dresser who have emerged on the jazz scene in recent years. And of course, there have also been some like Buster Williams, Eddie Gomez, Christian McBride, Marc Johnson, Miroslav Vitous, and Henry Grimes who have been with us for a while and continue to gather fans wherever they perform. Unfortunately, due to space limitations we can't offer profiles of each of these fine players, even though they and many others deserve much wider recognition. So keep their names in mind and explore their music on the Internet in order to get an idea of the kind of music they create.

There are, however, three bassists we are about to spotlight who have ascended to national recognition via their solo projects as well as their performances with many of today's top jazz talents.

John Patitucci exploded onto the Los Angeles jazz scene in the early '80s and made many of that city's bassists sit up and take notice (he probably sent many of them scurrying back to their practice rooms as well!). A native of Brooklyn, New York, he began playing the electric bass at the tender age of 10, and he added the acoustic bass five years later. His musical interests were extremely diverse at that time, allowing him to explore not only rock and pop, but also blues, classical music, and of course, jazz. Moving to California, Patitucci studied classical bass at San Francisco and Long Beach State universities. Taking up residency in Southern California, Patitucci became active in L.A.'s studio and jazz scenes and, in 1986, was voted by the National Academy of Recording Arts and Sciences as its most valuable bass player.

The list of jazz artists that John has recorded and played with is seemingly endless and includes his tenures with the groups of both pianist Chick Corea and saxophonist Wayne Shorter, as well as with Stan Getz, Wynton Marsalis, Michael Brecker, Tony Williams, and many others. The winner of two Grammy Awards as well as over two dozen Grammy nominations, Patitucci also leads his own groups and has recorded many CDs, which feature stellar bands and many of his compositions.

Interlude II: The Alembic Trio

Even with all of the worldwide acclaim and his secure place as a jazz star, John Patitucci is, above all, the same witty and affable guy I knew in the '80s, back in our L.A. days when we played together for a number of years in a great band called Seventh Avenue. He knew he was a very good bassist, but he was always looking for ways to challenge himself and move beyond wherever he was at the time. We wound up losing touch for many years. John was on the path he was meant to be on—worldwide fame and recognition as a true musical artist, and I watched from afar, happy to have known and played with him during his formative years.

We reconnected once I returned east to live and were finally reunited musically. I had mentioned to Dave Liebman that John and I had resumed our friendship, and we both agreed that it would be great if we three might be able to schedule a trio gig at the Deer Head Inn, a local and quite legendary jazz club. After comparing schedules, we were able to book a common date to concertize. And concertize we did.

John Patitucci, the bassist, is all about being right there, "in the moment." He created brilliant musical ideas, reacted to Lieb's and my musical statements, and lifted the trio off the ground in so many ways. Lieb, who is not exactly a slouch in that department, did the same and off we went, exploring uncharted territory in our three-way conversations, and taking the packed house full of listeners with us. Two sets of music, two standing ovations, and complete communion with our listeners. And this all was due in no small measure to John who, even after all of his fame as one of jazz's leading bassists, still knows how to share his absolute joy of making music with others.

We called ourselves the Alembic Trio. "Alembic," among other things, means "anything that transforms." And that is what John Patitucci is all

Figure 14.6. The Alembic Trio: from left to right, Dave Liebman, John Patitucci, and the author. Courtesy of Robert Victory.

about. He transforms himself into the music he plays. He transforms audiences with his complete sense of joy and his endless enthusiasm. And that night, he—and we—transformed ourselves into one breath of musical air and the audience into a single attentive body of listeners—the earmark of a true jazz experience.

Like John Patitucci, bassist Scott Colley moved to New York City from Los Angeles in the second half of the 1980s, in order to become a part of the vital, ever-changing New York jazz scene. He came well prepared, as a student of both composition and jazz studies at the California Institute for the Arts. In addition, he honed his technical and improvisatory skills by studying bass with jazz icon Charlie Haden and classical bassist Fred Tinsley, longtime member of the Los Angeles Philharmonic.

After moving to New York, Colley worked with singer Carmen McRae and trumpet giant Dizzy Gillespie, among other notables. Word traveled quickly about Colley's exemplary work as both a rhythm section accompanist and as a soloist, and he became one of the city's most in-demand bass players. Throughout the '90s and into the new millennium, Colley graced the recordings and live appearances of many of the finest players, from venerable and revered players such as guitarist Jim Hall, pianist Herbie Hancock, and the late saxophone genius Michael Brecker to exciting young players like saxophonist Chris Potter and drummer Antonio Sanchez, both of whom happen to be members of Colley's trio. Among the many other reputable jazz artists Colley has played with are trumpeter Dave Douglas, pianist Kenny Werner, vibraphonist Gary Burton, and guitarists Bill Frisell and John Scofield. To say that Colley is "in demand" among the upper echelon of jazz artists is an understatement.

Interlude III: Warmth and Spontaneity

As a bassist, Scott Colley has a warm and woody sound. His solos are often songlike and are always thoughtfully constructed and beautifully executed. I know from personal experience. We began our musical association in L.A.

and continued it in New York years later, where I was lucky enough to have him play on *OM/ShalOM*, my first recording as a leader. One of the wonderful things about Scott's playing is his ability to assimilate everything going on around him and still make it all sound so personal. At one point during the recording session—a very intense musical moment which involved both improvisation and the spoken word—Scott picked up his bow and played a "tremolo" (a wavering tone that is often used to express a great deal of feeling) that was chilling and deeply emotional. This was not written in the music; it was completely spontaneous on Scott's part. And he found exactly the right place to play it, between the end of one word and the beginning of another. I believe, as do many other listeners, that Scott's creative contribution on that track is one of the highlights of the recording. Scott, like John Patitucci, is so much more than a bass player. He is a musical sculptor who fashions notes and silences, all in the service of the music. To hear him in any setting is a gratifying experience, and to play music with him is a gift.

Many years younger than the other bassists profiled in this chapter, Esperanza Spalding has, in a very short time, attracted the attention of jazz listeners and critics both here and abroad. She is unique in that she is both an accomplished and imaginative bassist and an excellent singer. Her interests are wide ranging, and her recordings are both spirited and filled with all sorts of nuances and moods. No two tracks are ever alike; for example, on her Chamber Music Society CD, her music is, by turns, quirky, challenging, playful, and tonally colorful. In fact, if she were a painter, Spalding might initially create a canvas with broad strokes and vibrant colors, but then she might also express herself in deep blue-green hues and delicate lines and shapes. As a vocalist, she has a voice that is light and airy, yet capable of swinging and locking into both the meaning and the groove of a song. She is extraordinarily talented and has been recognized as such by both the critical press and the musical community—and even by President Barack Obama, who invited Spalding to perform as his guest when he received the 2009 Nobel Peace Prize in Oslo, Norway.

In February 2011 Spalding became the first jazz artist ever to win the "Best New Artist" award—an honor that thrust her even further into the national public eye and introduced her music to a much larger non-jazz

Figure 14.7. Esperanza Spalding. Courtesy of Carlos Pericás.

audience. Her ascent since that time has been steady and constant, and she continues to evolve as a bassist and also as a singer and a songwriter.

The bass has not only provided the "bottom and boom" in jazz groups since the early days of the music, but as rhythm sections evolved through swing and bebop and beyond, the bass has always been at the heart of the groove, where it is firmly ensconced even today. As Charlie Haden said in the quote at the beginning of this chapter, without the bass "the bottom kind of drops out of everything."

Getting Personal with John Patitucci

What advice would you offer a new listener who will be experiencing your music for the first time, either in concert or via one of your recordings?

[About experiencing jazz in a live setting:] I think that with jazz music, the best thing that can happen is that you see it "live." You can get really inspired from records as I did; but I remember as I was growing up and going to hear jazz, I had experiences that I still remember. Jazz is a visual as well as an aural music, so I think that the best thing you can do is to go see it "live"—whether it's me or anybody else for that matter. I think the communication between the musicians, the spiritual aspect of the music, and how that gets projected and shared with the audience—that's something you really can't get from a recording.

Figure 14.8.   John Patitucci. Courtesy of Gus Cantavero.

[About approaching the jazz experience with an open mind:] I think that the most common misconception which applies to listening to my music or any kind of jazz is that people somehow think that they have to understand everything, like intellectually, which is absolutely untrue. I think you can just react viscerally and emotionally to my music, or any music, in fact. A lot of times, people have this impression that jazz is complicated and they'll never understand it, so it sort of scares them before they even have a chance to listen to it. My music is pretty melodic and lyrical; it's very rhythmically based and oriented. React to the feeling of it emotionally and don't worry about understanding anything. The soulful element of it—the feeling, emotion, the power of the rhythm—these are the things that transcend anybody's familiarity or nonfamiliarity with the music.

What would be the first recording of yours that you would recommend for an initial listening experience and as a good introduction to your music?

It's kind of a toss-up between *Songs, Stories, and Spirituals* and *Communion*, because there's a vocal element on both of those as well, which sometimes helps people connect with the music. *Songs* is more of a concept record.

[To new listeners:] In my music, the blues is in there, there's different ethnic traditions, there's Brazilian and African overtones in the music heavily, there's some grooves, some swinging. Don't underestimate your ability to connect with this music and try to come to it with an open mind, because a lot of times in our society, there've been some really weird, stereotypical, ridiculous handles put on jazz music. I think that if you are open minded, you'll find all kinds of things you would enjoy in it.

SELECTED BASSISTS' WEBSITES: FROM THEN 'TIL NOW

Note: Only official sites are listed. Use Google for all others.

Milt Hinton: www.milthinton.com
Charles Mingus: www.mingusmingusmingus.com
Scott LaFaro: www.scottlafaro.com
Charlie Haden: www.charliehadenmusic.com
Ron Carter: www.roncarter.net
Eddie Gomez: www.eddiegomez.com
John Patitucci: www.johnpatitucci.com
Scott Colley: www.scottcolley.com
Drew Gress: www.drewgress.com
Christian McBride: www.christianmcbride.com
Esperanza Spalding: www.esperanzaspalding.com

RECOMMENDED READING

Milt Hinton

Hinton, Milt, and David G. Berger. *Bass Line: The Stories and Photographs of Milt Hinton*. Philadelphia: Temple UP, 1988. Print.
Hinton, Milt, David G. Berger, and Holly Maxson. *OverTime: The Jazz Photographs of Milt Hinton*. San Francisco: Pomegranate ArtBooks, 1991. Print.

Charles Mingus

Mingus, Charles. *Beneath the Underdog*. New York: Vintage Books, 1991. Print.
Mingus, Sue Graham. *Tonight at Noon: A Love Story*. Cambridge: Da Capo Press, 2003. Print.

Scott LaFaro

LaFaro-Hernandez, Helene. *Jade Visions: The Life and Music of Scott LaFaro*. North Texas Lives of Musicians Series, #4. Denton: U of North Texas P, 2009. Print.

Ron Carter

Ouellette, Dan. *Ron Carter: Finding the Right Notes*. New York: ArtistShare, 2009. Print.

Jaco Pastorius

Milkowski, Bill. *The Extraordinary and Tragic Life of Jaco Pastorius*. Anniversary edition. San Francisco: Backbeat Books, 2005. Print.

15

I GOT RHYTHM III

Give the Drummer Some!

The universal language of man isn't music. It's rhythm. That's the only thing people all over the world understand. The drum. The beat: boom, boom, boom. The person who sits behind the drum set gives us the foundation, the heartbeat of jazz.

—Chico Hamilton

A LITTLE PREFACE TO A *BIG* CHAPTER

Drums and other instruments in the percussion family are much more than objects that anyone can hit and think that the sound that comes out is music. Far from it. In fact, the master jazz drummer Max Roach said it best:

You can't take the instrument lightly! Relatively new to the world of music, the drum set is very difficult to really master. There's so much to the whole process. Just the coordination of wrists, arms, and legs, in various rhythmic circumstances, is challenge enough.

—From *Drummin' Men: The Bebop Years* by Burt Korall
(Oxford University Press, 2002)

It would be easy to write an entire book about the drums in jazz, instead of a single chapter. In fact, the esteemed jazz writer Burt Korall has written not just one book about jazz drummers, but two complete volumes in his Drummin' Men series published by Oxford University Press—and those two excellent books profile the great drummers from the beginnings of jazz only through the bebop era. Hopefully, Korall will add to the series, since there is a lot more ground to cover—over a half century more, to be exact.

In this large chapter we will give the new jazz listener/experiencer an introduction to a number of the greatest jazz drummers in jazz history, as well as look at some of the rising stars currently on the scene. Regrettably, some great players will inadvertently be omitted; however, the Korall books, as well as Joachim Berendt's excellent volume *The Jazz Book*, will offer additional interesting and pertinent information about the players profiled here and others who deserve wider recognition and a place in your music collection.

FROM BEGINNINGS TO BOP

The Forefathers: Baby and Zutty

The first use of drums in jazz came not in the form of the drum set but as a "drum section," which was made up minimally of a snare drummer, a bass drummer, and a cymbal player, although sometimes in the absence of a cymbal player, the bass drummer played a cymbal mounted face up on his bass drum, clapping it with the mounted cymbal with his left hand, while his right kept time on the bass drum with a mallet.

The drum set as we know it did not just spring into existence overnight. Early drummers were known to have played the bass drum and snare drum simultaneously, using one hand on each. Understandably, the process was cumbersome and did not allow for a lot of creativity or variety of tonal colors. However, in the early part of the 20th century, the bass drum pedal came into existence, followed thereafter by the "hi-hat" or "sock cymbals," which allowed the newly liberated drummer to play the bass drum with one foot, while the other foot would depress a pedal that would clap the two small cymbals together, creating a "chik-chik" sound. These two advancements freed the drummer up, enabling him to concentrate on using his hands to play not only the snare drum but also a variety of cymbals, tom toms, woodblocks, cowbells, and other novelty instruments, in order to create specific moods.

Two of the best of the early drummers—if not the best—were Baby Dodds and Zutty Singleton, both from New Orleans. They were instrumental in moving the drums from a very low status to a position of respect and authority. Prior to Dodds and Singleton, the drums were frequently perceived as an "adjunct" feature in a band; that is, they provided rhythm and some novelty effects—little else—making them "less than" musicians. An old joke handed down over generations goes something like this:

Somebody asks a band leader: "How many do you have in your group?"

The band leader replies: "Six musicians—and a drummer."

Baby Dodds and Zutty Singleton changed all of that by bringing the drums to the forefront as a solo instrument and by showing the world that drummers were capable of so much more than merely providing a beat for the rest of the group. Thanks to them, the drummer became a more integral part of a jazz band—a "colorist" as well as a beat-keeper. He would poke and prod soloists, using the time-honored call-and-response approach so essential to all jazz music. He would also provide a much wider tonal palette by employing a variety of sounds in addition to the existing drums and the hi-hat cymbals, such as wood blocks, temple blocks, cow bells, Chinese tom toms, and a variety of Chinese and Turkish cymbals.

Baby Dodds (1898–1959) was a wonder, and his contributions to drumming and jazz continue to influence drummers today. Fortunately, we are able to hear him talking about drumming, demonstrating his amazing technique, and playing several solos, thanks to the recordings produced by Frederick Ramsey for Folkways Records in 1951. These recordings are not only superior as samples of Dodds's drumming virtuosity but are also windows into the bygone era of the 1920s. While Dodds's thoughts and stories are entertaining, it is his flawless and colorful drumming that will really stay with you. His first solo, called "Spooky Drums No. 1," begins with the traditional "roll off," which was a common parade drum introduction to many a march. From there, Dodds moves into a repeated rhythmic pattern using his drum rims, woodblock, and cowbell, creating an almost hypnotic effect. It is a joyous and jumping little romp that can stay with the listener long after its two-plus-minutes duration. Baby Dodds played with tremendous drive, and even though the recording techniques of the day

Figure 15.1.   Baby Dodds. Courtesy of the William P. Gottlieb Collection.

did not favor drummers, we can still hear Dodds's power behind both the soloists and the groups with which he played.

To compare the other New Orleans drumming master Zutty Singleton (1898–1975) to Baby Dodds would be like comparing a juicy McIntosh apple to a delicious mango. Both were innovative and thoroughly musical drummers—yet they were markedly different from each other, in their approaches to playing the drum set. Whereas Dodds's drumming seemed quite martial and was frequently filled with "ruffles and flourishes" as he moved back and forth from the snare drum to the tom toms, Singleton's attack was a little lighter and perhaps more buoyant, and always swung. Both men were consummate ensemble players and managed to support the other band members while exhibiting their own uniquely personal styles.

Figure 15.2.   Wire brushes.

Singleton also was one of the first—if not the first—to use specially made wire brushes on the drums (see figure 15.2), in order to create a sustained swishing sound by dragging the brushes over the snare head in clockwise and counterclockwise motions.

Like Dodds, Singleton worked with many of the greatest jazz musicians of that day, including Louis Armstrong, Fats Waller, Sidney Bechet, and many others. He also was one of our first drum soloists and, like his contemporary, moved the concept of drum solos into the foreground, not as displays of technique, but as complete musical statements that always retained the feeling of the songs that their solos were based upon. It is accurate to conclude that Baby Dodds and Zutty Singleton were our first great drummers and that their influence has been mighty and lasting throughout all of jazz's illustrious history.

Interlude I: Independence Day

One of the things that make drumming so unique is the concept of independent coordination. In order to understand what that is, you can conduct this little experiment:

1. Pat the top of your head in a steady medium tempo rhythm with your left hand.
2. Using your right hand, rub your stomach in a circular, clockwise motion.
3. Continuing the head patting and stomach rubbing, begin tapping your right foot twice as fast as you are patting your head.

Note: If you are left-handed, you can reverse hands and foot above to make it easier. However, to really master this exercise you should be able to perform it either way.

Now you can see how the drummer's creative talent and independent sense of time helps him meet the challenges of jazz's rhythmic complexities. Drummers use both hands with sticks, brushes, and other beaters, and they use their feet on the bass drum and hi-hat pedals respectively. As you might guess, drumming is a lot more involved than just banging away on drums and cymbals.

The Sons: Chick, Big Sid, Papa Jo, Gene, and Buddy

While there have been many great drummers in the Dodds-Singleton lineage—men such as Dave Tough, Ray Bauduc, George Wettling, and Ray McKinley—we will focus upon five of the greatest and most memorable drummers of the transitional era, from early jazz to swing.

Of the five names in the heading above, two (Jo Jones, Buddy Rich) have been the subjects of biographies, and one (Gene Krupa) has been the subject of not only biographies, but also a full-length motion picture. The remaining two could easily become the subjects of books as well, given their legendary status in the concentric worlds of jazz and jazz drumming. However, this is a listener's companion and not biographical research. The object here is to introduce you to these fine players, in order that you might further explore their music and read more about them as well.

Chick Webb (1905–1939) was small in stature, but a giant when it came to jazz drumming. He, more than anyone else, set the gold standard for swing drumming all through the 1930s, and while there were certainly a number of great drummers playing during that period, none of them could approach Webb's dazzling virtuosity or technical skill. All the more amazing, considering that as a child, Webb suffered severe physical trauma as a result of an accident that left him with irreversible damage to his vertebrae—injuries that would stunt his growth and cause him a lifetime of pain.

A native of Baltimore, Webb moved to New York in 1924 and within several years began to establish himself as a force to be reckoned with. He formed small bands first, which grew into larger bands, and ultimately into a formidable big band—one that welcomed all comers: visiting bands like Count Basie's or Benny Goodman's aggregations. In each friendly "battle" of the big bands, Webb's group won, hands down. And Webb himself was revered by many fine drummers, among them the equally legendary Gene Krupa:

> I found direction when I first heard Chick. He changed everything around me when I first came to New York. . . . Chick had drive and ingenuity and magnetism that drew drummers by the dozens to where he was working. All of us in that "learnin' groove" in the 1930s were enlightened by him. (8)

While Big Sid Catlett (1910–1951) was not known as a virtuoso or an innovator in the same way that Chick Webb was, he was a drummer who was ultimately revered for his ability to move from one style of jazz to the next and sound at home in any musical situation, whether it was early jazz, swing, or bebop. Catlett's sense of rhythm, pacing, and almost telepathic level of communication with his band mates made him the drummer of choice in many diverse small- or large-ensemble settings, from Louis Armstrong and Jack Teagarden to Charlie Parker and Dizzy Gillespie. In essence, he was a team player who would submerge his ego for the good of the music he was performing at any given time.

Catlett was initially influenced by both Baby Dodds and Zutty Singleton; however, it was Singleton's smoothness, finesse, and inventiveness that exerted a stronger pull upon Catlett's developing musical sense. This is very evident when watching Catlett play, thanks to a number of excellent YouTube videos. A large man, as his name implies, Catlett nonetheless played with the gracefulness and accuracy of a ballet dancer. And as many a knowledgeable drummer will tell you, Big Sid had a beautiful "touch." That is, even though he could play with lightning speed and at full-tilt volume, the way he would hit the drums and cymbals brought out their best tonal qualities.

Figure 15.3.   Big Sid Catlett. Courtesy of the William P. Gottlieb Collection.

One of the most beautiful things about jazz—and many other forms of music as well—is the desire of the musicians to pass along to the next generation both their knowledge and experience and, in many cases, their innovations. In ancient and tribal cultures, before music theory and nota-tion, the art of making music was passed from generation to generation orally, often in a master-apprentice relationship. In jazz, that would hap-pen in several ways: one would be to hear and absorb a master musician's work through recordings and to be able to see their work as transcribed for instructional books. Another would be through personal contact, including live performances and conversations. A third way would be to get to know a musician through his or her writings, if in fact that musician also happened to write memoirs. A number of fine players across generations have written about their lives in jazz, including Duke Ellington, Eddie Condon, Charles Mingus, Bill Crow, Dave Liebman, and many others. One of the most readable and colorful windows into the jazz life was created by "Papa" Jo Jones (1911–1985), one of our best drummers. Jones was unique as both a jazz artist and a human being. There was and has never been anyone quite like him on either front. Fortunately, Jones told his story to the eminent writer Albert Murray via a series of recorded conversations that took place from 1977 to 1985, which have since been transcribed by editor Paul Devlin for *Rifftide: The Life and Opinions of Papa Jo Jones* (University of Minnesota Press, 2011).

While other drummers concerned themselves more with the technical aspects of drumming, Papa Jo Jones, like Chick Webb, placed a high value on musicality, even though he was a superb technician and a powerful drummer in every respect. As mentioned elsewhere, Papa Jo was one of the key members of Count Basie's "All American Rhythm Section." Unlike other big swing bands of the day whose stock in trade was excitement and power, the Basie aggregation created excitement by swinging in a natural, unforced, relaxed manner. Jones used his tremendous facility to help create an irrepressible groove that would have listeners tapping their feet. Papa understood the importance of the entire rhythm section and its relationship to the other sections in the band. He was also one of the first drummers to emphasize the importance of tuning the drums carefully in order to achieve a solid blend with the other players in any group with which he was associated. And in terms of innovation, it was Papa Jo who used the hi-hat cymbals, creating rhythms with sticks rather than with only his left foot; emphasized the importance of keeping the beat on his cymbals, rather than the snare drum; and moved away from the ponderous heaviness of playing the bass drum on every beat.

Jones's creative developments exerted tremendous influence upon generations of drummers and altered the course of drumming history. In the words of jazz writer and critic Bob Blumenthal: "How many others in jazz history both epitomized their own era and made essential contributions to the next?" (*Boston Phoenix*, October 3, 1978).

Born and raised in Chicago, Gene Krupa (1909–1973) was groomed by his parents to become a priest. Fortunately for us, he was bitten by the jazz bug early and bought his first set of drums at age 11. He subsequently abandoned the idea of priesthood and turned to the drums and what would become his lifelong love of jazz. While he was not the first drum soloist in jazz, he was certainly the first to play extended solos—an innovation, given that most drum solos before Krupa were short "drum breaks" and flourishes. Krupa would use a musical motif and take his time developing it, building tension all the while and taking his audiences with him on the journey. This was especially evident during his stint as the drummer for the Benny Goodman groups of the late '30s. Goodman's hit, "Sing, Sing, Sing," was an important vehicle for Krupa and a real crowd pleaser for the Goodman band, particularly at its triumphant 1938 Carnegie Hall concert. Krupa's flair for the dramatic, coupled with his technical prowess and his unerring sense of swing, helped bring the often stuffy Carnegie Hall patrons to their feet and dancing in the aisles on that magic night. And his charismatic, matinee-idol looks didn't hurt him any either! As a result, Krupa became a celebrity and, later on, the subject of both a biography and a movie called *The Gene Krupa Story*.

Figure 15.4. Gene Krupa. Courtesy of the William P. Gottlieb Collection.

In spite of all of the accolades he received from fans and the press, Gene Krupa had the deepest respect for his mentors as well as his contemporaries. He knew and loved the work of Baby Dodds and Zutty Singleton and was in awe of Chick Webb. One night, after a highly publicized "Battle of the Bands," which pitted Goodman's big band against Chick Webb's in a mock musical battle, Webb's group outplayed Goodman's, and Webb himself shone so brightly behind his drums that, after the musical dueling, Krupa bowed down to the little drummer and proclaimed him to be the undisputed "king."

In addition to performance, Krupa was also instrumental in developing tunable tom toms as well as an improved hi-hat system. In fact, as a result of these and other innovations, he has often been called the father of the modern drum set. He was also active as a teacher, lecturer, and spokesperson for the Slingerland Drum Company for many years.

After leaving Goodman's band, Krupa started his own large and small groups and ventured into newer musical territory, hiring bop-oriented arrangers like saxophonist Gerry Mulligan to write for his big band. His drumming style changed and became more modern in the coming years, but through all of the changes in the music happening in the '40s and '50s Krupa always emphasized swinging over everything else. As a result, his bands were always well received by listeners, both here in the United States and abroad. He toured with his small groups through the middle '60s and retired from playing for three years before returning to the drums and public performance in 1970, where he continued playing until his death three years later. Krupa's contributions to jazz and to drumming, along with those we have profiled thus far, have laid the foundations for generations of drummers to come. All you need to do is listen to the 1938 Goodman Carnegie Hall concert to feel the enormous impact and presence that Krupa had on musicians and listeners alike.

No discussion of jazz drumming in the swing era would be complete without casting a spotlight upon Buddy Rich (1917–1987), who was quite possibly the most technically accomplished jazz drummer to ever sit behind a drum set. The key here is the word "jazz." While there have been and continue to be jazz-rock drummers who have embraced Rich's technical virtuosity and held it as a gold standard, few if any have been able to best Rich's blinding speed and his ability to support an ensemble without overshadowing it with a lot of drum pyrotechnics.

Buddy Rich began playing the drums at the impossible age of around 18 months. His parents worked as vaudeville entertainers and, aware of his early affinity for the drums, brought Buddy into their show, where he became known as "Traps, the Drum Wonder." According to his biography, he became a featured performer on Broadway at the tender age of four. As a young adult, Rich began his long career as a jazz musician, playing at the Hickory House in New York City in 1937. One thing led to another, and his reputation as a dynamic musician grew as time passed. Within a couple of years, he was playing with big bands led by trombonist Tommy Dorsey and clarinetist Artie Shaw, and as the '40s progressed into the '50s, he played with many jazz greats, including saxophonist Lester Young, trumpeter Dizzy Gillespie, pianists Art Tatum and Oscar Peterson, vibraphonist Lionel Hampton, and many others. He founded his exciting big band in the mid-'60s and toured and recorded with its various incarnations throughout the '70s.

Buddy was also known for his quick wit and his biting attacks on what he felt was disingenuous and amateurish in music. He was also a frequent and popular guest on talk shows like *The Tonight Show* and *The Merv Griffin Show*, and he even made a legendary appearance on *The Muppet Show*, where he played a drum battle with "Animal." This segment is accessible on YouTube and is still very funny today.

Buddy Rich received many awards and accolades for his contributions to drumming and jazz and is still held in the highest esteem as a master drummer, a consummate showman, and an astounding soloist. He passed away in 1987—almost a full seven decades after he began thrilling audiences as "Traps, the Drum Wonder." And what a drum wonder he was.

Interlude II: Two Encounters with Buddy

Sometimes, a personal story comes with a sequel. Meeting Buddy Rich twice is one of those rare occasions when you get a chance to respond years later to a comment that someone made to you much earlier in your life. Meeting Buddy Rich twice is the theme of this little memoir.

I

When I was 15 years old and just a couple of years into playing the drums, my drum teacher—a wonderful old guy and ex-drum corps champion named Vincent Mott—invited me to go with him to a weekend matinee to

hear the amazing Buddy Rich and his small group at the Johnina Hotel's
Dream Bar on Miami Beach. Apparently, from what I was told, Buddy had
a home in North Miami, and whenever he came into town for a stay, he'd
play at the Dream Bar. So naturally I was excited, elated, and terrified to
be meeting one of the best drummers alive.

We got ringside seats next to the drums. I remember sitting in stunned
silence, watching and hearing nothing but Buddy, his hands a blur as he
defied gravity and the rhythmic permutations of us ordinary musical mor-
tals. I never saw anyone play that fast or with that much finesse—and still
haven't, really. Buddy was unbelievable, and I could feel my jaw dropping
on the table with each solo he played.

When the set was over and Buddy came off the stage, he saw Vince and
came over to our table. My heart was in my throat! Vince introduced me
to Buddy as one of his star pupils, and Buddy in turn bought me a Coke. I
never forgot our conversation:

> Buddy: Kid, you know what will happen if you practice five hours a day, five
> days a week, for the next 25 years?
>
> Me: No, Mr. Rich . . . what?
>
> Buddy: You *still* won't be as good as me!

Both Vince and Buddy laughed, and I sat there stunned and speechless,
even though he was joking.

II

Fast-forward 25 years. I am in Lake Tahoe, playing a show with actress-
singer Debbie Reynolds. Buddy is performing in the large hotel lounge
with his big band. One night during our engagement, Buddy and his
daughter come to see Debbie's show. From my drums, I see them sitting
in the center of the room, close to the stage. Now in the show, there's a
couple of short drum solos; knowing Buddy is there, I tighten my snare
drum's wire snares and get out the heavy sticks. When my solo turns come,
I do my best Buddy Rich imitations and manage to pull them off without
having any major flubs, or even falling off the drum stool.

After the show, I'm backstage walking to the dressing room, when I see
Buddy coming toward me from the other end of the hall. He looks at me
and the following exchange happens:

Buddy: You're the drummer, right?

Me: Yes I am, Mr. Rich . . .

Buddy: You sounded good up there.

Me: Thank you, Mr. Rich. Now, let me tell you a little story.

I pressed on quickly, so he wouldn't have time to object:

> When I was 15 years old, Vince Mott took me to the Johnina Dream Bar on
> Miami Beach to hear you play. When you came off the stage, you bought me
> a Coke and told me that if I practiced five hours a day for the next 25 years
> . . . I *still* wouldn't be as good as you . . .

Buddy smiled and was silent, waiting for whatever would come next. So I
got right up in his face and said very quietly: ". . . and you know what, you
motherfucker? I'm *still* not as good as you!"

Buddy got this big grin on his face, laughed heartily, and gave me an
almost rib-cracking hug. I don't remember what exactly he said after that
and before he continued down the hall—but truthfully, it didn't matter.
We had come full circle, he and I . . . and nothing else needed to be said.
And I once again got the thrill of my life.

FROM BOP TO THE 21ST CENTURY

Bebop Drumming Pioneers

Just as bebop was a radical departure from the jazz of the swing era, so,
too, was the approach to drumming. One important thing to remember is
that with the advent of bebop, the notion of jazz as dance music became
somewhat antiquated. Bop was a listener's music—something to absorb as
an art form and not as a vehicle for tripping the light fantastic on the dance
floor. Accordingly, the bop rhythm sections were liberated from the strict
two- and four-beat rhythms of swing. Drummers in particular underwent
a dramatic stylistic change. Gone was the bass drum on all four beats in
every bar of music, as well as the strident stiffness that often crept into
the swing beat. These were replaced by a looser, more subtle feeling. The

drummer was now freer to interact with a horn soloist, or other members of the rhythm section. But how to deal with the newfound freedom? The drummers we're going to profile were top among those who took up the challenge of creating a new vocabulary for jazz drums. While ultimately many fine bebop drummers emerged on the scene, these five gentlemen in particular were responsible for laying the foundation that all others would ultimately follow.

Kenny Clarke and Max Roach were among the first to create a new language for jazz drummers. They each found a way to shift the rhythmic flow from the bass drum to the ride cymbal as a beat-keeping device. Both also developed a way to play syncopated accents on both the snare drum and the bass drum, where one drum would interact with the other to create a unified rhythmic figure. As an example, think of the old nursery rhyme, "Jack and Jill." If you play the melody of the song on your left knee with your left hand, except where noted below in CAPITAL letters (which would be played by tapping your right foot), you would have an idea of a bebop drum set pattern. Try it:

Jack and Jill WENT up a hill TO fetch a pail OF wa-ter
Jack fell down AND broke his crown, AND Jill came tum-BLING af-TER

With a little bit of practice, you would have the general idea of the kinds of musical "conversations" bop drummers would have with themselves, as their feet worked with their hands to spread the rhythmic patterns out over the entire drum set. This is much more than drumbeat calisthenics—it is the creation of rhythmic patterns, using both hands and feet, to contribute to intensity and drive in the music.

While both men were innovators of the first order, their individual styles were as different as night and day. Kenny Clarke (1914–1985) is considered a father of bebop drumming. His style was aggressive yet quite subtle, and he was a superb accompanist for both soloists and singers. In the 1950s, he was the original drummer with one of modern jazz's most beloved groups, the Modern Jazz Quartet, and in the decade before that he was the house drummer at Minton's Playhouse, which was the incubator for bebop innovators such as Charlie Parker, Dizzy Gillespie, Thelonious Monk, Bud Powell, and others. Ultimately, he relocated to France and was active on the jazz scene, with visiting American jazz musicians as well as many fine European jazz artists.

Many jazz musicians, historians, and critics agree that Max Roach (see figure 15.5) will always be known as one of the best of the many great jazz drummers in the music's 100-year history. But Roach was much more than a technically brilliant player. He was an artist whose interests were far ranging and in fact extended way beyond the stylistic parameters of bebop. Looking at Max's career, we can see that he was at the forefront of a number of important jazz milestones:

- He worked and recorded with Charlie Parker and Dizzy Gillespie at the dawn of bebop in the mid-'40s.
- He played drums on Miles Davis's historic *Birth of the Cool* sessions for Capitol Records in the late '40s.
- In the mid-'50s, he co-led one of bebop's most critically acclaimed small groups: the Clifford Brown–Max Roach Quintet, which featured saxophonists Harold Land and Sonny Rollins, among others.
- In the 1960s his support of the civil rights movement and his deep personal concerns about racial inequality in America led him to infuse political themes into modern jazz and world music, culminating in his genre-bending composition: *We Insist! The Freedom Now Suite* (Candid Records, 1960).

Roach also steadfastly refused to be pigeonholed stylistically in terms of his musical interests and approaches. He was much more than a bebop innovator. Not one to rest on his laurels, Roach engaged in many forms of musical expression. For example, in 1970 he founded jazz's first percussion ensemble, M'Boom, which featured other stellar jazz drummers and percussionists such as Joe Chambers, Freddie Waits, and Warren Smith. Roach was also intrigued by the duo format and in the '80s and '90s recorded and performed in tandem with avant-garde pianist Cecil Taylor, with saxophonists Archie Shepp and Anthony Braxton, with trumpeter Dizzy Gillespie (with whom he had worked and recorded in the '40s), and a number of other notable musicians and performing artists. He even recorded a duet in which he interacted musically with a recording of Martin Luther King delivering his historic "I Have a Dream" oration.

He also expanded his activities to include teaching and, in 1972, joined the faculty at the University of Massachusetts at Amherst, where he continued his association for more than three decades.

**Figure 15.5.   Max Roach, New York, 1940s. Courtesy of the William P. Got-
tlieb Collection.**

Roach also found other interesting avenues for his creative energies,
including the augmentation of his working quartet with the Uptown String
Quartet, led by his daughter, Maxine Roach; a brass quintet augmented by
his drums; an exploration with hip-hop artists; and amazing solo concerts
that were unlike anything anyone had ever heard. If anyone could sustain
an evening of solo drumming, it would be Max Roach—he was that musically inventive.

A recipient of eight honorary doctorates, a MacArthur Foundation Genius Grant, the French Grand Prix du Disque, and many other notable
awards and honors, Roach continued his creative journey until his death in
2007 at the age of 83.

Two good words to describe Art Blakey, both man and music, might be "rolling thunder." Indeed, Blakey was lightning, thunder, and storm. He played with tremendous drive and spirit. And when you watch him play on YouTube or on any one of the DVDs that feature him, you will also notice the great, energetic joy with which he communicates through his music. One gets the sense that, for Blakey, music and living were inseparable. He was once reputed to have said that music washes away the dust of everyday life. His approach to jazz certainly substantiated that perspective.

As a drummer, Blakey was largely self-taught. One of his early heroes was Chick Webb, for whom Blakey acted as a gofer and as a valet. Webb reinforced the importance of practice as important for any young musician seeking to improve himself as well as his potential. While Blakey was not someone who burst onto the jazz scene of the late '30s and '40s, he kept his eyes and ears open and tried to assimilate as much as possible from his mentors. He really began to hit his stride with the Billy Eckstine big band in the mid-'40s. It was almost like a baptism of fire for the young drummer, since the band boasted many of early bebop's best players, among them Charlie Parker and Dizzy Gillespie. Gillespie in particular took Blakey under his wing and made all manner of suggestions regarding approaches to accompanying soloists and playing time.

Another milestone in Blakey's early experiences was his friendship and musical relationship with pianist Thelonious Monk. Blakey's forceful drumming was the perfect foil for Monk's jagged, playful compositions and his slightly-left-of-center soloing. All of these playing experiences were instructive in that Blakey placed his emphasis more upon the art of accompaniment than upon the soloing and showmanship so valued by more than a few of his drumming contemporaries. Even so, when it came to soloing, Blakey brought a distinct personality to the art—one that had its roots in African and Afro-Cuban rhythms. Listening to an Art Blakey solo was akin to hearing and feeling something raw and primal, something exciting and yet quite musical. Plus, rather than showy technical forays or exhibits of showmanship, Blakey played in a simple yet powerful way and with a lot of heart and built his solos in a very dramatic fashion, almost as if he were telling a story through his instrument.

As great a musician as he was, it was his skill as a band leader that brought him even more squarely into the public eye. Blakey created his first edition of the Jazz Messengers in 1954. It was originally a cooperative group that featured pianist Horace Silver, tenor saxophonist Hank Mobley, bassist

Doug Watkins, and Blakey; however, as time passed, Blakey assumed the leadership, and for the next three-plus decades, Blakey and the Jazz Messengers, in its various incarnations, thrilled audiences and listeners with its hard-bop approach. Just as he was mentored as a fledgling jazz musician, Blakey in turn mentored many young musicians in the Messengers who went on to become great musicians and jazz stars in their own right. The list of Blakey alumni reads like a veritable who's who of jazz and includes trumpeters Clifford Brown, Donald Byrd, Lee Morgan, Freddie Hubbard, and Wynton Marsalis; saxophonists Benny Golson, Jackie McLean, Hank Mobley, Wayne Shorter, and Bobby Watson; trombonist Curtis Fuller; and many, many others.

Art Blakey played drums almost until his passing in 1990. Toward the end of his life, he was plagued by terrible illness, yet, according to his daughter, the minute Blakey sat down to play, it was as if he were completely cured—as if he were still the young man whose drums were the driving force for scores of great jazz artists who would always acknowledge their debt to him as a mentor and an inspiration.

Not all of the great early bebop drummers were pioneers and innovators like Kenny Clarke, Max Roach, and Art Blakey. Two of the greatest drummers who were rooted in the bop tradition, Philly Joe Jones and Roy Haynes, were both major stylists to come out of that era. Philly Joe Jones was a fiery, relentless swinger who played with what could be called controlled abandon. He was a superb accompanist and a dynamic soloist. Some of his finest work can be heard on John Coltrane's 1957 masterpiece *Blue Train* (Blue Note), on pianist Wynton Kelly's superb trio disc *At Midnight* (Vee Jay), on another great trio recording—this one by Bill Evans—called *California, Here I Come* (Verve), and on just about anything the first great Miles Davis Quintet recorded between 1955 and 1958. Jones, pianist Red Garland, and bassist Paul Chambers were the fuel that powered the particular rhythmic locomotive that supported Davis and saxophonist John Coltrane in their solos and ensemble playing. He also recorded numerous times with piano great Bill Evans. Jones also had a great sense of humor, as evidenced by his remarkable recording *Blues for Dracula* (Riverside). In addition to great playing all the way around, the title cut finds Jones doing an effective and funny imitation of the voice of Bela Lugosi, the actor who so grandly portrayed the vampire count in the original 1931 film *Dracula*.

After his stint with Miles Davis, Jones appeared on many of the finest bebop records to come out of the 1950s and '60s, primarily on Blue Note,

Riverside, Jazzland, and Galaxy Records. Jones remained active until his death in 1985. Today's jazz drummers hold Jones in very high esteem for his consistently excellent performances and his ability to fit into any situation and make it sound as though he'd been born into it.

At this writing, drummer Roy Haynes is 88 years young! If there is such a thing as a fountain of youth, Haynes has found it, bottled it, and stored it away for safekeeping. He is the eighth wonder of the jazz world. His career spans a mind-blowing 65-plus years, and he has played with everyone from Lester Young, vocalists Billie Holiday and Sarah Vaughan, to Miles Davis, John Coltrane, Stan Getz, pianists Thelonious Monk, Bud Powell, and Chick Corea, vibraphonist Gary Burton, guitarist Pat Metheny, and countless others. It's a fact that he is one of a handful of great drummers and has been one of the most recorded in all of jazz. He has also been—and continues to be—virtually uncategorizable, having played swing, bebop, postbop modern jazz, jazz-rock fusion, and avant-garde forms of the music. Like Art Blakey often did, Haynes often surrounds himself with younger players in order to keep fresh and energized. There is no single recording of Haynes that is considered a classic, because there are so many that are held in high esteem by a broad spectrum of jazz musicians.

Figure 15.6.   Roy Haynes. Courtesy of Chuck Koton.

As a stylist, Roy was known for his tight, crisp sound and the interplay between his snare drum and his bass drum. He developed what seemed like conversations between these two drums and created patterns that were songlike in their approach to both accompanying and soloing. He also liberated the hi-hat from the limitation of having to play on the second and fourth beats of each measure of music; instead, he used it on off beats and in unusual places to emphasize a particular phrase—very much like a horn player would do in his or her solo.

Haynes has won many awards and has been accorded many honors, including a Grammy for lifetime achievement and multiple awards from various jazz magazines; in 1995, he received the NEA's coveted Jazz Masters Award—the highest honor a jazz artist can receive in America. It is accurate to say that Roy Haynes represents creativity, energy, and longevity in jazz and that he has secured his place as a role model for all jazz musicians from every era.

THE JUGGLERS: ELVIN JONES, TONY WILLIAMS, JACK DEJOHNETTE

Just as swing-era drummers may not have known what to make of the new and innovative approaches to drumming developed and nurtured by the bebop drummers, so, too, might the boppers have been confounded by what was happening in the next wave of players. "Post-bop" had taken on new and freer modes of solo and group improvisation—an approach that was much more spontaneous and "in the moment," than the predictability of bop song structures, chord changes, and performance patterns (where groups would play the "head" or melody, then there would be designated solos, followed by call-and-response exchanges with the group's drummer). Among the most influential of post-bop groups were the John Coltrane quartet—then called "the classic quartet"—and Miles Davis's second great quintet. Two of the most radically innovative post-bop drummers came out of those bands: Elvin Jones with Coltrane, and Tony Williams with Davis. Both men, along with drummer Jack Dejohnette, sent a lot of drummers scurrying "back to the woodshed" to rethink their own ways of playing and improvising.

All three of these men revolutionized the way drummers perceive the act of playing jazz rhythms. As we all know, swing drummers often favored a danceable four-beats-to-the-bar rhythm, which—with the exception of a big band's showcase numbers—was the order of the day for rhythm sections during the swing era; and when jazz became no longer a dancer's music, and rhythm sections began breaking away from the rigidity of swing, they became looser and more spontaneous, albeit in a way that still honored traditional song and performance structures, as mentioned previously. However, the '60s saw the birth of the Coltrane and Davis groups, both of which revolutionized jazz and, more specifically, led the way to even greater freedom for horn players and most notably for pianists, bassists, and drummers. Perhaps I can explain the new rhythmic freedom this way: picture swing and bebop rhythms as a constantly flowing, steady, straight line. If you were to break up the constancy of that straight line, then rhythms might become choppier and less predictable—still moving forward, but zigging and zagging, walking, running, hopping, and jumping, somewhat like a heartbeat on a hospital monitor.

This is not to say that the new freedom is completely free. If you look at and listen to the three drummers who follow, you'll hear each one's acknowledgment of tradition in their playing; however, careful listening will reveal that traditional rhythmic approaches serve as springboards into unknown territory. Tradition is just a place to start. Or as someone once suggested: learn the rules first; then ignore them.

In some cases, once an artist learns the foundations of his or her art, he or she doesn't break rules as much as extend them in a way that mirrors tradition, yet restates it in new and exciting ways. Elvin Jones (1927–2004) is a case in point. A drummer whose powerful, unerring sense of swing (the feeling, not the era) came straight out of all jazz traditions, Jones nonetheless found new ways of mixing drumming styles from the bebop era with a very personal approach that utilized "polyrhythms," or quite literally, "many rhythms." Drawing largely from African rhythms as well as other sources, Jones forged a style that was both rhythmically complex and swinging. He could play one rhythm layered on top of another and put a third rhythm on top of that, and make it all work. It was a perfect synthesis whose end result was what sounded like multiple drummers, combining to form a divine locomotion; a powerful and often mesmerizing groove. It's no wonder that Elvin Jones was John Coltrane's favorite drummer. Jones matched Coltrane's energy level and, at times, transcended it. A wonderful example of how intensely and how perfectly their energies intertwined can be seen on both YouTube and on several

DVDs, including one called *The World according to John Coltrane*. The performance took place in the summer of 1965 in Belgium. The music is very intense and heartfelt, and the visual intercutting of Jones and Coltrane is amazing to watch. It really shows the depth of their musical relationship. The performance also shows the immensity of Elvin Jones's importance and voice in the quartet. Elvin's energies are what moved Coltrane into the higher realms of the stratosphere, and his amazing endurance in ultra-long performances is something to behold.

Elvin, knowing that Coltrane wanted to add a second drummer to the quartet, decided to leave the group in 1965. Throughout the remainder of

Figure 15.7.   Elvin Jones. Courtesy of Rick Laird.

that decade, he established himself as a leader and created a number of impressive groups, including a quartet featuring two saxophonists (Dave Liebman and Steve Grossman) and bassist Gene Perla. In fact, Elvin and Perla shared a special musical relationship, and Elvin said on more than one occasion that Perla was his favorite bassist.

Interlude III: Perla and Jones

Bassist Gene Perla played a trick on me. During a break from our first set at the Lafayette Bar, he said, "Come on out to the car. I want you to hear something." I wandered outside and got in the passenger seat. He slipped a CD into the player and said, "Tell me who you think the drummer might be." After a few minutes of concentrated listening, I was somewhat befuddled. "Well, it sure sounds like Elvin, but I never knew that Elvin recorded anything with a big band." "He didn't." Perla was all grins. "But . . . but that *is* Elvin, isn't it?" "Yeah, it's the master himself, but he never played with a big band." I grew impatient. "Well, this is becoming complicated." At that point, Gene Perla told me this story in a nutshell:

After the dissolution of the two-saxophone quartet, the drummer and bassist performed together in a variety of settings beyond Elvin's quartet. In fact, Perla brought Elvin into a recording studio at one point in 1986 and recorded a bunch of his compositions on electric piano, with the drummer as the only other participant. Later, after Elvin's death in 2004, Perla arranged all but one of those recorded songs for Germany's NDR Big Band, then removed his original piano tracks and replaced them with his own bass tracks. Miraculously, the band—all wearing headphones to be able to hear the prerecorded tracks with Elvin and Perla—recorded Perla's arrangements as though there actually were a bassist and a drummer present in the studio. In 2007, Perla effectively completed what he and Elvin had begun two decades earlier. The NDR Big Band turned in a brilliant performance, and the final product has been called *Bill's Waltz*. It's amazing to listen to it now and realize that Elvin Jones, even after his death, could make a recording that would resonate among drummers and listeners alike for a long time to come.

Elvin, like Art Blakey before him and like his other contemporary Roy Haynes, surrounded himself with young talent and helped them grow as budding jazz artists. His group the Jazz Machine, like Blakey's Jazz Messengers and Haynes's Fountain of Youth band, featured many promising young musicians, whom Elvin nurtured and inspired. All three of these master drummers passed the torch on to future generations, keeping the music alive.

Tony Williams came onto the scene in a much different manner. Unlike Elvin Jones, who had two other famous jazz siblings (pianist Hank and trumpeter Thad) all hailing from the Detroit area, Williams was born in Chicago and raised in Boston. Even though he began playing jazz in his early teens, he came into national prominence in 1963 at age 17, when he was invited by Miles Davis to join his group. More important, he would be there for the formation of Miles's "Second Great Quintet" just about two years later.

Williams brought an entirely new way of playing to the table. Thus far, drumming was based upon a very "linear" concept of rhythm. Let's look at what that means: when you are walking down the street for any length of time, you might be likely to get to a certain speed and stay there for a while. You even might hum a tune that's in sync with the walking tempo you've set for yourself. Drummers have done the same thing in terms of formally establishing a rate of speed or tempo and locking it in—that is, staying consistently in that tempo throughout a song. This was true in early jazz, in swing, in bebop, and beyond; when the tempo was established, it generally would remain at that speed for the bulk of the performance.

Tony Williams understood the linear concept and the consistency of tempo that was at its core. But even at his young age, he also understood that in order for music—like anything else in life—to continue evolving, there would have to be some risk and experimentation involved in order to create a new rhythmic vocabulary—a new way of spontaneously manipulating rhythms in such a way as to layer one tempo atop another and use this layering to move outside of traditional swing. As a result, Williams, at the tender age of 17, began revolutionizing how jazz drummers would play for years to come, shoring up the time, bouncing from one tempo to another like a basketball player moving across the court. Miles Davis, always perceptive when it came to his band members' strengths, allowed Williams and his rhythm section mates, pianist Herbie Hancock and bassist Ron

Carter, to nurture and develop this concept to a highly sophisticated degree. One of the most advanced and influential rhythm sections was born!

The classic Davis quintet was active from 1965 to 1968, and Williams stayed on through 1969, recording various projects with the trumpeter. That year, Williams formed one of the most engaging and intense jazz-rock groups in fusion's history. He enlisted the aid of his friend, organist Larry Young, and guitarist John McLaughlin. The group was called "Tony Williams' Lifetime," named after Williams's first Blue Note album as a leader. Williams expanded this group to include bassist Jack Bruce, who was the bassist for the power rock trio "Cream." Even though the group came under fire from more conservative jazz fans, it became one of the classic fusion groups and retains that position today.

Williams's drumming style became heavier and more thunderous, due largely to his desire to draw from contemporary rock music. This didn't mean that he lost his trademark intuitive sensitivities. He just reinvented them in this new idiom. Lifetime stayed together in various incarnations until the mid-'70s. At that point Williams reunited with former Davis Classic Quintet rhythm section mates Herbie Hancock and Ron Carter, as well as with saxophonist Wayne Shorter. They added trumpeter Freddie Hubbard in lieu of Davis, who was taking a hiatus from playing, and called the group V.S.O.P.

After that, Williams remained active in the fusion world, playing with various high-powered groups and always creating and recording some of the best jazz-rock on the planet, until his untimely passing in 1997—a true innovator and liberator who continues to influence scores of young drummers even today. We drummers are still trying to catch up to the many things that Williams played, either as an accompanist or as a soloist.

Unlike Elvin Jones and Tony Williams, Jack Dejohnette was and continues to be more than a master jazz drummer and (like Williams) a composer. Dejohnette began his musical life as a pianist and studied classical piano for over 10 years, beginning at age four. Drumming came later, in high school, and he became equally adept on both instruments. In fact, Dejohnette was known on the Chicago scene as both a pianist and as a drummer, and he worked in both capacities in all kinds of musical situations, from rhythm and blues to jazz to avant-garde improvised music. Because of his broad background, Dejohnette has always maintained an interest in and an appreciation of all types of music, including classical music, rock, hip-hop, world music,

music for meditation and contemplation, country music, and of course, all forms and eras of jazz. In his own words:

> As a child I listened to all kinds of music and I never put them into cat-
> egories. I had formal lessons on piano and listened to opera, country and
> western music, rhythm and blues, jazz, swing, whatever. To me, it was all
> music and great. I've kept that integrated feeling about music, all types of
> music, and just carried it with me. I've maintained that belief and feeling in
> spite of the ongoing trend to try and compartmentalize people and music.
> (www.jackdejohnette.com)

Possibly because of his incredible musical breadth as well as his extensive experience as a pianist, Jack Dejohnette has an amazing melodic sense as a drummer. Now, while drums—particularly jazz drums—are not widely known as melodic instruments, there have been drummers such as Jo Jones, Max Roach, and Tony Williams whose approaches to improvisation were quite songlike, specifically in the way they would develop a little melodic series of notes or a "line" and use it as a theme to be improvised upon. Dejohnette falls squarely in this category. While his jazz drumming influences are extensive, his interest in all manner of musical genres has informed his style in a most unique and imaginative way. All of this is powered by an enormous sense of inquisitiveness. Jack has never been one to stand still stylistically and is always looking for new forms of expression. Thinking "outside of the box" is what he does quite well, and as a result this has been an integral part of a wide variety of recording and performing projects.

Dejohnette has performed with many of jazz's greatest artists, including Miles Davis, John Coltrane, Bill Evans, Keith Jarrett, Herbie Hancock, John Abercrombie, Michael Brecker, Ornette Coleman, Stan Getz, Pat Metheny, Dave Liebman, Jackie McLean, and many others. True to his background and experience, he has been involved in a wide variety of musical endeavors, including duets with guitarist Bill Frisell, reedman John Surman, and Gambian kora player Foday Musa Suso; the long-standing trio with pianist Keith Jarrett and bassist Gary Peacock; and "Trio Beyond," which includes organist Larry Goldings and guitarist John Scofield. Add world musicians into the mix and you have a drummer with one of the most diverse careers of this or any other generation. And, as if that weren't enough, in 2005 Dejohnette established his own record label, Golden Beams Productions, and has released a number of ethereal music projects, including Grammy-nominated *Songs in the Key of OM* and 2009 Grammy winner *Peace Time*.

In 2012, Dejohnette became a recipient of the coveted Jazz Masters Award from the National Endowment for the Arts for his contributions to the music and for his long-standing commitment to helping provide an ample musical legacy for generations to come.

There is much more to Jack Dejohnette than there is room here to explore. As a result, a visit to his website, www.jackdejohnette.com, will open up an enormous window into Dejohnette's brilliance as a drummer, a pianist, a producer, and a band leader. If there were 50 hours in a day, Jack would fill every single one of them with music.

BEYOND TIME: FROM RHYTHM TO FLOW

Perhaps one of the most radical developments in jazz drumming—and the music in general—took place in the early to mid-'60s with the advent of the "free jazz" movement. Drummers and bass players began to break away from traditional rhythmic pulse and syncopation and move into realms that were largely freer and more open—and devoid of any steady beat whatsoever.

Think of a stream flowing along on its way to a river—or for that matter, roaring river rapids on their way to a waterfall. While there is a steady, un-interrupted flow, there really isn't a discernible "rhythm"—that is, a repetitive series of regularly timed sounds, one after the other, that constitute what we know as "rhythm" or "pulse."

Just like these natural phenomena, free jazz rhythms can be less about "the rhythmic pulse" than about creating a "flow" of percussive sounds. In other words, the drummer was free to be able to play completely by intuition, without creating a groove in any traditional sense. There was still movement and forward motion, yet often there wouldn't be any place in the music where we could tap our feet, clap our hands, or snap our fingers. Even though this was a huge development in jazz, it was not all that well received, largely because many listeners were turned off by the lack of the rhythms they were so used to hearing in all styles of the music up to that point.

As a result of this enormously radical stylistic shift, drummers began to rethink their roles in the rhythm section (or should we say, the "non-rhythm section"?)—and the bass drum, the hi-hat cymbals, and the ride cymbal, so crucial in previous eras, became part of a palettte of sounds and shapes. More than ever, drummers became sonic "painters" who were liberated from what they may have seen as the tediousness of repetitive rhythm.

Among the first of these "free" drummers were James "Sunny" Murray and Milford Graves. Murray, in particular, was a pioneer whose long and fruitful relationship with pianist Cecil Taylor excited some listeners and infuriated others. Although he was capable of playing in traditional settings, Murray dispensed with the beat completely, favoring washes of sound alternating with percussive explosions—a perfect complement and foil to Taylor's breathtaking, rhapsodic pianistics. When you listen to their performances, either together or with various artists, you have to dispense with traditional notions and just go along for the ride. Murray came under fire from critics, listeners, and other drummers who claimed that he couldn't play his instrument; however, he had the conviction to pursue his new musical vision and ultimately won the respect of many more listeners, both stateside and in Europe.

Milford Graves is, simply put, an extraordinary human being as well as an innovative and imaginative musician. To call him a drummer is to describe only a small part of who he really is. For Graves, exploration of the many aspects of living takes precedence over merely making music. As a result, this worldly man has become a renowned role model among artists and listeners alike who are seeking something outside the jazz mainstream. Writer Mark Medwin, in a perceptive portrait of Graves in an article for allaboutjazz.com on June 22, 2009, offers these words:

> To label Graves as one of the pioneers of free jazz is to define his work in far too narrow a scope. Leaving aside, for the moment, his contributions to herbology, the martial arts, acupuncture and to the healing characteristics of music, his approach to the drums places him apart from many of those with whom he has so often been compared. Each phrase he plays resists simple categorization, whether in the service of fire-and-brimstone free improvisation or as heard in the melodies he conjures from skin, metal and wood. His appetite for learning is as enormous as his thinking is broad, but beyond learning and cultivation, feeling is of paramount importance to him. He states, "The drum is the heart" and his is music of the heart, figuratively and literally, with all its rhythmic intricacies and melodic subtleties.

Milford Graves was born and raised in New York City and played in all manner of groups before beginning his associations with "the new music" of saxophonist Albert Ayler, pianist Paul Bley, and many others. His ongoing interest in the roles of percussion in world music led him to intense study of the music of India and Africa, among other countries. Graves, like trumpeter Don Cherry, was one of jazz's first world music innovators. Now in his seventh decade, he continues his musical journey, collaborating and recording with newer creative artists such as saxophonist/composer/record producer John Zorn.

How many of us remember hammering out our versions of rhythm on Mom's pots and pans when we were children and wanted to play along with the music that captured our ears and imaginations? If you fall into that category, then you might also remember that as would-be drummers, we banged on anything: tin cans, cardboard boxes, tabletops—anything with a sound that intrigued us. As years passed, we either forgot about our musical efforts or went on to formalize them by becoming either amateur or professional musicians. In any case, the pots and pans were replaced by pianos, guitars, saxophones, trumpets—or drums. In other words, most of us musicians left the childhood world of sounds behind and graduated to real musical instruments. Most of us, but not all of us. Among classical composers, George Antheil, John Cage, and Harry Partch created music using "found objects" such as automobile brake drums and tin cans (Cage), sirens and airplane propellers (Antheil), or invented instruments such as the chromelodeon and cloud bowls (Partch).

In the world of jazz drumming, no one stands out in the use of "found objects" more notoriously than Holland's Han Bennink. In fact, to call Bennink a drummer is to tell only a small part of his musical story. Born in Amsterdam in 1942, Bennink says that his first musical instrument was a kitchen chair. Even though his father, who was an orchestral percussionist, provided him with some drums, Bennink continued to pursue what has amounted to a lifelong interest in a wide variety of sounds, including those that exist well outside of the musical sphere—which is to say that Bennink still plays on chairs and tables! Watching and listening to him play is an exercise in expecting the unexpected. We never know what he might use to make music. He has been known to play on the floor of a concert stage, using sticks and wire brushes, and he has used a common garden hose to create eerie windlike effects. He can also be seen on YouTube playing a drum set made up almost entirely of cheese wheels! Even though a Bennink performance can be lively and even humorous, this is not at all gimmickry; in fact, it is consistent with the musical paths followed by Cage, Antheil, and Partch—all architects of sound.

Bennink also brings a wonderful visual aspect to his performances, possibly because he is also an excellent visual artist, whose paintings, drawings, and found-object sculptures have been exhibited at various art galleries in Europe. He has also designed his own album and CD covers.

Above all, Han Bennink is a complete musician—and an accomplished one at that. He can swing mightily in the tradition of the great bop drummers like Kenny Clarke and Philly Joe Jones, and he can play in the free-flowing avant-garde style favored by Sunny Murray and Milford Graves. In the 1960s he recorded with jazz saxophone legends Dexter Gordon and Eric Dolphy and also performed with modern progressives such as German reedman Peter Brötzmann, British guitarist Derek Bailey, German pianist Misha Mengelberg, and American pianist and composer Myra Melford. Now in his 70s, Bennink plays with a kinetic yet playful energy and the unabashed joyousness of a musician half his age. To see and hear him is to truly experience improvised music being created in the hands of a master.

The year 2011 saw the passing of master drummer Paul Motian, who was truly an artist for the ages. At a time when technical brilliance has seemed to be the goal for many drummers, Motian went against the tide and followed his own vision of the way he felt that the drums should be played.

Like Roy Haynes, Motian was firmly rooted in the bebop tradition, and like Haynes, he moved beyond that tradition, perhaps even more radically. Known in the '50s as a fine bebop drummer, Motian became much more well known when he joined pianist Bill Evans and bassist Scott LaFaro to form the most legendary piano trio in all of jazz. The Evans-LaFaro-Motian collaborations were just that: rather than the conventional approach to piano trio playing, where the roles of the bassist and drummer were supportive and often took a back seat to the pianist's solo excursions, Evans, LaFaro, and Motian were engaged in true group interaction, sort of like a three-way conversation among friends. Motian's role was unique in that he didn't always play constantly; he would drop out, then wait a moment or two before adding his musical "commentary" to whatever interaction was happening between the piano and the bass. Certainly, no other drummer was playing like Motian at that time. His approach was fresh and imaginative.

But his tenure with Bill Evans was only part of a long and fascinating musical life. Toward the end of the '60s, he played with folk singer Arlo Guthrie, most notably at the legendary Woodstock Festival. He moved on into the '70s as a member of pianist Keith Jarrett's American quartet, which featured Jarrett's original compositions. The music was eclectic and contained elements of rock, gospel, free jazz, and Middle Eastern sounds—all of it uniquely Jarrett. And Motian's sheer adaptability and musicality was in evidence throughout each recording. His approach to playing was open and free, and he managed to fit into many musical situations without sacrificing his emerging identity.

The next phase of Motian's musical life found him performing and recording with forward-thinking pianist Paul Bley in a trio setting, usually with bassists Gary Peacock or Charlie Haden. The music was often edge-of-your-seat group improvising, almost like riding on a roller coaster: a slow climb followed by a plummet into the abyss. Motian credited Bley for really opening him up to the many possibilities of free playing. This new approach would remain at the heart of Motian's playing throughout the rest of his life. Unlike many other drummers, Motian would often underplay, almost like creating space between words in a poem or watercolors on a canvas. In fact, Motian was often likened to a master colorist who avoided clutter in favor of economy. The air was his canvas and the drum set was his medium.

The '80s found Motian leading a number of uniquely original groups including his Electric Bebop Band and a cooperative group with guitarist Bill Frisell and saxophonist Joe Lovano. The repertoire for both groups included originals by Motian; reconstructed versions of jazz classics by Bill Evans, Monk, and others; and Broadway show tunes. The common thread that ran through each group and recording was Motian's great musical sense. As pianist Ethan Iverson, a Motian alumnus, put it: "With Paul, there was always that ground rhythm, that ancient jazz beat lurking in the background" (Ben Ratliff, *New York Times*, November 23, 2011).

Indeed, Paul Motian was the past, present, and—in many respects—the ongoing future of modern jazz drumming.

WITH ALL DUE RESPECT . . .

While we have focused upon some of the leading exponents of avant-garde drumming, there are many other fine players whose work is worthy of mention and certainly merits your attention: Denis Charles and Andrew Cyrille, both of whom created vibrant music with pianist Cecil Taylor; the totally original Barry Altschul, who played and recorded with pianist Chick Corea and woodwind wizard and composer Anthony Braxton; Edward Blackwell, whose terrific momentum was an integral element in Ornette Coleman's quartet; Famoudou Don Moye, the imaginative, mind-bending drummer with the Art Ensemble of Chicago; Hamid Drake, whose breadth of knowledge of and experience with world music and modern improvised music has won him international acclaim; and outside of America, British drummers John Stevens and Tony Oxley, and South African drummer Louis Moholo.

TIME OUT!

A word or two about the late Joe Morello. A mainstay in the immensely popular Dave Brubeck Quartet for over 12 years (1956–1968), Morello recorded 60 albums with Brubeck. He also won *DownBeat* magazine's polls as best drummer for five consecutive years. Morello had a dazzling technique, but he always accompanied and soloed with tremendous taste and with a great deal of musicality as well.

RECENT RUMBLINGS

Happily, there is no shortage of free-thinking drummers in today's jazz and creative music scene. Among the most important of the current crop are Jim Black, whose highly influential work is by turns totally unique, powerful, lively, humorous, and subtle; Joey Baron, who is equally at home weaving beautiful rhythmic tapestries with guitarists Jim Hall and Bill Frisell as he is with the demanding and exciting music of Dave Douglas and saxophonist John Zorn; Tom Rainey, who, like Paul Motian, has managed to insert himself comfortably into any musical situation, no matter how challenging; Dan Weiss, who is equally at home playing Indian ragas, rock, and post-bop jazz—all with an uncannily natural ease; Gerald Cleaver, whose sense of dynamics and musical shading, combined with his understanding of drumming history, make him one of the most in-demand drummers on today's creative music scene; Tyshawn Sorey, equally formidable as a drummer, composer, and trombonist, currently in the doctoral program at Columbia University; Matt Wilson, a master drummer of great breadth and depth who approaches every performance with daring, humor, and imagination, no matter what the setting; and John Hollenbeck, an extraordinarily gifted drummer, large- and small-group leader, and composer who has been accorded many honors both here and in Europe, not the least of which has been a Guggenheim Fellowship for composition.

Each of these fine musicians has a healthy respect for the past, as well as an ongoing curiosity about what may be lurking just around the corner up ahead. Follow them as they move forward into uncharted waters, and you may be intrigued, even amazed, at what they discover—and what you experience as a result of their discoveries.

It's been over a hundred years since the drums surfaced as an important and vital voice in jazz music. And as you can see, a lot has happened since the days of Baby Dodds and Zutty Singleton. However, one thing is for sure: the drums are the heartbeat of this music, and without them, jazz just wouldn't be the same.

Getting Personal with Jim Black

What advice would you offer a new listener who will be experiencing your music for the first time, either in concert, on YouTube, or via one of your recordings?

Simply listen and/or watch without any expectations, which is easier said than done most of the time. I would recommend that for anybody's music or art. What does the sound do to you? What does it make you think, feel . . . ? Follow it, listen to it unfold, stay with it until the end, then reflect on your feelings.

Figure 15.8.   Jim Black. Courtesy of Paul LaRaia.

Music is about emotion, vibe, mood, and atmosphere . . . that's all I want to be aware of when listening.

I don't believe in difficult music or that you need some sort of education to listen to something unfamiliar. Some of it's immediately attractive, and some of it doesn't make sense upon first hearing. Learning the inner game of music helps understanding in a different way after the fact, but hopefully you are moved by the music in the first place to want to hear it again and discover more. If it doesn't work for you the first time, be sure to try it again sometime in the future because our ears/minds change/evolve constantly.

What would be the first recording of yours that you would recommend for an initial listening experience and as a good introduction to your music?

AlasNoAxis on Winter & Winter. There's a lot of musical ground covered on that CD, a full range of sounds and intensities. I was trying to take what I liked about melody, harmony, rhythm, and color and then present it in a short song format. The other four *AlasNoAxis* CDs continue that exploration.

SELECTED DRUMMERS' WEBSITES: FROM THEN 'TIL NOW

Note: Only official sites are listed. Use Google for all others.

Buddy Rich: www.buddyrich.com
Louie Bellson: www.louiebellson.net
Art Blakey: www.artblakey.com
Jimmy Cobb: www.jimmycobb.com
Joe Morello: www.joemorello.net
Milford Graves: www.milfordgraves.com
Han Bennink: www.hanbennink.com
Rashied Ali: www.rashiedali.org
Joe Chambers: www.josephachambers.com
Jack Dejohnette: www.jackdejohnette.com
Lenny White: www.lennywhite.com
Alphonse Mouzon: www.tenaciousrecords.com
Adam Nussbaum: www.adamnussbaum.net
Jim Black: www.jimblack.com
John Hollenbeck: www.johnhollenbeck.com
Nasheet Waits: www.nasheetwaits.com
Ari Hoenig: www.arihoenig.com
Terri Lyne Carrington: www.terrilynecarrington.com
Dan Weiss: www.danweiss.net

RECOMMENDED READING

Art Blakey

Goldsher, Alan. *Hard Bop Academy: The Sidemen of Art Blakey and the Jazz Messengers*. Milwaukee: Hal Leonard, 2002. Print.

Baby Dodds

Dodds, Baby, and Larry Gara. *The Baby Dodds Story*. Rev. ed. Baton Rouge: Louisiana State UP, 1992.

Buddy Rich

Tormé, Mel. *Traps, the Drum Wonder: The Life of Buddy Rich*. Alma: Rebeats Press, 1997.

Collections

Korall, Burt. *Drummin' Men: The Heartbeat of Jazz—The Swingin' Years*. New York: Schirmer Books, 1990. Print.
Korall, Burt. *Drummin' Men: The Heartbeat of Jazz—The Bebop Years*. New York: Oxford UP, 2002. Print.

16

I GOT RHYTHM IV

A Little Discussion about Percussion

The possibilities of percussion sounds, I believe, have never been fully realized.

—Charles Ives

Oh, I'm not a percussionist. I just like to hit things.

—Tom Waits

THE WIDE, WIDE WORLD OF PERCUSSION

In the previous chapter, we introduced a drummer named Han Bennink and suggested that "to call Bennink a drummer is to tell only part of his story." As you may recall, this master drummer is known for playing floors, chairs, pots and pans, and even his Dutch clogs. His musicality manifests itself beyond the conventional drum set and expands into the realm of percussion, which is a world unto itself. For our purposes, we will look briefly at the role of percussion in jazz music from three distinct perspectives: Latin percussion, "atmospheric percussion," and the world of the vibraphone.

EL RITMO CALIENTE

Most jazz historians might agree that one of the first cross pollinations of jazz and Latin music happened in the 1940s when the master Cuban *conguero* Chano Pozo joined forces with trumpeter Dizzy Gillespie to create a new sound: the idea was to combine exciting, pulsating rhythms such as the *mambo, danzón*, and *son montuno* with the melodic and harmonic adventurousness of bebop. Many of the musicians back then dubbed this new hybrid music "Cu-Bop," and it became very popular among both jazz and Latin American music fans. Pozo was one of the first—if not the first—conga drummer to lift the conga drum out of its accompanying role and into the role of soloist. He was also a fine composer, whose musical compositions were already popular in Cuba at the time he departed that country for the rich musical soil of New York City. He became a sensation as a member of Dizzy's big band in the late '40s and would have continued along that path had it not been for his untimely murder in 1948 as a result of some dispute with an underworld figure in a Harlem bar. However, Chano Pozo, in a few short years, set the stage for the continued evolution of Latin jazz—his influence pervasive and his music timeless.

Other great conga drummers migrated from Cuba to the United States as well. Armando Peraza arrived in New York City in 1949 and became an in-demand fixture on the jazz and Latin scenes thriving at that time. He played with both Dizzy Gillespie and Charlie Parker, toured with a variety of bands, and finally settled in San Francisco where he ultimately wound up playing with the pianist George Shearing's quintet, vibraphonist Cal Tjader's Latin jazz group, Dave Brubeck, and many others. Peraza, also an exceptionally good bongo drummer, went on to record and perform with both prominent jazz and rock artists. The latter group included rock stars Carlos Santana, Eric Clapton, and Frank Zappa. Peraza's gift was (and is) that he could fit comfortably into a wide variety of musical situations; as a result, his popularity has grown considerably over the years and he is revered by younger generations of drummers, percussionists, and other instrumentalists and vocalists. Carlos "Patato" Valdez and Mongo Santamaría were two other influential Cuban conga drummers whose technical skill and virtuosity are the stuff of which legends are made. Valdez was active in New York jazz circles and performed with many famous jazz artists, beginning in the mid-'50s. He was also instrumental in helping to develop the first hand-tunable conga drums (earlier congas could be tuned using intense heat). He also composed music for television (*The Cosby Show*) and the movies (*The Mambo Kings*). Mongo Santamaría was not only known for his mastery of the conga drums and other Latin percussion instruments, but also as a composer. Two of his most famous compositions have been staples of jazz repertoire for years: "Afro Blue," which was made famous by saxophonist John Coltrane, and "Watermelon Man," immortalized first by pianist Herbie Hancock, then by countless others. Mongo and his various bands found successful ways of combining elements of rhythm and blues, jazz, and salsa into a tasty musical stew that listening and dancing audiences loved. Indeed, Latin jazz—like swing music before it—became very popular because much of it was and still is danceable.

Other fine *congueros* include Francisco Aguabella, Ray Barretto, Ray Mantilla, Giovanni Hildalgo, Poncho Sanchez, Ray Armando, Luis Conte, Don Alias, and the phenomenal Alex Acuña, who is equally formidable on drum set, congas, and many other Latin percussion instruments.

SONIC VISIONARIES

The role of Latin groove master established by many of the names you see in the previous section began to expand and change in the late '60s as percussionists, especially those from Brazil, became part of the ever-evolving jazz scene during that period in the music's history. Most notable among these were Airto Moreira and Dom Um Romão, both of whom brought a brand-new dimension to jazz percussion. Rather than concentrate on creating grooves, Airto and Dom were colorists—painters of sounds, whose broad sonic palettes were ever changing. Each had an arsenal of instruments such as shakers, tambourines, whistles, hand drums, frying pans, and more exotic Brazilian instruments such as the *berimbau* (pronounced "beer-im-baw") and the *cuica* (pronounced "kwee-kah"), pictured in figures 16.1 and 16.2.

Without going into too much detail, we can say that the *berimbau* has a single "wire" that is often played with a coin and a stick in order to control the pitches and create rhythmic patterns, respectively. The little shaker—called a "*caxixi*" (pronounced "ca-shi-shi")—is also played simultaneously. You almost have to have three hands to play this instrument. To watch some great *berimbau* playing, visit YouTube to see how the instrument is played using the coin, the stick, and the *caxixi*.

The *cuica* comes in a variety of sizes (such as the two in figure 16.2) and is, like the *berimbau*, a totally unique instrument. The small knot at the top of a *cuica* fastens a thin stick inside the can-like body of the instrument, and when this stick is rubbed with a small piece of wet rag, the result is a series of sounds that can mimic anything from the creaking of a door opening to a dog barking to a baby weeping. It is a truly extraordinary instrument, and there are those who can play entire melodies on it. The pitches are changed by applying pressure to the head with one hand, while rubbing on the stick with the other.

Airto Moreira is a master of both instruments, and the late Romão was also. The quality that made both of these percussionists special was their innate ability to find the right instrument to play at exactly the

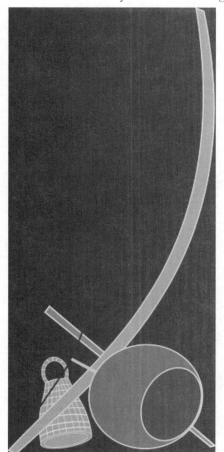

right time. This was especially evident in the earliest recordings of Weather Report, where the music was both sparse and multilayered, thanks to the creative visions of the band's coleaders, saxophonist Wayne Shorter and keyboardist Josef Zawinul. Airto was the percussionist on the first recording, and Romão on several subsequent records. The percussion was not a gimmicky, add-on feature, but an integral part of the group, helping to create a tapestry of sound that brought a lot of sonic richness to the band. Airto lent those same

Figure 16.1. A *berimbau*.

Figure 16.2. A *cuica*.

qualities to the bands of Miles Davis and Chick Corea, among others from the late '60s onward. Both men opened the doors for other like-minded percussionists, and as a result, creative percussionists began to spring up into the public eye and ear with increasing regularity.

Today, it's not uncommon for percussionists from all over the world to add their unique and exciting sounds to many jazz or world music performances. Some of the finest are Philippine American Susie Ibarra, Japan's Satoshi Takeishi, India's Trilok Gurtu, Puerto Rico's Manolo Badrena, Denmark's Marilyn Mazur, Brazil's Naná Vasconcelos, and Los Angeles's Munyungo Jackson, to name only a few. All are masters of musical colors and textures and add great depth and feeling in any jazz and world music settings. Since much percussion music can be visually interesting as well as sonically, it is highly recommended that the curious listener experience these and other master percussionists on YouTube for a more complete picture of their artistry. Munyungo Jackson, in particular, is one of the most responsive and musical percussionists on the scene today. Not only does he use a dazzling array of percussion instruments, but he also employs children's toys, hand-claps, foot stomps, and vocal effects to create completely original sound colorations, in addition to both Latin and world percussion instruments.

Figure 16.3.   D. Munyungo Jackson. Courtesy of Garry Corbett.

GOOD VIBES: THE VIBRAPHONE IN JAZZ

The vibraphone, or "vibes," has had a somewhat curious history in jazz, perhaps in part due to its unusual nature. It is a percussion instrument by definition, since one must strike it in order to produce a sound. In fact, the same can be said of the piano, because if you depress a piano key, a small wooden hammer on the inside of the piano strikes a tuned wire or string to create a note.

There are other similarities between the vibes and the piano with regard to layout; namely, the configuration of the keyboard is the same on both instruments. The black keys on the piano fall into alternating groups of twos and threes situated above the white keys; the same alternated pattern can be seen on the vibes; so when you look at the two keyboards side by side, as shown in figures 16.4 and 16.5, you see this arrangement.

 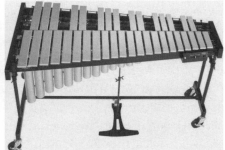

Figure 16.4.   Piano keyboard.   **Figure 16.5.   Vibraphone "keyboard."**

The vibraphone was originally manufactured in the United States in 1921, and it first caught the attention of the listening public as a novelty instrument, much like its smaller predecessors, the wooden xylophone and the metal glockenspiel. Even though all three mallet instruments helped supply a wide palette of tonal colors for vaudeville bands, the vibes began to attract particular attention in the early to mid-'20s.

The vibraphone sound is one that has traditionally been associated almost exclusively with jazz, although it has been used in other stylistic settings from time to time, including classical, country, and rock music.

Interlude: An Experiment in Good Vibrations

If you don't think you've ever heard the vibraphone before, try this little experiment:

> Using cloth tape, attach a large cotton ball (often used for removing makeup) or a couple of layers of moleskin or felt to a pen or pencil and gently strike a wine goblet in various places (holding the goblet by its stem). It is a gentle, ringing, crystalline sound that is pleasant to the ears.
>
> Next, take an ordinary pencil and strike the goblet gently with the eraser in the same general locations as you did with the cotton ball. The sound is different—but could you explain how you think it differs from the first sounds? Is it a harder sound? A softer sound?
>
> What you are hearing is a series of sounds created from the vibration of the goblet, when struck gently by your two "mallets." You now have an idea of several kinds of sounds the vibraphone is capable of making.

In terms of a typical vibraphone sound, one set of vibes may vary from another quite subtly—perhaps in ways many of us can't really hear; however, as we have just discovered in our experiment, what we use to strike the vibes makes quite a big difference in the sounds we are able to produce. In fact, you could hear a half-dozen vibists play the same exact instrument and sound completely different from one another. There are two distinct reasons for this: first, many vibists use mallets made from various materials to create different sounds and feelings. Yarns of different thicknesses, differences in cores around which the yarn is woven, and the size of the mallet head are just three ways that the sound can differ. A second way one vibes player can be distinguished from another might be the velocity with which he or she strikes the aluminum bars. Just like with the drums or the piano, a musician's touch helps determine the kind of sound produced from the instrument. In classical music, for example, you can hear pianist Mitsuko Uchida play a Mozart sonata, and then listen to the same sonata played by Vladimir Horowitz. The contrast is palpable, since both great pianists depress the keys with different velocities. That is the beauty of experiencing all music. Most people bring something different and quite personal to the table, no matter the instrument or the setting.

Another variable that may distinguish one vibraphonist from another is how he or she adjusts the speed of the oscillator. Most vibraphones are equipped with an electric motor that controls the fluctuations of small oscillating discs housed at the top of each of the tubes seated below every vibraphone bar. The speed of these discs also controls the rate of speed of the instrument's "vibrato," from very fast to quite slow.

EARLY VIBRAPHONE MASTERS:
ADRIAN ROLLINI, RED NORVO, LIONEL HAMPTON

There were three men who were the true pioneers of the vibraphone in jazz, beginning in the late '20s.

Adrian Rollini was, by all accounts, a virtuoso musician who excelled on a variety of instruments. Born in New York in the early 20th century, he began as a child prodigy on the piano and was actually giving recitals at age four. As a teenager, Rollini played in a variety of jazz groups. Ultimately, he became especially well known as a master of two of the more obscure instruments of the day: the vibraphone and the bass saxophone. The latter instrument—although rarely played in jazz—served as a good replacement for the tuba in early jazz bands. Rollini not only fulfilled the tuba's role as a rhythm section instrument (which would later be replaced by the string bass), but he was also an accomplished soloist, making the bass sax sound as though it was born to jazz.

Rollini was as accomplished on the vibraphone as he was on the bass saxophone. His sound was light and airy, and his technique nimble and flawless. He played both single-note runs and two-mallet chords. His vibes had a motor that powered small fans which turned in each of the tubes housed beneath every bar (see figure 16.5), giving the vibes a lovely, fluttering quality. Rollini performed and recorded with the likes of trombonist Jack Teagarden and trumpeter Bix Beiderbecke, and with a number of his own ensembles as well.

Born in a small town in Illinois in 1908, Red Norvo came to the vibraphone via the xylophone and the marimba, two mallet instruments with wooden bars which predated the vibes by a considerable period of time. He became active with various bands during the mid-'20s and made the switch to vibes sometime later. Norvo was the first vibist in jazz to use the three- or four-mallet technique, where the left hand would hold two mallets and the right either one or two mallets. This gave Norvo the ability to play multiple notes ("chords") simultaneously, creating a fuller, shimmering blanket of sound like none other. In addition to finding new ways of playing, Norvo was also a musician who would stay ahead of the curve by presenting jazz in new contexts. One of his most fondly remembered of these was his drummerless trio, which featured vibes, guitar, and bass. While a number of fine jazz artists passed through Norvo's trio, one of the most memorable units featured the guitarist Tal Farlow and a very young Charles Mingus on bass. This particular edition of the group recorded two discs for Savoy Records that are still available today and are worth a listen.

Norvo and his various groups recorded and performed with a number of the greatest singers to come out of the swing era, including Billie Holiday, Frank Sinatra, Dinah Shore, and his wife, Mildred Bailey. He also worked with swing and big-band icons Benny Goodman and Woody Herman, and even organized recordings that featured bebop legends Charlie Parker and Dizzy Gillespie. Known throughout his life as "Mr. Swing," Norvo has left a lasting mark on jazz as one of the most imaginative musicians of his day, and certainly one of its best vibists.

While Rollini and Norvo were certainly important figures in the inception of the vibraphone in jazz, the man who really put the instrument on the map was Lionel Hampton. Unlike either Rollini or Norvo, Lionel Hampton came to the vibraphone from the drums—and in a most unique way.

During a recording session with Louis Armstrong, Hampton noticed a vibraphone sitting in the studio and, on a break, began playing it. Armstrong liked what he heard, and Hampton wound up recording one song, playing vibes on the session. Soon after, clarinetist and band leader Benny Goodman heard Hampton and invited him to join his newly formed quartet, along with pianist Teddy Wilson and drummer Gene Krupa. It is worth noting that this is the group that broke the color barrier of racially segregated jazz bands by including Wilson and Hampton in its lineup. It was a bold move, a daring gamble that paid off greatly, given the positive reception of the quartet by both audiences and critics.

As a vibraphonist, Hampton was a dazzling technician and a brilliant improviser who was exciting to watch and a joy to hear. When you watch "Hamp" play on DVD or YouTube, one thing you will notice is the exuber-

Figure 16.6. Lionel Hampton, 1946. Courtesy of the William P. Gottlieb Collection.

ance he brings to the music. Listen to the quartet's performance on "China Boy" from Goodman's 1938 Carnegie Hall concert. Blinding speed and accuracy are the order of the day, especially in Hamp's bravura performance.

As a band leader, Hampton led one of the most exciting big bands in jazz history, featuring a bunch of great soloists as well as Hampton himself. The band was also a springboard for musicians who went on to achieve jazz immortality. Musicians such as trumpeters Clifford Brown, Art Farmer, Fats Navarro; saxophonists Dexter Gordon, Illinois Jacquet, and Red Holloway; and singers Joe Williams, Dinah Washington, Betty Carter, and Aretha Franklin—all graced the Hampton bandstand with their presence.

Along with Louis Armstrong and Dizzy Gillespie, Hamp became known as one of America's "Jazz Ambassadors." He toured Europe, Africa, and the Middle and Far East, spreading the joyful message and magic of jazz wherever he went. As a result, he became known the world over as one of jazz's greatest performers. He was also honored by Presidents Dwight Eisenhower, George H. W. Bush, and Bill Clinton for his musical and diplomatic contributions.

Hampton was also deeply concerned with the future of the music, and as such, he became an integral force in the development of the jazz curriculum in higher education. Specifically, his involvement with the University of Idaho resulted in the establishing of the Lionel Hampton School of Music and the realization of his dream to help support the future of jazz and music education.

These accomplishments are only the tip of the very large Hampton iceberg. An extraordinary musician and human being, Hamp's place in jazz and in this country's cultural history is unquestionable.

BAGS' GROOVE: MILT JACKSON

The advent of bebop in the '40s gave us the first and most stylistically modern vibraphonist in the person of Milt Jackson. He was arguably the most influential vibist in modern jazz history, and he set the standard for generations of vibraphonists to follow. Born in Detroit in 1923, Jackson was originally schooled as a guitarist, then as a pianist. In high school, Jackson switched to the vibraphone and its wood-barred cousin, the marimba. It was around that time that Jackson first saw Lionel Hampton and his band perform at the Michigan State Fair. Hampton was the reason Jackson decided to concentrate solely upon the vibraphone as his main instrument. However, even though Hampton was an inspiration for the younger vibist, he was not a musical influence. Jackson was totally absorbed by the new direction music was taking in the form of bebop, and as a result, he became the man who would translate bop's melodic, harmonic, and rhythmic innovations onto the vibraphone. It was only natural that he develop important relationships with Charlie Parker, Dizzy Gillespie, and Thelonious Monk at that time. In fact, his association with Gillespie as a member of the trumpeter's legendary big band led to a number of small groups, notably a Gillespie sextet and his own quartet, which was basically Jackson plus the rhythm section for Gillespie's big band: pianist John Lewis, bassist Ray Brown, and drummer Kenny Clarke. This group became known as the Modern Jazz Quartet. Brown and Clarke left and were replaced by bassist

Figure 16.7.   Milt Jackson with bassist Ray Brown, late 1940s. Courtesy of the William P. Gottlieb Collection.

Percy Heath and drummer Connie Kay, and the second and most famous edition of the MJQ was born.

In jazz, as we know by now, many of the musicians were given nick-names by their fellow musicians and friends; throughout this book you've seen colorful names like "Satchmo," "Prez," "Lady Day," and "Bird." And as we also know, these nicknames come from tidbits about the musicians themselves, usually modes of dress or physical characteristics. The latter of these applies to Milt Jackson, who was given the nickname of "Bags," which refers to the bags under his eyes accrued as a result of going to all-night jam sessions upon returning to Detroit from his stint in the navy.

Stylistically, Bags's sound on the vibes was unique for its time for a number of reasons. First of all, his sound was soft and supple. He used mallets that were not as hard and percussive as Lionel Hampton's, and he favored the use of two mallets, rather than the three or four used by Red Norvo in his chordal approach. Second, Bags preferred a very slow oscillating speed. So rather than the fast, fluttering vibrato preferred by the early masters, his vibrato was slow and undulating, sounding like a sea anemone looks underwater as it flows back and forth in the current.

Musically, Bags favored the blues, which he played with a deep, swinging groove in lots of different settings and with many great musicians through the years. As a member of the MJQ, he was the major voice of the group, whose sound, with Bags's vibes in tandem with John Lewis's delicate piano playing, was instantly recognizable to musicians and listeners alike. Thanks to Bags, the MJQ became one of the most popular of all modern jazz groups during its 30-plus years of existence. And Milt Jackson remains an icon and model for many vibists to this day.

MALLETS IN WONDERLAND

Here are a few pocket portraits of some of jazz's most creative and gifted vibraphone masters and stylists, some well established and others deserving wider recognition:

Gary Burton is a veritable vibraphone virtuoso and one of the most skilled four-mallet players in jazz. He is a beautifully lyrical improviser, who has reached deeply into the vibraphone to extract its purest glasslike sounds. A self-taught musician, Burton recorded for the first time at age 17 in Nashville. Shortly thereafter he joined Stan Getz's quartet. He also created some of the first jazz-rock fusion records with his own quartets. Many great players came through the Burton groups, including guitarists Pat Metheny and Mick Goodrick. Burton made many fine recordings, including many memorable duo recordings with Chick Corea, Steve Swallow, and many others.

One of the most creative and daring of all vibists, Bobby Hutcherson began playing the vibes as a teenager and was largely self-taught. Just as Lionel Hampton inspired Milt Jackson to play the vibes, Milt Jackson, in turn, was a source of inspiration for Hutcherson in choosing the instrument as the one he wished to pursue. Upon moving to San Francisco from Los Angeles, Hutcherson soon began turning heads via his first records. Beginning in the 1960s, he began recording as a sideman and eventually as a leader for Blue Note Records during one of its most fruitful and exciting periods. Hutcherson was the object of much critical acclaim and garnered a worldwide reputation as a forward-thinking and brilliant soloist. His recordings from the earliest to the most recent are marvels of virtuosity and imagination.

When one thinks of Latin jazz, one invariably thinks of Cal Tjader, even though he was a master of other jazz styles as well. Tjader grew up in Northern California and was an accomplished drummer and percussionist (especially the bongo drums). After getting out of the army in 1946, he returned to San Francisco and ultimately connected with two other young musicians destined for greatness: pianist Dave Brubeck and saxophonist Paul Desmond. With Tjader on drums, they added a bassist and formed the Dave Brubeck Quartet. As a member of the pianist George Shearing's quintet, Tjader played both vibes and Latin percussion instruments. As a result of his tenure with Shearing, Tjader's interest in and ultimate attraction to Latin music intensified considerably, particularly after visiting New York City and hearing many of the great Latin bands. Once back on the West Coast, he formed the first of his Latin jazz bands and became well known as a Latin jazz artist, even though he was also a consummate bop-oriented jazz player. He went on to win much popular acclaim as well as a Grammy in 1980 for his record *Amazonas*. As a vibist, his sound was similar to Jackson's in terms of mellowness and provided a great contrast to the exciting Latin rhythms pulsating underneath his solos.

Unlike the vibraphonists we've profiled thus far in this section, Karl Berger stands alone in terms of his sound and approach to improvisation. A six-time poll winner in *DownBeat* magazine, Berger was influenced greatly by such disparate sources as Ornette Coleman and Don Cherry, world music of all types, free jazz, and contemporary improvisational music. As a vibist, Berger is easily identifiable as both a mallet virtuoso and as an improviser. His sound on the Bergerault vibraphone is bright and bell-like, and his solos are often composed of cascades of notes skittering into the air like a flock of swallows heading in four different directions at once. And it all swings madly, crazily, and joyfully—all trademarks of the Berger musical persona. Like Ornette, Berger is well rooted in the art of simplicity and economy in his compositions, and one can feel a great sense of humanity and community in his music. Indeed, Berger's career as director of the legendary Creative Music Studio in Woodstock, New York, and as a teacher and a leader of large improvisational ensembles over the years bears this out—especially upon viewing his 2011 Stone Workshop Orchestra's performances available on YouTube.

Berger has performed and recorded with musical giants as diverse as Lee Konitz, Don Cherry, John McLaughlin, Dave Brubeck, Dave Holland, and many others. In addition to his mastery of the vibraphone, Berger is also an accomplished pianist who was well established as such in his native Germany in the early '60s, before moving to New York. And as if that wasn't enough, he holds a PhD in musicology and has taught all over the world as an artist-in-residence, visiting professor, and program director. He is as creative and imaginative as a teacher as he is as a musician. To call Karl Berger a visionary would not be an exaggeration.

THREE RECENT VOICES:
STEVE NELSON, JOE LOCKE, STEFON HARRIS

The future of the vibraphone in jazz is secure. While there are more than a few gifted young vibraphonists on the scene today, these three have been lauded repeatedly for their brilliant technique and masterful playing on both vibes and the marimba. It is fair to say that while all three are very much individualists in terms of their compositions, song choices, and solo styles, each has absorbed their predecessors thoroughly.

Steve Nelson has an absolutely beautiful, velvet-like sound and really takes his time building his solo statements. His sound is most reminiscent of Milt Jackson's, and he manages to sustain that sound even on the most hard swinging and intense performances. He is an adept multi-mallet player and is heard to great advantage on his own discs as well as those of bassist Dave Holland.

Joe Locke seems to thrive upon playing in many different settings. While he, too, pays homage to Milt Jackson, he also tips his hat to Bobby Hutcherson in terms of adventurousness. Locke can play virtually anything put in front of him, from mainstream jazz to post-bop to Brazilian and Latin music. And while he may alter his approach as a soloist from recording to recording, the core of his musicality always comes shining through. His is a glistening, melodious sound, and he is also fun to watch, because he always manages to make the most demanding articulations look effortless.

The *Los Angeles Times* has called 39-year-old vibraphonist and composer Stefon Harris "one of the most important young artists in jazz," and he has been the object of much praise from jazz critics and listeners alike. To experience him "live" on YouTube or, better yet, in concert is to witness sheer energy and—like Nelson and Locke—complete and utter virtuosity on both the vibraphone and the marimba.

Harris has been the recipient of many awards as both a soloist and a composer. His recordings have repeatedly been nominated for Grammy Awards and have won awards from the Jazz Journalist Association; *Jazz Times*, *JAZZIZ*, and *DownBeat* magazines; and a multitude of other publications, festivals, and associations. He has also been awarded multiple composition commissions and has had his work performed in a variety of settings.

As a soloist, his work can be described in two words: "passionate" and "dazzling." This is not to say that he is a flashy technique-for-technique's-sake player. To the contrary, Harris understands the value of the quiet simplicity of a single note hanging in the air at the end of a phrase, as well as he does the intensity of a cascade of notes summoned forth in the heat of the moment when the rhythm section is boiling beneath him and the listeners are on the edge of their seats.

Without a doubt, we will be hearing much more from Steve Nelson, Joe Locke, and Stefon Harris as time passes. Don't hesitate to see, hear, and let their music captivate you if the opportunity arises.

A FINAL WORD

There have been and continue to be many fine vibraphonists on the scene who have not been profiled here, but whose contributions to jazz are certainly such that you will want to add them to your listening list. These include the past masters Marjorie Hyams, Teddy Charles, Lem Winchester, and Walt Dickerson; today's masters Terry Gibbs, Mike Mainieri, Roy Ayres, David Friedman, Dave Samuels, and Jay Hoggard; and tomorrow's masters Matthias Lupri, Mark Sherman, Chris Dingman, and Matt Moran.

Getting Personal with Joe Locke

What advice would you offer a new listener who will be experiencing your music for the first time, either in concert, on YouTube, or via one of your recordings?

Figure 16.8. Joe Locke. Courtesy of R. Andrew Leply.

There is quite a broad stylistic range in my music. My recordings with pianist David Hazeltine, bassist Essiet Essiet, and drummer Billy Drummond (*Mutual Admiration Society* and *Mutual Admiration Society 2*) are coming out of the tradition, with a strong emphasis on swinging. My work . . . in *Four Walls of Freedom* was much more contemporary and compositional in nature, as is the music I am currently playing with the Joe Locke/Geoffrey Keezer Group. The new CD, *Signing*, has no straight-ahead [swinging] jazz on it at all.

I also love vocalists and vocal music. My *Storytelling* CDs feature singer Mark Ledford with songs by such non-jazz artists as Steve Winwood, Bill Withers, Neil Young, Bob Dylan, Michael Jackson, and Richard Thompson. *For the Love of You*, featuring vocalist Kenny Washington, is also a vocal album but is much more jazz-focused.

So, in short, I would have to say that on any given recording or any given concert, a listener is getting one or some parts of what I am about musically, but not the whole picture. There is a lot I want to express—different things at different times.

For an interesting contrast in styles, check out the YouTube video of "Van Gogh by Numbers" by the Locke/Keezer Group; then watch "Verrazano Moon" with Kenny Washington, Geoffrey Keezer, George Mtaz, and Clarence Penn [also on YouTube].

What would be the first recording of yours that you would recommend for an initial listening experience, and as a good introduction to your music?

I made a few duo recordings with the wonderful pianist Frank Kimbrough. I think the first one of that series, entitled "Saturn's Child," would be a good introduction to my music, because it really showcases my way of playing—riding in and out of the time [the rhythmic pulse] and floating over the beautiful carpet that Frank lays down. It is a very lyrical recording and also features both of us as composers.

SELECTED PERCUSSIONISTS' WEBSITES: FROM THEN 'TIL NOW

Note: Only official sites are listed. Use Google for all others.

Airto Moreira: www.airto.com
Francisco Aguabella: www.franciscoaguabella.com
Poncho Sanchez: www.ponchosanchez.com
Luis Conte: www.luisconte.com
Trilok Gurtu: www.trilokgurtu.net
Susie Ibarra: www.susieibarra.com
Munyungo Jackson: www.munyungo.com
Marilyn Mazur: www.marilynmazur.com

SELECTED VIBRAPHONISTS' WEBSITES: FROM THEN 'TIL NOW

(Only official sites are listed. Use Google for all others.)

Terry Gibbs: www.terrygibbs.com
Gary Burton: www.garyburton.com
Cal Tjader: www.caltjader.com
Mike Mainieri: www.nycrecords.com
Dave Samuels: www.dsamuels.com
Joe Locke: www.joelocke.com

Stefon Harris: www.stefonharris.com
Mark Sherman: www.markshermanmusic.com
Matt Moran: www.mattmoran.com
Chris Dingman: www.chrisdingman.com
Matthias Lupri: www.matthiaslupri.com

RECOMMENDED READING

Latin Jazz

Fernández, Raúl. *Latin Jazz: The Perfect Combination*. San Francisco: Chronicle Books, 2002. Print.
Roberts, John Storm. *The Latin Tinge: The Impact of Latin American Music on the United States*. 2nd ed. New York: Oxford UP, 1999. Print.

Lionel Hampton

Hampton, Lionel, and James Haskins. *Hamp: An Autobiography*. New York: Amistad Press, 1993. Print.

Terry Gibbs

Gibbs, Terry, and Cary Ginell. *Good Vibes: A Life in Jazz*. Lanham: Scarecrow Press, 2003. Print.

17

I GOT RHYTHM V

The Guitar

The guitar has had a long and colorful history in jazz. Perhaps the earliest guitar players who predated jazz were the country and blues musicians, who sang and often accompanied themselves on guitar and occasionally— in the case of the blues musicians—on neck-strap harmonica.

THE RHYTHM PLAYERS

An interesting facet of the history of jazz guitar is that, at first, guitars were used in jazz bands primarily as rhythm instruments; that is, they would strum the chords to a song in rhythm, but never really play a solo on it. The main reason for this role was that back in the early days of jazz, the guitar (like its predecessor, the banjo) was unamplified and, therefore, its ability to project sound was severely limited—particularly stacked up against the overpowering volume of the horns and the drums. The first really notable "rhythm jazz guitarists" were men like Eddie Condon—colorful, witty, and totally dedicated to the preservation of the music of the '20s and '30s. Another great jazz guitarist from that era was Eddie Lang; although he was quite capable of playing rhythm guitar, he was an early advocate for the guitar amplifier, and he was one of the first to use it. His best work was in tandem with the formidable violinist Joe Venuti.

Perhaps the best known of all rhythm guitarists was Freddie Green, who was at the very heart of the rhythm section in the Count Basie band from 1937 until 1984, the year of Basie's death. Green set the standard for rhythm guitar playing, and while he rarely played solos, his strong but unobtrusive playing was the glue that held the pianist, the bassist, and the drummer together—so much so that guitarists became a regular part of the rhythm sections of many big bands in the swing era.

One interesting observation about rhythm guitar playing is how similar the role of the rhythm guitarist in rock and funk groups is to that of the rhythm section guitarists of the swing era. Basically, they both served the same function by providing a rhythmic "anchor" for others in both the rhythm section and the larger ensemble. While the traditional role of the rhythm guitarist in today's jazz exists on a much smaller plane compared to its role in earlier eras, its flame continues to burn brightly in various styles of rock and roll as well as in the blues and country music. So if you accept this observation, you might well say, for example, that master rock rhythm guitarists like Chuck Berry, Cornell Dupree, Jimmy Page, Pete Townsend, and of course, Keith Richards, dip way into the grooves they play to help unify the overall feeling of their groups. All in all, the role of the rhythm guitarist is to "fill the middle" layer of sound and lock the groove into place. Not exactly in the spotlight, he or she is absolutely essential to the musical success of the group, just as Freddie Green was with the Basie Band.

FROM BACKGROUND TO SPOTLIGHT: THE GYPSY KING

We can't begin to discuss jazz guitar in any complete way without acknowledging the greatness of two major innovators. First, the Gypsy guitarist Django Reinhardt. A brilliant musician who emerged from the French gypsy culture in the early part of the 20th century, Reinhardt's life was anything but ordinary. He lived in a caravan for most if not all of his life and began a brilliant career that was cut short for a while, as a result of a caravan fire that caused extensive damage to one of his legs and his left hand. As a result, Reinhardt had to relearn the guitar without the full use of two of his fingers. Even so, he created a two-finger system that he could use on the fret board (the neck) of the instrument, and his mastery of this homegrown system allowed him to play with lightning agility and complete control. Reinhardt's influences were varied. While

he came out of the European Gypsy tradition, Reinhardt was also influenced by jazz musicians like saxophonists Coleman Hawkins and Charlie
Parker, and by French classical composers like Debussy. Django's playing has been described as exciting and romantic, his solos consisting
of sweeping cascades of notes tumbling into each other. His mastery
catapulted him into the stuff of legend among musicians and listeners,
well beyond his death in 1953. Perhaps his most famous recordings were
made with a group known as the Hot Club of France, which consisted
initially of three guitars, violin, and bass. These lively, brilliant recordings
have been restored and remastered over the years and continue to bring
pleasure to many listeners today.

**Figure 17.1. Django Reinhardt. Courtesy of the William P. Gottlieb Col-
lection.**

OTHER ACOUSTIC MASTERS

Arguably, Django Reinhardt exerted a great influence upon future generations of acoustic jazz guitarists. His accompaniments and solos were of
particular influence on other European, American, and South American
guitarists. For example, in Europe, the great Belgian virtuoso Philip Cath-
erine and the Frenchmen Biréli Lagrène and Christian Escoudé are very
well known in both the jazz and guitar worlds. South America—notably
Brazil—has produced many fine acoustic guitar players, including Baden
Powell, Bola Sete, and Egberto Gismonti. And in America two of the preeminent masters were Laurindo Almeida, a Brazilian living in America,
and Charlie Byrd. Both men were well versed in both jazz and classical
traditions and were major proponents of the bossa nova movement in the
United States in the early '60s. Byrd, in particular, championed the music
of Antonio Carlos Jobim, Joao Gilberto, Ivan Lins, Milton Nascimento, and
many other fine Brazilian composers and performers. His 1963 recording
Jazz Samba, with tenor saxophonist Stan Getz, is still considered a classic
today by many jazz and bossa nova fans worldwide.

Interlude: Byrd in Flight

The call came while I was still in grad school at the University of Maryland—studying by day, playing any gig I could get, from weddings and up-
pity country clubs in Bethesda to jazz clubs and restaurants in the District.
The phone was ringing as I walked in the door. The voice at the other end
was relaxed and had a slight Southern twang to it: "Hi, Mike, this is Charlie
Byrd. I was wondering if you'd like to go to South America with me next
month. It'll be three to four weeks and I think you'd enjoy the countries
we'll be playing in." I was almost speechless . . . almost. I did, however,
manage to get one word out: "Sure!"

Of course I knew who Charlie was, and I knew that he was one of the
few guys at that time in the early '70s who played the acoustic guitar exclusively. Even his amplified guitar was acoustic. I also knew that Charlie,
along with Stan Getz, helped bring the songs and rhythms of the Brazilian
bossa nova to this country around 10 years earlier, and that they had a huge
hit with their *Jazz Samba* album.

A month or so later—and after only a couple of rehearsals and warm-up gigs—off we went on a U.S. State Department tour, which began in Panama and ended up in Argentina. Charlie was a class act: a gracious and dryly witty leader, charming and relaxed with audiences, and always up for a good joke. Best of all, he was the consummate musician. A former student of the legendary Andrés Segovia, Charlie was equally at home in both classical and jazz realms. In fact, one segment of each of our shows was devoted to one or two classical guitar solos. I would sit on stage right during those pieces, mesmerized by his stunning virtuosity.

And he captivated audiences wherever we played. For example, one night in Rio de Janeiro—our first appearance in Brazil—we opened the set with "Desifinado," which was a hit for Charlie and Getz. I thought it was going to be a disaster; I mean, there we were—Charlie, his brother Joe (on bass), and me—three gringos playing our version of a bossa nova for 500 Brazilian music lovers. (Is there anyone in Brazil who doesn't love music?) All I could think of was me sitting back there behind the drums, playing my pathetic bar mitzvah band version of the bossa beat. Yet, at the end of the song, the crowd cheered, and by the end of the night, we had 500 new friends!

The tour was amazing, both musically and spiritually. We played on the remnants of a stage in a burned-out stadium, for at least a thousand music-hungry people, a short time after the devastating 1972 earthquake that hit Managua, Nicaragua. I think we must have played four or five encores, and each time, the audience cheered and threw flowers on the stage. We also performed in Buenos Aires for an audience that included the famous composer and musician Astor Piazzola, and we even sat in an airport in Panama, waiting for hours for a flight to Colombia—along with another legendary musician and Charlie's friend, sitar virtuoso Ravi Shankar. It was through Charlie that I was exposed to many great musicians like Piazzola and Shankar, who really were in awe of him, as I was of all of them.

Our final gig together took place years later in Ojai, California, when Charlie came to play at a retreat called Wheeler's Hot Springs, out in the middle of practically nowhere. I was excited to see him again after so many years and to have another opportunity to make music with him, this time as a more mature and musical drummer. It was a magical evening and felt like no years had passed at all. Charlie played better than ever, and you could have heard a pin drop during his 90-minute set. The amazingly resonant tones from his acoustic guitar rang bell-like through the room, and the capacity crowd was held spellbound by Byrd's virtuosity.

At the end of the night, I drove Charlie down a winding, rutted dirt road to one of the guest cabins where he was staying. He stood on the porch waving good-bye, a single lightbulb swaying gently in the breeze above his head. Frankly, it was a lonely scene there in my rearview mirror as I pulled away: this musical giant who'd concertized all over the world—from Carnegie Hall to a Cartageña, Colombia, bull ring—this musical innovator and world-class performing artist, all alone out here on the porch of a weathered old cabin. Charlie was, however, an old road warrior and was used to the ups and downs of the jazz life—so it probably bothered me more than it bothered him that he was staying the night in a rustic dump.

Charlie Byrd left us a year or so later, and though I miss him, I feel comfort in knowing that we had one last chance to have a musical conversation, there on the little bandstand out in the middle of practically nowhere, where I imagine the beautiful resonances of his guitar still floating lazily in the California night air.

PLUGGING IN: CHARLIE CHRISTIAN

The second major figure who inspired the transition of the guitar from a rhythm instrument to a solo voice took that transition to another level by amplifying his sound. Whereas Django Reinhardt played and recorded mostly on an unamplified "hollow body" guitar, Charlie Christian—while not the first guitarist to do so—used an amplified version of the instrument. In either case, the term "hollow body" refers to the construction of the guitar in such a way that the instrument resonates more deeply, since there is a hollow area inside helping to give more fullness to chords that are being strummed or notes being played individually.

Charlie Christian was a marvel. Like Django Reinhardt, he had a totally unique style, although Christian embraced the blues tradition and bebop as well as swing. In fact, his were the first guitar solos to model themselves after those of both swing and bebop horn players. For example, if you listen to a Charlie Christian solo and follow that by listening to a solo by tenor saxophonist Lester Young, you will be able for the most part to hear the similarity between the two in terms of swinging sequences of notes that flow effortlessly into your ears. Christian's guitar sound was clear and

Figure 17.2. Charlie Christian. Courtesy of the William P. Gottlieb Collection.

warm and was one he favored over the sometimes metallic tinniness of an unamplified acoustic guitar. His sound was immediately attractive to band leader Benny Goodman, who hired Christian in 1939. The guitarist's reputation quickly grew, and he played and recorded a number of bebop records with Dizzy Gillespie, Thelonious Monk, and others. Unfortunately, Charlie Christian died in 1942, at not quite 26 years old. However, in his brief time as a musician, he managed to revolutionize the world of jazz guitar playing, as well as subsequent generations of players.

SIX-STRING BOP: THE NEXT GENERATION OF JAZZ GUITARISTS

Charlie Christian's innovations as a soloist laid the foundation for many other fine guitarists, as they worked to develop their individual styles and approaches to jazz improvisation. Among the first of these to move in the new direction was Billy Bauer, who, as a student of the influential pianist and teacher Lennie Tristano beginning in the mid-1940s, played long and often complex lines, much in the same fashion as two other famous students of the Tristano school, saxophonists Lee Konitz and Warne Marsh. While he was very influential, Bauer was also quite humble, and he preferred the role of sideman to that of being a leader. As a result, he avoided the spotlight and began concentrating upon teaching, which he did until his passing in 2005.

As we have seen in the art of jazz, a musician's style and approach to the music is almost always built upon the shoulders of his or her predecessors and the foundations that they established. Billy Bauer came from Charlie Christian in terms of amplification and sound, and from pianist Lennie Tristano in terms of the approach to soloing and composition. But Bauer is also part of the roots of the family tree that gave us great jazz guitarists like Barney Kessel, Jimmy Raney, Kenny Burrell, Tal Farlow, Johnny Smith, Herb Ellis, Grant Green, and Jim Hall—all products of the jazz of the '50s and beyond. Listening to each of these men, you may be struck by the warmth of each one's sound and the smoothness of each one's approach to stating melodies and playing solos.

While these and others are among the finest guitarists of their time, there are two who have lived into the new millennium. Jim Hall has one of the most beautiful guitar sounds ever recorded—clear as glass and beautifully rounded and warm. Couple that with his elegant and intelligent improvisations, and you have a true master of the instrument. Hall's musical history includes his early work with drummer Chico Hamilton's group, and with clarinetist/saxophonist Jimmy Giuffre's intriguing trios with either Bob Brookmeyer on valve trombone or bassist Ralph Peña; his later work includes a duo with Brookmeyer, and his own groups, notably his various trios, and his memorable duo with ex–Miles Davis bass virtuoso Ron Carter. Hall is recognized and revered by contemporary masters such as Pat Metheny and Bill Frisell, and he has recorded with each.

The other living guitar master is Kenny Burrell. Like Jim Hall, Burrell has been on the scene since the 1950s, and he is considered by many to be one of the finest guitarists in jazz. He has appeared on several hundred recordings as both a participant and a leader. In an article for the online jazz website All about Jazz, Burrell says, "My goal is to play with good tone, good phrasing, and to swing. I strive for honesty in playing what I feel." The guitarist has worked in many kinds of instrumental settings, from trio (with bass and drums) to large ensemble; he also made a terrific recording with saxophonist John Coltrane (for Prestige Records) that should be on every guitar player's list of must-haves.

In addition to his well-deserved reputation as a world-class guitarist, Burrell has also been involved in jazz education, notably as the director of jazz studies at the University of California, Los Angeles, and as the founder and president emeritus of the Jazz Heritage Foundation. Burrell is deeply committed to the preservation and sustenance of jazz as a creative art form and has successfully balanced a life of making music and building future audiences for it. By all accounts, he is a warm and congenial man who has been a role model, not only for guitarists but for all jazz musicians.

TWO TORCHBEARERS: WES MONTGOMERY AND PAT MARTINO

Among modern jazz guitarists, Wes Montgomery is held in very high esteem. One of the things that distinguished Montgomery from many other fine jazz guitarists was the use of his thumb, rather than the more conventional guitar pick. In creating this unconventional way of playing, he was able to play "octaves," which means that he could play the same note simultaneously on two different strings—one higher and one lower. There's another example of an octave on the piano keyboard below. Press the "middle C" key on a piano (below left), and at the same time press the next C key, seven white keys to the right of the middle C; the sound you'll hear is called an octave. Note where the two Cs are shown in figure 17.3.

In the world of the jazz guitar, Wes Montgomery had "the gift of style" and was immediately identifiable. The result of his unorthodox way of playing the instrument was a totally unique sound—quite mellow and pure. Montgomery was especially active in the late '50s and '60s, and his recording *Smokin' at the Half Note* is one of the most influential jazz guitar albums of all time. Wes Montgomery continues to be a pervasive influence on many guitarists even today, well beyond his death in 1968.

One of the guitarists who absorbed Montgomery's technique and went on to forge his own unique way of playing is Pat Martino. His life story is the stuff movies are made of and is a shining example of how a person can survive a devastating health experience through sheer will and the love of music.

Born in Philadelphia in 1944, Pat Martino was exposed to jazz by his father, who was a local singer and sometime guitarist. Martino got to hear

Figure 17.3. Piano keyboard.

and meet Wes Montgomery, John Coltrane, and many others. As a result of a nurturing family and firsthand exposure to the music, Martino immersed himself in the guitar, beginning at age 12. Less than a decade later, he signed with Prestige Records, and the jazz world began to take notice. However, in 1976 Martino began suffering seizures and was diagnosed with a life-threatening brain aneurysm. After multiple surgeries and with almost no memory of either his family or playing the guitar, he began the long road back to recovery. It wasn't easy, by any means. In terms of the guitar, Martino had to start from square one and learn the instrument all over again! He did this by studying his old recordings and by practicing the fundamentals of the instrument for hours and hours. Fortunately for both Pat Martino and his legion of fans, he finally returned to the jazz scene in 1987, with a recording called "The Return"—certainly an auspicious and joyous occasion as well as a testament to determination and the power of music and family.

As a guitarist, over the course of his career Pat Martino has investigated all of the stylistic nooks and crannies of jazz. He recorded a superlative ballad album: a series of duets with electric pianist Gil Goldstein (*We'll Be Together Again*); a series of exciting fusion performances with his group on *Joyous Lake*; and many other projects, from organ-guitar-drums trios to larger groups such as some all-star quintets.

On his website, Martino offers the following philosophical perspective about his students and fans: "The guitar is of no great importance to me. The people it brings to me are what matter. They are what I'm extremely grateful for, because they are alive. The guitar is just an apparatus" (www.patmartino.com).

INNER-MOUNTING FLAMES:
MAHAVISHNU, SCOFIELD, METHENY, AND ABERCROMBIE

The cross-pollination of jazz and rock has created very fertile ground for new avenues of expression. And while many instruments figure prominently in the "fusion" of these two musical genres, the electric guitar may well be at the top of the list. This might be because rock guitarists like Jimi Hendrix and Eric Clapton and blues guitarists like Hendrix, B.B. King, and Stevie Ray Vaughan had a significant impact upon members of jazz's guitar-playing community. And the sonic explorations of pioneer Les Paul laid the groundwork for almost everyone in the electric guitar world.

Some early experimentation merging jazz with rock began largely with a guitarist named Larry Coryell, whose work in the mid-'60s with vibraphonist Gary Burton and his own group, The Free Spirits, was an integral part of fusion's beginnings. Coryell's solos combined jazz phrases with rock guitar sounds to intriguing effect. Not surprisingly, Coryell's approach influenced other young guitarists at that time, most notably John McLaughlin in England. Active initially with British rock bands and jazz groups, McLaughlin rose to prominence in 1969 when he moved to the United States in order to join drummer Tony Williams's Lifetime, which was composed of Williams, McLaughlin, and organist Larry Young. To call this trio a fusion group is to do it an injustice, since it really covered a lot more ground than either jazz or rock. The music still sounds fresh today.

McLaughlin also attracted the attention of Miles Davis, whose own visions of the music were changing radically. As a result, the guitarist became a part of Miles's legendary *In a Silent Way* and *Bitches Brew* sessions (in 1969 and 1970, respectively), as well as subsequent Davis recordings, including *A Tribute to Jack Johnson*, *Big Fun*, and *Live-Evil*.

There were other recordings with a variety of ensembles as well. However, it was the Mahavishnu Orchestra that brought McLaughlin front and center into the public eye and ear as a band leader in 1972. This band was one of the first really influential fusion groups in the history of jazz-rock, and its unorthodox instrumentation (guitar, violin, keyboards, electric bass, and drums) and musically complex compositions set it apart from other fusion bands at that time. Fueled by Billy Cobham's energetic and virtuosic drumming, the Mahavishnu Orchestra, indeed, sounded at times almost as though it were a 90-piece ensemble. This was often very loud music; but it also beautifully crafted and brilliantly played. The group recorded from 1972 to 1975, and its second incarnation released two other projects almost a decade later.

McLaughlin's spirituality (he was a student of Sri Chinmoy) as well as his musical inquisitiveness led him to form an ensemble called Shakti in the mid-'70s. Unlike the Mahavishnu Orchestra, this group was all acoustic and delved into Indian classical music. Aside from the guitarist, the group was composed mainly of some of India's finest musicians.

"Shakti" means "energy," and this group had energy to spare. The music varied quite a bit and moved from gently contemplative to furiously intense. Shakti, along with trumpeter Don Cherry's various ensembles, was arguably one of the earliest groups to fuse jazz and world music. After the group disbanded in 1978, McLaughlin went on to record and perform with a diversity of musicians and ensembles and, to this day, has never stood still long enough to be pigeonholed into one genre or another.

Another guitarist who, like McLaughlin, continues to cross stylistic boundaries—albeit in a very different way—is John Scofield, whose playing is extremely original and inventive. He plays very much in the modern jazz idiom, yet his sound is often similar to that of a really good rock guitarist like Eric Clapton or a blues master like B.B. King. His solo lines are often long, loping, funky affairs, which combine the fat melodic solo phrases of a tenor saxophonist like Sonny Rollins with the raw sound of many of rock's more accomplished guitar soloists.

Scofield's initial inspirations as a young guitarist were rock and blues guitarists, and he carried those influences into his education at the Berklee College of Music, the famed jazz school in Boston. He first received wide exposure in the mid-'70s as a member of the fusion band of drummer Billy Cobham and keyboardist George Duke; however, his first recording was earlier, a live concert with jazz icons Gerry Mulligan and Chet Baker—quite at the opposite end of the stylistic spectrum. Anything Scofield does, he does well, and he has the gift of a recognizable voice on the guitar, no matter what the setting. He recorded with bassist Charles Mingus, and he played with vibist Gary Burton's quartet in 1977. A year or so later, he began his career as a solo artist, recording albums that were each unique and conceptually different from the previous one. His unique voice graced both the concert stage and recordings of Miles Davis from 1982 to 1985. He even recorded with Kansas City swing and blues legend Jay McShann.

After his stint with Miles, Scofield continued to lead his own groups, and he has made over 30 recordings as a leader, making music with the likes of guitarists Pat Metheny and Bill Frisell; bassists Steve Swallow and Charlie Haden; drummers Adam Nussbaum, Jack Dejohnette, and Bill Stewart; saxophonists Dave Liebman, Joe Lovano, and Joe Henderson; and pianists Herbie Hancock and Brad Mehldau—a veritable who's who of modern jazz greats.

Beyond his skills as the consummate guitarist, Scofield is also a unique composer. His tunes can often be quirky and lively or somber and reflective; all are ingeniously written and fun to play. Their titles alone make you want to listen to them. Here is a sampling: "So Sue Me," "Fat Lip," "I Can See Your House from Here," "Low Blow," and "Yawn."

Above all, John Scofield has not limited himself to any one style of music. He continues to be inspired by a cross section of genres in a variety of settings. Even so, the Scofield sound and style is instantly identifiable, once you've listened to him for a while. His music always welcomes us and invites us back for more each time.

Like both John McLaughlin and John Scofield, guitarist Pat Metheny has managed to carve a unique and adventurous niche for himself in the world of jazz and beyond. Not only is he as readily identifiable as the two John's, but like them, he has also explored many aspects and dimensions of his instrument and has expanded the notions of what jazz is and what it has the potential to be. Winner of 18 Grammy Awards and countless other honors, Pat Metheny continues to be one of the most diverse and interesting musicians on the contemporary jazz scene.

Metheny was born and raised in Kansas City, Missouri, and began studying the guitar at age 12. Three short years later, he was actively involved in the KC jazz scene. The first gig that offered a great deal of exposure for Metheny was as a member of vibist Gary Burton's quartet in the mid-'70s. (As mentioned above, John Scofield also played with Burton's quartet, though after Metheny's stint with the group.) Metheny's first album as a leader was called *Bright Size Life* (1975, ECM Records) and featured the guitarist with the brilliant electric bassist and innovator Jaco Pastorius and the equally gifted drummer Bob Moses. Metheny had arrived!

Over the years, Metheny began to expand traditional notions of jazz by exploring other styles of music—all the while maintaining his personal sound and his lyrical, hornlike approach to improvisation. He has collaborated with some of the most vital artists in contemporary music, regardless of genre: classical composer Steven Reich, Brazilian singer/songwriter Milton Nascimento, popular music icon David Bowie, and jazz legends Ornette Coleman and Jim Hall. He has written all types of music for solo guitar and small and large ensembles, and he has been a sonic explorer and innovator, among the first—if not the first—to utilize the guitar synthesizer. He has also played an important part in the development of totally new and unique musical instruments, from the 42-string Pikasso guitar to his version of the multi-instrument, Orchestrion. This latter "instrument" has its roots in the 19th century and has many variations. In short, it is a series of connected robotic instruments (such as drums and percussion, orchestra bells, chimes, and many more), all controlled by a single source—in this case, Metheny's guitar; yet through it all there is his distinctive solo

Figure 17.4. Pat Metheny. Courtesy of Jimmy Katz.

voice, which is always at the heart of his music. No matter what the setting, expect the unexpected with Pat Metheny.

The unexpected has also always been at the heart of the music of guitarist John Abercrombie. He, too, is a true "original" in that he—like the other three guitarists profiled—has a sound and style that is very recognizable. That's one of the beautiful things about jazz: we can listen to all four of these guitarists, and although each one is playing basically the same instrument, each one has his own personal style and approach to the instrument and to his soloing. Abercrombie sounds ethereal at times, almost otherworldly, yet there is a kind of gentleness in his playing that can be very appealing to guitar-loving jazz listeners. Someone once said that "his solos kind of sneak up on you." That might mean that each time you listen to an Abercrombie solo on CD or MP3, you might hear something different with each progressive listening experience.

Like his other three contemporaries, John Abercrombie is, as stated on his website, "a restless experimenter, working firmly in the jazz tradition while pushing the boundaries of meter [rhythm] and harmony." An early recording artist on ECM, the famed German new music label, Abercrombie led a number of imaginative and exciting ensembles, including Gateway, a trio featuring bassist Dave Holland and drummer Jack Dejohnette; another trio with Dejohnette and Mahavishnu Orchestra keyboardist Jan Hammer; and other small ensembles that featured many well-known musicians. His current group is a quartet that features the violinist Mark Feldman, the bassist Thomas Morgan, and the drummer Joey Baron. Much of the music this group plays is thoughtful, contemplative, and at the same time playful and just slightly aloof.

To have the experience of watching and listening to Abercrombie play a solo is to witness a man lost in the folds of the music that he is creating, purely in the moment and deeply personal—the epitome of another jazz artist who is 100 percent music, through and through; one who brings listeners into the experience of his music in a gentle and inviting way.

DEFYING CATEGORY AS AN ART:
BILL FRISELL, NELS CLINE, MARC RIBOT

It's easy and even comfortable for listeners to want to put musicians into stylistic little boxes; for example, jazz fans may be apt to say that Kenny Burrell is a bebop player, John McLaughlin is a fusion player, Jim Hall is a main-stream player, and so on. This tendency exists even more blatantly in rock, when we say that "Musician X" plays one of the following: industrial, retro, grunge, house, techno, heavy metal, punk-rock, folk-rock, alt-rock, country-rock . . . and so on. Of course, this kind of categorization can be blatantly unfair to many musicians who, at the end of the day, would not want to be put in some category, usually just to sell their recordings. Many musicians would like you to enjoy what they have to offer without imprisoning it in some singular genre. In fact, there are the artists who are quite comfortable being completely uncategorizable. Perhaps it actually might even free them up to explore the outer reaches of any style at any given time.

Guitarists Bill Frisell, Nels Cline, and Marc Ribot are three musicians who seem to fit that description quite well. Whereas with the preceding four master guitarists, even though we can expect the unexpected from one recording project to the next, Frisell, Cline, and Ribot may just as easily vary their guitar stylings and approaches from one recorded track of a project to the next, pushing the envelope each time, thereby keeping us on the edge of our seats as they carry us along from track to track.

One word that seems to come to mind when talking about Bill Frisell is "Americana." Frisell has dug deeply into American roots music, most notably rural folk, country, and bluegrass music, and has found a natural way to bring jazz sensibilities into play. As a result, he has created a style of guitar playing that is intriguing, adventurous, and quite attractive—all without sounding pretentious or artificial. Frisell has brought his unique musicality to a great many diverse musical endeavors and has done so with great success. He was a long-standing member of a trio (and sometimes quartet) with saxophonist Joe Lovano and drummer Paul Motian. He has two working trios currently and has recorded many fine CDs with a wide variety of artists in various genres. His website discography is a veritable who's who of jazz, folk, and country artists. Frisell has been called a musical chameleon because of his ability to blend into any musical situation and sound as if he were born to it. About his philosophy of playing music, Frisell (www.billfrisell.com) told the *Village Voice*:

> I like to have fun when I play and I like comedy—but it's not a conscious thing. I'm basically a pretty shy person and I don't dance or get into fights. But there are all these things inside me that get out when I perform. It's like a real world when I play, where I can do all the things I can't do in real life.

A revealing comment, which not only sums up Bill Frisell's feelings about his music but might also speak for many other men and women who have invested their lives in the art of creating music on a deeply personal level.

Nels Cline is a marvel. Put one of his CDs in your player, and you'll notice that on one track he'll be playing a swinging straight-ahead jazz composition. The next track may begin quietly with just dribs and drabs of guitar colorations, very sparse wire brushes on a snare drum, and bowed string bass. However, after a minute or two, guitar, bass, and drums begin to bubble and brew and increase in intensity, to the point that Nels and his two band mates create and sustain a wall of sound—one that eventually changes into a Jimi Hendrix–style psychedelic riff. Another track might be purely electronic sounds and the clicking of drumsticks on wood and metal, and yet another may feature only the electric guitar playing a simple, childlike melody. Welcome to the world of Nels Cline, raconteur of sounds and silences. Like McLaughlin, Scofield, Metheny, and Abercrombie, Cline has an insatiable curiosity that drives him forward; his influences are many and come from a wide range of musical styles, including contemporary classical music, cabaret, all forms of rock music, country music, film music, and of course, many styles of jazz. In addition to guesting with other groups, leading his own bands (such as the instrumental trio he calls—oddly enough—"The Nels Cline Singers"), and doing many recording projects, Cline is a member of the popular Grammy-winning band Wilco, with whom he also plays and records.

An artist of very few boundaries, Cline embraces all manner of experimentation. In addition to the many musicians he works with, Cline has collaborated with poets, spoken word artists, filmmakers, and painters. Throughout his musical life, Cline's path has been a natural one, and he offers his music to us all with a great deal of warmth, as well as a dollop of oblique, wry humor.

As is the case with Nels Cline, the music of guitarist Marc Ribot offers listeners a glimpse of the past, present, and future—all at the same time. That is, Ribot draws his creative materials from the past and brings them up into the present moment, and through his own experimentation with sounds and riffs, manages to create new and fresh musical ideas that can be quite accessible without blatantly copying anyone else's musical styles. For example, we might hear him play a Chuck Berry–like guitar riff that may dissolve into pure electronic dissonance, or we may hear him playing a sensual sort of Latin groove like "El Gaucho Rojo" with his group, Los

Cubanos Postizos. In a solo setting, Ribot's sense of timing, drama, and a sort of whacky humor comes shining through on an old standard like "Dinah"; and when we hear his raw, funky guitar with singer-songwriter Tom Waits, firing up the groove on a song like "Filipino Box Spring Hog," we can understand and appreciate the enormous breadth of Ribot's musical vision. Like Nels Cline, Marc Ribot is a musical sojourner who uses music's history, its humor, and its current possibilities to create something new and stimulating. Ribot says, "Going forward means going back to some degree. I trust that desire to go back and find fun."

OTHER IMPORTANT VOICES

There are so many other wonderful guitarists currently on the scene, and it's frustrating to say only a few words about them; however, it is nonetheless important that listeners know that these great guitarists are as near as your computer, and that you can hear them and purchase their music, if you like what you hear. Mick Goodrick has been on the scene for many years and continues to be a vital voice on the instrument. First a student at Berklee College of Music and then a professor, Goodrick's sound and style have influenced many other guitarists, including Pat Metheny; in addition, some of his more illustrious students have included John Scofield, Bill Frisell, and Mike Stern. Vic Juris, though not as well known as those profiled earlier, is a true guitar master, who has, in his long and critically acclaimed career, made recordings of the highest quality, most notably with saxophonist Dave Liebman. Kurt Rosenwinkel is another original voice and an imaginative young composer and improviser. One attractive characteristic of Rosenwinkel's playing is his unique ability to be able to sing his solos as he is playing them. Steve Cardenas, an alumnus of the late drummer Paul Motian's ensembles, is also creating music that draws from a variety of styles, which he has managed to synthesize into a very personal and lyrical style. On the West Coast, Larry Koonse has been turning heads for quite a while with his beautiful sound and adventurous rhythmic approach to soloing. Other great young players include Adam Rogers, Sheryl Bailey, Ben Monder, Julian Lage, Mary Halvorson, and Peter Bernstein— all certainly worth a listen.

Getting Personal with John Scofield

What advice would you offer a new listener who will be experiencing your music for the first time, either in concert, on YouTube, or via one of your recordings?

First of all, I would say that it's the same advice for any jazz music and not just my own. And when I answer this question, I have to think back to what turned me on to jazz to begin with, you know. And I listened in the beginning for the melodies and for the rhythm . . . the rhythm that turned me on. I had already gotten into rhythmic music through rock and roll and blues and was way into that as a kid, I guess like we all were then. And then through blues—because B.B. King's shuffle music is a kind of jazz—through that blues and understanding that rhythm—that led me to swing, you know.

Figure 17.5. John Scofield. Courtesy of Nick Suttle.

So I would say, get into the rhythm of it, and then just listen for the beautiful melodies that are in there, because everybody likes melody, right? Sometimes it's in the "heads" of the composition [the statement of the original melody]. Sometimes, the great thing about this music is that in the solos—sometimes the best things are not thought out; they're just stumbled upon in the solos. Some of the most beautiful phrases happen. I think everybody who plays [jazz] gets to that.

Jazz is different from pop music because we allow this stuff to unfold. . . . There're going to be moments that are not as happening as other moments. And I think that's the thing about jazz. I think the listener has to really want it. Most people that get to it because they heard about this form of music that is fulfilling and stimulating in a way that other kinds of music aren't . . . it's just gonna take a little bit more of your brain space.

When I got my first jazz records, one of them was *The Shape of Jazz to Come* by Ornette Coleman. I didn't realize that they were not playing on the [traditional] 32-bar form . . . so I got kinda lost and all that; but I just loved the melodies so much that it spoke to me!

What would be the first recording of yours that you would recommend for an initial listening experience, and as a good introduction to your music?

Can I choose three? (laughter) They're in different bags [styles], because I do kind of run to different things, you know.

A lot of people that aren't jazz aficionados like the record I made called *A-Go-Go*, which is kind of funk-jazz, you know, whatever you call it; and I think that was a good example of a group that really jelled; and the tunes were nice and it just worked for us.

And then there's a record—it might be a little dense for some people; but as far as my guitar playing, I did a "live" trio record with [electric bassist] Steve Swallow and [drummer] Bill Stewart, "live" at the Blue Note, that's called *En Route*, and as you know, "live" records capture the stuff . . . the hotter moments that sometimes don't happen in the studio.

And then, I guess there's a record of mine that a lot of people say they liked; that's me with [saxophonist] Joe Lovano . . . it's a quartet, so it's a different, bigger sound than just the trio. And I think my tunes were good on this record, compositionally—and that's called *Time on My Hands*.

Also, on YouTube there's some stuff of mine that I like that's actually from a commercial DVD, and I think that the whole DVD is on YouTube. It's just called *John Scofield: The Paris Concert—Live at the New Morning*.

SELECTED GUITARISTS' WEBSITES: FROM THEN 'TIL NOW

Note: Only official sites are listed. Use Google for all others.

Freddie Green: www.freddiegreen.org
Wes Montgomery: www.wesmontgomery.com
Jim Hall: www.jimhallmusic.com
Jimmy Raney: www.jonraney.com
Laurindo Almeida: www.laurindoalmeida.com
Pat Martino: www.patmartino.com
Vic Juris: www.vicjurisjazz.com
Larry Coryell: www.coryelljazz.com
Pat Metheny: www.patmetheny.com
John Abercrombie: www.johnabercrombie.com
John Scofield: www.johnscofield.com
John McLaughlin: www.johnmclaughlin.com
Bill Frisell: www.billfrisell.com
Peter Bernstein: www.peterbernsteinmusic.com
Sheryl Bailey: www.sherylbailey.com
Steve Cardenas: www.stevecardenasmusic.com
Kurt Rosenwinkel: www.kurtrosenwinkel.com
Ben Monder: www.benmonder.com
Julian Lage: www.julianlage.com
Adam Rogers: www.adamrogersmusic.com
Marc Ribot: www.marcribot.com
Nels Cline: www.nelscline.com
Mary Halvorson: www.maryhalvorson.com

RECOMMENDED READING

General

Alexander, Charles, ed. *Masters of the Jazz Guitar: The Story of the Players and Their Music*. London: Balafon Books, 1999. Print.
Sallis, James, ed. *The Guitar in Jazz*. Lincoln: U of Nebraska P, 1996. Print.

Charlie Christian

Broadbent, Peter. *Charlie Christian: Solo Flight—The Story of the Seminal Electric Guitarist*. 2nd ed. Blaydon on Tyne: Ashley Mark, 2003. Print.

Grant Green

Green, Sharony Andrews. *Grant Green: Rediscovering the Forgotten Genius of the Jazz Guitar*. San Francisco: Backbeat Books, 1999. Print.

Pat Martino

Martino, Pat, with Bill Milkowski. *Here and Now: The Autobiography of Pat Martino*. Milwaukee: Backbeat Books / Imprint of Hal Leonard Corp., 2011. Print.

Pat Metheny

Niles, Richard. *The Pat Metheny Interviews*. Milwaukee: Hal Leonard Books, 2009. Print.

Wes Montgomery

Ingram, Adrian. *Wes Montgomery*. 2nd ed. Blaydon on Tyne: Ashley Mark, 2008. Print.

Django Reinhardt

Dregni, Michael. *Django: The Life and Music of a Gypsy Legend*. New York: Oxford UP, 2004. Print.

18

THE SINGER AND THE SONG

Never sing a song the same way twice.

—Billie Holiday

Forgive me if I don't have the words.
Maybe I can sing it and you'll understand.

—Ella Fitzgerald

PRELUDE

Believe me, I've worked with singers . . . lots of them, from the divine to the earthbound. But one thing's for sure. All of them, almost to a person, had the desire and the courage to get up there on the bandstand and, as Ella Fitzgerald said above, to express themselves in a way that maybe they couldn't do in conversation. There's something magical about that when it's really right and there's no pretense attached to it.

When I first moved to Los Angeles, I was lucky enough to snag a gig in a rhythm section whose role was to accompany singers who would sign up to perform two tunes each at a five-night-a-week club showcase called

"Pandemonium." And believe me, it was often as chaotic as the name suggests, since we would talk through a lot of music (without actually rehearsing it), and play for six to ten singers a night. I don't remember much about
those who really needed to find a more constructive use of their time other
than obliterating the Great American Songbook. But I do fondly recall the
ones who could give you the chills—those who had genuine talent and
a real feel for jazz and true and personal expression—singers who really
caressed each word of a lyric and truly captured the essence of the song.
Among these, there was a suave, yet tough-looking guy named Mike Batis,
who sang "Somewhere over the Rainbow" with such subtle conviction and
poignancy that you believed every bit of the longing he was feeling. Another great singer was Pamela Stonebrook, a tall and willowy blonde who
made us all believe it when she sang "Anywhere I Hang My Hat Is Home."
And then there was the MC and organizer of the showcases, an imposing,
gentle giant of a man named David Walker, who was quite simply one of
the best ballad singers I ever worked with. It's sad to think none of these
three fine vocalists ever received the recognition and exposure they so
richly deserved. Yet there it is: the reality of the music business. Three of
the best singers you never heard of . . .

WHAT EXACTLY IS A JAZZ SINGER?

Just as there is a wide variety of instrumental styles in music, there are
also a great many ways to sing a song. As listeners, we have many vocal
genres to choose from as we experience music in our daily lives. We may
enjoy great opera singers like Audra McDonald, folk singers like Jonathan
Edwards, blues singers like B.B. King, rockers like Bonnie Raitt, or totally
uncategorizable singers like Tom Waits, Delbert McClinton, Norah Jones,
and Queen Latifah. All have wonderful gifts to offer us; however, jazz singing, by way of comparison, has its own unique approach to the art of the
song that is very much worth exploring.

There has always been a lot of debate about what makes a vocalist a
"jazz" singer. One camp suggests that someone who sings jazz should also
be able to use his or her voice as a vehicle for improvisation; another camp
says that it's all in the phrasing—that a jazz singer is someone who can
swing the lyrics and syncopate the phrasing of the words in such a way that

a performance would capture the essence of jazz. Who is right? Let's look briefly at the validity of each point of view.

When a singer finishes singing the lyrics to a song and follows those lyrics with a wordless, horn-like solo, this is called "scat singing," or "scatting." Legend has it that the first scat singing happened quite accidentally, when a singer forgot the lyrics to a song and substituted nonsense syllables, just to be able to get through a performance. Whether or not this is true remains to be seen; however, it is what scat singing is all about—when the singer uses his or her voice as a musical instrument, rather than as a way to tell a story using both music and words. While it may be true that scatting existed as a novelty effect somewhat earlier, the first singer to really put scat singing on the jazz map was Louis Armstrong, beginning back in 1926 with his scat vocal on a song called "Heebie Jeebies." He improvised a solo, not using his trumpet or cornet, but his voice. That solo and his subsequent scat vocals created a foundation that scatting singers have been building upon ever since.

Pops was a great jazz singer in another way—one that typifies the flip side of that coin where the singer doesn't attempt to scat sing on any given song. He or she merely pays great attention to how to phrase the lyrics in such a way that they swing. More specifically, a jazz vocalist may sing a series of words that sound as though they might have been played by, say, a trumpeter (like Armstrong) or saxophonist. That might mean singing a little bit behind or ahead of the beat or singing some of the words using syncopated rhythms (see chapter 2 for a brief review of rhythm and syncopation). It might also mean altering some of the original notes in the melody just as a horn player, for example, might do in his or her statement of it. In these ways, a singer is actually improvising by making up new ways to sing the melody, so much so that sometimes the end result may be an instantaneous "countermelody," one that might not even sound like the original song. For example, listen via the Internet to the great Billie Holiday sing the song "Them There Eyes," from her July 5, 1939, Columbia Records recording. Unlike the original notes on the sheet music, "Lady Day" sings:

> I fell in love with you, first time I looked into
> [sings these words mostly on one note] them there eyes.
>
> You had a certain little cute way of flirtin' with
> [this line also] them there eyes.

They make me feel so happy,
[almost speaks these two words] They make me feel so blue;

I'm fallin'—no stallin',
fallin' in a great big way for you.

My heart is jumpin', you started somethin',
[speaks previous three words] with them there eyes.

You'd better look out, little brown eyes, if you're wise.

They sparkle—they bubble,
. . . get you in a lot of trouble. [omits "They're gonna . . ."]

Ahhhhhhhhhh, Baby . . .
[somewhere between speaking and singing] Them there eyes . . .

Music and Lyrics by Maceo Pinkard, William Tracy, and Doris Tauber
© 1930 Bourne Co.

After the tenor saxophone, trumpet, and alto saxophone solos, Lady Day reenters with the melody and sings it a completely different way, altering the notes and rhythms from both the original and the way she sang it before the solos. This is the product of a highly creative mind at work. There is no scat singing here, nor does there have to be. Billie's genius, like Louis Armstrong's, was that she created instantaneous variations in both the melody and the rhythm of this and many other songs. And she swung relentlessly and effortlessly every time.

FRANK SINATRA, TONY BENNETT: JAZZ SINGERS?

It is an indisputable fact that Frank Sinatra and Tony Bennett are two of the most revered singers in the history of American popular music. But are they jazz singers? Neither one is a scat singer—even Sinatra's "Doo-be-doo-be-doo's" don't really contain the basic elements of scatting. However, both have recorded with many of jazz's greatest musicians, most notably Sinatra with Duke Ellington and Count Basie, and Bennett with the Basie band and pianist Bill Evans.

Without a doubt, Frank Sinatra embodied the spirit of jazz in his choice of songs and, most important, in the way he sang them. His approach to a song was relaxed, and his fusing of melody and lyrics was flawless.

Sometimes singers talk about "breath control"; how much breath do you need to sing one phrase, before you have to take another breath? Sinatra was a master of breathing, and you will never hear him on any recording struggling to take in air at the end of a phrase; he made singing sound utterly effortless. Have a look at this master singer at work on YouTube in a segment called "Frank Sinatra in the Studio, 1965" as he records "It Was a Very Good Year" before an in-studio audience. He sings with the same control and ease that trumpeter Miles Davis mastered in the latter's lyrical work with arranger Gil Evans in the late '50s.

Tony Bennett stands shoulder-to-shoulder with Sinatra in similar ways. Like the latter, Bennett has a rich voice and a penchant for knowing which songs to include in his gigantic repertoire. And also like Sinatra, his phrasing is relaxed, assured, and always swinging. Neither man merely stood in front of a large or small band and sang; they made themselves part of the music by listening to their accompanying musicians and capturing the overall feeling of the performance.

And Tony Bennett continues to deliver these qualities even today. At this writing, Bennett is 87 years young and continues to explore unique ways to present his song stylings, most notably in his recent series of genre-bending duet recordings with a wide variety of singers from country, pop, and rock genres, including James Taylor, k. d. lang, Tim McGraw, Willie Nelson, Paul McCartney, Aretha Franklin, Lady Gaga, the late Amy Winehouse, and many others. Bennett clearly inspires these fine song stylists to greater heights by his mere presence and staggering ability to make every song he sings sound like it was written especially for him.

So are Frank Sinatra and Tony Bennett jazz singers? A fine singer from Los Angeles by the name of Julie Kelly suggested to me recently that both men are beyond category. They simply are who they are, and rather than attempt to pigeonhole them into one stylistic box or another, we should just sit back, relax, and enjoy their musical offerings. At the end of the day, that's really not a bad idea.

WHERE DID JAZZ SINGING COME FROM?

In chapter 3 of this book we suggested that during the time of slavery, field hollers were often made up largely of a form of "call and response" that was established between a singer and those who responded to him or her.

We suggested further that this call-and-response approach was also commonplace in the black Baptist churches, most notably in the South. The spirit of jazz in its infancy loomed over the fields, the churches, and the revival tent meetings.

People of color sang together for a variety of reasons: to show their devotion to God and a belief that a better life was coming; to communicate encoded messages among themselves; to get through a day a little faster picking cotton in the fields; and to be able, on a much broader level, to create a sense of community in order to help them survive the tremendous oppression they faced on a daily basis. To lift every voice and sing was to signify spiritual self-worth, as well as the will to overcome cruelty and injustice.

It was upon this foundation that gospel music and spirituals, the blues, and eventually jazz, were born. The evolution of jazz singing has the blues and, to a lesser extent, African American church music at its roots. However, of the three genres, jazz singing has been the most dynamic in terms of stylistic changes, whereas the blues, for example, has basically moved back and forth from traditional acoustic to electric, rock-influenced styles. Even so, jazz and blues singing are inextricably intertwined. There are some great jazz singers who can also sing the blues, and vice versa.

What this chapter seeks to do is to give new listeners a sense of direction by introducing some of the singers who have set the gold standard for jazz singing throughout its history—men and women like Louis Armstrong and Billie Holiday, whose creativity and imagination have inspired generations of singers to follow, as well as those in more recent times whose contributions to the art of jazz singing are only beginning to be felt and recognized as important and vital to the art.

Like other chapters in this section that deal with musical instruments and their masters, this one is meant to merely open the door for new listeners, rather than to provide a comprehensive historical survey and analysis of jazz singing. The idea is to whet your appetite by offering snapshots that will hopefully entice you to visit the nearest record store or website in order to sample much of the fine vocal jazz that's out there waiting for you.

EARLY JAZZ SINGERS

The first notable jazz singers were women who came from the blues tradition. Most experienced listeners agree that Bessie Smith and Ethel Waters were the most notable. Both had powerful voices and yet paid great attention to the nuances and feelings of a song's lyrics. Bessie Smith, aside from being known primarily as a great blues singer, was also considered a jazz singer because of her ongoing musical relationships with legendary jazz musicians like Louis Armstrong and pianist James P. Johnson. In fact, even though she recorded with both men at different times, it was her emotionally powerful recording of "St. Louis Blues" in 1925 with Armstrong that is among the most memorable of early jazz vocal recordings.

"St. Louis Blues" was also recorded by Ethel Waters and showcases Waters's total immersion into the song. Like Bessie Smith, she infused the song with great depth of feeling—but she also put a lot more drama into the lyrics, half-singing and half-talking the lyrics at various times and using the kind of syncopation favored by horn players throughout. Waters, like Smith, had a commanding presence as a vocalist, yet her voice was not as husky; however, whatever she may have lacked in weightiness, she more than made up for with the imaginative way she altered the lyrics and rhythmic phrases of any given song. Listen to her rendition of "Am I Blue?" and you will hear those improvisations. Our discussion of how Billie Holiday altered a song's lyrics, melody, and phrasing should give you a pretty good indication of the influence Ethel Waters had and continues to have upon other great jazz singers who would succeed her for more than the next 90 years.

We can't leave the subject of early jazz singers without mentioning pianist/organist Thomas "Fats" Waller, whose vocals were often quite humorous in terms of both subject matter ("Your Feet's Too Big," "The Reefer Song") and tone ("Crazy 'bout My Baby"). Even though he came after Bessie Smith and Ethel Waters and was active from the late 1920s through the early '40s, Waller—along with Cab Calloway and a few others—bridged the gap between early jazz and swing vocalists. Even though he infused humor into much of his music and vocal delivery, Waller was a phenomenal pianist, and it remains a joy to hear his piano, organ, and vocals today. Whether you're faced with a gray, gloomy day or are hopelessly gridlocked in traffic, listen to some Fats Waller. He'll put a smile on your face and help you walk "on the sunny side of the street."

JAZZ VOCALISTS IN THE SWING ERA

The swing era was a time for big-band vocalists to flourish. Talented singers like Helen Forrest, Martha Tilton, Ray Eberle, Dick Haymes, and of course, Frank Sinatra traveled and recorded with the likes of Benny

Goodman, Artie Shaw, Tommy Dorsey, and Glenn Miller. The role of big-band singer was a peripheral one. When you see posed photographs of many of the big bands of the day, you'll notice that on either the left or right side of the stage sat the band's vocalist—either a man or, more often, a woman. In some cases, a band might feature both a man and a woman. The band singers would sit through a number of "instrumental" numbers (those that didn't have any vocals) and wait their turn at the microphone. If a band played four sets of music on any given evening, a portion of each set was given over to vocal features.

While all of the singers listed above were truly fine vocalists, none—with the exception of Sinatra—could really be called jazz singers, based upon our determinations of what a jazz singer may be. There were, however, a handful of great jazz singers who gained popularity and critical notice during the swing era. Frank Sinatra sang first with trumpeter Harry James's band, and then with Tommy and Jimmy Dorsey's bands, where he gained immense popularity. Of course he went on to achieve fame as one of America's greatest singers, as well as being an Academy Award–winning actor, among many other accomplishments.

Billie Holiday sang with both Count Basie and Artie Shaw, in addition to her own groups and those of pianist Teddy Wilson. The story of her incredibly difficult and tumultuous life has been the subject of a number of biographies, as well as a film named after her autobiography, *Lady Sings the Blues*. There was a youthful exuberance, sensuality, and playfulness in much of her work, which as a result of the ravages of her drug, alcohol, and relationship problems, was replaced by a kind of world-weariness that reflected itself in the diminished strength and tone quality of her voice. Even so, the Billie Holiday you hear in her 1950s recordings is darkly beautiful in its way. There has always been a feeling of truthfulness in her delivery. You got the feeling that this Billie was talking directly to you, telling her story in such a personal and, in some ways, subtly painful fashion. She has been and continues to be praised as a major figure in jazz history—a musical storyteller, and one of the most individualistic of all jazz singers.

Mildred Bailey was featured with bands led by Paul Whiteman, Benny Goodman, and by husband Red Norvo. While not as well known as Holiday, her feathery voice and her remarkable sense of swing were nonetheless very distinctive, and together with vibraphonist Norvo, the two were known as "Mr. and Mrs. Swing."

Figure 18.1. Billie Holiday, "Lady Day." Courtesy of the William P. Gottlieb Collection.

Jimmy Rushing, also known affectionately as "Mister Five-by-Five" ("five feet tall and five feet wide"), was a much-beloved jazz and blues singer who sang with Count Basie's big band steadily from 1935 to around 1950. Rushing was on many of Basie's most famous and popular recordings. After leaving Basie, he performed and, in some cases, recorded with a wide variety of jazz greats, including pianists Thelonious Monk and Dave Brubeck, and he won many jazz polls both in the United States and in Europe.

And of course, there is the magnificent Ella Fitzgerald, "The First Lady of Song," who bridged the gap between swing-era vocal stylings and bebop-influenced singing. Ella first came to the listening public's attention in the mid-'30s. Her story has a true fairy-tale quality to it: In 1934—at age 17 and nearly destitute—she entered and won a talent contest at Harlem's Apollo Theater. The following year, Ella came to the attention of drumming dynamo Chick Webb, who hired her to be the main vocalist in his big band. It was with the Webb band that Ella recorded "A-Tisket, A-Tasket," which became a million seller and catapulted her into national prominence. With the arrival of the '40s and the birth of bebop, Ella easily assimilated the language of bop into her broad musical vocabulary. She was featured with Dizzy Gillespie's big band and also began her lifelong friendship and association with the legendary jazz promoter Norman Granz, whose 1946–1957 concert tour series "Jazz at the Philharmonic" (JATP) featured many of jazz's finest performers, including Ella Fitzgerald.

Figure 18.2.   Ella Fitzgerald and Dizzy Gillespie. Courtesy of the William P. Gottlieb Collection.

In her lifetime, Ella recorded over 200 albums (including her famous "Songbook" series, which featured the music of many of our finest composers and songwriters) and was revered by both fans and critics alike. She was the recipient of many honors and awards, including the National Medal of Arts, awarded to her by President Ronald Reagan in 1987. She had a magnificent voice and fantastic technical and interpretive skills. Above all, at the heart of her singing there was unbridled joy and a true and genuine ability to "sing what she couldn't say."

JAZZ VOCALISTS IN THE BEBOP ERA

As mentioned previously, Ella Fitzgerald (see figure 18.2) helped build the bridge for us that extends stylistically from swing to bebop. She was one of the first bebop scat singers, and she was able to hone her skills working with bop master Dizzy Gillespie and as a member of the JATP touring groups. Another pioneering bebop vocalist was a man named Lee Brown, who was better known as Babs Gonzales. He was a tireless promoter of this new music and epitomized its hipness both musically and visually. Because of his quirky character, Gonzales became more of a bop "character" to the listening public, rather than a singer. In the latter arena, he was a bit more limited and excelled more as a scat singer and "personality," rather than as an accomplished vocalist.

In addition to Ella, there are some notable female singers who appeared beginning in the late '40s, who were influenced by the radical break with swing-era jazz and in turn had a definite impact upon the art of jazz singing from that time forward. One such singer was Sarah Vaughan, who could not only scat sing excellently—and did so with bebop greats such as Bird and Diz—but who was equally at ease singing up-tempo tunes as well as ballads from the Great American Songbook. There seemed to be nothing Sarah (or "Sassy," as she was called by her fellow musicians and her fans) couldn't do. Later in her career, she expanded her repertoire to include songs by rock icons like the Beatles and by Brazilian stars like Antonio Carlos Jobim, as well as collaborations with Count Basie, Stan Getz, and Milton Nascimento.

Another fine singer worth hearing is Anita O'Day, who was often called a "musician's singer," in that she was a favorite among musicians. Anita had a cool and totally evolved style that was outwardly relaxed yet intensely

**Figure 18.3.   Sarah Vaughan, New York, 1946.
Courtesy of the William P. Gottlieb Collection.**

swinging at the same time. Her first important gig was with drummer Gene Krupa's big band in the early '40s, where Anita, together with trumpeter Roy Eldridge, recorded an instant jazz hit called "Let Me Off Uptown." Following Benny Goodman's lead, Krupa had a racially mixed band, and it was a daring yet ultimately beautiful musical moment to have a swinging white female vocalist and a great black trumpet jazz giant collaborate on a song that would become immensely popular for years to come.

Anita O'Day was not only an extraordinary singer but also an equally amazing human being. Like her idol Billie Holiday, Anita battled drug addiction and almost died from a heroin overdose in 1967. Remarkably, she kicked the habit completely and went on to resume her life as a jazz singer; she sang until her death in 2006 at age 87. Her autobiography, *High Times, Hard Times*, is an intimate window into her personal and musical lives, as well as a firsthand chronicle of jazz in both the late-swing and bebop eras. A few years after her death, Anita was the subject of an award-winning, Grammy-nominated documentary called *Anita O'Day: The Life of a Jazz Singer*. Anita O'Day lived "the jazz experience," and we are fortunate to be able to see and hear her artistry and to read about the jazz life in her own words.

Another female song stylist who can stand shoulder to shoulder with those discussed so far is Dinah Washington, who was nicknamed "The Queen of the Blues"—a misleading moniker, especially since of all the singers profiled thus far (with the possible exception of Sarah Vaughan), Dinah was the most versatile in terms of mastery of a number of diverse styles. She was a powerful jazz and blues singer, but also an excellent pop singer as well. Dinah was an extremely effective rhythm and blues "crossover" artist, which meant that in addition to her career as a jazz vocalist, she excelled at R & B. In fact, Dinah won a Grammy in 1959 for her rendition of "What a Difference a Day Makes." Her voice had a beautiful urgency to it, and her phrases were articulate yet bluesy—her sound was all her own, and like Ella, Sarah, and Anita, she had the gift of an immediately identifiable sound.

There were other fine vocalists who thrived during the bebop era. Nat "King" Cole and Mel Tormé were both excellent musicians before becoming known as jazz singers. Tormé was an accomplished drummer, and Nat Cole was a fine pianist who played with many great jazz giants, including Lester Young and Lionel Hampton. Both men had exceptionally smooth singing styles, and because of their excellent musicianship, they were able to forge solid jazz and popular music styles. Tormé was called "The Velvet Fog," due to his smoky but pure tenor voice, and Cole had a silky smooth, easily identifiable approach; as a result both won many fans, especially Cole, who had his own television show on NBC in 1956–1957.

Other great jazz singers emerged in the '40s and '50s: the great baritones Billy Eckstine (whose big band included Charlie Parker and Dizzy Gillespie), Joe Williams (one of Count Basie's best-loved vocalists), Johnny Hartman (a great balled singer and the only singer to share album honors in the early '60s with John Coltrane), and Mark Murphy, who is perhaps the most distinctive of this quartet of singers. Murphy bends and stretches notes and phrases as though they were made of putty. His voice lies somewhere in the baritone-bass range and has a dusky, streetwise quality to it that is irresistible. A recipient of multiple awards and honors, Murphy has retired from touring and recording. His website sums him up perceptively:

> Listening to Mark Murphy, you will instantly understand that this artist is singing his life. The words, the notes, the intention of the song are all a part of the artist himself. (www.markmurphy.com)

ALL ALONE: A FEW WORDS ABOUT CHET BAKER

None but the lonely heart
can know my sadness;
alone and parted,
far from joy and gladness.

—Excerpt from a poem by Johann Wolfgang von Goethe

The classical composer Tchaikovsky set Goethe's poem to music, and the end result is something both haunting and beautiful. If we come to believe that the words and notes of a song are part of who an artist is, then we must talk about Chet Baker, since it is impossible to separate Baker the person from Baker the musician. And the words "haunting" and "beautiful" come to mind when listening to Chet's singing. There has never been anyone quite like him in the jazz world.

A bit of background: Chet Baker's life was like something out of a storybook—one with an unhappy ending. A native of Yale, Oklahoma, he migrated at an early age to California and achieved fame in the early '50s as a jazz sensation and an embodiment of "cool," thanks largely to his talent and his boyish good looks. Chet played with the original Gerry Mulligan quartet, a pianoless group that became a sensation, which led to his winning the *DownBeat* jazz poll in 1954, placing him ahead of jazz icon Miles Davis. The world, in short, was at Chet's door. However, his lifelong addiction to heroin was ultimately his undoing and was the cause of his slow and painful decline as both an artist and as a human being. Chet Baker died in 1988 as the result of a mysterious fall from a second-story window ledge in a hotel in Amsterdam—the terrible end to a once-promising life. There have been a number of biographies about Baker, as well as a film documentary called *Let's Get Lost*, in which he took part.

The astonishing thing about Baker's singing is how closely tied it was to his trumpet playing, in terms of both his delicate and almost fragile sound as vocalist and trumpeter, and the quality of his soloing as an instrumentalist and a scat singer. Unlike other jazz singers who used syllables or nonsense words in their scat solos—phrases like "ool-ya-coo" and "dee-ba-doo-bop"—Baker truly sounded like he was playing trumpet with his voice. That is, his scat singing seemed more natural and less contrived than that of many of his contemporaries. Pianist Phil Markowitz, who made some extraordinary quartet records with Baker in Paris in the late '70s, had this to say about working with him:

> Working with Chet Baker was an apprenticeship of the highest order. We were young and he took us on, and was patient and taught by example. Perfect phrasing, time feel like a taught rope, and the most intent listener I have ever seen on the bandstand. No show—just pure intense feeling and concentration on the task at hand. His singing was an exact clone of his playing. Even at the older age, still the ebullient young tone and feel that he had earlier in his youth.

Like Billie Holiday's later work, Chet's vocals throughout his career took on an aura of melancholy that has touched the hearts of many listeners. His early recording of "I Get along without You Very Well" in the mid-'50s and his heartbreaking rendition of "She Was Too Good to Me" over two decades later sound very much like someone who had indeed lived some very sad moments. Hearing Baker sing songs like these provides us with a window into the heart of sadness. "None but the lonely heart" are accurate words that describe a singer who truly stands alone in the world of song.

WE'RE HIP: DAVE FRISHBERG AND BOB DOROUGH

I'm hip. I'm no square.
I'm alert, I'm awake, I'm aware.

From "I'm Hip" © 1964 (renewed), Swiftwater Music/Aral Music
Lyrics: Dave Frishberg, Music: Bob Dorough

By now, it should be obvious that jazz mirrors the feelings of those who create it, as well as those who listen to and experience it. We also know that it runs the gamut of emotions, and can be sad, wistful, contemplative, angry, happy, and even silly. While many songs that jazz singers include in their repertoire have been written by others, there is a small number of artists who both write and perform their own work. Two of the most respected singer-songwriters in jazz are Dave Frishberg and Bob Dorough. And as their song attests, both are "alert . . . awake . . ." and "aware," and are two of the liveliest and most imaginative treasures in the world of jazz tunesmiths.

Dave Frishberg is a diminutive and rather professorial-looking gentleman; however, as a pianist, he can swing the doors off a barn, and as a writer of songs, he has few peers. Born in Minnesota in 1933, Frishberg moved to New York City in 1957 and found work as a solo pianist. He ultimately wound up playing with many of New York's finest, including saxophonists Al Cohn, Zoot Sims, and Ben Webster; drummer Gene Krupa; and singer Carmen McRae. A move to Los Angeles in 1971 brought Frishberg squarely into the city's legendary jazz scene, where he ultimately became quite popular among both musicians and listeners. While his skills as a pianist were considerable, it was ultimately his songwriting and vocal renderings of his songs that really put Frishberg on the map.

Many of Frishberg's songs are left-of-center, witty, and playful, even though they may deal with both the lighter and darker sides of the human condition. The titles of his songs are often offbeat as well, including "I'm Hip" (in collaboration with Bob Dorough's music), "Excuse Me for Living" (sarcasm raised to new heights), "My Attorney Bernie" (a satirical look at lawyers' lifestyles), "Too Long in L.A." (about the nightmare of the city's freeway system and the diminishing quality of day-to-day living in the Golden State), and one of his most famous songs, "Van Lingle Mungo," in which all of the lyrics are made up of the names of baseball players.

While he is arguably a critically acclaimed master of musical wit, Frishberg has written some attractive ballads as well. Most notable among them is a song called "You Are There," one of the most touching songs ever written about love, longing, and perhaps loss. For this song, Frishberg's words have been linked to a melody written by the legendary composer/arranger Johnny Mandel. One of the loveliest and most poignant renditions of this song—one well worth seeking out—was recorded by singer Irene Kral and pianist Alan Broadbent on an album on Choice Records called *The Gentle Rain*. It is considered by many to be among Dave Frishberg's finest songs. The Kral album is available in a variety of places on the Internet, as is Frishberg's own lovely version on his live duo album with Dorough called *Who's on First?* (Blue Note Records).

Like Dave Frishberg, Bob Dorough is a gifted singer/songwriter whose work is by turns wickedly funny and sweetly heartfelt. Frishberg speaks of Dorough with admiration:

I've always been impressed by the excellence of his work. He doesn't know how to write bad. He's just a terrific writer, and very intent upon being excellent. (*Jazz Times*, January–February 2001)

Figure 18.4.   Bob Dorough. Courtesy of Garth Woods.

Bob Dorough is sort of the Willie Nelson of jazz singer/songwriters. At age 88, he is ageless, energetic, audaciously funny, and he exhibits an effusive sense of joy and happiness about his life in music. Like Frishberg, he is a trenchant observer of the human condition and all of the foibles and follies that go along with it. Bob is a country boy from Cherry Hill, Arkansas, who brings new meaning to hipness; that is, Bob is "hip" without even trying.

Interlude: Bobbin' Along

The first time I met Dorough was at the Deer Head Inn, northeastern Pennsylvania's venerable old jazz club. I was new to the area, having relocated recently from Los Angeles, and wanted to check out what I had understood to be one of America's oldest jazz venues—and a favorite destination of great players coming out from New York City and Philadelphia. The Deer Head was also known as a great watering hole for "locals" like Bob Dorough, Phil Woods, Dave Liebman, Bill Goodwin, and other jazz greats.

Even though I've forgotten who was playing there that night, I remember the ponytailed guy at the door, collecting the cover charge. I also remember saying something to him like "You know, your voice sounds really familiar," to which he thrust out his hand and said, "Bob Dorough!" I said something dumb, like "Are you the club's regular gatekeeper?" Bob laughed heartily and said, "Only when they can't get anyone else."

Here was the man behind the legend, the guy who was one of the only vocalists ever invited to sing two of his original songs on a 1962 Miles Davis record and whose composition "Devil May Care" was also recorded by the great trumpeter around that time. He was also the musical director, composer, and performer for the immensely popular kids' television show *Schoolhouse Rock!* in the '70s and '80s. (Remember learning the multiplication tables set to music?) And here he was, taking my $12. That night was the beginning of a treasured friendship and some real musical adventures, which have included playing duo (thanks to a no-show bass player) for a fundraiser promoting the arts; singing and scatting a tune with him at the Deer Head's weekly jam session; and working with him in the recording studio, playing drums on his "We the People" project. Bob is an easygoing, regular kind of guy who happens to possess enormous musical talent. He's a poet, a two-fisted pianist, a teacher, and above all, a witty and compassionate man who's a pleasure to be around. Most of all, he's ageless, and his songs are timeless gifts that keep on rewarding you each time you hear them.

After graduating from the University of North Texas, Bob migrated to New York City at the beginning of the '50s, where he immersed himself in that city's dynamic jazz scene, as both a pianist and a singer. Twenty or so years down the road came the phenomenon of *Schoolhouse Rock!* where Dorough's jazzy voice and music helped countless kids learn—among other things—their multiplication tables, with catchy, funny songs like "Naughty Number Nine" and "My Hero Zero." Dorough has a special rapport with kids of all ages, and he never fails to inspire and spread pure joy during all his performances.

One of the things that makes Bob Dorough so unique is the quality of his voice. He bends and changes pitches in unpredictable places; he whispers, grumbles, chortles, sings falsetto—he even speaks his lyrics at times, rather than singing them. And he makes it all seem like he's singing only for you, as though he might be sitting on the back porch with you after dinner, spinning a tale or two about life's ups and downs. Part of the attractiveness in Bob's voice and delivery comes from his background. The regional twang in his voice—like that of earlier singer-songwriter Georgia-born Johnny Mercer—has a pleasing quality in the way that it combines hip jazz phrasing and rural folksiness.

Both Dave Frishberg and Bob Dorough have created their own little corner of the jazz world, and taken either separately or together (as in their live duo concert recording mentioned above), they offer many hours of pleasure for listeners who enjoy stylish jazz singing and songwriting.

BEYOND CATEGORY: A HANDFUL OF GREAT JAZZ SINGERS

As we have discovered, there have been a great many individualists who have made their mark in the jazz world by following their own special paths. To try to fit these creative artists into a comfortable stylistic compartment is a futile effort at best, since some artists are completely beyond category. This is especially true in the world of jazz singing, which boasts a remarkable variety of vocalists, beginning—as we've seen—with Louis Armstrong and Billie Holiday. While we've met some real individualists thus far in this chapter, there are many others who are worth a listen, due largely to the original and evocative way each approaches the art of the song. Here is a handful for your consideration.

In 2012, Sheila Jordan was honored by the National Endowment for the Arts by being named a Jazz Master. Such a prestigious award has been a long time coming for Jordan, now in her eighth decade. Jordan has always been a complete individualist, and her uncompromising approach to jazz singing had, until recently, won her a small but devoted following. Jordan has the ability to move from one note to another in truly unexpected ways. She swoops and glides in and around the chord changes like the eagle in Tennyson's poem: up into the airstream, then diving into the abyss, only to swoop up once more. Even that's not an accurate description of Jordan's imaginative way with words and music. It has always been and will always be her own unique vision of singing. As of late, the listening public has finally begun to catch up to her visionary creativity. Her work with pianist Steve Kuhn's quartet and especially her adventurous duet recordings with bassists Harvie Swartz (aka Harvie S) and Cameron Brown are great examples of Jordan's art, yet they are only the tip of her creative iceberg.

Another totally original singer, Britain's Norma Winstone, came into view in the late 1960s jazz scene in London, at Ronnie Scott's legendary jazz club. Even though Winstone began her career singing more conventional material, she gradually became involved in more exploratory kinds of improvised music, including "wordless vocals," where her voice—like Kay Davis's voice on Duke Ellington's 1945 version of "Mood Indigo"— was used primarily to provide additional tone colors in combination with other instruments. However, Winstone did more than just sing wordless melodies; she also improvised freely. This was a radical departure in jazz singing, since it was not scatting but the creation of "free-form" singing— that is, vocal improvising without the restraints of chord changes or even syncopated phrases. In addition to developing and mastering this technique, Winstone has also become an important lyricist, creating the words for original compositions by a variety of well-known jazz artists.

Betty Carter was one of the most expressive singers in jazz and also one of the most distinctive, especially in how she was able to alter a melody, substituting her note choices for the notes in the original song.

Such alterations can be quite risky if a singer tries to substitute one note for another and lands on the wrong note—say, a B-natural instead of a B-flat. The end result might sound out of place or "sour," even to the inexperienced ear. Betty Carter was so musically skilled that she could give a standard song like "Misty" an almost completely different melody, so much so that the only way a listener would know it was the same song would be to hear the lyrics.

Betty's road to jazz's upper echelon was a long one, often fraught with frustration at not being able to fully pursue her musical vision. While she was much loved by fellow musicians and experienced listeners, Betty was confounded by critics who couldn't grasp what she was doing as a jazz singer. As a result, she struggled for a number of years to be heard and appreciated as a true jazz artist. Her integrity paid off when she was invited to collaborate with singer Ray Charles. That collaboration yielded some fine recordings, most notably their rendition of "Baby, It's Cold Outside," which was an enormous hit and catapulted Betty Carter into national prominence. A well-known and highly respected jazz vocalist over the years, Betty was awarded a National Medal of Arts in 1997 by President Bill Clinton. She passed away a year later, but she has left us with a substantial body of work to enjoy, both on CD and video.

Like Betty Carter, Jimmy Scott didn't become well known overnight as a jazz singer. Unlike many of today's musical personalities from all genres, Scott (as well as many of the other singers profiled in this chapter) did not have the kind of support from a strong management machine, which has become almost always necessary for success (frequent bookings, substantial CD and MP3 sales, and effective publicity, among other things). In fact, it took Jimmy Scott over 70 years to achieve national prominence. He has recently been the subject of books and magazines, as well as a documentary called *Jimmy Scott: If You Only Knew*, which won an Audience Award in 2004.

Scott's voice is pure magic. Because a disability limited his growth to just under five feet and also caused a lack of normal physiological development, Scott's vocal range is somewhere in the region of alto, rather than the usual tenor or baritone ranges common to adult male singers; however, the undeniable beauty of his voice and the great emotion with which he renders a song have been known to bring listeners to tears. To put it another way, Jimmy strikes a real and true chord with all who hear him. He reaches down deeply into us and helps us connect with ourselves—our happiness, as well as our personal losses. His Grammy-nominated comeback album, called *All the Way*, was a critical sensation and thrust him squarely into his rightful place as one of jazz's most endearing voices. Jimmy Scott has been called "The Golden Voice of Jazz." Listen to him and you will immediately know why that description is accurate.

Other great song stylists deserving wider recognition are Abbey Lincoln and Nina Simone, both of whom, in addition to more conventional repertoire, wrote and sang songs protesting racial and gender inequality long before it became a widespread practice. Both Lincoln and Simone were also incredible song stylists who knew how to use body language as well as evocative lyrics to be able to tell a musical story. Another is Irene Kral, whose lovely alto voice lent itself well to ballads, and whose stunningly beautiful duo albums with pianist Alan Broadbent remain jazz classics long after her untimely death in 1978. Like Dinah Washington before her, Nancy Wilson excels in a broad range of styles in addition to jazz, including blues and pop tunes. Two of her most popular and best-selling recordings continue to be *The Swingin's Mutual* with pianist George Shearing and *Nancy Wilson/Cannonball Adderley*, two classic examples of how in tune a versatile and accomplished singer can be with great instrumentalists. Wilson also hosted her own Emmy-winning television show in the '70s, and she has been the host of National Public Radio's Jazz Profiles series since 1995. Finally, there is Shirley Horn, who was one of the most exquisite ballad singers of all time. Like Betty Carter, Horn was also an accomplished pianist who led a trio for years—much of that time in her native Washington, D.C. Trumpet legend Miles Davis, upon hearing Horn, invited her to open for him at the Village Vanguard in New York City. They remained friends for years, and in 1990, Miles appeared on Shirley's album *You Won't Forget Me*. And she certainly didn't. Her 1999 album *I Remember Miles* won a Grammy Award for Best Vocal Performance.

A WORD OR TWO ABOUT VOCAL GROUPS

Whenever people get together to sing, each voice becomes part of a whole and has the responsibility to blend with the other voices in order to create an overall sound—much like playing a chord on the piano. Some voices carry the melody and others the harmonies. This is true whether we're listening to the Mormon Tabernacle Choir, a barbershop quartet like Old School, a doo-wop group like Little Anthony and the Imperials, or a rock group like Crosby, Stills, and Nash—and of course, jazz vocal groups, which, like vocal groups in the post–doo-wop rock world, weren't as common as those in other genres.

Large and small jazz vocal groups have flourished in recent years on college and university campuses, and there are schools like the University of Miami in Florida that have maintained excellent programs for years. It may be fair to suggest that group jazz vocalizing in higher education may well have been a healthy by-product of the earlier innovators in the field. Three such early vocal groups were the Rhythm Boys, which featured Bing Crosby; the Pied Pipers, which was both a vocal group featured with Tommy Dorsey's Orchestra and a backup group for Frank Sinatra; and the Mel-Tones, a group led by the prodigious singer-instrumentalist Mel Tormé. All thrive on both group harmonies and solos from each member.

The year 1957 saw a distinctive rebirth of the jazz vocal group with the advent of Lambert, Hendricks, and Ross, which featured the collective and solo voices of Dave Lambert, Jon Hendricks, and Annie Ross. Each member of the trio complemented the other in terms of style, and their ability to blend their voices was remarkable. They often engaged in vocalese, which is essentially putting words to previously recorded instrumental solos (the vocalese style was created initially by singer Eddie Jefferson and further developed by King Pleasure). Annie Ross's most famous vocalese effort was her composition "Twisted," in which she put words to a composition written by the bebop tenor saxophonist Wardell Gray, and to his saxophone solo as well. Lambert, Hendricks, and Ross won a Grammy Award for their *High Flying* album in 1962. Ross departed later that year and was replaced by Yolande Bavan. There were three more recordings before the trio finally disbanded in 1964.

Other vocal groups followed, including France's Swingle Singers, whose eight voices often performed *a cappella* (which means "without accompaniment") or sometimes with only a bassist and a drummer. Their precursor, the Double Six of Paris, utilized six singers and multitracked ("overdubbed") additional voices to double the number of voices, giving their recorded performances a choir-like effect. Singers Unlimited was the brainchild of vocal arranger Gene Puerling and began as a quartet of voices created to record commercials. Ultimately, they moved into the performance arena, as an a cappella group, featuring Puerling's brilliant and now-classic vocal arrangements. They also recorded with a variety of musicians and utilized multitracking as well, to create a wide range of tonal colors and moods. The Manhattan Transfer, an enormously popular American group formed in the early '70s, was a quartet of singers who also used overdubbing and added synthesizers as well. Their version of Weather Report's "Birdland" became an instant classic and won the group a Grammy. Finally, the New York Voices, unlike the others profiled, has followed a different path—one that doesn't feature the vocalese approach of words attached to solos. Instead, the group favors lyrics, scat solos, and horn-like vocal ensemble backgrounds and riffs. So a listener might hear a lead vocalist singing a melody or scatting a solo, while the voices in the background support the singer, much as a sax or brass section in a big band would play behind a soloist. The group also uses voices to create entire ensemble passages—another common characteristic of big-band music.

THE SCENE TODAY: SOME ESTABLISHED VOICES

The downturn in the recording industry, which has contributed to the slow demise of record companies, has come about largely as a result of our ability to download music from the Internet. The record-buying public is fast becoming the downloading public. Reacting to this trend, many musicians across genres have taken it upon themselves to produce commercially available CDs and MP3 downloads. This means that the artist is financially responsible for producing the project—from the recording to the layout and design of the disc or download. This phenomenon has been widespread, particularly in the independent ("indie") rock and jazz worlds.

Many jazz artists have formed their own labels or have offered their music to small, independent jazz labels. One result of this has been the ever-growing volume of jazz artists who have recorded and released their work into the world. And with that growth, as well as websites such as spotify .com, we as listeners are able to hear a much broader range of music than ever before from artists we might never have heard of otherwise. All this is a way of saying that there seem to be many more jazz vocalists on the scene today than in pre-Internet years; and as a result, this next section will offer a smattering of them, with the hope that you will further explore their music as well as the music of others you have yet to discover.

There are many wonderful male and female vocalists on the scene today, and all are worth hearing. As you experience the song stylings of whichever singers you choose, listen to each one perform in a variety of musical settings in order to get a better feel for his or her approach to jazz singing.

Among the more established of today's jazz voices are Grammy winners Al Jarreau, George Benson, and Bobby McFerrin, all of whom have highly individualistic approaches to the art of the song. Al Jarreau has a light and airy voice and pays great attention to nuance, subtlety, and feeling in his vocals. He has, over the years, gravitated toward the adult contemporary pop genre, although he is perfectly capable of more traditional approaches to jazz singing. In recent years, he has also been involved on projects promoting children's literacy through music. George Benson is, first and foremost, a skilled jazz guitarist—one who has recorded some great straight-ahead jazz records as well as some stellar collaborations with other jazz stars, including Miles Davis. Benson's Warner Brothers recording *Breezin'* was a major turning point in his career, as it featured his vocal on a song called "This Masquerade." The album topped the charts and went platinum in sales, catapulting Benson into fame and many more jazz and pop recordings. He has won 10 Grammy Awards and has been honored as a Jazz Master by the National Endowment for the Arts. Bobby McFerrin can only be described as a one-man orchestra. He can sound like Miles Davis's muted trumpet or like Armando Peraza's conga drums. His musical vision is virtually boundless; as his website puts it:

> Listening to Bobby McFerrin sing may be hazardous to your preconceptions. Side effects may include unparalleled joy, a new perspective on creativity, rejection of the predictable, and a sudden, irreversible urge to lead a more spontaneous existence. (www.bobbymcferrin.com)

McFerrin is an extraordinarily daring vocalist who is able to defy musical gravity, thanks to his superior musicianship. In 1984, before reaching national prominence, McFerrin recorded a solo voice album—no other instruments were used. He used his voice for each instrument—without any overdubbing or electronic trickery.

A breakthrough hit for him came with the release of his album *Simple Pleasures* and his song "Don't Worry, Be Happy," which consisted of McFerrin's voice overdubbed eight times. No instrumental accompaniment; all Bobby—all the way.

Over the years, Bobby McFerrin has won 10 Grammy Awards and has collaborated with the likes of pianists Chick Corea and Herbie Hancock and cellist Yo-Yo Ma. He has also been active as a conductor and works with choral groups in the United States and abroad.

The beauty and spirit of Sarah Vaughan burns brightly in the person of Dee Dee Bridgewater, whose 2011 mostly ballad release *Midnight Sun* is an extraordinary experience in heartfelt balladry. "Extraordinary" is an apt description of this artist, whose work spans almost four decades, beginning with her association with the Thad Jones/Mel Lewis Jazz Orchestra in the '70s, as well as her performances with such luminaries as Sonny Rollins, Dizzy Gillespie, and Max Roach. Much of Dee Dee's subsequent work has been praised by critics and listeners alike. She has recorded many albums, many of which she produced herself.

Bridgewater's artistic energies have not been limited to jazz. She has had extensive experience as an actor/performer in musical theater and won a Tony Award in 1975 for her performance in *The Wiz*. She is also a Goodwill Ambassador for the United Nations in that body's drive to end world hunger—and as if that weren't enough, Dee Dee has hosted National Public Radio's *Jazz Set* for over a decade.

THE SCENE TOMORROW: SOME RECENT VOICES

Look out! There are some other fine singers on the horizon, waiting for you to discover them, so they can turn your head around. Here are some of them, in no particular order.

Dianne Reeves, in addition to coming out of the tradition of Sarah Vaughan, Carmen McRae, and other great singers of that era, puts her own spin on style by infusing her rhythm and blues roots. Four of her recordings have each won a Grammy, and she has appeared in many kinds of settings, from small groups to symphony orchestras like the Boston Pops.

Canadian Diana Krall came into prominence in the early '90s. She has a smoky contralto voice and is a very good jazz pianist. Diana studied at Berklee College of Music in Boston and with bassist Ray Brown and pianists Jimmy Rowles and Alan Broadbent in Los Angeles. Her first album was released in 1993 in Canada. Diana won a Grammy six years later for her rendition of "When I Look into Your Eyes," on the Verve album of the same name. She married Elvis Costello in 2003, and thanks to his encouragement, began writing songs as well as collaborating with him on new material. Their musical association culminated a year after their marriage with a new album of music called *The Girl in the Other Room* for the Verve label.

Roseanna Vitro exudes personality both on and off stage, and it is very clear that she loves to sing—especially with top-flight musicians like the late drummer Elvin Jones, bassists Buster Williams and Christian McBride, and pianists Kenny Werner and Fred Hersch. Her recordings represent a broad diversity of musical interests, including tributes to Ray Charles, Bill Evans, and homages to Brazilian music and the blues. Her 2011 Grammy-nominated recording is a tribute to singer-songwriter Randy Newman and is simply called *The Music of Randy Newman*. The thread that runs through all of Roseanna's recordings is the tremendous passion and vitality she puts into each performance. Whether it be a rousing blues shouter, a silky smooth bossa nova, or a burning straight-ahead tune, Roseanna is at the center of it all, the glue that holds the heart of music together.

She also served in 2009 as a Jazz Ambassador, sponsored by Jazz at Lincoln Center and the U.S. Department of State, and was awarded the same position five years earlier by the Kennedy Center for the Performing Arts, co-sponsoring with the U.S. Department of State. As a part of her ambassadorship, Roseanna performed, taught, and gave workshops internationally and, as a result, has received broad exposure as a true world-class vocalist.

Two young singers whose intriguing, eclectic, and wholly original approaches to both singing and composition are Esperanza Spalding and Gretchen Parlato. We have already profiled Spalding as an up-and-coming bassist in an earlier chapter; however, her songs and vocals are wholly original affairs and, like her bass playing and instrumental compositions, emphasize nuance and texture in addition to syncopation and groove. The mix is like a delicious *cioppino*, full of sonic flavors that will lodge themselves into your memory long after the recording has ended. A new listener—or a seasoned listener who has yet to experience Esperanza Spalding—will want to begin by listening to her "Societies," that is, her breakout disc, *Chamber Music Society*, and her funkier follow-up recording, *Radio Music Society* (both on the Heads Up label). Her vocals on both discs are light as a feather yet contain an urgency that belies their breathiness. And Spalding's rhythmic skills as a bassist inform her singing as well, allowing her to effortlessly execute syncopations that many other singers would not even begin to attempt.

Gretchen Parlato, like her friend and sometimes singing partner Esperanza Spalding, is fearless when it comes to wholly original interpretations of a standard or a classic song from the jazz repertoire. For example, elsewhere in this book, we have mentioned the Bill Evans composition "Blue in Green," as played by Miles Davis (and Evans with his trio): its moody, melancholy, and thoroughly beautiful melody and solos. Parlato has recorded a totally unique version of the song on her album, *The Lost and Found* (ObliqSound)—a rhythmic shape shifter which finds Parlato's beautiful, plaintive voice floating over the constantly morphing rhythm section, creating a stunningly and yet quietly intense effect as the song progresses. And Gretchen makes it sound easy.

Other excellent female singers recording and performing today include Cassandra Wilson, Kate McGarry, Patricia Barber, Jane Monheit, Karrin Allyson, Madeline Peyroux, Denise Donatelli, Tierney Sutton, Nancy Reed, and Julie Kelly.

The list of male jazz singers on the scene today is not quite as extensive as the roster of female vocalists; however, these are some of the more prominent gentlemen turning a phrase:

Kurt Elling, a singer whose formidable control and virtuosity have earned him a Grammy for Best Jazz Vocal Album, as well as 10 nominations, is a master of every facet of what makes a singer great. The *New York Times* referred to him as "the standout male vocalist of our time," and the *Washington Post* called him "dynamic, daring, and interesting." Elling not only sings standards but also writes and performs his own songs. He is also a master of vocalese and composes and performs his own word versions of instrumental solos, such as his utterly astonishing take on John Coltrane's "Resolution" from the latter's classic album, *A Love Supreme*. To label Elling as daring would certainly be an understatement. To call him a brilliant vocal stylist would be accurate.

A lesser known but equally appealing singer is Dwight Trible. In fact, to call him a singer is hardly an accurate description of who he really is. For sure, Dwight has a rich, full baritone voice that not only soars and glides above an ensemble, but he also knows how to "play the silence": that is, to use silent moments to give the notes he sings more emphasis, more feeling, more meaning. To call him a singer, then, is to tell only part of the story. Dwight is a poet, a spoken word performer, and an intensely spiritual man, much in the same way we think of John Coltrane as spiritual. In fact, Dwight has been a member of ex-Coltrane saxophonist Pharoah Sanders's group for some time now and adds the perfect dimension to Pharoah's transcendent musical explorations. To play music with Sanders, Trible, pianist William Henderson, and bassist Trevor Ware was one of the musical highlights of my musical and spiritual life. Dwight Trible deserves to be heard by a much wider audience. His voice and music are filled with eternal peace and hope for a better world—his message clear and his voice sweet and strong.

Other male singers worth investigating are Giacomo Gates and Kenny Washington, who both possess clear and resonant voices, and are wonderful interpreters of many great old and new songs; daring experimenters

Theo Bleckmann and JD Walter, who use electronics and other found objects in interesting and creative ways; and newcomer Gregory Porter—a name to watch and a voice to definitely hear. The future is *now*, and these vocalists, both older and younger, are out there, paving the way and building upon the traditions created by Satchmo, Lady Day, Sarah, Ella, Frank, Tony, and so many others. The singer and the song are inseparable. The music of the voices and their stories will always be with us, if we are open to the richness of the experiences that they offer us.

Getting Personal with Dwight Trible

What advice would you offer a new listener who will be experiencing your music for the first time, either in concert, on YouTube, or via one of your recordings?

For me the word "jazz" means spontaneous creativity. The advice that I would give to someone hearing me for the first time:

We cannot insist that creativity must always follow the path that we have grown accustomed to.

It's like a bird soaring free doing its own thing—a spiritual thing. Be open to it and maybe we can learn something new together.

Figure 18.5. Dwight Trible. Courtesy of J. P. Shaw.

What would be the first recording of yours that you would recommend for an initial listening experience and as a good introduction to your music?

I am attempting to give a glimpse of the sum total of my present and past life experience.

The record of mine that I would recommend is my latest: *Cosmic*.

The reason: I have struggled to get my spirit's truth on recordings as I have demonstrated and been able to achieve in a live performance setting. I don't feel that I have done it completely yet, but this record has come the closest so far.

Getting Personal with Roseanna Vitro

What advice would you offer a new listener who will be experiencing your music for the first time, either in concert, on YouTube, or via one of your recordings?

I'm not certain that you give people advice on how to listen to your music. I have found there are many elements that go into "whether" a person likes your music or not: the venue you're playing in; the band you're singing with; and the music that you're interested in at that time.

For singers especially, a lot depends on "who" the listener has been exposed to. First we're assuming that the listener likes music, or they wouldn't have put themselves in front of you or put your record on. If you're with a good band and you have a good sound system and it's a club where audiences come to listen to music, your chances are good that the listener will enjoy you. I always tell my students that you have about two songs for the audience to decide if they want to hear more or not. If you sing with conviction and you begin with an easy-to-relate-to piece, plus look at the audience to invite them in, it usually turns out pretty good. It's the same with a recording. It only takes a spot listen to a couple of tunes to determine if you enjoy the sonic sound of the singer you're listening to.

What would be the first recording of yours that you would recommend for an initial listening experience and as a good introduction to your music?

If the listener is a bebop or post-bop jazz fan, I would recommend *Softly* (1994, Concord CD), with Fred Hersch, Jay Anderson, Tom Rainey, George Coleman, Tim Ries, and Mino Cinelu. It is a nice cross section of material with a beautiful sound.

One of my most popular recordings was *Passion Dance* (1996, Telarc). There is a large cast of musicians because my husband, great recording engineer Paul Wickliffe, was closing his studio, Skyline in Manhattan. This CD was born from a jam session to say good-bye to Paul's studio, and it features many great musicians such as pianists Kenny Werner and Larry Willis, bassists Christian McBride and Ratzo Harris, drummers Elvin Jones and Clarence Penn, guitarist Vic Juris,

Figure 18.6.   Roseanna Vitro. Courtesy of John Abbott.

vibraphonist Steve Nelson, and many others. What a moment that was. Wow. I have stories on each CD.

I have recorded 12 albums with the greatest musicians in the world. Each recording is different, plus I have four tribute records: *Catchin' Some Rays: The Music of Ray Charles*, *Conviction: Thoughts of Bill Evans*, *The Time of My Life: The Music of Steve Allen*, and *The Music of Randy Newman* (the Grammy-nominated one). On each recording, whether a tribute or not, I study the music I'm interested in and choose the players that I feel would best suit my project and then work with the band or pianist to create the arrangements. So I've given my heart and my best in each case. The rest is up to the listeners' ears.

SELECTED SINGERS' WEBSITES: FROM THEN 'TIL NOW

Note: Only official sites are listed. Use Google for all others.

Louis Armstrong: www.satchmo.net
Billie Holiday: www.billieholiday.com
Ella Fitzgerald: www.ellafitzgerald.com
Anita O'Day: www.anitaodaydoc.com
Mark Murphy: www.markmurphy.com
Chet Baker: www.chetbakertribute.com
Dave Frishberg: www.davefrishberg.net
Bob Dorough: www.bobdorough.com
Sheila Jordan: www.sheilajordan.com
Jimmy Scott: www.jimmyscottofficialwebsite.org
Norma Winstone: www.normawinstone.com
Nina Simone: www.ninasimone.com
Irene Kral: www.irenekral.com
Al Jarreau: www.aljarreau.com
Bobby McFerrin: www.bobbymcferrin.com
George Benson: www.georgebenson.com
Dee Dee Bridgewater: www.deedeebridgewater.com
Dianne Reeves: www.diannereeves.com
Diana Krall: www.dianakrall.com
Roseanna Vitro: www.roseannavitro.com
Esperanza Spalding: www.esperanzaspalding.com
Gretchen Parlato: www.gretchenparlato.com
Kate McGarry: www.katemcgarry.com
Tierney Sutton: www.tierneysutton.com
Julie Kelly: www.juliekelly.com
Jane Monheit: www.janemonheitonline.com
Karrin Allyson: www.karrin.com
Denise Donatelli: www.denisedonatelli.com
Kurt Elling: www.kurtelling.com
Giacomo Gates: www.giacomogates.com
Kenny Washington: www.kennywashingtonvocalist.com
Dwight Trible: www.dwighttrible.com
Theo Bleckmann: www.theobleckmann.com
JD Walter: www.jdwalter.com
Gregory Porter: www.gregoryporter.com

RECOMMENDED READING

Note: The books included here represent only a small sampling of the many fine portraits of jazz's master singers, beginning with those whose names are synonymous with the swing era. For additional readings, visit the websites listed in the previous section and google other names in this chapter to learn more about many other excellent vocal artists who populate the jazz world.

GENERAL

Balliett, Whitney. *American Singers: Twenty-Seven Portraits in Song*. Jackson: UP of Mississippi, 2006. Print.

Crowther, Bruce, and Mike Pinfold. *Singing Jazz: The Singers and Their Styles*. San Francisco: Miller Freeman Books, 1997. Print.

Yanow, Scott. *Jazz Singers: The Ultimate Guide*. Milwaukee: Backbeat Books, 2008. Print.

Ethel Waters

Waters, Ethel, with Charles Samuels. *His Eye Is on the Sparrow: An Autobiography*. Cambridge: Da Capo Press, 1992.

Billie Holiday

Clarke, Donald. *Wishing on the Moon*. Cambridge: Da Capo Press, 2002. Print.

O'Meally, Robert. *Lady Day: The Many Faces of Billie Holiday*. Cambridge: Da Capo Press, 1991. Print.

Frank Sinatra

Hamill, Pete. *Why Sinatra Matters*. Boston: Back Bay Books, 2003. Print.

Kaplan, James. *The Voice*. New York: Anchor Books, 2011. Print.

Ella Fitzgerald

Nicholson, Stuart. *Ella Fitzgerald: The Complete Biography of the First Lady of Jazz*. Updated ed. New York: Routledge, 2004. Print.

Sarah Vaughan

Ruuth, Marianne. *Sarah Vaughan* (Black American Series). Los Angeles: Holloway House Publishing Company, 1994. Print.

Anita O'Day

O'Day, Anita, with George Eells. *High Times, Hard Times*. New York: Limelight Editions/Hal Leonard Publishing, 1989. Print.

Nat Cole

Epstein, Daniel Mark. *Nat King Cole*. Boston: Northeastern UP, 2000. Print.

Tony Bennett

Bennett, Tony. *The Good Life: The Autobiography of Tony Bennett*. New York: Pocket Books, 1998. Print.

Evanier, David. *All the Things You Are: The Life of Tony Bennett*. Hoboken: Wiley, 2011. Print.

Nina Simone

Simone, Nina, with Stephen Cleary. *I Put a Spell on You: The Autobiography of Nina Simone*. Cambridge: Da Capo Press, 1993. Print.

Jimmy Scott

Ritz, David. *Faith in Time: The Life of Jimmy Scott*. Cambridge: Da Capo Press, 2003. Print.

Chet Baker

DeValk, Jeroen. *Chet Baker: His Life and Music*. Berkeley: Berkeley Hills Books, 1989. Print.

Gavin, James. *Deep in a Dream: The Long Night of Chet Baker*. Chicago: Chicago Review Press, 2003. Print.

Johnny Hartman

Akkerman, Gregg. *The Last Balladeer: The Johnny Hartman Story*. Lanham: Scarecrow Press, 2012. Print.

19

IS JAZZ ENTERTAINMENT
OR IS IT ART?

CAN ART BE ENTERTAINING? CAN ENTERTAINMENT BE ART?

In order to even begin thinking about these questions, we need to look briefly at what we mean by the word "entertainment." According to *The Oxford English Dictionary* (aka the OED), entertainment can be defined as "the act of occupying a person's attention agreeably; amusement," and as "a thing which entertains or amuses someone, [especially] a public performance or exhibition designed to entertain people."

Now, a little definition goes a long way; it would appear that "entertainment," then, can be anything from enjoying a night at the circus, a rock concert, or a Harry Potter movie, to pleasurably savoring a performance of Shakespeare's *A Midsummer Night's Dream* or swooning at a ballerina's graceful movements during Tchaikovsky's *Swan Lake*. The latitude given to defining the concept of entertainment is enormous; however, it may well boil down to the notion that entertainment is a phenomenon that has been created expressly for the pleasure of an audience.

That being said, we must now ask ourselves another, more complex question: What is art? Turning once again to the safety of the OED, we may define art as "a pursuit or occupation in which skill is directed towards the production of a work of imagination, imitation, or design, or toward the gratification of the aesthetic senses." The OED further suggests that art may then also be seen as "the products of any such pursuit." Translating that into plain English, we may say that artists are those who creatively use imagination, as well as some manner of design or structure, in order to produce visual arts like painting and sculpture, and performing arts such as music, dance, and film and theater arts. And often, artists begin their journey under the influence of other artists—those who provide inspiration via their own artworks. And this is where imitation comes into play. Artists—especially those who are less experienced—look to other artists and artworks for inspiration—and if they're truly committed to their artistic growth, these artists will break away from their influences in order to create their own unique vision of the world.

So then, can art exist that entertains as well as evokes or pleases the senses? Can any form of art be expressly created to attract and bring a degree of pleasure to an audience? Look at paintings by the accomplished and imaginative artist Norman Rockwell, who painted many scenes depicting the smallest moments in American life. Chances are that viewing one or more of his works will be a pleasurable experience. Likewise, seeing a film like 2010's *Avatar* can bring pleasure (the story itself) and can simultaneously appeal to our aesthetic senses (the visual beauty of the film and its engaging musical score). And in the world of "popular" music, Tom Waits's *Mule Variations* and Joni Mitchell's *Blue* both offer stories of other times and places, while still providing many musical pleasures for their listeners. These are but a few examples of how art, by our definition, can in fact bring pleasure (entertainment) to those willing to spend some time with it. So at the end of the day, it may well be that art can and does entertain, and that which we know as entertainment can also be quite artistic in nature. As you might guess, the line between the two can be a blurry one at best! In the final analysis, what is important is whether or not you find the work deeply fulfilling, perhaps in a way that even you can't explain.

TWO SIDES OF THE SAME COIN: A FEW EXAMPLES OF JAZZ AS ART AND ENTERTAINMENT

Sometimes, as we have seen in the jazz world, musicians such as Louis Armstrong and Duke Ellington were both artists and entertainers; that is, they offered not only an amusing or pleasurable experience for listeners, but also the artistic creation of both written and improvised masterpieces, utilizing the building blocks that are essential to much of jazz music: melody, harmony, syncopated rhythms, and improvisation. Armstrong, for example, was very aware of his audiences and strove to both inspire and entertain them. His music and vocals were lively and quite often promoted a sense of joyousness and excitement among listeners—yet, he was a consummate virtuoso as a trumpeter and a powerful and creative soloist as well. Duke Ellington was one of America's greatest composers and led a magnificent big band. Like Armstrong, he was able—through his creative imagination—to transport listeners to faraway times and places. By creating concert pieces like "Far East Suite" and "Black and Tan Fantasy" that utilized the tonal colors of every instrument at his disposal, Ellington could take us on a musical journey to Japan, the Congo, or New Orleans, among many other locales that were the subjects of his compositions. Duke's genius was that he was also able to create swing music that would bring an audience to its feet and out into the aisles, where they would be able to dance to compositions like "Take the A-Train" and "Rockin' in Rhythm."

As we have learned in earlier chapters, Dixieland and swing styles of jazz became immensely popular forms of entertainment among people from all walks of life. Early jazz was heard in brothels, bar rooms, and dance halls, and swing-era jazz was also—if not more so—enormously popular with dancers as well as listeners. However, as we discovered in chapter 4, after the swing era had run its course in the 1940s, the music seemed to move away from the perception that it should "entertain" its audiences and move toward the notion of jazz as a bona fide art form, one that offered a new and challenging role to audiences—primarily as listeners. Beginning with bebop, jazz began serving an entirely different purpose and, over the decades, has sought to create a deeper, more lasting, and meaningful bond between musician and listener. So then, is there room for both jazz that entertains and jazz that seeks to transform its listeners in some way? And is it possible that jazz, taken as a whole, can or should do both? These are difficult questions that we may not be able to answer but should certainly be thinking about as we continue on our journey as active listeners.

There have always been areas within each era of jazz that have sought to entertain audiences as well as to evoke and inspire listeners' feelings. In the bebop era, Dizzy Gillespie most notably connected with his listeners with his on-stage antics and his often outrageous dress—but once he got their attention, it became clear that he was all about the music. Dizzy showed us that even though jazz was indeed an art form, there was no reason why you couldn't have a good time with it, either as a musician or as a listener. Later on in the 1950s and '60s, groups led by drummer Art Blakey, pianist Horace Silver, and organist Jimmy Smith, among others, played "soul" jazz, which often concentrated on funky, finger-snapping grooves. And in the '60s and '70s, avant-garde groups like Sun Ra and his Arkestra and the Art Ensemble of Chicago showed us that new and radically different music could also be visually appealing and entertaining. Still, the majority of jazz music created since the swing era focused less on entertaining audiences and more on challenging them to sit and listen. This was problematic to an extent, since audiences were used to participating as dancers, not merely sitting and listening.

JAZZ ON THE SCREEN: SOME THOUGHTS ON SIGHT AND SOUND

Jazz has been featured on film in five distinct ways.

As a Short Subject

These kinds of films were, as their name implies, not full-length features; but rather, they were "fillers," in that they—much like newsreels and cartoons—were created to offer audiences short features that would lead up to the showing of a full-length feature film. Often, a jazz performance would be the focus of the short film (which was also called a "soundie") and would feature such luminaries as Louis Armstrong, Bessie Smith, Duke Ellington, Chick Webb, Benny Goodman, and many others. You can view any number of these entertaining little films on YouTube. They are valuable as windows into the past and are often the only visual documentation we have for certain significant jazz artists.

As Part of a Larger Film

Often, feature films would incorporate jazz performances into their story lines, albeit in rather vague ways—almost as though the producers were looking for some excuse to feature jazz as a small part of the film. This was almost commonplace during the swing era, when it was not unusual to see the big bands of Benny Goodman (*Holiday Hotel*, 1939), Duke Ellington (*Cabin in the Sky*, 1943), Artie Shaw (*Dancing Co-Ed*, 1939), and Count Basie (*Swingin' the Blues*, 1941), among others.

As the Subject of a Dramatic Film

Films about jazz, and more specifically about the lives of the musicians who play it, are often "romanticized"; that is, they portray the jazz life in a fictionalized way, creating and sustaining stereotypes that lead viewers and listeners to believe that jazz musicians are, more often than not, troubled drug addicts or alcoholics who give up everything for the sake of their art. While this has been true in some cases, it is an inaccurate portrayal of jazz musicians as a whole. Some of these films include *Young Man with a Horn* (1950) and *The Man with the Golden Arm* (1956).

Other films about jazz include biographies, which vary in terms of accuracy. These include *The Benny Goodman Story* (1955), *The Gene Krupa Story* (1959), *Lady Sings the Blues* (1972), and *Bird* (1988). These last two films are about the lives of singer Billie Holiday (as portrayed by Diana Ross) and saxophonist Charlie Parker, respectively. This last film was directed by Clint Eastwood, himself a jazz aficionado and sometime pianist, and is fairly accurate in the way that it portrays Bird's short life and his brilliant contributions to jazz.

A final film that deserves mention here has been called the best film ever made about the jazz life. *Round Midnight* (1986) was made by the esteemed French director Bertrand Tavernier, and it featured the legendary saxophonist Dexter Gordon in the lead role. Gordon had no previous acting experience before tackling this part; yet he was totally believable as Dale Turner, an American jazzman who relocated to Europe where he was revered by French jazz fans. The character was based partly upon Gordon himself, as well as saxophonist Lester Young. *Round Midnight* is unique in that the cast is also peopled by real musicians including pianist Herbie Hancock, vibraphonist Bobby Hutcherson (both of whom acted in the film as well), guitarist John McLaughlin, bassist Pierre Michelot, and drummers Billy Higgins and Tony Williams. It is a beautiful film visually and reflects Tavernier's love for the music and those who play it.

As the Subject of a Documentary Film

Fortunately for jazz fans, there have been some very fine documentary films about jazz. One of the first and best of the genre is called *Jazz on a Summer's Day* (1959). Produced by Bert Stern and Aram Avakian, this film beautifully captures the legendary 1958 Newport Jazz Festival, which featured a stellar lineup of jazz greats, including Thelonious Monk, Gerry

Mulligan, Louis Armstrong, Dinah Washington, and many others. Another fine jazz documentary was called *Last of the Blue Devils* (1979). This film, which sought to capture some of Kansas City's most famous jazz musicians in their twilight years, was directed by filmmaker Bruce Ricker. Ricker also collaborated with actor/director/pianist Clint Eastwood to produce an extraordinary documentary about the extraordinary pianist and composer Thelonious Monk, called *Thelonious Monk: Straight, No Chaser* (1988). There are many other jazz documentaries that are well worth a look, including intimate profiles of Dave Brubeck, John Coltrane, Miles Davis, Art Blakey, Sun Ra, Chet Baker, Louis Armstrong, and others. And last but not least, we must include the valuable 2001 in-depth historical series, *Jazz*, by filmmaker Ken Burns—a good if not all-inclusive guide to the evolution of the music from its beginnings to fairly recent times.

As the Soundtrack for Movies and Television

Quite a few movies have featured jazz as background music, even though the story lines may not have been about jazz itself. Some examples of movies that have great jazz soundtracks are *I Want to Live* (1958), which featured saxophonist Gerry Mulligan, trumpeter Art Farmer, and trombonist Frank Rosolino; *Anatomy of a Murder* (1959), which featured a beautiful score by Duke Ellington; *The Pawnbroker* (1964), which included an exciting soundtrack composed by Quincy Jones; Spike Lee's *She's Gotta Have It* (1986), with a jazz soundtrack composed by Lee's father, the bassist Bill Lee; and the Robert Altman film *Kansas City* (1996), which included music by Count Basie and Lester Young as part of the soundtrack.

A number of television dramatic series have likewise used jazz music to heighten the intensity of the action, this time on the small screen. Jazz soundtracks for TV were fairly common in the '50s and '60s, with some of the more prominent shows being *Peter Gunn* (1958), with music by Henry Mancini; *Richard Diamond* (1957), featuring a soundtrack by Pete Rugolo; and the lesser-known *Johnny Staccato: The Jazz Detective* (1959), featuring the music of Elmer Bernstein. All three of these series featured some of the greatest jazz musicians who were prominent in both the studio and club scenes in Los Angeles during those years. Many television aficionados credit the jazz soundtracks for much of the effectiveness and success of each series, with the *Peter Gunn* shows being the most critically acclaimed.

BREEZIN': IS SMOOTH JAZZ REALLY JAZZ?

You hear it when you're on hold for 20 minutes with the phone company. You hear it on elevators, and in department stores, restaurants, and car dealerships. You hear it on soundtracks for movies. There are radio stations whose playlists are dedicated solely to "smooth jazz." So what then is it? Let's have a look.

The history of this genre of music may well have begun sometime in the mid-1960s when jazz record producer Creed Taylor and others collaborated with the eminent and innovative guitarist Wes Montgomery, on a series of projects that featured Montgomery playing songs by the Beatles, Simon and Garfunkel, Burt Bachrach, and other pop performers and songwriters of the day. Often, he played only the melody of each song without really improvising, and the recordings were "sweetened" with string and/ or horn section backgrounds to make them sound fuller and perhaps more commercial. Many jazz listeners and critics saw these efforts as being far beneath Montgomery's masterful jazz playing, and he was accused of "selling out," that is, fashioning and recording material that would be suitable for airplay on AM radio—which would conceivably boost record sales and provide a more lucrative living for Montgomery. In any case, other musicians who were interested in earning more money than any jazz club could offer jumped on the bandwagon and began recording similar albums. Trumpeters Freddie Hubbard and Chet Baker, saxophonist Stanley Turrentine, and especially guitarist George Benson—all well-known and respected jazz musicians—recorded for a variety of record labels that attempted to cash in on what appeared at that time to be a trend that featured jazz greats interpreting pop songs. At worst, the recordings were dreary, and at best they only minimally compromised the integrity of the artist being recorded.

With the advent of jazz-rock fusion music, the concept of playing funky, often danceable grooves seeped into the smooth jazz genre. However, whereas fusion music also emphasized rhythmic complexity, harmonic density, and the often daring use of electronics, smooth jazz remained "smooth" in nature, offering uncomplicated, unobtrusive, almost polite grooves undergirding simple melodies and harmonies. Unlike fusion music or acoustic jazz—or many other forms of music, for that matter—smooth jazz does not demand much of the listener. This is not to say that it is not "good" music. Duke Ellington suggested that there are only two kinds of music—good music and "the other kind." He was also purported to have said that if it feels good and sounds good, then it *is* good. So then, it's unfair for some diehard jazz fans to accuse smooth jazz of being "the other kind" of music and to label its practitioners as insipid, bland jazz wannabes. On the contrary, smooth jazz musicians such as saxophonists Dave Koz and Kenny Gorlick (aka "Kenny G"), guitarists Earl Klugh and Stanley Jordan, and keyboardists David Benoit and Jeff Lorber are all accomplished musicians who have elected to compose and play this style of music. The question is why. Do smooth jazz musicians play it for the pure joy and love of doing so? Or is turning a significant profit at the core of their decision to play it? Do these questions really even matter, if we take to heart Duke Ellington's perception about what "good" music is?

The larger issue regarding smooth jazz is whether it is jazz at all. There has been an inclination to call this music "adult contemporary pop," which is as misleading as it is vague, when you consider that "adults" these days (anyone older than 25—a totally arbitrary designation at best) may listen to anyone from the Beatles or Joni Mitchell or Crosby, Stills, and Nash to Pink Floyd, Wilco, or Coldplay. So to hang the "adult contemporary pop" label on smooth jazz tells us nothing. However, as smooth-sounding as smooth jazz may be, it is certainly not any genre of jazz we have been discussing in this book.

Interlude I: Introducing Smooth Jazz to College Students

When teaching a course that deals with how to listen to jazz, one of the worst things a teacher can do is to let his or her bias get in the way of offering a fair-minded and open approach to every style of the music being presented. So when I was presenting the unit on smooth jazz, I took special care not to express my preferences one way or the other, even though quite a number of students wanted to know what I thought of the music. I replied that what I thought of the music was of no particular importance at that time. My only goal was to expose them to this kind of music and let them decide if they liked it or not.

So we listened to a good cross section of smooth jazz recordings by Earl Klugh, Stanley Jordan, Dave Koz, the Rippingtons, and others. I then asked students what they liked and/or disliked about the music. I suspect that those who said they hated it might have been bucking for a higher grade in the class, but there was no telling. Quite a few said that it wasn't jazz, while others said that it reminded them of anything from a romance with Angelina Jolie to watching the sun sink into the Pacific while standing on a cliff in Malibu with George Clooney. One of my students, Carolyn, even said that it was great music to listen to while she was doing the dishes after dinner or sitting in a Jacuzzi with a glass of cabernet. Fair enough. Feels good . . . sounds good . . . *is* good. I asked Carolyn if she thought that what she had been hearing was jazz. She hesitated, looked at me quizzically, and said, "I'm not sure . . . I don't think so . . . but I still like it." At that point, most students said that while the music was like a cool breeze on a warm day, it wasn't jazz; the problem was that they didn't really have a label for it. Another student, sensing Carolyn's discomfort, suggested that while what we heard was nice music, it didn't demand much in the way of active listening. Carolyn—and the class—agreed completely, letting me nicely off the hook!

Interlude II: The Kenny G Experiment

Another semester, while covering the smooth jazz segment, I introduced the music of Kenny G by playing excerpts of six tracks in the exact sequence of appearance on one of his CDs. I didn't shuffle the order of the tracks; I merely played them in the order in which they were originally presented. As each track rolled into the next, I noticed that some students were laughing and others were squirming in their seats, looks of bewilderment on their faces. When the music was over, I then asked the students to give me their impressions of what they just heard. These were some of their responses:

> "Every tempo and every groove was exactly the same as the next."
> "All the tracks sounded like one song."
> "Kenny G is playing the same solo on every track."

So then I asked the class: "Did Kenny G play his instrument in tune and did he have a 'pretty' sound?" Most members of the class answered yes. "Was he improvising? Was he 'having a conversation' with his bandmates?"

Most students believed that he wasn't improvising, that he was merely playing "licks," or learned, unspontaneous phrases.

"Based upon what we've learned in this course so far, is this music jazz?" Everyone in the room agreed that while Kenny G's music was "smooth," and mellow, it wasn't really jazz as we had experienced it thus far in the class. I persisted: "Then what *is* it?" One student called it "mellow mood music." And that's as close as we got to what most of the students felt was an accurate label.

AHHHH . . . NEW AGE MUSIC

There has not been as much confusion about differentiating between jazz and so-called new age music. Jazz is nowhere in the name, and quite a bit of new age music is so meditative and peaceful in nature that it really bears no overt relationship to jazz. However, the irony is that—unlike smooth jazz—there can on numerous occasions be a significant amount of improvisation found in new age music. Among acoustic musicians like guitarists Will Ackerman (who created Windham Hill Records) and Alex de Grassi, pianists George Winston and Liz Story, bassist Michael Manring, and groups like the Paul Winter Consort, Oregon, and others, the art of improvising is essential to their music. De Grassi's second record for Windham Hill was called *Slow Circle* (1979) and is still considered by many listeners to be a masterwork of solo acoustic new age music. Each track is composed up to a point, but after the melody has been stated, the rest is improvised. The whole of each piece is structurally quite similar to a jazz performance: theme—improvised variation—theme. De Grassi's tone is glasslike and pure, and his improvisations like small melodies unto themselves.

So what, then, is the difference between a typical Alex de Grassi performance and a solo acoustic performance by another virtuoso, jazz guitarist Pat Metheny? Listen to *Slow Circle* and then experience Metheny's *One Quiet Night* (2001). You would be hard-pressed to say that one recording is by a new age artist and the other by a jazz artist. Labeling either man as this or that type of musician is a superfluous and unfair task at best. Labels become totally useless here. So, you may well ask, what's the point of calling one type of music one thing and a second type of music another, if they seem to be indistinguishable, as in this case?

We tend to compartmentalize and stereotype people, styles of living, schools of art, music, film, and other cultural characteristics, mostly for our own comfort—so when we visit amazon.com, for example, we can differentiate between country and bluegrass music, impressionist and expressionist art, drama and comedy, and so on. Putting these things in categories helps us locate them faster and easier than if we merely categorized them as "country music," "French and German painting," or "theater or film art." However, in the realm of music, once we arrive at our destination, there may well be a fine line between two styles of music that is almost imperceptible, as we have seen from the examples above.

AT THE END OF THE DAY

One of the exciting things about listening to jazz—or for that matter, a lot of other types of music—is that in many cases, the lines drawn between the styles tend to blur. So rather than try to figure out the minute differences between them, or whether you are being entertained or inspired, just sit back, relax, and let the music envelop you. Don't worry about styles and labels and what you think the intent of the artist might be. At the end of the day, it's really all about the music itself and little else. Good music doesn't belong to any one exclusive category; it is what it is: simply good music. It can be both entertaining and evocative. And if it resonates for you on a deeply personal, inexplicable level, then so much the better. You will have arrived as a listener!

RECOMMENDED READING

Yanow, Scott. *Jazz on Film: The Complete Story of the Musicians and Music on Screen*. Milwaukee: Backbeat Books, 2004. Print.

20

THE SHAPE OF THINGS TO COME

Jazz in the 21st Century

Jazz in the new century continues to be an anomaly. Some critics question its ability to survive as a human art in a hyper-technological age. There are times that the future has looked extremely bright for jazz, and other times when it has looked hopelessly bleak, depending upon who you read or speak to about it. As an example of the ups and downs of the discussion, consider this: before its demise in 2008, the International Association for Jazz Education (IAJE) hosted annual conferences in New York, Los Angeles, Toronto, and other cities, which were often attended by thousands of students, jazz musicians, educators, writers, and listeners. During each conference, jazz clubs and other venues in the hosting city were usually overflowing with listeners, and the illusion seemed to exist that jazz was "making a comeback" into the musical mainstream and that its future as a vital part of American culture was secure. However, with the exception of the IAJE conference, it was not probable that many musicians and jazz educators would see the situation of jazz in the new millennium as anything but dismal. For example, the IAJE conference held in Los Angeles in 2005 was brimming with attendees, and as a result of the conference, clubs in the vicinity, like L.A.'s esteemed Jazz Bakery, were overflowing with listeners on those evenings. However, it was "business as usual" the rest of the year, because in a large metropolitan area like Los Angeles, competition for audiences was (and presumably still is) fierce. One musician was overheard saying that many of the conference attendees were only part-time jazz fans whose support of the music was confined to the annual conference events.

Getting to the heart of the matter, we need to have a look at jazz's survival from a number of perspectives, and we need to also look at the level of commitment among the musicians, the fans, the record companies, and the venues that have labored to keep the music alive.

NEW YORK CITY: THE JAZZ CORNER OF THE WORLD

With so many distractions as well as so much competition for the consumer dollar, it becomes more and more challenging to draw in great numbers of listeners to jazz venues. New York City seems to stand a little apart from that observation, since the jazz scene there seems generally to thrive in many areas of the city. Richard OKon has been an important fixture on the New York jazz scene for over four decades, and very few people know the music as well as he does. OKon's love affair with jazz began sometime in his early teens and has never dimmed. Beginning as a jazz drummer, he ultimately embarked upon a lifelong career in management of jazz groups, and he is particularly well known in the New York jazz community as an experienced and knowledgeable jazz club manager. Some of the legendary New York clubs OKon has been associated with are the Blue Note, the Iridium, and Birdland. No one can describe the recent history or current state of jazz in New York City more perceptively than OKon does here:

> Twenty years ago, there were probably the same number of jazz clubs in the city, but there seemed to be a larger group of elder statesmen with better name recognition, who would attract a larger and more diverse audience. While there are quite a few really good musicians who have come up in the last two decades, they don't have the same name recognition to the general public and, in general, can't fill the [jazz] rooms for multiple nights.
>
> While the metropolitan area is diverse and has many area jazz fans, the clubs can't exist with only their support. So jazz clubs here in New York City are more or less in two tiers: the major clubs are generally larger, can charge higher admission fees, and can pay more to the artists performing there. The smaller clubs charge lesser fees and are limited in what they can pay the artists.

When asked about the nature of New York jazz audiences, OKon suggested:

> The vast percentage of patrons of the larger clubs are tourists from all over
> the world. The smaller venues tend to attract more of a local audience who
> want to see and hear some of the up-and-coming musicians. There are also
> different categories of people that visit the clubs. Some are big fans of the
> music and will visit a number of clubs while in New York to see and hear
> artists they enjoy listening to. Others have some knowledge of the music,
> but don't get to see live shows on a regular basis back in their hometowns.
> And still others know only a little about the music, but feel they have to
> visit a place that is well known by their friends back home (perhaps just
> out of curiosity).

In terms of future trends of jazz in New York City, OKon believes that the
city's jazz community will continue to thrive:

> There are new night clubs opening all the time [and] almost all of them are
> of the smaller scale. This is good because it gives the up-and-coming musi-
> cians a place to show their wares and continue to perfect their art. There are
> many wonderful young musicians coming on the scene, and as long as they
> have patience, there's no reason why they too can't prosper.

THE LIFE AND DEATH OF A JAZZ CLUB

Unfortunately, New York City has proven to be the exception rather than
the rule among American cities and towns from coast to coast. Sometimes
it seems that one minute, there is a new jazz club opening in Anytown,
USA, and the next minute, it is a thing of the past. A club's demise can also
happen to more established venues as well, as in the case of Charlie O's, a
little neighborhood jazz bar and grill in Los Angeles that opened its doors
in 2000 and enjoyed an 11-year run. Here is its story.

Charlie O's: Requiem for a Jazz Club

Bad news, as they say, travels fast. Several days ago, one of the most beloved jazz clubs in Los Angeles closed its doors for the last time. Charlie
O's was a victim of the recession, plain and simple. Although the venerable
club had a loyal fan base and was a great meeting place for L.A.'s many fine

Figure 20.1. Charlie O's Jazz Club, Los Angeles, California, R.I.P.

jazz musicians and their fans, there was just not enough support from the community at large to keep the club afloat.

Los Angeles is a funny and fickle town when it comes to jazz. At this writing, the *Los Angeles Times* seems for the most part to have abandoned writing about local jazz events altogether, with the exception of obituaries, occasional nods to isolated performances here and there, or the promotion of major concerts in large venues. In terms of the local club scene, many legendary venues have come and gone over the years, primarily because of the demographics of the city. L.A. is so spread out that it has become progressively more difficult to maintain a sense of community, not only for jazz musicians and listeners, but also for creative artists in general. A sad reality is that, after a day of doing penance on the city's many freeways, people generally don't like driving across town—or even only a few miles—to do anything, let alone go hear live jazz. Living and working in Southern California can really wear you out.

Which brings us to the 11-year odyssey of Charlie O's. It was the dream of Charlie Ottaviano and his wife JoAnn Abatangelo to have a neighborhood bar and grill where people could come out and enjoy live jazz in an intimate and homey setting. No expensive cover charge or drink minimum. Just good food, good company, and great music. The club opened in 2000, starting small with music one night a week. However, word traveled fast, and soon Charlie's was operating full tilt, offering jazz every night and featuring many of the best players from L.A.'s considerable pool of great—and in many cases, legendary—jazz musicians. Plus it afforded listeners the opportunity to not only experience the music, but also to be able to meet and socialize with these fine musicians. And it was not unusual to see students from college jazz classes in attendance, taking notes and asking the musicians questions about the music. In short, Charlie O's became a gathering place for all ages and folks from every walk of life, from movie stars like Clint Eastwood to regulars who would prop themselves up at the bar and let the music and camaraderie fill some void that only they could know.

Charlie Ottaviano died in 2008, yet JoAnn was determined to carry on by herself, in honor of his memory and because she realized how important the club was to the musicians and listeners who made it a regular part of their lives. As the country spiraled into a recession, she and her dedicated staff labored mightily through some very lean times; somehow through it all, every performing musician continued to get paid at the end of the night, and each member of her staff drew a weekly paycheck. Unfortunately, in 2009 JoAnn was diagnosed with a serious illness. Her brother Mike stepped up to the plate and assumed responsibility for operating the club during the long stretches of her convalescence; so somehow, Charlie O's remained afloat, despite the tremendous obstacles which it faced. Yet at the end of the day, it simply became too difficult to keep the club afloat. Middle-class folks were tightening their purse strings in order to survive a dismal economy, and spending an evening at a jazz club became a luxury that many could not afford. As a result, Charlie O's dimmed the stage lights and closed its doors forever on the last day of August 2011.

After moving back to the East Coast, I had begun making a yearly trek back to Los Angeles during the summers, and I would invariably reunite with Charlie, JoAnn, and all of my L.A. friends. In the last three years of the life of the club, I appeared there with various "reunion quartets" composed of some of the city's finest musicians. When I played at the club in July 2011, I had the distinct feeling that it would be the last time. As is usually the case with drummers packing up their equipment, I was among the last to leave that night. I remember how lonely the place felt without the musicians and listeners who, only an hour earlier, filled the room with music, applause, laughter—life. And I remember for no particular reason thinking that Charlie O's days were numbered. Unfortunately, I was right. It was the end of a lovely run and of the dream of two people to bring jazz to their community—and in drummer Art Blakey's words, to allow the music to "wash away the dust of everyday life."

SOME SUCCESS STORIES

Regardless of the fact that the life of a jazz club too often seems to be a short one, there have been success stories, like the venues that have managed to keep their doors open indefinitely in spite of economic conditions, competition for customers, and technological distractions. One of these has been the venerable Deer Head Inn in the Pocono Mountains of Pennsylvania. The country's oldest continuously running jazz club in the same location, the Deer Head, has been operating for over 60 years and presents the music four nights each week. Being less than two hours from New York City, it attracts world-class jazz musicians from the city, as well as those like saxophonists Dave Liebman and Phil Woods, singer/songwriter Bob Dorough, and drummer Bill Goodwin, who have made the Poconos their home.

Other jazz venues that have gathered a loyal following and have withstood the test of time include Baker's Keyboard Lounge in Detroit (over 75 years), Yoshi's in San Francisco (over 40 years), Wally's Café in Boston (over 65 years), and Blues Alley in Washington, D.C. (over 45 years). The music and the environment in these and other jazz venues continue to attract new listeners, as well as many return audiences.

GETTING AWAY FROM THE COMPUTER
AND OUT OF THE HOUSE

Taking a wider view, we have to look at the current state of the music from a number of different perspectives. What does it take to move us from the comforts of home and our big-screen televisions, video games, and the Internet, out into the world of live performance? Jazz clubs are, by and large, social places where alcoholic and nonalcoholic beverages (and sometimes food) are served. Other venues for the music include small theaters, coffeehouses, art galleries, and even movie theaters. So what, then, keeps listeners (and prospective listeners) from venturing out into the night to hear a jazz performance? Of course, as mentioned a few moments ago, the major technological distractions are always there. As a result, here's a dialogue you might have with yourself:

> You #1: I'd like to go out tonight to relax and hear some live jazz at the XYZ Club.

> You #2: Why? You can watch any of 200 TV channels, a pay-per-view movie, or you can play the latest Black Ops video game. You don't have to shower, get dressed, and drive to the XYZ Club. Everything you need is right here in this house.

> You #1: Yeah, but that's not the same as checking out some live jazz! This book I've been reading says that as far as jazz goes, there's no substitute for actually feeling the excitement of being there.

> You #2: Hey—you can see some jazz performances on pay-per-view or even on YouTube, without having to spend the money for admission to the club and for a couple of drinks . . . especially when we are trying to be careful about how and where we spend our money.

> You #1: OK, I know that . . . but going out once or twice a month to the XYZ Club isn't going to cost that much! Less than a movie, after you factor in the popcorn, candy, and a soda. And, frankly, seeing and hearing a jazz performance on our TV or laptop isn't the same as having the experience of being right there in the room with other listeners, just a few feet away from the band as they're playing. Now that's a real-life experience!

> You #2: So what makes that so special, as opposed to checking a concert out at home? I don't get it . . .

> You #1: Well, for one thing, experiencing live jazz benefits everyone. The club might make enough money to turn a modest profit. The musicians make some money and have a place to play; and we reap the benefits of being in the room, soaking up the vibe, and listening to the musicians create this music! I mean, how are we going to help keep this music alive by sitting home?

Truly, it is a matter of supporting live music that helps sustain it, and in the long run, our enjoyment of it. Because without a venue in which to create jazz for listeners, musicians would wind up playing only for themselves and maybe a few friends. After evolving for over a century, America's singularly original art form deserves better than to be trivialized by the distractions of home entertainment. This is not to say that there is anything inherently wrong with HD-TV, Xbox, and other recreational technology. They can be fun and certainly have their place in our lives; however, it would do well to strike a balance between these diversions and being out in the world of real people who create real art, right there on the spot. Art is most certainly not a diversion or distraction. It can and often does offer a way of being better in touch with the world in which we live. To experience jazz in a live setting, then, is to put us on the road which can bring us in closer touch with our own emotions, if we are open to that possibility.

MEETING THE CHALLENGE: KEEPING THE MUSIC ALIVE

Apart from its base of loyal listeners, today's jazz community faces some serious obstacles to its survival as an art form in America and, quite possibly, in the world. The following sections offer a look at a few of these obstacles, as well as some of the positive work that is being done to overcome them.

The Self-Produced Jazz Artist: Beginnings

Two artists who many consider to be the first jazz musicians to create independent record labels featuring primarily their own music were Andrew White and Sun Ra. A native son of Washington, D.C., White was—and is—a wonder. He is a triple-threat musician who has played tenor and alto saxophones with many well-known jazz figures, oboe with a number of national orchestras, and electric bass with artists as diverse as Stevie Wonder, the Fifth Dimension, and Weather Report. Perhaps he has not received the recognition he deserves because he never wished to compromise his music at the hands of others. He created his independent label, Andrew's Music, in 1971, and has released over 40 recordings to date. Always the Renaissance man, White has over the years created a mini-arts empire, also creating and selling music scores, transcriptions, and his 850-page autobiography. That he is not better known is a real crime, given his immense talent.

Sun Ra, a fine keyboardist and a legendary leader of some of the most unusual and uniquely uncategorizable ensembles in all of jazz, started perhaps the first true independent record label back in the 1950s, with El Saturn records. While initial quantities of his records were limited— sometimes only 50 copies at a time—Ra managed to record, package, and sell his discs throughout the lifespan of his large ensemble, which he called his "Arkestra." There have been entire books written about Sun Ra, who, in his approach to music, was an American original, like Thelonious Monk. Sun Ra recorded prolifically throughout his long career and managed to bring his music to a wider audience through his memorable, self-produced recordings.

Four Success Stories

With the slow demise of the major record companies and labels, and with the popularity of downloading music from a wide variety of sites like Amazon, iTunes, Pandora, and Spotify, musicians have had a rough go of it, and they have relinquished the hope of securing a recording contract, since most of those seem to be a thing of the past. A great and innovative group can often become discouraged after spending time and money recording its music and sending a demo to two dozen record companies, only to be summarily ignored by folks who may not have listened to more than one minute of the music, if any.

Creative musicians have responded to this frustrating situation in a number of ways. One such example is the Jazz Compass label. Created in 1999 by guitarist Larry Koonse, trumpeter Clay Jenkins, bassist Tom Warrington, and drummer Joe LaBarbera, four prominent world-class jazz musicians based in Los Angeles and New York, Jazz Compass sought initially to release quality jazz recorded by ensembles led by all four men; their goal has been to "present their music as they envision it, without compromise." Their first recordings for Jazz Compass—one by each man—were released in 2000, and they have been gradually expanding their catalog to include other artists as well. It's very clear that their effort is all about presenting the best jazz possible, and the fact that they have managed to thrive for over a decade speaks well of their level of commitment to both the music and their listeners. This is a prime example of musicians taking control of recording and releasing their own music, and seems to be a significant trend among jazz artists in the new millennium.

We can't talk about jazz artists who take control over the recording, manufacture, and distribution and marketing of their music without bringing the name and accomplishments of trumpeter/composer Dave Douglas into the light. A prolific and imaginative composer and trumpeter, Douglas studied at Berklee College of Music, the New England Conservatory of Music, and New York University. Since the early '90s, he has released more than 30 recordings that explore a wide range of music, including a tribute to the legendary pianist and composer from the 1930s and '40s, Mary Lou Williams; a series of large and small ensembles that explore klezmer and Balkan music, the music of Miles Davis, and much more. Douglas has also composed some lively and beautiful music for a brass ensemble he calls Brass Fantasy—and that only scratches the surface of his talent and abilities. Apparently, others have taken notice as well, as Douglas has been accorded many honors, including a Guggenheim Fellowship, the Aaron Copeland Award, the Mid-Atlantic Arts Foundation's Jazz.NEXT Grant, and many other awards from jazz magazines and organizations.

In 2005 Douglas and associate Mike Friedman founded Greenleaf Music, which, according to its website, "concentrates on releasing jazz, post-jazz, and world music." Greenleaf's mission has been to honor "creativity in musical expression," and it presents the music of a number of other artists in addition to Douglas. The Greenleaf Music website is user friendly and interactive, and interested listeners can hear some samples of recordings from the Greenleaf catalog.

Another musician who has created an outlet for his and others' music has been saxophonist John Zorn. Beyond being a saxophonist, Zorn has many credits as a producer and as a composer, and he operates in a much wider spectrum than just jazz; for example, he has left his imprint upon styles as diverse as punk rock, klezmer, classical, world, and film music—all in a highly unique avant-garde, experimental fashion. As a producer, he established Tzadik Records in 1995, which has released more than 400 recordings under a number of categories, including "Radical Jewish Culture," "Film Music," "Archival Series" (which features Zorn's own performances), and the "Oracle Series," which documents the compositions and performances of female musicians. Zorn's amazing versatility as well as his insatiable curiosity and high level of commitment were no doubt factors in his being awarded a MacArthur Fellowship in 2006. On top of that honor, Zorn was awarded Columbia University's William Schumann Award, which recognizes "the lifetime achievement of an American Composer whose works have been widely performed and have generally been acknowledged to be of lasting significance." Zorn's work, radical as it may be, may certainly be worth a listen.

One other shining example of artist autonomy and vision—this one a bit more "homegrown"—comes from Brooklyn-based saxophonist/clarinetist Chris Speed, who founded Skirl Recordings in 2006, as a way of recording his own projects and also those of his friends and musical associates scattered throughout the Brooklyn communities like Park Slope and Kensington. Like much of today's cutting-edge improvised music, Speed and friends cover a wide range of musical styles—always challenging, unpredictable, and interesting.

The Hope of Being Heard

Many other jazz musicians, as well as musicians who play other types of music, have recognized the difficulty of presenting their music to a wider audience—especially these days, where dreams of being signed to a recording contract with an established label have all but evaporated. Musicians' response to this bleak situation has been to record, package, and distribute their own music, often at great personal expense. The dilemma here is that once a band has released its CD, then what? The easiest solution is to try to sell the CD at gigs, even though on-site sales are generally spotty. Of course, the band can market it on the Internet via iTunes, Amazon, and CD Baby and can also announce the CD's release on Facebook and other social networking sites. However, there are two challenges that independent artists are faced with as they attempt to sell their recordings on the Internet. One is that listeners will not gravitate toward a particular artist or recording automatically, unless they have heard the artist before, either on another recording or live at a jazz club. Second, with the advent of CD duplicating and packaging companies like Discmakers, anyone with some working capital can release a "jazz" CD. There is virtually no quality control. This is very much akin to the self-publishing industry that has sprung up in recent years, in which an "author" with only a modicum of talent may pay to have his or her work published. Whether genuine vision and the literary skills to back it up are present seem often to be secondary considerations—and again, the method is to pay a company to release one's product into the world. Of course, there are many fine self-released works in both the jazz and literary worlds. Yet, in terms of jazz, how would you be able to differentiate between the work of a talented jazz musician and the work of an amateur? That's where this listener's companion can be helpful. It can point you in the right direction—as it is hopefully doing here and now—and offer some paths that you might wish to follow in your quest to discover personal meaning in this music.

The Independent Record Label Producer

While singular artists have produced and released their own recordings, as we have learned from the previous section, and prolific artists like Dave Douglas, John Zorn, and Chris Speed have created record labels that prominently feature their own music as well as the music of others, the role of independent producers—who have created and sustained labels that feature the work primarily of multiple artists (John Zorn may fall in both this category and the previous one)—is quite different and in many ways may be more demanding and costly. In the jazz world, there are many small labels that continue to release quality works by lesser-known musicians, even though the chances of making a lot of money from such ventures may be fairly slim. Often, these labels survive for no reason other than sheer will and their unflagging belief in the music they are presenting to the listening public. To get an idea of just how many of these independent record labels exist, all you need to do is google "independent jazz record labels" for further exploration. Fortunately, a number of indie label websites have sample excerpts that you can hear, in order to get a brief flavor of their music. And it is always possible that Amazon, CD Baby, or other similar sites may list indie CDs that offer audio samples as well. A few of the many labels worth investigating are Sunnyside, OmniTone, Atavistic, Aum Fidelity, Arkadia, Challenge, Criss Cross Jazz, Dragon, Sharp Nine, and Cryptogramophone.

Interlude: Staying Alive: Cryptogramophone Records

What began as one man's tribute to a fallen friend and mentor became an independent recording label of astonishingly high quality. Each Cryptogramophone disc is lovingly produced and features a unique artistic design. The Crypto catalog offers an amazing diversity of approaches to improvised music, all brilliantly recorded. None of this would have been possible without the guiding hand of Jeff Gauthier. This is how it all happened:

Figure 20.2. Cryptogramophone Records. Courtesy of Cryptogramophone Records.

Gauthier, an accomplished and versatile violinist, was born and raised in Los Angeles, where he studied with Armand Roth, first violinist with the Los Angeles Philharmonic. His love of jazz and rock came early, and upon hearing jazz-rock violinists Jean-Luc Ponty and Jerry Goodman with the Don Ellis Orchestra and the Mahavishnu Orchestra, respectively, Gauthier found himself at the beginning of his lifelong path as an improvising musician. He continued his musical studies at the California Institute of the Arts, where he was exposed to contemporary classical music as well as world music. All of this exposure helped Gauthier begin to congeal a very broad musical outlook, which even today is reflected in the great diversity of the Crypto CDs he produces.

It was at the end of his college studies that Gauthier met the brilliant bassist/composer Eric Von Essen, with whom he developed an intense musical kinship. Eventually, they were joined by two other gifted young players, twin brothers Nels and Alex Cline (guitarist and drummer, respectively). They formed a group called Quartet Music, which featured Von Essen's compositions and music that was at once eclectic, thought-provoking, and stimulating.

Tragically, Von Essen died in 1997 while teaching in Sweden. Only in his early 40s, the bassist left an appreciable body of music and a modest recording history, including four discs by Quartet Music. As a tribute to his friendship with Von Essen and to the latter's gifts as a composer, Gauthier, along with the Cline brothers and many other fine Los Angeles musicians, set out in 1998 to record three albums of Von Essen's music. Knowing that it would be very difficult to attract the interest of the mainstream record companies at that time, Gauthier became his own producer and decided to release the records himself. And that was how Cryptogramophone was born!

The label features a dazzling array of cutting-edge artists, including Nels Cline (who continues to gain national and international recognition for his work as both a guitarist and an improviser), Gauthier's own Goatette Ensemble, pianist/composer Myra Melford, violinist Jenny Scheinman, and ex–Miles Davis and Herbie Hancock sideman Bennie Maupin, whose brilliant recordings for Crypto have been well received by critics and fans alike from around the world.

Gauthier's outlook for the future of this music is simple and direct:

> I believe that people who create improvised music have to find ways to reach the next generation of listeners pretty quickly, or serious music is in danger of becoming marginalized—it may not be rediscovered for many years. This has to happen on every level, from the music itself, to the ways people listen to and appreciate music. (www.popmatters.com)

Reaching Out via Technology

It's an indisputable fact that the Internet is here to stay. And it is also a fact that the life of jazz can be further enhanced by the use of cyber-technology. To believe otherwise is dangerous to the life of the music and those who make it, since it is no longer an option to assume that jazz will always survive, since it has long been considered one of America's national treasures. Neither can we assume that it will continue to exist because many colleges and universities offer jazz studies majors and have jazz history and appreciation classes as part of general education curricula. As a colleague so aptly put it, "That just won't fly the plane anymore."

Quite a few jazz musicians now have websites that offer many fine links, which feature their biographies, musical philosophies, photos, videos, listening samples, itineraries, and related merchandise, including CDs, books, and links to MP3 downloads. While this is an excellent start, the big question is: How do we musicians make you listeners aware that our websites even exist? In fact, how do we make you aware that *we* exist? With millions of websites available to you, how would you know how to navigate the web directly to our site?

An example: now that you have read much of this book and you know my name, it would be easy for you to google it, and the first entry would probably be the link to my website. Once there, you could learn more about my background and my activities as both a jazz musician and a writer. But say, for the sake of argument, that I was someone named Joe Cool, and I had a comparable website—but I was not the author of this book. How would you ever find me on the Internet? You wouldn't even know to look! The point is, we musicians can't expect potential listeners to just show up on our cyber-doorsteps and become immediate fans. So you can see that there are challenges to be met and obstacles to be overcome if jazz music and its practitioners are going to thrive in a hyper-technological society.

There are some musicians and fans who are taking positive steps on the Internet to help promote both the music and those who play it. One group that goes by the singular fictional name of "Lester Perkins" has created a donation-driven jazz video search engine called Jazz on the Tube, which offers many legendary and obscure performances generated by YouTube. So if you think you'd be interested in hearing and seeing Miles Davis perform, there are many videos available for viewing. If you decide to become a subscriber to Jazz on the Tube, you can enjoy jazz videos that the group will send to you on a semi-regular basis—usually on the birthday of one of its featured artists. It's a great way of enjoying some jazz during your day and is also a wonderful tool for learning more about artists mentioned in this and other books and periodicals about jazz.

Another even more adventurous nonprofit endeavor has been undertaken recently by a young and imaginative jazz fan named Adam Schatz, who—thanks to a massive fund drive and some very generous patrons—has developed an ingenious website called "Search and Restore." In short, Schatz has found a way to bring many of New York's established and up-and-coming players into the public eye. Search and Restore is, in a sense, an enormous repository of live performances videotaped in many locations in New York

City, from established jazz venues like the Blue Note to some unlikely locations like the Six Point Brewery. It also serves to link the artists with fans via the artists' websites—an important feature in today's Internet world.

According to Schatz, the main purpose of creating and developing such a site is so that listeners can hear and see music that they in all likelihood didn't know existed. Schatz sees Search and Restore as a "brand new, ever growing point of discovery for the new jazz and improvised music community." Not only is the site updated daily with newly recorded videos, but it also alerts visitors to upcoming events that will be taking place around the city. While this is a great way for folks in the metropolitan area to find out where the music is happening (and often be able to see a video of a group that is slated to perform), it also serves the purpose of exposing many fine new artists to a broader audience—potential listeners who live in other cities, states, and countries. Admittedly, much of the music falls into the avant-garde category, but it also provides many rewards for those looking for something new and adventurous. Even so, there are also more conventional artists featured on some of the videos as well. A curious listener can get lost in much of the music presented on Search and Restore. The experience of sampling the talents of so many different groups at a single sitting is exhilarating—and beneficial for both listener and artist.

Such examples of jazz outreach are exemplary, but they are only the beginning. As the music itself continues its 100-plus-year metamorphosis, so do the methods of delivery—from 78, 45, and 33-1/3 rpm (revolutions per minute) records, through reel-to-reel and cassette tapes, through compact and mini-discs, to MP3 downloads and beyond. This may well be only the beginning of the next hundred years of the growth and development of jazz music. Yet, you the listener are at the core of the jazz experience. As long as you see jazz as a personal transaction between those who play and those who listen and respond, the mode of delivery becomes secondary to how one human being, telling his or her story through the vehicle of a piece of wood or brass or metal, reaches into your being and shakes your very foundation. In this way, life becomes just a little bit richer, more mysterious, and at the end of the day, maybe more fulfilling as well.

AFTERWORD

By now, you should know how much I love this music, as both musician and listener. That has been the primary reason for giving my life over to it, and spending the better part of three years writing this book. Like Doug Ramsey, Dave Liebman, Terry Teachout, David Remnick, the late Bob Brookmeyer, and many others, I have been concerned that jazz is losing its audience. To be able to share our love for this music with you, we musicians play and play and tell our stories, hoping that you will look, listen, and be a part of the human tapestry that is constantly unfolding. The truth is, we jazz folk can't go this route alone. To play this music only for ourselves is sort of like having a conversation sometimes with empty air. But to be able to offer our humanity and share our life experiences with you through our melodies, harmonies, and rhythms can bring validation that we are all alive and celebrating our existence as compassionate and whole human beings.

Others have said these things better than I, so I want to leave you with a few of their thoughts, with the hope that you might stick around and enjoy the ride, from the end of one song into the beginning of the next:

> A jazz man should be saying what he feels. He's one human being talk-
> ing to others, telling his story—and that means humor and sadness, joy,
> all the things that humans have.
>
> —Bob Brookmeyer

Music, for me, has always been a place where anything is possible—
a refuge, a magical world where anyone can go, where all kinds of
people can come together, and anything can happen. We are limited
only by our imaginations.

—Bill Frisell

We are You.

—Karl Berger

GLOSSARY

Many areas of human activity—from journalism to sports to the arts and sciences and popular culture—have their own linguistic terminologies. Jazz music is no exception. What follows is a small sampling of terms that have been coined by jazz musicians over the years. Some of these have become so commonly used, outside of jazz, that they have been accepted as mainstream cultural lingo.

bebop. A school of jazz that emerged in the mid-1940s that differed from swing in that it was less dance oriented and more performance based. This was the first era of jazz to be called "modern."

bomb. A pronounced, syncopated accent played by a drummer, usually on the bass drum.

bread. Money (also "dough," "scratch," "moolah," and others).

burn. (verb) To play at a very high, often exciting level (also "wail").

chart. The jazz musician's term for what is written as a musical arrangement of an original composition or a standard (often well-known) melody.

chops. Technical and/or improvisational skill on a musical instrument; the facial area, including the eyes, ears, nose, cheeks, and mouth.

chorus. A single "playing through" of a song's structure, either by stating its melody or by following this structure while playing a jazz solo.

comp. (verb) To accompany a soloist by playing the chords of the melody underneath his or her solo.

cool. A phrase coined by Lester Young, meaning a state of hipness. Examples: "That's cool"; "Don't blow your cool." Also, a "cool jazz" is a softer, less aggressive school of jazz.

counterpoint. Two or more musical lines of approximately equal importance sounding at the same time; intersecting musical statements.

dig. (verb) To understand someone or something; to enjoy someone or something. Examples: "I can dig it"; "You dig?"

dues. What something costs; in jazz terms, usually something a musician has to go through in order to reach a goal. Example: "She's paid her dues, but now she's famous."

funky. A state of soulfulness; a catchy, syncopated groove; dirty or gritty.

gig. A performance for which the musicians are paid, e.g., a concert, a dance, etc.

groove. (noun) A repetitive rhythmic feel; (verb) to play a rhythmic feel repeatedly.

head. The melody or prewritten theme of a piece of music.

hot. Exciting, emotional, extroverted (as it relates to a jazz performance).

jam. (verb) To improvise.

jam session. A musical get-together where improvisation is stressed.

polyrhythms. Several rhythms sounding or being played at the same time.

rhythm section. A group of musicians in a band whose responsibility it is to accompany the soloist(s); usually consists of a chordal instrument such as piano or guitar, and bass and drums.

riff. (noun) A musical phrase; a theme; a melodic fragment; (verb) to jam with other musicians.

solid. Good, affirmative, positive, substantial. For example, Musician 1: "The gig pays $5,000." Musician 2: "Solid, man. I can use the bread."

syncopation. The displacement of rhythm in music, a crucial aspect in creating jazz.

wail. (verb) To improvise at an optimal and impressive level (also "burn").

APPENDIX A

Surfing the Jazz Net

As we have discovered throughout this book, with the advent and use of computer technology there are more than a few ways to experience jazz. Here are some of the most common and useful ways to continue nourishing your jazz experiences.

A SAMPLING OF JAZZ WEBSITES

In addition to the musicians' websites listed at the end of many chapters in this book, there are also interesting and useful sites that serve as repositories for musicians, listeners, writers, photographers, and graphic artists. Here are a few of the more well-established jazz websites for you to explore.

All about Jazz (allaboutjazz.com)

Founded by Michael Ricci in 1995, the award-winning All about Jazz website has been a labor of love on the part of many hands, including writers, editors, graphic designers, and of course, the musicians themselves. Every era and style of jazz is well represented, and the site is rich with essays, free downloads, videos, podcasts, musician and band profiles, links to other sites, jazz-related photo and art galleries, forums, events calendars, guides to festivals, clubs, and concert venues, and much more.

Jazz Corner (jazzcorner.com)

Another excellent jazz website, Jazz Corner was founded in 1996 by Lois Gilbert, and it features jazz news, jazz radio and videos, podcasts, musician profiles, and bulletin boards and is a repository for musicians' and jazz organizations' websites.

Jazz Review (Jazzreview.com)

The 1997 brainchild of Morrice Duane Blackwell, Jazz Review's subtext under its logo is "Where people talk about jazz." True to its name, this site's major emphasis is upon reviews of both recordings and live performances. There are also links to a variety of resources, as well as a virtual "jazz community," where listeners can enter into discussions about all facets of the music.

Jazz.com

This website is similar to the two previous sites in terms of its breadth of interesting information for musicians and new and seasoned listeners alike. You will find interviews, CD and concert reviews, forums where listeners can weigh in on all aspects and eras of the music, articles written by musicians about their favorite musical role models, and much more. One component unique to this website is the inclusion of Lewis Porter's *Encyclopedia of Jazz Musicians*, an enormous wealth of biographical and artistic information about literally hundreds of jazz musicians.

Jazz on the Tube (Jazzonthetube.com)

Calling itself "the Internet's jazz video search engine," Jazz on the Tube was established by a group of jazz lovers who collectively call themselves "Lester Perkins." What they have done is to create an enormous library of links of YouTube jazz videos, which are organized generally by the artist or group. Visitors are encouraged to use either the site's directory or its search engine to discover the many treasures that await their eyes and ears. The site's philosophy is simple:

> Before the advent of the Internet and online video the only reliable way to SEE jazz was to go to a live show. This is still the best way to see the music, but if you want to see the many great musicians who are no longer with us (and the living ones who aren't playing tonight in your town), we've created Jazz on the Tube as the Internet's search engine for jazz videos.

Please note that since computer technology is so dynamic and since things on the Internet change so quickly, some jazz resource sites above—or even various artists' websites listed throughout this book—may have already been revised, expanded, or even replaced by newer sites; hence, the listings in this and other sections are merely springboards to get you involved and to provide some incentive to explore further on your own.

OTHER JAZZ-RELATED INTERNET RESOURCES

Websites like Pandora and Spotify offer significant help to jazz listeners by providing an incredibly wide range of listening opportunities from all eras of jazz, from the most commonly heard performances to some of the most obscure. Both maintain "Internet radio," which has the capability to bring listener and music closer together much more quickly than ever before.

Controversy

Even so, controversy surrounds sites like Pandora and Spotify for a number of reasons. First is the issue of "royalties" disbursed to the musicians whose recordings have been made accessible online. It appears that, in general, the amount of compensation is infinitesimally small, almost negligible. Second, there is the ongoing issue of piracy. Illegal file sharing among listeners trivializes the efforts and artistry of the musicians whose music is being traded back and forth, the end result being zero profit for the recording artist. This is a tragedy, especially when oftentimes these days, many musicians shoulder the expense of releasing their music in either CD or downloadable MP3 format, only to have it "stolen" by people who don't wish to purchase the music, even at a reasonable cost. Sadly, this is unethical behavior which is very difficult to discourage or curtail. And it disrespects the efforts of the artists and takes money out of their pockets.

What You Can Do

If you explore Spotify, Pandora, or other similar sites, and find a song or CD that you would like to own, please—for the sake of the musicians—purchase it from Amazon, CD Baby, iTunes, or other similar marketplaces. By doing so, you'll be helping the artists create even more quality music in the future!

YOUTUBE

Without a doubt, YouTube has been one of today's most important Internet tools for enhancing the jazz experience. Jazz on the Tube (mentioned previously) has utilized YouTube videos and maintains a treasure trove of them; however, YouTube itself offers much more in the way of jazz performances. You just have to seek them out. One way to do this is creating a list of the jazz artists you are curious about and, starting perhaps with Google, looking for videos. Results of a Google search often include links to videos. So if, for example, you google Miles Davis, you will see some thumbnail photos of YouTube videos available for viewing.

Another way to explore a jazz musician's video performances would be to go directly to youtube.com, type in his or her name, and select the video you wish to watch. More and more musicians are also creating their own YouTube "channels," which allow them to select and offer video performances for potential viewing. Most musicians who maintain YouTube channels usually inform fans and potential viewers via their websites or via social or professional networking sites such as Facebook or linkedin.com, respectively.

SELECTED MUSICIANS' WEBSITES

Short of meeting a musician personally or hearing a jazz group perform live, musicians' personal websites are often the next best thing to being there. Some sites are simple and direct with a few sound samples (or links to sound samples), while others are quite elaborate with embedded videos, animation, hyperlinks to other sites and access to their CDs, MP3 downloads, and other merchandise. One thing most if not all musicians' websites seek to do is to introduce the artist to you in a way that personalizes and encourages contact and seeks to motivate you to explore his or her music further.

While selected musicians' websites have been included at the end of many chapters in this book, there are many, many more worth visiting. All you need is the name of the artist, and a jazz resource site like allaboutjazz .com or a search engine like Google will guide you to his or her domain, allowing you to enter a whole new musical world.

A FINAL THOUGHT . . .

While Internet sources—as well as recordings and DVDs—are all excellent resources and certainly worth your time, they really can't replace the thrill of experiencing the music up close and personal—either in the intimate setting of a jazz club or in the more formal setting of a concert hall. There is nothing quite like the give-and-take of a live jazz experience to open up your mind and nourish your soul. When you experience live jazz, you can feel the electricity dancing in the air around you! It can be that exciting and emotionally moving, if you open yourself up to it.

We jazz musicians do what we do in order to communicate our feelings to you, and in order to bring our very personal perceptions of life into this world—with the hope that you will become part of our journey, as we may hopefully become part of yours.

APPENDIX B

CDs and DVDs

THE CASE FOR COMPACT DISCS

There is no doubt that the CD has become an endangered species, whose popularity has diminished with the advent of downloading. Whether or not it will go the way of the cassette, the eight-track, and vinyl (which has been making a small comeback) remains to be seen. While there are more than a few recording industry folks who seem to believe that their demise is imminent, there are others who believe that CDs will survive, even if their mass production continues to decline.

The convenience of downloading an MP3, either by the song or an entire recording, is undeniable. To have an entire collection of songs and albums in one enormous yet compact repository would seem to be a real plus. Imagine—thousands of songs at your fingertips on your iPod or iPad or smartphone. On the other hand, there continue to be those who enjoy buying CDs, for three reasons:

1. The attractiveness of the cover art and the convenience of a pull-out booklet
2. The program notes, personnel, photographs, and the recording infor- mation in the booklet

3. The pleasures of a "physical collection" of compact discs in a hands-on music library

Frankly, you can have the best of both worlds by buying CDs for an in-home listening collection, and by downloading songs, either from a CD or from a legitimate online source such as Amazon or iTunes, into your MP3 player for listening on the go. It all depends upon what you believe your needs might be. Along those lines, there are many lists of CDs that claim to include the most essential recordings in the jazz canon. Among the best of these are the lists offered by the *New Yorker* magazine and National Public Radio. Even so, these lists and many others vary considerably, leaving new listeners a bit overwhelmed. One suggestion would be to use either of the two lists mentioned and, as time permits, take a spin through spotify.com or itunes.com and listen to songs from CDs recommended by either or both lists. A much smaller annotated list of "desert island" recordings has been included in this book for your information and interest.

Independent CD Labels: Keeping the Music Alive

There are—astonishingly enough—over 200 jazz record (CD) labels in existence at this writing. Many of these are small, independent labels like Cryptogramophone, Skirl, Challenge, and Clean Feed records—high-quality companies often created by the artists themselves for the sole purpose of bringing their work into the light. With the slow disappearance of major jazz labels, these small companies continue to be the life blood of new jazz and improvised music. To access a list of many of these labels, your best source is New York's Downtown Music Gallery. Proprietors Bruce Lee Gallanter and Manny "Lunch" Maris oversee what has become New York's (and possibly the world's) premier jazz and improvised music record store and one of the world's most complete mail order services for jazz of almost every stripe. To get an idea of the enormity of their operation, you can explore their website at www.downtownmusicgallery .com. There you will find newsletters about new music releases, profiles of little-known as well as famous musicians, and much more. And if you live in New York or plan to visit, then the DMG should be on your list of must-experience destinations. Either way, Bruce, Manny, and their helpful staff will guide you in a variety of directions, broadening your experiences and expanding your musical horizons.

DVDs: Jazz Sights and Sounds for Your Music Library

If you decide to build a music library comprising jazz artists whose music appeals to you, then the inclusion of DVDs would be a distinct plus. After all, the jazz experience, as we now know, is often an experience of both sight and sound. To maintain DVDs as part of your jazz collection would be to complement that which we hear with that which we can see. DVDs can also provide a context that often is elusive to try and capture within the confines of a recording studio. In other words, musicians in live concert or club performances do not have to deal with the restraints of formal recording. As a result, jazz musicians are often much less inhibited in a live setting than they might be when they're wearing a set of headphones and worrying about "getting a good take."

Thanks to both the vision of both semiprofessional and professional filmmakers, as well as modern technology, we are fortunate to have many, many jazz DVDs available for either renting or acquiring for our music collections.

Jazz DVDs fall into two main categories: the first group focuses upon jazz masters as well as famous jazz groups, and it features performance footage (some of which hasn't been seen for over half a century). Fortunately, there are many fantastic concerts on film available to us, many of which have been excerpted on the aforementioned website jazzonthetube .com. While such sample footage is valuable and serves as a good introduction to a musician's art, it is the complete concert, club, or festival footage presented on many jazz DVDs that really offers the ultimate on-screen experience.

The Jazz Icons Series

According to its website (www.jazzicons.com), the Jazz Icons Series is "an ongoing DVD series featuring full-length concerts and in-studio performances by the greatest legends of jazz, filmed all over the world from the 1950s through the 1970s." Produced by the award-winning Reelin' in the Years Productions producers David Peck and Phil Galloway, each DVD's footage quality has been uniformly excellent, and the concerts themselves feature a wide range of jazz masters, including Count Basie, Dizzy Gillespie, John Coltrane, Thelonious Monk, Art Blakey and the Jazz Messengers, Chet Baker, Ella Fitzgerald, and many others. There are, at this writing, five different boxed sets available, with anywhere from six to nine

DVDs in each set. If you are interested in only one or two artists initially, you may purchase DVDs from any series individually as well, from Amazon and a few other sources listed on Google.

The Idem Home Video Series

A decidedly eclectic catalog, the Idem Home Video Group includes four different series of DVDs: The Swing Era, 20th-Century Jazz Masters, True Giants of Modern Jazz, and the Jazz Casual Series. The catalog is quite large, and its strength lies in its tremendous diversity of styles and genres of jazz. Most DVDs are from concerts, one exception being jazz critic Ralph J. Gleason's incredible *Jazz Casual* television series, which filmed in San Francisco and aired from 1961 to 1968. Twenty-eight 30-minute episodes, many featuring interviews with jazz legends, were televised on an occasional basis. All are available from Idem at this time.

Another exception to the various Idem concert series was a single historic one-hour television show called *The Sound of Jazz*, which was filmed in New York City and aired nationally in December 1957. The show featured many swing-era stars as well as post-swing artists such as Thelonious Monk and Gerry Mulligan. The most memorable point in the show reunited tenor saxophone legend Lester Young and the equally legendary Billie Holiday for one song. The two, who were formerly close friends, had been estranged for years, and this show brought them back together one last time for a moving performance of a blues song called "Fine and Mellow." Prez's solo coupled with Lady Day's vocal proved to be a crystalline moment in the history of jazz. Both passed away within two years of that historic reunion.

Jazz History and Related DVDs

The second group of DVDs makes up a much smaller but no less important group in the jazz canon. The films in this group focus upon jazz history, jazz culture, and jazz philosophy and aesthetics.

Among the DVDs that offer a historical perspective are Ken Burns's *Jazz*, a 10-disc set covering the music from its origins through what Burns called "the present," which unfortunately is woefully lacking in terms of completeness, even for the year 2000 when this series first aired. Many musicians and critics expressed concern that the final DVD of the set excluded many modern artists and failed to bring the music fully up to the millennium. There has also been the feeling that *Jazz* was biased toward certain performers at the expense of others. Whatever the case, there is some remarkable footage throughout the films, particularly those that covered the music through the swing era.

A more well-rounded (and a lot shorter) history comes from Naxos Jazz's *Masters of American Music: The Story of Jazz*. Originally made in 1993 and released by Naxos in 2009, this 98-minute film is more complete in terms of jazz's historic continuum than the Burns series. A collaboration between Matthew Seig, who directed the film, and jazz journalist Chris Albertson, this DVD is a winning combination of film clips, photographs, interviews, and of course, the music itself, which moves quickly but accurately from era to era, culminating in free jazz and jazz-rock fusion. Many of the interviews offer pertinent and interesting information and anecdotes about some of jazz's most famous and often most colorful musicians.

Made perhaps as a rebuttal to the Burns series, *Icons among Us: Jazz in the Present Tense* (Paradigm Studios) was originally telecast in 2009 as a four-part series for the Documentary Channel and ultimately pared down to a feature-length film, which was released that same year to very positive reviews from a number of reputable jazz journalists, including John Kelman at allaboutjazz.com, who has asserted that *Icons among Us* is far and away the best series about jazz ever produced. Featured throughout the film are many of today's most inspired and inspiring creative musicians, including pianist Matthew Shipp, bassist/vocalist Esperanza Spalding, trumpeter Nicholas Payton, guitarist Bill Frisell, and drummer Brian Blade.

Directed by Lars Larson and Michael Riviora, the overall thrust of the series and its companion film is highly philosophical and posits that jazz is not so much "exclusive" music as it is "inclusive" music that by definition includes musicians from across races, world cultures, and genders—that is, the world of jazz is big enough to accommodate all improvising musicians, irrespective of race, gender, and cultural background. And the further contention is that such inclusiveness offers exciting possibilities for audiences, who can now experience the music on a much broader scale than ever before. *Icons among Us* doesn't thumb its nose at jazz's long history; rather it suggests that history, while offering a firm foundation for the music, should not serve to confine either musicians or listeners to a narrow set of stylistic boundaries, grounded only in the past. Nicholas Payton, early in the film, sums its message up nicely when he admonishes listeners to "let go of everything you've seen and heard to experience the truth."

A FINAL WORD

Whether you wish to have a physical jazz listening/viewing library or your entire library on your iPad, iPod, or smartphone, the two most important things you can do are to keep it maintained and updated with new sounds; and to purchase your music through your local record shop (if your town is lucky enough to have one), or online via Amazon, CD Baby, iTunes, or a similar entity, in order to help support those who made the effort to create and record the music and bring it to you.

WORKS CITED

Armstrong, Louis. *Louis Armstrong in His Own Words: Selected Writings.* Ed. Thomas Brothers. New York: Oxford University Press, 1999. Print.

———. *Satchmo: My Life in New Orleans.* New York: Prentice Hall, 1954; rpt. New York: Da Capo Press, 1986. Print.

Avakian, George. "A Gentle Gentleman of a Man." *Jazz Magazine* Oct. 1964: 14. Print.

Berendt, Joachim-Ernst, and Günther Huesmann. *The Jazz Book: From Ragtime to the 21st Century.* 7th ed. Chicago: Lawrence Hill Books, 2009. Print.

Blumenthal, Bob. "A Beat for All Seasons—Jo Jones Returns to Sandy's." *The Boston Phoenix* 3 Oct. 1978. Print.

Brase, Wendell. "Teamwork Principles." *A Model for Sustaining Administrative Improvement.* University of California, Irvine. 15 Jan. 1998. PDF file.

Brookmeyer, Bob. Liner notes. *Kansas City Revisited.* United Artists Records. 1958. LP. Reissue, EMI Music/Mosaic Records, 2004. CD.

Burnett, John. "Art Tatum: A Talent Never to Be Duplicated." NPR. 5 Nov. 2006, NPR.com. Web.

Carter, Ron. "Press Kit." roncarter.net. n.d. Web. 9 June 2012.

"Corporation." Def. 1. *The Pocket Oxford Dictionary.* 8th ed. 1992. Print.

Crow, Bill. *From Birdland to Broadway: Scenes from a Jazz Life.* New York: Oxford UP, 1992. Print.

———. "Re: Democracy." Message to the author. 16 Jan. 2012. E-mail.

Dejohnette, Jack. "Biography." jackdejohnette.com. n.d. Web. 11 Oct. 2011.

Haden, Charlie. "Charlie's NEA Master's Award Speech." Lincoln Center, New York. 10 Jan. 2012. charliehadenmusic.com. n.d. Web. 2 Feb. 2012.

Jones, Jo, and Albert Murray. *Rifftide: The Life and Opinions of Papa Jo Jones*. Ed. Paul Devlin. Minneapolis: U of Minnesota P, 2011. Print.

Kaufman, Bob. "Walking Parker Home." *The Jazz Poetry Anthology*. Eds. Sascha Feinstein and Yusef Komunyakaa. Bloomington: Indiana UP, 1991, 100–111. Print.

Korall, Burt. *Drummin' Men: The Heartbeat of Jazz—The Bebop Years*. New York: Oxford UP, 2002. Print.

———. *Drummin' Men: The Heartbeat of Jazz—The Swingin' Years*. New York: Schirmer Books, 1990. Print.

Layman, Will. "The Little Label That Could: An Interview with Cryptogramophone's Jeff Gauthier." popmatters.com. 13 Apr. 2007. n.d. Web. 17 Jan. 2012.

Lees, Gene. "Dave Frishberg and Bob Dorough: Dave's on First and Bob's on Deck." *Jazz Times* Jan.–Feb. 2001. Print.

Liebman, Dave. Personal interview. 20 Nov. 2011.

Markowitz, Phil. "Re: A Request." Message to the author. 13 June 2012. E-mail.

Martino, Pat. "Biography." patmartino.com. DL Media. n.d. Web. 18 Oct. 2012.

Maupin, Bennie. Personal interview. 11 October 2011.

Medwin, Mark. "Milford Graves: Timepiece." allaboutjazz.com. n.d. Web. 22 June 2009.

Metheny, Pat. Liner Notes. *Jaco Pastorius*. Sony Records reissue. 2000. CD.

Morgan, Lee. Spoken introduction to "Close Your Eyes." perf. Art Blakey and the Jazz Messengers. *At the Jazz Corner of the World*. Blue Note, 1994. CD.

Murphy, Mark. "Bio." markmurphy.com. n.d. Web. 3 Apr. 2012.

Nachmanovitch, Stephen. *Free Play: The Power of Improvisation in Life and the Arts*. New York: Putnam, 1990. Print.

OKon, Richard. "Re: piece." Message to the author. 16 Jan. 2012. E-mail.

Schulman, Bruce J. *The Seventies: The Great Shift in American Culture, Society, and Politics*. Cambridge: Da Capo Press, 2002. Print.

Shadwick, Keith. *Bill Evans: Everything Happens to Me—A Musical Biography*. San Francisco: Backbeat Books, 2002. Print.

"Sonny Rollins: The Official Website of the Saxophone Colossus." sonnyrollins .com. Monthly Updates. Web. 5 Oct. 2012.

Teachout, Terry. *Pops*. New York: Houghton Mifflin Harcourt, 2009. Print.

Woods, Phil. Message to the author. 13 Sept. 2011. E-mail.

OTHER SOURCES

No one book is the be-all-end-all book about jazz. There are many fine volumes that have been written which offer personal insight, historical perspective, and critical viewpoints; and there are wonderfully painted word portraits of the men and women who have made jazz their life's work (many of which are mentioned at the end of chapters 7–18). If you would like to learn more about the jazz music and musicians, you can build a modest but comprehensive library of jazz-related books, either as e-books or as print books. If you use an e-reader, chances are that you may collect both formats, since a number of important volumes may not be available electronically at this point. In any case, here are a number of very readable books on jazz by some of our best writers.

Jazz Stories

Jazz is as much about stories off the bandstand as well as on it. The following books offer wonderfully funny and sometimes heart-wrenching stories about the day-to-day lives of jazz musicians, and they bring the players vividly to life in ways that will stay with you long after you've turned the last page.

Condon, Eddie. *We Called It Music: A Generation of Jazz*. Cambridge: Da Capo Press, 1992. Print.

Crow, Bill. *From Birdland to Broadway: Scenes from a Jazz Life*. New York: Oxford UP, 1992. Print.

———. *Jazz Anecdotes*. New York: Oxford UP, 1990. Print.

Enstice, Wayne, and Paul Rubin. *Jazz Spoken Here: Conversations with 22 Musicians*. Cambridge: Da Capo Press, 1994. Print.

Hentoff, Nat. *The Jazz Life*. Cambridge: Da Capo Press, 1978. Print.

Jack, Gordon. *Fifties Jazz Talk: An Oral Retrospective*. Lanham: Scarecrow Press, 2010. Print.

Janus, Cicily. *The New Face of Jazz*. New York: Billboard Books, 2010. Print.

Margolick, David. *Strange Fruit: The Biography of a Song*. New York: Ecco Press, 2001. Print.

Ratliff, Ben. *The Jazz Ear: Conversations over Music*. New York: Times Books, 2008. Print.

Shapiro, Nat, and Nat Hentoff. *Hear Me Talkin' to Ya: The Story of Jazz as Told by the Men Who Made It*. New York: Dover, 1956. Print.

Taylor, Arthur. *Notes and Tones: Musician to Musician Interviews*. New York: Coward, McCann, and Geoghagen, 1977. Print.

Selected Jazz History and Criticism

Critical essays and histories are sometimes written in heavy-handed and rather dry prose that may be effective in one's battles with insomnia; however—and happily—such is not the case with many books written by jazz historians and critics, who are often musicians themselves. If you are looking for further grounding in these two richly mined areas, here are some of the better books to offer both historical and critical—and highly readable—perspectives of the music.

Balliett, Whitney. *Collected Works: A Journal of Jazz, 1954–2000*. New York: St. Martin's Press, 2000. Print.

Berendt, Joachim-Ernst, and Günther Huesmann. *The Jazz Book: From Ragtime to the 21st Century*. 7th ed. Chicago: Lawrence Hill Books, 2009. Print.

Fernandez, Raúl. *Latin Jazz: The Perfect Combination*. San Francisco: Chronicle Books, 2002.

Giddins, Gary. *Visions of Jazz: The First Century*. New York: Oxford UP, 1998. Print.

Kirchner, Bill, ed. *The Oxford Companion to Jazz*. New York: Oxford UP, 2000. Print.

Morgenstern, Dan. *Living with Jazz: A Reader*. Ed. Sheldon Meyer. New York: Pantheon Books, 2004. Print.

Shipton, Alyn. *A New History of Jazz*. London: Continuum Books, 2001. Print.

Sidran, Ben. *Talking Jazz: An Illustrated Oral History*. San Francisco: Pomegranate ArtBooks, 1992. Print.

Other Jazz Books of Interest

These books, like the music itself, offer a rich diversity of glimpses into the jazz world. Here, we will find the beautiful photography of "The Judge," bassist Milt

Hinton; Ashley Kahn will take us behind the scenes of the creation of two of jazz's most immortal recordings; Sam Stephenson will take us back to New York in the late '50s, where we will visit the musically fertile and exciting loft scene through intimate photographs and vivid writings—and these are only a few of the riches awaiting you as you embark on these jazz journeys.

Hinton, Milt, and David Berger. *Bass Line: The Stories and Photographs of Milt Hinton*. Philadelphia: Temple UP, 1988. Print.

Hinton, Milt, David G. Berger, and Holly Maxson. *OverTime: The Jazz Photographs of Milt Hinton*. San Francisco: Pomegranate ArtBooks, 1991. Print.

Kahn, Ashley. *Kind of Blue: The Making of the Miles Davis Masterpiece*. New York: Da Capo Press, 2000. Print.

———. *A Love Supreme: The Story of John Coltrane's Signature Album*. New York: Viking Press, 2002. Print.

Lange, Art, and Nathaniel Mackey, eds. *Moment's Notice: Jazz in Poetry and Prose*. Minneapolis: Coffee House Press, 1993. Print.

Nachmanovitch, Stephen. *Free Play: The Power of Improvisation in Life and the Arts*. New York: Putnam, 1990. Print.

Ramsey, Doug. *Jazz Matters: Reflections on the Music and Some of Its Makers*. Fayetteville: U of Arkansas P, 1989. Print.

Stephenson, Sam. *The Jazz Loft Project*. New York: Knopf, 2009. Print.

Whitehead, Kevin. *Why Jazz?—A Concise Guide*. New York: Oxford UP, 2011. Print.

Jazz Periodicals in the 21st Century

Walk into any shop that sells magazines and journals and you will discover that print versions of jazz magazines are fast becoming a thing of the past. While two of these—*DownBeat* and *Jazz Times*—continue at this writing to be fairly accessible in print format, others, including the excellent *Jazzwise* from the UK and Canada's venerable and adventurous *CODA Magazine*, are not as easy to find; however, the good news is that these and other jazz-related magazines and newspapers are also available as online periodicals and will often deliver jazz news to your computer on a daily basis. To explore further, check out these websites:

Cadence: www.cadencejazzmagazine.com
CODA: www.coda1958.com
DownBeat: www.downbeat.com
Jazz Inside: www.jazzinsidemagazine.com
Jazz Times: www.jazztimes.com
Jazziz: www.jazziz.com
Jazzwise: www.jazzwisemagazine.com
New York City Jazz Record: www.nycjazzrecord.com

NAME INDEX

Abercrombie, John, 377
Adams, Park "Pepper," 220
Adderley, Julian "Cannonball," 192–93, 264
Akinmusire, Ambrose, 135
Akoustic Band (Chick Corea), 264
Alessi, Ralph, 97, 134–35
Ali, Rashied, 171
Allen, Geri, 97
Almeida, Laurindo, 196, 366
Altschul, Barry, 272
Anderson, Ray, 97, 157
Armstrong, Louis, 39–41, 43, 91–92, 98, 113–14, 116, 120, 128, 141, 143, 209, 353, 387, 420–21
Art Blakey and the Jazz Messengers, 57, 73, 128, 130, 150, 175, 182, 191, 325–26
The Art Ensemble of Chicago, 422
Association for the Advancement of Creative Music (AACM), 155
Ayler, Albert, 171–72, 175

Bach, Johann Sebastian, 14, 83–84
Bailey, Mildred, 393
Baker, Chesney "Chet," 57, 116, 195, 219, 398–99
Baraka, Amiri (LeRoi Jones), 60
Baron, Joey, 340
Barron, Kenny, 97
Basie, William "Count," 24, 93, 98, 100, 102–6, 108, 116, 128, 150, 156, 163, 182, 248, 393
Bauer, Billy, 369–70
Bechet, Sidney, 39, 209, 211, 225
Beiderbecke, Leon "Bix," 42, 113–16, 120
Bellson, Louie, 182
Bennett, Tony, 260, 388–89
The Bennie Maupin Ensemble, 19–23, 239
Bennink, Han, 337–38, 344
Benson, George, 72, 409
Berger, Karl, 357–58
Berne, Tim, 9, 203–4

Bernstein, Steven, 135
Berry, Leon "Chu," 64
Bickert, Ed, 195
Bigard, Barney, 98, 226
Binney, David, 205
The Black Artists' Group, 220
Black, Jim, 97, 230, 340
Blade, Brian, 97, 177
Blake, Eubie, 39
Blakey, Art, 57–58, 73, 131, 177, 182,
    257, 325
Blanchard, Terrence, 132
Blanton, Jimmy, 98, 283
Bleckmann, Theo, 111
Bley, Paul, 271–72
Bloom, Jane Ira, 218
The Blue Devils, 102
Bluiett, Hamiet, 219–221
Bolden, Buddy, 39, 91, 113
Bradford, Bobby, 229
Braxton, Anthony, 90, 156, 201, 210,
    218
Brecker, Michael, 8, 131, 180–81
Brecker, Randy, 131, 180–81
Bridgewater, Dee Dee, 409–10
Broadbent, Alan, 274, 277–78, 406
Brookmeyer, Bob, 6, 12–13, 57, 84,
    103, 107, 108–11, 128, 150–54, 164,
    192, 219–20
Brötzmann, Peter, 175
Brown, Clifford, 93, 120, 127, 166
Brown, Garnett, 154
Brown, Lawrence, 145–46
Brown, Ray, 286–87
Brubeck, Dave, 94, 105, 195, 275
Bryant, Clora, 201
Burrell, Kenny, 370–71
Burton, Gary, 67, 356, 373
Byrd, Charlie 165, 366–68
Byrd, Donald, 58, 129, 191, 220
Byron, Don, 229

Cage, John, 129
Calloway, Cabell "Cab," 98
Candoli, Conte, 107
Cardenas, Steve, 380
Carney, Harry, 219–21
Carter, Benny, 187–89, 191–92
Carter, Betty, 404–405
Carter, John, 229
Carter, Ron, 70, 97, 124, 131, 262,
    293–95
Catlett, Big Sid, 314–315
Chambers, Paul, 124, 126, 150, 210,
    258
Charles, Ray, 405
Cherry, Don, 129–30, 135, 168, 173,
    197, 373
Christensen, Jon, 268
Christian, Charlie, 368–69
Christlieb, Pete, 182
Circle (Chick Corea), 263
Clarke, Kenny, 49, 50, 93, 120, 251,
    322
Clarke, Stanley, 71
Clayton, Wilbur "Buck," 102, 116
Cleaver, Gerald, 340
The Clifford Brown–Max Roach
    Quintet, 166
Cline, Nels, 378–79
Cobb, Arnett, 172
Cobb, Jimmy, 97, 124, 258
Cohen, Anat, 229
Cohn, Al, 163
Cole, Nat "King," 248, 397
Cole, William "Cozy," 118
Coleman, George, 182
Coleman, Ornette, 9, 41, 64, 94,
    129–30, 179, 191, 197–99, 200, 256,
    272, 292
Collette, William "Buddy," 163, 234
Colley, Scott, 96–97, 302–303
Collins, Rudy, 122

Coltrane, Alice, 171, 173, 270
Coltrane, John, 4, 7, 8, 18, 62–64, 74,
    82, 94, 124, 128, 129–30, 134, 150,
    163, 168–72, 175, 179, 181–82, 191,
    199–200, 203, 212–17, 238, 253,
    255, 258, 270, 328–30
Coltrane, Ravi, 183
Condon, Eddie, 41, 93, 363
Corea, Armando "Chick," 68, 71, 96,
    130, 181, 203, 263–64, 348
Coryell, Larry, 67, 373
Cranshaw, Bob, 168
Creole Jazz Band, King Oliver's, 91
Crow, Bill, 80
Cuscuna, Michael, 171

Daniels, Eddie, 228
Danielsson, Palle, 268
The Dave Brubeck Quartet, 195, 340,
    357
Davern, Kenny, 228
Davis, Dr. Art, 173, 201
Davis, Eddie "Lockjaw," 172
Davis, Miles, 55–57, 67–71, 73–74, 79,
    85, 93–96, 108, 113, 116, 124–27,
    135, 166, 170, 177, 182, 193, 197,
    202, 214, 217, 239, 251, 257–58,
    262–63, 268, 295, 326, 332–33, 348,
    406
Davis, Steve (bass), 268
Davis, Steve (trombone), 157
De Francesco, Joey, 273–74
DeFranco, Boniface "Buddy," 142,
    228
De Grassi, Alex, 428
Dejohnette, Jack, 97, 263, 328, 333–35
Dennis, Willie, 107, 155
Desmond, Paul, 9, 116, 195–96
Dickenson, Vic, 145
Dodds, Warren, "Baby," 309–12, 341
Dodds, Johnny, 40, 225

Dolphy Eric, 9, 19, 130, 199–201,
    234–35, 237–38
Donaldson, Lou, 193, 205
Donegan, Dorothy, 249–51
Dorham, Kenny, 120, 128
Dorough, Bob, 29, 399–403, 435
Dorsey, Jimmy, 104, 226–27
Dorsey, Tommy, 104, 141–42
The Double Six of Paris, 407
Douglas, Dave, 97, 133–36, 230,
    438–39
D'Rivera, Paquito, 228

Eastwood, Clint, 190, 423–24, 434
Eckstine, Billy, 397
Edison, Harry "Sweets," 102, 116
Ehrlich, Marty, 205, 230
Eldridge, Roy "Little Jazz," 117–20
Elektric Band (Chick Corea), 264
Elling, Kurt, 412
Ellington, Edward K. "Duke," 9, 14,
    39–40, 43, 74, 79, 86, 98–100, 105,
    117, 128, 143, 163, 187–88, 203,
    209, 219–20, 226, 238, 248, 420–21,
    425–26
Ellis, Don, 129, 134
Eubanks, Robin, 157
Evans, Bill 94, 126, 256, 258–61, 264,
    291, 326
Evans, Gil, 55–57, 108, 111, 125, 156,
    210

Farmer, Art, 128
Feather, Leonard, 15
Ferguson, Maynard, 105
Fitzgerald, Ella, 128, 394–95
Fontana, Carl, 155
Foster, George "Pops," 282
Fountain, Pete, 228
The Free Spirits, 373
Freeman, Bud, 41

Freeman, Russ, 57
Frisell, Bill, 97, 378–79
Frishberg, Dave, 399–400
Fuller, Curtis, 148, 150

Garbarek, Jan, 218, 268
Galbraith, Barry, 118
Garland, William "Red," 124, 257–58
Garner, Errol, 257
Garrett, Kenny, 9, 202–3
Garrison, Jimmy, 62–63, 82, 171, 268
Gauthier, Jeff, 441–43
The Gerry Mulligan Concert Jazz
    Band, 87–88, 98, 103, 106–7, 220
Getz, Stan, 57, 108, 150, 163–65, 182,
    366
Gillespie, John Birks "Dizzy," 24, 49,
    51, 93, 104–5, 118, 120–24, 127–28,
    146, 182, 189, 192, 248, 251, 345,
    353, 421–22
Gilmore, Steve, 192
Giuffre, Jimmy, 108, 163, 228, 272
Goldings, Larry, 274
Golson, Benny, 181–82
Gomez, Eddie, 264, 292
Gonsalves, Paul, 98
Gonzales, Babs (Lee Brown), 395
Goodman, Benny, 41, 44, 47, 93, 98,
    100–102, 146, 192, 210, 226–27,
    352–53, 369
Goodrick, Mick, 380
Goodwin, Bill, 27–31, 192, 435
Gordon, Dexter, 24, 93, 181, 262, 423
Gordon, Wycliffe, 157
Gorelick, Kenny ("Kenny G"), 72,
    427–28
Gowans, Brad, 150
Grappelli, Stephane, 93
Graves, Milford, 336–37
Green, Freddie, 102, 364
Greer, Sonny, 98

Gress, Drew, 96
Griffin, Johnny, 163
Grimes, Henry, 168
Gryce, George General "Gigi," 193

Haden, Charlie, 97, 197, 267, 292–93
Hagans, Tim, 132
Hall, Jim, 97, 168, 195, 260, 370
Hamilton, Chico, 199, 200
Hamilton, Jimmy, 226
Hampton, Lionel, 352–54, 356
Hancock, Herbie, 17, 30, 67–68,
    70–71, 124, 131, 177, 181, 203, 239,
    261–63, 295
Hargrove, Roy, 97, 131–32
Harrell, Tom, 132
Harris, Bill, 145–46, 150
Harris, Stefon, 359
Harrison, Jimmy, 145
Hart, Billy "Jabali," 97, 262
Hartman, Johnny, 397
Havens, Richie, 60
Hawkins, Coleman "Hawk," 8, 50–51,
    64, 98, 102, 117–18, 161–64, 166,
    172, 179, 210, 219–20, 272
Haynes, Graham, 134–135
Haynes, Roy, 97, 134, 263, 326–28
The Headhunters, 68, 239
Heard, John, 24–25
Heath, Albert "Tootie," 182
Heath, Jimmy, 182
Hemphill, Julius, 203, 205, 220
Henderson, Eddie, 262
Henderson, Fletcher, 39, 86, 98, 101,
    163
Henderson, Joe, 82, 130, 163, 177–78,
    203
Henderson, William, 173
Herman, Woodrow "Woody," 104,
    164, 182, 227
Hession, Jim, 245

Higginbotham, J. C., 145
Higgins, Billy, 168
Hines, Earl "Fatha," 115, 248
Hinton, Milton "Milt," 118, 284–87, 289
Hodges, Johnny, 9, 98, 164, 187–89, 191, 209
Holiday, Billie, 24, 163, 387–88, 392–93, 423
Holland, Dave, 97, 292
Hollenbeck, John, 111, 341
Holman, Willis "Bill," 105
Horn, Paul, 234
Horn, Shirley, 406
The Hot Club of France, 93, 365
Hot Five and Hot Seven, Louis Armstrong's, 91
Hubbard, Freddie, 130, 203
Hurst, Robert, 73
Hutcherson, Bobby, 356–57
Hyman, Dick, 118

Iyer, Vijay, 96

Jackson, Darryl Munyungo, 20–22, 348
Jackson, Milt, 354–56
Jamal, Ahmad, 257, 275
Jarreau, Al, 409
Jarrett, Keith, 90, 127, 265–68, 292–93
Jefferson, Eddie, 407
Jenkins, Clay, 132, 134, 438
Johnson, James "J. J.," 93, 146–47, 150, 166
Johnson, James P., 39, 245–46
Jones, Elvin, 62–63, 82, 107, 150, 171, 217, 268, 328–32
Jones, Hank, 107, 150, 180, 257
Jones, Jo "Papa Jo," 102, 316
Jones, "Philly Joe," 124, 258, 286, 326–27
Jones, Quincy, 128, 192

Jones, Thad, 107, 150
Joplin, Scott, 16, 37
Jordan, Clifford, 182
Jordan, Sheila, 97, 404
Juris, Vic, 36, 380

Kelly, Julie, 389
Kelly, Wynton, 258
Kenton, Stan, 104–6, 146, 220
Keppard, Freddie, 91, 113
Knepper, Jimmy, 154
Konitz, Lee, 9, 57. 97, 116, 182, 194–96, 210, 256, 369
Koonse, Larry, 380, 438
Kral, Irene, 406
Krall, Diana, 410
Krupa, Gene, 41, 102, 104, 117, 219, 316–18
Kuhn, Steve, 97, 268

LaBarbera, Joe, 438
Lacy, Steve, 155, 210–12, 216–17, 271
LaFaro, Scott, 260, 290–91
Lake, Oliver, 205, 220
Lambert, Hendricks, and Ross, 407
Lang, Eddie, 363
LaRoca (Sims), Pete, 268
Lateef, Yusef, 231, 234
Laws, Hubert, 235
Lewis, George (trombone), 155–56
Lewis, John, 197
Lewis, Mel, 107
The Liberation Music Orchestra (Charlie Haden), 293
Liebman, David, 8, 9, 69, 96–97, 181–83, 215–17, 221–22, 236, 435
Lifetime, (Tony Williams' Lifetime), 68, 273, 333, 373
Lincoln, Abbey, 406
Little, Booker, 129, 134
Locke, Joe, 358–61

Lovano, Joe, 97, 178–81, 378
Lovano, Tony "Big T," 179

Mahanthappa, Rudresh, 9, 97, 204–6
The Mahavishnu Orchestra, 68, 71, 373
Mangelsdorff, Albert, 156–57
The Manhattan Transfer, 408
Mann, Herbie, 233–34
Manne, Sheldon "Shelly," 105
Margitza, Rick, 183
Marino, Tony, 28, 30
Markowitz, Phil, 398–99
Marsalis, Branford, 73, 130, 183, 218
Marsalis, Delfeayo, 157
Marsalis, Ellis, 130
Marsalis, Wynton, 73, 78–79, 81–82, 130–31
Marsh, Warne, 57, 182, 256, 369
Martino, Pat, 371–72
Maupin, Bennie, 19–23, 68, 173, 238–41, 262–63, 443
McBride, Christian, 73
McCaslin, Donny, 9, 183
McCurdy, Roy, 24–25
McDuff, Brother Jack, 179
McFerrin, Bobby, 409
McGettrick, Curt, 221
McLaughlin, John, 68, 96, 373–74
McLean, Jackie, 9, 57, 188, 190–91, 193
McPartland, Jimmy, 41
McPartland, Marion (*Piano Jazz*), 276
McPherson, Charles, 205
McShann, Jay, 44
Mela, Francisco, 180
Melford, Myra, 443
The Mel-Tones (vocal group), 407
Menza, Don, 23–26, 182
Metheny, Pat, 97, 375–77, 428
Miley, James "Bubber," 98, 117

Miller, Mulgrew, 73
Mingus, Charles, 49, 61, 93–94, 182, 191, 199–200, 237–38, 256, 287–90
Mintzer, Bob, 183
Mitchell, Joni, 175, 181, 214, 263, 298
Mitchell, Nicole, 236
Mitchell, Richard "Blue," 58, 120, 129
Mitchell, Roscoe, 218
Mobley, Hank, 57, 181–82, 191
The Modern Jazz Quartet, 195, 354–56
Mole, Irving "Miff," 141–42
Moncur III, Grachan, 154–55
Monk, Thelonious, 49, 93–94, 120, 128–129, 134, 166, 192, 211, 220, 251–55, 325, 424, 438
Montgomery, Monk, 296
Montgomery, Wes, 371–72, 425
Moody, James, 10, 122, 181–82, 234
Moran, Jason, 96
Moreira, Airto, 346–48
Morello, Joe, 340
Morgan, Lee, 58, 67, 120, 128, 191
Morton, Ferdinand "Jelly Roll," 37, 244, 246
Most, Sam, 231, 233–234
Moten, Benny 44
Motian, Paul, 180, 264, 267, 291, 293, 338–39, 378
Mulligan, Gerry, 55, 57, 87–88, 107–8, 128, 154, 192, 195, 219–20
Murphy, Lyle, 239
Murphy, Mark, 397
Murray, David, 163, 175, 240
Murray, Sunny, 336
Mwandishi (Herbie Hancock Sextet), 239, 262

Nance, Ray, 117
Nanton, Joe "Tricky Sam," 98, 144, 157

Nascimento, Milton, 175
Navarro, Theodore "Fats," 120
Nelson, Steve, 358–59
The New Art Orchestra, 108–10
The New York Art Quartet, 155
The New York Voices, 408
Newsome, Sam, 218
Newton, James, 235
Niewood, Adam, 28–29
Norvo, Red (née Kenneth Norville), 351–52, 393
Nussbaum, Adam, 10

O'Day, Anita, 395–97
OKon, Richard, 431–32
Oleszkiewicz, Darek "Oles," 20–22
Oliver, Joe "King," 39, 91, 113, 141
The Original Dixieland Jazz Band, 91
Ory, Edward "Kid," 141, 157

Page, Walter, 102, 282–83
Parker, Charlie "Bird," 9, 18, 29, 49, 50–52, 54–55, 61, 93, 116, 120, 134, 146, 179–80, 188–94, 210, 227, 248, 251, 254–55, 423
Parker, Evan, 210, 218
Parlato, Gretchen, 411–12
Pastorius, Jaco, 296–99
Patitucci, John, 177, 264, 300–302, 304–306
Peacock, Gary, 267
Peplowski, Ken, 228
Pepper, Art, 105, 193, 196
Peraza, Armando, 345
Perez, Danilo, 177
Peterson, Oscar, 257
Pettiford, Oscar, 49, 93, 283–84
Piano Jazz (Marion McPartland), 276
The Pied Pipers (vocal group), 407
Portal, Michel, 240
Potter, Chris, 9, 183

Potter, Tommy, 251
Powell, Earl "Bud," 49–50, 93, 251, 255–57
Pozo, Chano, 105, 345
Priester, Julian, 154, 262

Quartet West (Charlie Haden), 274, 293
Quinichette, Paul, 163

Rainey, Tom, 340
Ranier, Tom, 24–25
Rava, Enrico, 132
Red Hot Peppers, Jelly Roll Morton and his, 91
Redman, Dewey, 267, 293
Redman, Joshua, 9, 183
Reeves, Dianne, 410
Rehak, Frank, 155
Reider, Jim, 88
Reinhardt, Django, 93, 364–66, 368
Return to Forever, 68, 264
Ribot, Marc, 96, 378–80
Rich, Bernard, "Buddy," 142, 182, 192, 318–21
Richmond, Dannie, 289
Ridl, Jim, 6
Roach, Max, 49–50, 61, 93, 166, 251, 308, 322–24
Roberts, Marcus, 73
Robinson, Perry, 229
Rollini, Adrian, 351–52
Rollins, Sonny "Newk," 8, 24, 57, 90, 93, 97, 130, 163, 166–68, 175, 179, 182, 191, 272
Romao, Dom Um, 346–48
Roney, Wallace, 131
Roseman, Josh, 97, 157
Rosenwinkel, Kurt, 96, 380
Rosnes, Renee, 10
Rosolino, Frank, 105, 148–49

Ross, Annie, 407
Rouse, Charlie, 182, 253
Rudd, Roswell, 97, 155, 157–58
Rushing, Jimmy, 393
Russell, Charles "Pee Wee," 41, 226

Saft, Jamie, 274
Sandoval, Arturo, 132
Santamaria, Mongo, 345
Saxophone Summit, 181
Scheinman, Jenny, 443
Schifrin, Lalo, 122
Schneider, Maria, 110–11
Scofield, John, 96, 178, 374–75,
    381–82
Scott, Jimmy, 405–406
Scott, Tony, 228
Scott-Heron, Gil, 60
Shakti (John McLaughlin), 373–74
Shank, Clifford "Bud," 196, 231
Shavers, Charlie, 142
Shaw, Artie, 44, 46–47, 93, 100–101,
    104, 210, 226–27
Shaw, Woodrow "Woody," 130
Shearing, George, 406
Sheldon, Jack, 57
Shepp, Archie, 63–64, 67, 155, 171–
    72, 175
Shorter, Wayne, 8, 68, 70, 96–97, 124,
    131, 163, 175–77, 182, 214–17, 262,
    265
Silvano, Judi, 180
Silver, Horace, 57–58, 73, 129–30, 257
Simon, Paul, 181
Simone, Nina, 406
Sims, John Haley "Zoot," 107, 163
Sinatra, Frank, 180, 181, 388–89, 392
Singers Unlimited, 407
Singleton, Arthur "Zutty," 309–12, 341
Smith, Bessie, 390–91
Smith Wadada Leo, 97

Smith, Dr. Lonnie, 179, 273
Smith, Jimmy, 58, 273
Smith, Johnny, 164
Smith, Marvin "Smitty," 73
Smith, Willie "The Lion," 39, 246–47
Sorey, Tyshawn, 340
Spalding, Esperanza, 180, 303–304,
    411
Spaulding, James, 205, 234
Speed, Chris, 9, 97, 183, 230, 440
Stafford, Terrell, 132, 134
The Standards Trio (Keith Jarrett),
    267
Stanko, Tomasz, 132
Steig, Jeremy, 234
Stenson, Bobo, 97
Stewart, Rex, 98, 117
Stitt, Sonny, 193
Strozier, Frank, 193, 205
Sun Ra, 422, 437–38
Sung, Helen, 96
Surman, John, 97, 218, 221
Swallow, Steve, 272, 296
The Swingle Singers, 407

Tabackin, Lew, 236
Tatum, Art, 247–48
Taylor, Cecil, 67, 172, 210, 271–72,
    336
Tchicai, John, 155
Teagarden, Jack, 141–43
Terry, Clark, 88, 98, 107–8, 117,
    128–29, 192
Terry, Sue ("Sweet Sue"), 29
Teschmacher, Frank, 41
Test, Billy, 28–30
The Thad Jones-Mel Lewis Jazz
    Orchestra, 107–8, 220
Thornhill, Claude, 108
Timmons, Bobby, 58
Tizol, Juan, 145

Tjader, Cal, 357
Tormé, Mel, 397
Torres, Nestor, 236
Tough, Dave, 41
Trible, Dwight, 412–414
Tristano, Lennie, 182, 192, 194, 196, 256, 270–71, 369–70
Turre, Steve, 157
Tyner, McCoy, 62–63, 82, 171, 268–70

V.S.O.P., 333
Valdez, Carlos "Patato," 345
Valentin, Dave, 236
The Vanguard Jazz Orchestra, 108
Vaughan, Sarah, 128, 134, 395–96, 409
Vitous, Miroslav, 263
Vitro, Roseanna, 410–11, 414–15

Waller, Thomas "Fats," 39, 90, 245, 247–48, 273, 391
Walton, Cedar, 97
Ware, David S., 175
Warrington, Tom, 438
Washer, Bill, 28–29
Washington, Dinah, 397
Washington Jr., Grover, 205
Waters, Ethel, 390–91
Watts, Jeff "Tain," 73
Weather Report, 68, 71, 177, 214, 265, 298, 347, 437
Webb, William "Chick," 104, 313–14, 325, 394

Webster, Ben, 64, 163–64, 172, 179, 210
Weckl, Dave, 264
Weiss, Dan, 340
Wess, Frank, 231–32
White, Andrew, 437
Wilbur, Bob, 228
Williams, Buster, 262
Williams, Charles "Cootie," 98, 117
Williams, Mary Lou, 248–49
Williams, Tony, 68, 70, 96, 124, 131, 262, 295, 328, 332–33
Wilson, Matt, 340
Wilson, Nancy, 406
Wilson, Steve, 205, 218
Wilson, Teddy, 248
Winding, Kai, 93, 146
Winstone, Norma, 97, 404
Woods, Phil, 27, 190–93, 435
Woodyard, Sam, 98
The World Saxophone Quartet, 220

Yahill, Sam, 274
Young, James "Trummy," 145
Young, Larry (Khalid Yasin), 273
Young, Lester "Prez," 8, 12, 51, 102, 120, 134, 150, 161–64, 179, 182, 194, 210, 219, 228, 368, 423

Zawinul, Josef (Joe), 68, 96, 175, 214, 264–65
The Zawinul Syndicate, 265
Zorn, John, 439, 441

TITLE INDEX

A-Tisket, A-Tasket, 394
Afro-Blue, 62–63, 346
Ain't Misbehavin', 246
Alabama, 62–63
Alone and I, 262
Alone Together, 29
Am I Blue? 391
Anthropology, 11

Babble On, 296
Baby, It's Cold Outside, 405
Better Get It in Your Soul, 289
The Bird with the Coppery Keen
    Claws, 111
Birdland, 408
Black and Tan Fantasy, 421
Blue Bossa, 128
Blue in Green, 126–27, 411
Blue Rondo à la Turk, 195
Boo Boo's Birthday, 255

Brilliant Corners, 254
Bye, Bye, Blackbird, 125

California Dreamin', 196
Caravan, 145
Chameleon, 30
Cherokee, 51
Chim, Chim, Cheree, 213
China Boy, 353
Composition "173," 202
Cottontail, 164
Crazy 'bout My Baby, 391

Devil May Care, 402
Don't Be That Way, 102
Don't Worry, Be Happy, 409

Early Autumn, 164
Eat That Chicken, 289
El Gaucho Rojo, 379

The Entertainer, 37
Epitaph, 289
Evidence, 254
Excuse Me for Living, 400

Fables of Faubus, 289
Fall, 177
Far East Suite, 421
Fat Lip, 374
Filipino Box Spring Hog, 380
Footprints, 177
Friday the Thirteenth, 254

The Girl from Ipanema, 164
Greensleeves, 213
Groovin' High, 123–24

Heebie Jeebies, 387
Honeysuckle Rose, 246

I Can See Your House from Here, 374
I Can't Get Started, 212
I Didn't Know What Time It Was, 30
I Get Along without You Very Well,
    399
I Got It Bad and That Ain't Good, 188
I'm Getting Sentimental over You,
    142
I'm Hip, 400
I'm Just Wild about Harry, 39
Imagine, 33
India, 214
I Remember You, 28
Isotope, 83
I Think My Wife Is a Hat, 296
It Was a Very Good Year, 389

The Joint Is Jumpin', 246
Just the Way You Are, 192
Just You, Just Me, 254
Justice, 254

King Porter Stomp, 101

Ladies in Mercedes, 296
Let Me Off Uptown, 396
Let My People Be, 87
Lord, Don't Let Them Drop That
    Atomic Bomb on Me, 289
A Love Supreme, 94
Low Blow, 374

Maple Leaf Rag, 16, 37
The Maze, 262
Meditations on Integration, 289
Mercy, Mercy, Mercy, 264
Misty, 405
Mood Indigo, 100, 404
Moonlight in Vermont, 164
Mumbles, 128
Music for a Great City, 33
My Attorney Bernie, 400
My Favorite Things, 171, 213
My Funny Valentine, 12
My Hero Zero, 403
My Wild Irish Rose, 266

Naughty Number Nine, 403
Nefertiti, 177
New Love, 109
Night and Day, 24

One O'Clock Jump, 104
Ornithology, 255

Penumbra, 22
Perdido, 145
Poinciana, 275
Puttin' on the Ritz, 39

Raise Four, 254
The Reefer Song, 391
Resolution, 412

Rhythm-a-ning, 255
Rockin' in Rhythm, 421
Round Midnight, 254

St. Louis Blues, 391
Satin Doll, 79
She Was Too Good to Me, 399
Shuck That Corn Before You Eat, 34
Sing, Sing, Sing, 317
Skippy, 254
So Sue Me, 374
Spooky Drums No. 1, 310
Straight, No Chaser, 255
Swing Low, Sweet Chariot, 35

Take Five, 195, 275
Take the A Train, 238, 421
Tapping Things, 22

Them There Eyes, 387–88
This Is the Moment, 128
This Masquerade, 409
Too Long in L.A., 400
Trillium R, 202
Trinkle, Tinkle, 254
Twisted, 407

Van Lingle Mungo, 400

Watermelon Man, 17, 262, 346
The Well-Tempered Clavier, 83–84
West End Blues, 91–91, 114
When I Look into Your Eyes, 410

Yardbird Suite, 29
Yawn, 374
You Are There, 400
Your Feet's Too Big, 246, 391

RECORDING INDEX

Adventures in Blues (Stan Kenton), 105

Adventures in Jazz (Stan Kenton), 105

Adventures in Standards (Stan Kenton), 105

Adventures in Time (Stan Kenton), 105

The All Seeing Eye (Wayne Shorter), 177

All the Way (Jimmy Scott), 406

Amazonas (Cal Tjader), 357

At Midnight (Wynton Kelly), 326

Big Fun (Miles Davis), 239, 373

Big Stuff (Gil Evans), 210

Birth of the Cool (Miles Davis), 55, 57, 108, 124, 146, 219, 323

Bitches Brew (Miles Davis), 68, 95, 125, 214, 239, 263–64, 373

Blue Train (John Coltrane), 128, 150, 326

Blues for Dracula (Philly Joe Jones), 326

Breezin' (George Benson), 409

Bright Size Life (Pat Metheny), 296, 375

California, Here I Come (Bill Evans), 326

Chamber Music Society (Esperanza Spalding), 303, 411

Charles Mingus Presents Charles Mingus, 237

City of Glass (Stan Kenton), 105

Come Sunday (Charlie Haden–Hank Jones), 293

Concert in the Garden (Maria Schneider), 110–11

Conversations with Myself (Bill Evans), 260

Crossings (Herbie Hancock), 262

Cuban Fire (Stan Kenton), 105

Don Juan's Reckless Daughter (Joni Mitchell), 298

Doo Bop (Miles Davis), 125

Duster (Gary Burton), 67

E.S.P. (Miles Davis), 262

Echo Canyon (James Newton), 235

Filles de Kilimanjaro (Miles Davis), 67–68, 125

Focus (Stan Getz), 164

A Gathering of Spirits (Saxophone Summit), 181

The Gentle Rain (Irene Kral with Alan Broadbent), 400

The Girl in the Other Room (Diana Krall), 410

Hejira (Joni Mitchell), 298

High Flying (Lambert, Hendricks, and Ross), 407

I Remember Miles (Shirley Horn), 406

In a Silent Way (Miles Davis), 68, 125, 214, 263–64, 373

Intermodulation (Bill Evans–Jim Hall), 260

Introducing Paul Bley, 272

Intuition (Bill Evans–Eddie Gomez), 260

Jack Johnson (aka A Tribute to Jack Johnson) (Miles Davis), 239, 373

Jaco Pastorius (Jaco Pastorius), 299

Jazz Samba (Stan Getz–Charlie Byrd), 368

Joys and Desires (John Hollenbeck), 111

Kenton/Ritter (Stan Kenton–Tex Ritter), 105

Kenton/Wagner (Stan Kenton), 105

Kind of Blue (Miles Davis), 70, 94,124, 126, 170–71, 193

The Köln Concerts (Keith Jarrett), 266

Last Date (Eric Dolphy), 19

Live at the Fillmore (Miles Davis), 263

Live-Evil (Miles Davis), 373

Looking Ahead (Cecil Taylor), 271

The Lost and Found (Gretchen Parlato), 411

A Love Supreme (John Coltrane), 94, 171, 412

The Melody at Night with You (Keith Jarrett), 266

Midnight Sun (Dee Dee Bridgewater), 409–10

Miles Ahead (Miles Davis–Gil Evans), 108, 125

Miles in the Sky (Miles Davis), 67

Mingus (Joni Mitchell), 298

The Music of Randy Newman (Roseanna Vitro), 411

Mwandishi (Herbie Hancock), 262

My Favorite Things (John Coltrane), 213

Nancy Wilson–Cannonball Adderley, 406

Now He Sings, Now He Sobs (Chick Corea), 263

OM/ShalOM (Michael Stephans), 303

On the Corner (Miles Davis), 239

One Quiet Night (Pat Metheny), 428

Outward Bound (Eric Dolphy), 199, 295

Page One (Joe Henderson), 178

Penumbra (Bennie Maupin) 442

Pilgrimage (Michael Brecker), 181

Porgy and Bess (Miles Davis–Gil Evans), 108, 125

Radio Music Society (Esperanza Spalding), 411

Reflections (Steve Lacy), 211

The Return (Pat Martino), 372

The Shape of Jazz to Come (Ornette Coleman), 292

The Sidewinder (Lee Morgan), 67, 128

Simple Pleasures (Bobby McFerrin), 409

Sketches of Spain (Miles Davis–Gil Evans), 108, 125

Slow Circle (Alex de Grassi), 428

Smokin' at the Half Note, (Wes Montgomery), 371

Something Else (Ornette Coleman), 197

Songs in the Key of OM (Jack Dejohnette), 335

Sound Grammar (Ornette Coleman), 197

Stan Getz–Bob Brookmeyer, recorded fall 1961, 164

Stay Out of the Sun (Bob Brookmeyer–Michael Stephans), 154

Steal Away (Charlie Haden–Hank Jones), 293

Super Nova (Wayne Shorter), 177

The Swingin's Mutual (Nancy Wilson–George Shearing), 406

Takin' Off (Herbie Hancock), 262

This Is Our Music (Ornette Coleman), 292

Tijuana Sketches (Charles Mingus), 289

Time Further Out (The Dave Brubeck Quartet), 105

Time Out (The Dave Brubeck Quartet), 94, 105, 195

Together Again (Tony Bennett–Bill Evans), 260

The Tony Bennett–Bill Evans Album, 260

A Tribute to Miles (various artists), 131

Under the Missouri Sky (Charlie Haden–Pat Metheny), 293

Undercurrent (Bill Evans–Jim Hall), 260

We Insist! The Freedom Now Suite (Max Roach), 323

We'll Be Together Again (Pat Martino), 372

West Side Story (Stan Kenton), 105

When I Look into Your Eyes (Diana Krall), 410

When the Heart Emerges Glistening (Ambrose Akinmusire), 135

Where (Ron Carter), 295

Who's On First? (Dave Frishberg–Bob Dorough), 400

You Won't Forget Me (Shirley Horn), 406

ABOUT THE AUTHORS

Michael Stephans leads several distinct but interrelated lives. A well-known and respected jazz drummer, Stephans has performed and/or recorded with a wide array of internationally famous artists, including reed players Bennie Maupin, Pharoah Sanders, and NEA Jazz Masters Dave Liebman and Phil Woods; the late trombonist/composer/NEA Jazz Master Bob Brookmeyer; pianists Uri Caine and Alan Broadbent; bassists John Patitucci and Scott Colley; vocalist/composer Bob Dorough; and many others. As a college professor, he holds a doctorate in education, and masters' degrees in English and education. He is currently in residence at Blooms-burg University of Pennsylvania, where he teaches writing.

Doug Ramsey, who wrote the foreword, is the author of *Take Five: The Public and Private Lives of Paul Desmond* and *Jazz Matters: Reflections on the Music and Some of Its Makers*. He is a winner of the Lifetime Achievement Award of the Jazz Journalists Association. His most recent book is *Poodie James*, a novel. His award-winning blog *Rifftides* is at www.dougramsey.com.

Dave Liebman, who wrote the preface, has had a career spanning more than four decades, beginning in the 1970s as the saxophonist/flutist in both the Elvin Jones and Miles Davis groups, continuing as a leader since. He has played on nearly 300 recordings, with over 100 under his leadership or co-leadership. In jazz education, he is a renowned lecturer and author of several milestone books. He is founder and artistic director of the International Association of Schools of Jazz (IASJ). He has received numerous awards for his work and was recognized in 2011 by the National Endowment of the Arts as one of its Jazz Masters.